Voices of the Apalachicola

The Florida History and Culture Series

UNIVERSITY PRESS OF FLORIDA

Florida A&M University, Tallahassee
Florida Atlantic University, Boca Raton
Florida Gulf Coast University, Ft. Myers
Florida International University, Miami
Florida State University, Tallahassee
New College of Florida, Sarasota
University of Central Florida, Orlando
University of Florida, Gainesville
University of North Florida, Jacksonville
University of South Florida, Tampa
University of West Florida, Pensacola

The Florida History and Culture Series
Edited by Raymond Arsenault and Gary R. Mormino

Al Burt's Florida: Snowbirds, Sand Castles, and Self-Rising Crackers, by Al Burt (1997)
Black Miami in the Twentieth Century, by Marvin Dunn (1997)
Gladesmen: Gator Hunters, Moonshiners, and Skiffers, by Glen Simmons and Laura Ogden (1998)
"Come to My Sunland": Letters of Julia Daniels Moseley from the Florida Frontier, 1882–1886, by Julia Winifred Moseley and Betty Powers Crislip (1998)
The Enduring Seminoles: From Alligator Wrestling to Ecotourism, by Patsy West (1998)
Government in the Sunshine State: Florida Since Statehood, by David R. Colburn and Lance deHaven-Smith (1999)
The Everglades: An Environmental History, by David McCally (1999), first paperback edition, 2001
Beechers, Stowes, and Yankee Strangers: The Transformation of Florida, by John T. Foster Jr., and Sarah Whitmer Foster (1999)
The Tropic of Cracker, by Al Burt (1999)
Balancing Evils Judiciously: The Proslavery Writings of Zephaniah Kingsley, edited and annotated by Daniel W. Stowell (1999)
Hitler's Soldiers in the Sunshine State: German POWs in Florida, by Robert D. Billinger Jr. (2000)
Cassadaga: The South's Oldest Spiritualist Community, edited by John J. Guthrie, Phillip Charles Lucas, and Gary Monroe (2000)
Claude Pepper and Ed Ball: Politics, Purpose, and Power, by Tracy E. Danese (2000)
Pensacola during the Civil War: A Thorn in the Side of the Confederacy, by George F. Pearce (2000)
Castles in the Sand: The Life and Times of Carl Graham Fisher, by Mark S. Foster (2000)
Miami, U.S.A., by Helen Muir (2000)
Politics and Growth in Twentieth-Century Tampa, by Robert Kerstein (2001)
The Invisible Empire: The Ku Klux Klan in Florida, by Michael Newton (2001)
The Wide Brim: Early Poems and Ponderings of Marjory Stoneman Douglas, edited by Jack E. Davis (2002)
The Architecture of Leisure: The Florida Resort Hotels of Henry Flagler and Henry Plant, by Susan R. Braden (2002)
Florida's Space Coast: The Impact of NASA on the Sunshine State, by William Barnaby Faherty, S.J. (2002)
In the Eye of Hurricane Andrew, by Eugene F. Provenzo Jr. and Asterie Baker Provenzo (2002)
Florida's Farmworkers in the Twenty-first Century, text by Nano Riley and photographs by Davida Johns (2003)

Making Waves: Female Activists in Twentieth-Century Florida, edited by Jack E. Davis and Kari Frederickson (2003)

Orange Journalism: Voices from Florida Newspapers, by Julian M. Pleasants (2003)

The Stranahans of Ft. Lauderdale: A Pioneer Family of New River, by Harry A. Kersey Jr. (2003)

Death in the Everglades: The Murder of Guy Bradley, America's First Martyr to Environmentalism, by Stuart B. McIver (2003)

Jacksonville: The Consolidation Story, from Civil Rights to the Jaguars, by James B. Crooks (2004)

The Seminole Wars: The Nation's Longest Indian Conflict, by John and Mary Lou Missall (2004)

The Mosquito Wars: A History of Mosquito Control in Florida, by Gordon Patterson (2004)

Seasons of Real Florida, by Jeff Klinkenberg (2004)

Land of Sunshine, State of Dreams: A Social History of Modern Florida, by Gary Mormino (2005)

Paradise Lost? The Environmental History of Florida, edited by Jack E. Davis and Raymond Arsenault (2005), first paperback edition, 2005

Frolicking Bears, Wet Vultures, and Other Oddities: A New York City Journalist in Nineteenth-Century Florida, edited by Jerald T. Milanich (2005)

Waters Less Traveled: Exploring Florida's Big Bend Coast, by Doug Alderson (2005)

Saving South Beach, by M. Barron Stofik (2005)

Losing It All to Sprawl: How Progress Ate My Cracker Landscape, by Bill Belleville (2006)

Voices of the Apalachicola, compiled and edited by Faith Eidse (2006), first paperback edition, 2007

Floridian of His Century: The Courage of Governor LeRoy Collins, by Martin A. Dyckman (2006)

America's Fortress: A History of Fort Jefferson, Dry Tortugas, Florida, by Thomas Reid (2006)

Weeki Wachee: City of Mermaids, A History of One of Florida's Oldest Roadside Attractions, by Lu Vickers and Sara Dionne (2007)

City of Intrigue, Nest of Revolution: A Documentary History of Key West in the Nineteenth Century, by Consuelo E. Stebbins (2007)

The New Deal in South Florida: Design, Policy, and Community Building, 1933–1940, edited by John A. Stuart and John F. Stack Jr. (2008)

Pilgrim in the Land of Alligators: More Stories about Real Florida, by Jeff Klinkenberg (2008)

Disorder in the Supreme Court: Scandal and Reform in Florida, by Martin A. Dyckman (2008)

Voices of the Apalachicola

Compiled and Edited by Faith Eidse

Published on Behalf of the Northwest Florida Water Management District

Foreword by Gary R. Mormino and Raymond Arsenault

Planning, editorial, and research assistance by Lucinda Scott, Georgann Penson, Duncan Cairns, Dan Tonsmeire, Bill Cleckley, George Fisher, Graham Lewis, David Clayton, Maria Culbertson, and the Apalachicola National Estuarine Research Reserve (Woody Miley, Erik Lovestrand, Frances Ingram, and Maria Parsley).

Maps by Ferdouse Sultana and Gary Settle

University Press of Florida
Gainesville · Tallahassee · Tampa · Boca Raton
Pensacola · Orlando · Miami · Jacksonville · Ft. Myers · Sarasota

Copyright 2006 by Northwest Florida Water Management District
First paperback edition, 2007
Printed in the United States of America on acid-free paper

12 11 10 09 08 07   6 5 4 3 2 1

Library of Congress Cataloging-in-Publication Data
Voices of the Apalachicola / compiled and edited by Faith Eidse;
foreword by Gary R. Mormino and Raymond Arsenault.
p. cm.—(The Florida history and culture series)
"Published on behalf of the Northwest Florida Water Management District."
A collection of oral histories of the Apalachicola River and Bay.
Includes bibliographical references and index.
ISBN 0-8130-2864-7 (acid-free paper) (cloth)
ISBN 978-0-8130-3212-2 (acid-free paper) (paper)
1. Apalachicola River Valley (Fla.)—History—Anecdotes. 2. Apalachicola River Valley
(Fla.)—Social life and customs—Anecdotes. 3. River life—Florida—Apalachicola River—
Anecdotes. e. Apalachicola River Valley (Fla.)—Biography—Anecdotes. 5. Oral history.
I. Eidse, Faith. II. Northwest Florida Water Management District (Fla.) III. Series.
F317.A6V65   2005
975.9'92—dc22   2005053159

The University Press of Florida is the scholarly publishing agency for the State Univer-
sity System of Florida, comprising Florida A&M University, Florida Atlantic University,
Florida Gulf Coast University, Florida International University, Florida State University,
New College of Florida, University of Central Florida, University of Florida, University of
North Florida, University of South Florida, and University of West Florida.

University Press of Florida
15 Northwest 15th Street
Gainesville, FL 32611-2079
www.upf.com

Contents

Maps

Figures

Foreword

Voices of the Apalachicola appears as the latest volume in a series devoted to the study of Florida history and culture. During the past half century, the burgeoning population and increased national and international visibility of Florida have sparked a great deal of popular interest in the state's past, present, and future. As the favorite destination of hordes of tourists and as the new home for millions of retirees, immigrants, and transplants, modern Florida has become a demographic, political, and cultural bellwether.

A state of vast distances and distant strangers, Florida needs more citizens who care about the welfare of this special place and its people. We hope this series helps newcomers and old-timers appreciate and understand Florida. The University Press of Florida established the Florida History and Culture Series in an effort to provide an accessible and attractive format for the publication of works related to the Sunshine State.

As coeditors of the series, we are deeply committed to the creation of an eclectic but carefully crafted set of books that will provide the field of Florida studies with a fresh focus and encourage Florida researchers and writers to consider the broader implications and context of their work. The series includes monographs, works of synthesis, memoirs, and anthologies. And, while the series features books of historical interest, we encourage authors researching Florida's environment, politics, and popular or material culture to submit their manuscripts as well. We want each book to retain a distinct personality and voice, but at the same time we hope to foster a sense of community and collaboration among Florida scholars.

Voices of the Apalachicola is an extraordinary achievement. Faith Eidse and her team of transcribers and interviewers have compiled one of the finest collections of oral histories ever completed in Florida; indeed, the individual life histories simply soar, taking the reader to special places: Whiskey George Creek, Tate's Hell, Alligator Point, and Johnson's Slough.

"Tell us about the river." Thus begins a magical relationship between interviewer and interviewee. Soulful and sonorous, bittersweet and melancholic, the personal reminiscences represent soundings from the Apalachicola River. The British historian Arnold Toynbee once remarked that the riverbank marked one of the best vantage points to study history. From Jackson, Gadsden, Calhoun, Liberty, Gulf, and Franklin county sloughs, steep-head ravines, and barrier islands, voices tell of American gunboats, stern-wheelers, and oyster skiffs. Voices include Creek chief Andrew Boggs Ramsey, who "walks softly in two worlds"; Neel Yent's memories of panthers; Judge David Taunton, "defender of swamp dwellers"; Tom Corley, the Mark Twain of the Apalachicola; Billy Kersey, "road builder through Hell"; the Walkers, "catfish trap makers"; L. L. Lanier, "honey philosopher"; Boncyle Land, "turpentine legend"; and Don Ingram, who milled "old-as-Christ cypresses."

The Apalachicola is neither the longest nor the most celebrated Florida river, but it is Florida's first in flow and it is certainly the richest. In the sheer vitality and variety of its flora and fauna, its commerce and people, the Apalachicola is a mighty river. Its history is equally compelling. *Voices of the Apalachicola* eloquently illustrates the confluence of humanity and nature. The book proudly takes its place alongside a growing list of Florida river studies.

The Apalachicola River Valley is a parable of modern Florida. Life on and along the river was hard, but the locale was remarkable in its fertility. Men and women adapted to and imposed upon the forest and water a rich and unique culture and lifestyle. Alas, as is happening all too often in Florida, a way of life is vanishing. *Voices of the Apalachicola* allows us to remember tall tales of oystermen and turpentiners, deadhead loggers and worm grunters.

Raymond Arsenault and Gary R. Mormino, Series Editors
University of South Florida, St. Petersburg

Preface

In Praise of Natural Wonders

Three exquisite moments during my travels along the Apalachicola reveal the natural wonders of this near-pristine, but threatened, river valley, so often extolled in these oral histories.

One was the black bear raised up on hind legs, feeding at dusk on a golden branch in the Apalachicola National Forest. Lucinda Scott slowed the truck. She had transcribed many of these oral histories, and we both longed to see a bear, once so populous that early settlers baked biscuits with their grease.

The bear dropped onto four huge paws and turned, ears pricked, eyes shiny onyx. It was about 3 feet high, medium-sized, half-grown. As if sensing our delight, it sauntered across State Road 65 in front of us. It paused along a trail leading to East Bay and turned again, engaging our animated faces inside our rolling cage. I could have sworn it skipped as it disappeared into the forest. We had not brought a camera, but it didn't matter. The moment lives on.

Another pure moment was the day my son, his friend, and I slogged into a vast pitcher plant prairie 4 miles north of Sumatra. At first I saw only the yellow-green trumpet pitcher plants awash in sunlight, many still bearing heavy blossoms. But my son's friend had studied carnivorous plants in sixth grade, and he looked closer, deeper. He found tiny sundew rosettes and glistening dew threads in the mud all around us. Here and there northern pitcher plants grew, their flared bronze lips luring bugs to a bowl filled with rainwater. Wetlands are disappearing at alarming rates, and my heart leaped at the resilience of these rare gems.

A third awe-inspiring moment was experiencing the river vista opening on the Garden of Eden Trail atop the Apalachicola Bluffs and Ravines Preserve, which felt like gazing into eternity. Here Kodiak-sized beardogs, giant ground sloths, and armadillos the size of small cars once roamed. Then, as now, rainwater flowed from high in the Appalachians over the ancient "fall line" at Columbus, which had erupted when the supercontinent of Gondwanaland collided with the supercontinent of Laurasia and formed the even larger Pangaea. This continent, for many millions of years, included all the land on earth. Raindrops fell, and I inhaled their earthy scent. Time and petty concerns receded. Cares melted away.

This Apalachicola River and Bay oral history project reached out to dozens of longtime residents of the river basin and recorded their spoken histories before their experiential knowledge of the river could pass from memory.

In the sense that you can't "hear" their words, these aren't technically "oral" histories. But we listened and wrote the text to reflect spoken dialect. Also, in the sense that we directed their reminiscences to the river and bay, these memories are specifically focused. In addition, we edited for relevance to life on the river and bay. Contributors approved the final cuts, so we eliminated distracting ellipses that indicated missing words.

Exceptions to oral reminiscences are those of Neel Yent and Pearl Porter Marshall, who wrote down their stories and the stories that were passed down orally to them. We thank their heirs for giving us permission to publish excerpts here. Boncyle Land recorded an oral history before she died, and her heirs have made that transcript available to us as well. Other interviews were provided by river and bay researchers (James Barkuloo) and project managers (Dan Tonsmeire and Ace Haddock). Several were recorded by Frances Ingram and Maria Parsley of the Apalachicola National Estuarine Research Reserve.

We are aware that local knowledge sometimes gets lost, and that memory is sometimes unreliable. We acknowledge that oral histories are subject to error, since experience is subject to interpretation and events can be altered by memory lapse. Also, hearsay, or secondhand tellings, such as, "My father said . . . ," further remove readers from the experience. We tried to verify accounts with historical records, often relying on the dedicated librarians at the State Library of Florida. Northwest Florida Water Management District directors and staff also reviewed and edited this project. Thank you, Georgann Penson, Douglas Barr, Duncan Cairns, Maria Culbertson, Graham Lewis, George Fisher, Tyler Macmillan, and Dan Tonsmeire.

As an extra precaution, since taped speech is sometimes misunderstood, we sent written oral histories to speakers to verify their accuracy. We thank them for their diligence and spirit. They know the river better than outsiders ever could.

Our method was to identify lifestyle communities and their notable or veteran members. We asked open-ended or specific questions that permitted wide-ranging or detailed responses. Our request to "tell us about the river" encouraged free-flowing perceptions of life and changes on the river. "What do you remember about the 1929 flood?" elicited vivid, five-sense recall.

How people traveled before bridges and paved roads, where they went by rail or ferry, and what they packed, revealed lives that were once more survivalist, isolated, and localized.

Oral histories encouraged lively, subjective responses in character-enlarging vernacular rather than a textbook delivery of "just the facts." By ordering chapters according to livelihood, we attempted to deliver cohesive contexts. We tried to focus on each interviewee's special knowledge, to probe deeply, and to convey a living, breathing journey along the Apalachicola River and Bay.

Acknowledgments

We thank the individuals interviewed for this collection, or their estates, for permitting us to tape, transcribe, and use their stories for public information and education purposes. Other uses of these recollections will require permission from the individuals themselves or their estates. The section on restoring Tate's Hell first appeared as part of a feature in *Tallahassee* magazine.

Introduction

Stories of Historic Change

The wise, hardy, often amusing stories of average families who have spent most of their lives on the Apalachicola River and Bay reveal firsthand how the river has changed over time. These families have seen cycles of diminished river flow as the century turned, threatening both plant and animal life. During winter and spring floods, the river's flow may be abundant. Yet during drought, and when upriver demands result in even lower flows for extended periods, Florida must fight for water to keep fish and oysters alive in the bay.

The system once ran deep, swift, and narrow, seasonally contributing a majority of its flow to surrounding floodplains. But natural river scouring and deposition processes—combined with human impacts such as damming, channel dredging, and spoil banking—have decreased slope and increased meander. They have disconnected sloughs and tributaries needed for freshwater nurseries and spawning. Also, because dams tend to block detritus (organic particles) required for the food chain, flooding below the Jim Woodruff Lock and Dam is ever more essential to restart detrital transport to the bay.

This oral history is intended to illuminate practical local wisdom and insights that might otherwise be lost. The people who spent much of the last century on the river and bay, or in its forests, swamps, and floodplains, describe the basin's historical, ecological, health, and environmental changes. This project recognizes their valuable perceptions and often unique takes on a myriad of issues. Seafood workers, who have netted shrimp for decades, know the influence of freshwater inflows and aquatic plant and animal life on the size and quantity of their catch, as well as the pressures of overfishing. Their stories increase our awareness and reshape fragmented knowledge of this remarkable system.

Basin management has been directed by human hands, yet for those managers there is often no substitute for practical, observed local knowledge, which all too often disappears. Tom Corley, the last Apalachicola steamboat pilot licensed as first-class, and Edward Tolliver, Apalachicola's first black mayor, died within weeks of telling their stories. Lavere Walker,

Joe McMillan, and General Robert Howell followed, though their stories live on in these pages. Neel Yent, Pearl Porter Marshall, and Boncyle S. Land recorded their stories shortly before their deaths, and their heirs permitted us to include them, as well.

Stories of a river as it existed in the 1930s and 1940s, before major development in upstream states impacted the Apalachicola basin, are preserved here. The advent of hydropower and the age of dams reveal how our desire to manage water flow for electricity, transportation, recreation, safety, and the economy sometimes came at the price of natural resources. Our purpose is to record, listen, and provide a public forum as development impacts Apalachicola's historic way of life. Perhaps these memories will help guide our actions in the future and teach us not to repeat our errors.

1

Botanical Eden,
Cultural Battleground

The Apalachicola River is recognized as one of the six most biodiverse regions of the United States.[1] It was also a final frontier of Indian and settler battles. Early botanists traveled intrepidly in these exotic woods, discovering plants new to science. Here northern plants, descending on the current, met southern plants ascending during climate shifts. They reproduced, evolved, and dispersed, creating a botanical Eden.

Large portions of the river's forested floodplain, also Florida's largest, are protected by state and federal governments and private entities. The basin's range of habitats gives it the highest species density of amphibians and reptiles on the continent, north of Mexico.[2] It is home to 135 listed species tracked by the Florida Natural Areas Inventory.[3] Between blended forests of cypress, gum, beech, and saw palmetto, the river rolls, ample in wet season, exposing a sandy shore during dry season.

The river valley's unrivaled steepheads grow the only native *Torreya taxifolia* evergreen anywhere.[4] These steep streamheads drop vertiginously from otherwise relatively flat terrain. Their constantly flowing groundwater environs harbor uniquely adapted salamanders and evergreens, creating a refuge from climatic extremes. Florida yew and dusky salamander occur naturally in these cool refuges.

The Lower Creek Apalachicolas—not to be confused with the Apalachees, their linguistic cousins to the east[5]—ruled, traded, and spread out from this region. Their descendants sought refuge in this basin rather than trek westward. They were called the "Bogot" people, meaning "the last people and their last refuge." They reemerged when the forest was opened for timbering, according to Chief Andrew Ramsey ("Haco" in Muskogee), interviewed in the next chapter. They keep their culture alive near Blountstown, celebrating four annual busks (festivals) at Pine Arbor Tribal Town in one of the least populous regions of Florida. Even the basin's population density is changing, however, as timberland converts to development, and oyster houses give way to condominiums.

Fig 1.1. In this undated photo, visitors stand on Rock Bluff in Torreya State Park. Photo courtesy of Florida State Archives.

Today it is the increasing frequency and duration of low flows, coupled with growth pressures, that threaten riverine life. Thirty-eight species of fish that require inundated floodplains to spawn and survive, struggle under these conditions. When water levels drop for long periods, as they did from 1997 to 2001, so does the extent of aquatic habitat. Reduced flows can also encourage invasive plants to flourish and may increase forest fire threats.[6]

Ceremonial mounds that once lifted the river's early inhabitants above floodwaters have stood well beyond the river's reach for years. Three dozen mounds, some of them burial mounds dating to A.D. 200–700, were built by Indians of the Woodland period who thrived on this waterway. The mounds were mapped in the early 1900s by archaeologist Clarence B. Moore, who found here the original "killed" pottery (clay pots punctured before firing and buried with human skeletons), a practice that spread throughout the Southeast.

One of Moore's most interesting finds was a burial mound at the Chipola Cutoff containing forty-two folded skeletons and fifty-one clay pots.[7] Archaeologist Jon L. Gibson sees in the Chipola Cutoff pottery blends evidence of Euro-American contact and cultural undoing at the zenith of a cultural cycle. Under foreign influence and in quest of European goods,[8] divisions

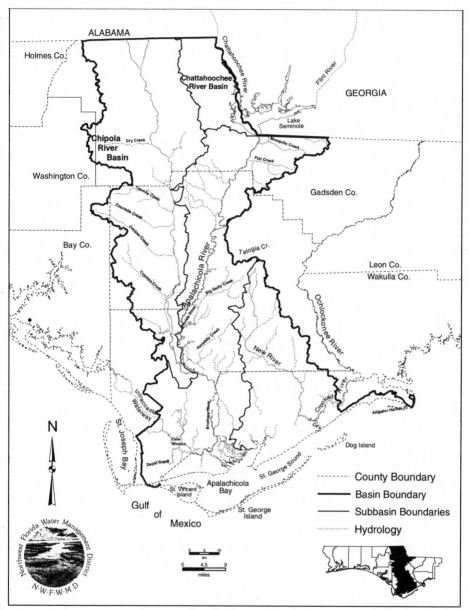

Map 1.1. Apalachicola River and Bay Watershed

between Upper and Lower Creeks grew into alliances with Spain and England. Devastating battles ensued.

The Apalachicolas were allied with Spain and controlled southwest Georgia and parts of southeast Alabama until they were invaded by Upper Creeks and the English during the years 1702–7. They were transported to the Savannah River, but most returned fifteen years later. Apalachicola Fort was established west of the Chattahoochee at its confluence with the Flint River.[9] Apalachicola, the port city on the bay, was named a century later, in 1831, by European settlers.

According to Muskogee legend, Apalachicola Fort became the capital of the eighteenth-century Muskogee Creek confederacy of fifty-five tribal towns.[10] It was a white town where no blood was to be spilled.

Yet in 1763—the year Spanish Florida came under British control for twenty years—several European traders and their Creek families took shelter under fire in the council house at Apalachicola Fort and were burned to death by angry Muskogees. Apalachicola lost its prestige as a white town and later erected a red war post. For ten generations, its citizens could not speak out, vote, or lead national assemblies, according to Muskogee shaman Charles Daniels-Sakim.

When the United States won the American Revolution twenty years later, Florida was returned to Spain. Meanwhile, Creek Indians forayed into north Florida and became known as Seminoles, or "runaways." They also welcomed and intermarried with escaped slaves, forging a significant alliance. During the War of 1812, in which the United States declared war against Great Britain, Spain hoped to retain Florida and created alliances with these Creeks and Seminoles. The Creeks attacked southwest Alabama, the United States counterattacked, and the Creek War ensued.[11]

General Andrew Jackson crushed the Creeks at the Battle of Horseshoe Bend in Alabama and forced them to surrender extensive lands in southwest Georgia and Alabama. Jackson then seized and evacuated settlers from Pensacola, where William Augustus Bowles had organized the "State of Muskogee" and carried on a pirating trade.[12] Jackson went on to rout the British at New Orleans on January 8, 1815.

A British fort at Prospect Bluff on the upper Apalachicola River, built to recruit escaped slaves and Native American fighters, was burned with hot cannon shot by order of the U.S. Navy's J. Loomis on July 27, 1816. Of the three hundred ex-slave men, women, and children and twenty Choctaw warriors, a handful survived and were bound into slavery.[13] Two chiefs were executed "on the spot" for having earlier tarred and burned alive a captured U.S. Navy crewman.[14] Retaliation came in November 1817 when Lt. R. W.

Fig. 1.2. The Apalachicola Bluffs and Ravines, a refugium of species listed as threatened or endangered, as seen from the Garden of Eden Trail. Photo by Faith Eidse.

Scott's party, in an open army boat, was attacked by Indians near River Junction (Chattahoochee), leaving few survivors.

In 1818, Jackson again invaded Florida, igniting the First Seminole War, also a continuation of the Creek War. Near the British fort, Duncan Mc-Krimmon was taken hostage but spared when a young Native American woman, Millie Francis, begged for his life. She later received a Congressional Medal for bravery. Shaman Sakim, interviewed in the next chapter, calls her "Florida's Pocahontas" and claims to be her descendant. Secretary of State John Quincy Adams persuaded Spain to give up control of Florida in the 1819 Adams-Onís Treaty.[15]

To reward several Native American chiefs for guiding Andrew Jackson in routing the Seminoles at Miccosukee in 1817, the 1823 Moultrie Creek Treaty gave land along the Apalachicola to chiefs John Blount and Tuski Haco Cochrane (Chief Ramsey's ancestor). Land near Sneads was given to the Mulatto King and Emathochee. Within twelve years, a pursuant treaty was negotiated at the Duval House in Tallahassee. The chiefs surrendered title to lands for assurances that whites would not invade their homes. After they gave up their guns in friendship, however, their slaves, livestock, and family members were kidnapped, perhaps by slave-hunters.[16]

The Second Seminole War lasted seven years (1835–42) and involved ten thousand Muskogee Creeks resisting removal. These southeastern remnant tribes, often mixed with those of African ancestry, were fighting for freedom and survival. The war ended not with a peace treaty but rather because so many had died, fled to remote hammocks, been sold out or tricked, or eventually moved to Oklahoma.[17]

Eighteen Creeks crossed into Gadsden County, Florida, on April 23, 1840, and killed a settler mother and three children at Sand Ridge. Her twenty-year-old son, John K. McLane, survived what has been called the "last Indian massacre in Florida." Victims were buried in a single grave at Sycamore cemetery.[18]

"I don't know for sure, but [those Creeks were] prob'ly the Haco people coming down," said Chief Ramsey.

The United States acquired Florida, and much of the Apalachicola River basin was given up in land cessions to settle Indian debts with Panton, Leslie, and Company. This became part of the 1.5-million-acre Forbes Purchase awarded to Thomas Forbes, a surviving founder of the trading empire. His subsequent sale to Colin Mitchell was eventually approved by the U.S. Supreme Court in 1835, despite years of litigation. Mitchell sold the land in parcels to settlers.[19]

In the end, the Muskogees who could be found were shipped west, though some may have returned to their "continuous fire" near Blountstown, where a flame was carried by lantern to the ceremonial mound and back again and kept continuously burning. By the end of the Seminole Wars, Native American land was surveyed and ready for sale.[20]

In 1836, Apalachicola became the third-largest cotton port on the Gulf of Mexico until railroads diverted cotton at Columbus, Georgia, and River Junction, Florida. Apalachicola revived itself at century's turn as a profitable sawmill exchange[21] and, in recent years, has been remodeled as a quaint fishing and resort town. Its oysters are famous at raw bars around the nation.

The bay is barrier-rimmed by St. George Island, Dog Island, St. Vincent, and Cape St. George. It is shallow enough that moderate winds can completely mix fresh- and salt water.[22] But periodic droughts (such as those in 1930, 1954, 1986, and 1999) can reduce flow to a quarter, or less, and cause the death of entire oyster bars.[23]

It doesn't help that Metro Atlanta's water use increased from 459 million gallons per day in 1990 to 606 million gallons a day in 2000, according to the U.S. Geological Survey,[24] "If you continue to have this kind of growth in the metropolitan Atlanta area," said Corps colonel Robert Keyser at a public meeting in 2002, "we need another water supply."[25] The Big River is one of few major river systems in the United States with a large metropolis, Atlanta, near its headwaters.

Also, four large Chattahoochee River dams hold three to four months' rainfall to support authorized hydropower and navigation uses, as well as water supply for recreation and to augment low flows. South Georgia draws from the Flint River and aquifers and returns only small portions of the 1.5 billion gallons its crops consume each day during the growing season.[26] These demands deplete the Apalachicola River of a third of its flow during low cycles.[27]

Shoaling in the river decreases the available shipping channel and has led to the practice of holding back water in upper basin reservoirs to create a single release, or "navigation window," to float waiting barges. This creates weeks of reduced river flow in which fewer acres of floodplain are connected to the river channel than if there had been no withholding at all.[28]

Will we, its beneficiaries, make the right decisions for the Big River? Negotiations among Alabama, Georgia, and Florida over sharing water ended without agreement on August 31, 2003. "Florida was unwilling to accept only minimum flows, plus whatever else the upstream states were not able to consume or store," said David Struhs, then Department of Environmental Protection secretary. Florida will seek to entrust protection of the river's historic flows to the nation's highest court.

2

River Roots

*I've known rivers ancient as the world
and older than the flow of human blood in human veins.
My soul has grown deep like the rivers.*
Langston Hughes

The Archaics of the Apalachicola were river travelers. They knew the Big River and its many tributaries like we know our highways and interstates today. Family clans paddled downstream, carved reed flutes, and answered birdsong. They camped at villages along the way and joined the stomp dance. They paddled to the Gulf of Mexico and the mouths and hearts of other rivers, trading knowledge as they went.[1]

These early Indian tribes organized seasonal busks (festivals) to nurture emerging beliefs and maximized skills of hunter, salt distiller, and meat preserver. Game smoked in earthen pits was divided among many families as sustenance for the winter.

Creek chief Andrew Ramsey (Haco) and Muskogee shaman Charles Daniels-Sakim, featured in this chapter, are the legacy of an ancient river culture that fed body, mind, and spirit. River travelers ignited rich exchanges over twelve millennia that spread crafts, ritual, and identity across what is now the tri-state region (Alabama, Georgia, Florida) and the entire Southeast.[2]

Beneath Lake Seminole, a fiber-stamped potsherd was radiocarbon-dated to 1200 B.C., suggesting that cultural influences had already expanded from the Atlantic Coast. Also, chalky ceramics of the St. Johns complex, 1200–500 B.C., were found in the Jim Woodruff Reservoir.[3]

During the Woodland period, 1000 B.C.–A.D. 700, river dwellers tilled the loamed forest floor, where tender shoots were protected from the sun. The culture became known as Weeden Island and used slash-and-burn agriculture throughout the basin.[4] Chiefdoms emerged, and Ft. Walton culture evolved. Permanent settlements grew to control and protect large plots of land.

Refugee groups speaking different languages moved into the river valley. Yet a confederacy emerged, dominated by speakers of the Muskogee dialect. European Americans referred to all of them as Creeks because of their river-dwelling tendencies.[5] In the end, Euro-American settlers overran Indian land, often violating treaties.

Given the Seminole wars and Indian removal, it was surprising to find in Blountstown a titled Creek chief, descended from an unbroken line. It was even more surprising to find a medicine maker who taught Muskogee-Creek language and ceremony. Ritual lives on at Pine Arbor Tribal Town, a north-west Florida community with a ceremonial square ground near Blounts-town. The discovery of a descendant of Andrew Jackson's soldiers near Wewahitchka filled a historic frame. The stories of Chief Ramsey, Shaman Charles Daniels-Sakim, and Judge David Taunton paint a picture of frontier living on the Apalachicola River before roads, bridges, and railroads, before rural electrification and development.

Creek Chief Ramsey: Walking Softly in Two Worlds

Chief Andrew Boggs Ramsey is large, well over 6 feet tall. He wears glasses and has a Ph.D. in education. Chief in one culture, educator in another, he nonetheless walks softly in two worlds. His name appears on a bilingual Muskogee-Creek/English historical marker at the Blountstown Courthouse as the last in an unbroken line of titled chiefs. Born in 1932, he is a direct descendant of the original permanent settlers of Blountstown—Creeks forced out of Alabama by wars in 1810. A former reigning matriarch married to the tribal chief, Polly Parot was his great-great-great-grandmother.

Ramsey prepared adults for General Education Development exams; served as an elementary school principal for eight years; earned a Ph.D. in 1970; and was promoted to the Calhoun County office as teacher trainer and project planner. His project plan was one of only seven funded in the state.

Chief Dr. Andrew told his story on May 24, 2001, at his ancestral home on Blountstown's Central Avenue.

"My grandfather never wore shoes, but he always had that pair of new shoes. He'd get dressed and pick up his pair of new shoes, take them to the store, put 'em on the shelf. Wagons would just go through the back of [that trading post], and they would load there. When he left that night, he'd pick up his shoes [and] walk home barefoot. Indian people didn't wear shoes," Ramsey said simply, though his grandfather apparently didn't want to be judged for lacking them.

My Grand-father never wore shoes.

Fig. 2.1a. Creek chief Dr. Andrew Boggs Ramsey, wearing tie and shell medallions, at his ancestral home in Blountstown. Photo by Faith Eidse.

"The big house used to be right here in front of this one. It burned in 1938." Ramsey presented a map with a large communal house on what is now his front yard. "Yeah, the big house had a room in the middle of it that would [sleep] two hundred people. I was born there, and my mother was born there.

"That little brick house [in the front yard] is my grandmother's. And when they rebuilt, she still lived outside. She never did move in and live inside, 'cept for sleepin'. She cooked outside, she sat outside, she did all of her work outside. Everything was outside.

"You're right in the middle of a [former] Indian village. When they put this road through, they cut it right in half.

"At that time it was Blunt-em-tvlofd. Blunt—his—town. The . . . Muskogee alphabet's sounds are different [*t* is *d*, *c* is *j*]. Moravian missionaries put it into writing, and so we use the [same] letter symbols [as] in English, but they have different sounds."

Speaking Muskogee, Ramsey said: "I'm Creek, my name's Andrew Ramsey, and I'm Wind Clan. My wife is Bird Clan." He added in English: "So all our children are Bird Clan. See, we're a matriarchal society, and you get your clan from your mother. Our grandchildren, they're their mother's clan. I have one set of grandchildren that are Deer Clan and one set that are Snake Clan.

"It's incest to marry into your own clan. So when you see a pretty girl, you ask her what [her] clan is, and if she says 'Wind,' you just walk on. She says 'Bird,'"—the chief nudged his wife—"you get busy."

"Your father's people're not kin to you, really. See, your father rears his sister's children. I was taught how to fish by my mother's brothers. In fact, my Uncle Bert was medicine man at Pigpen Square—that's a religious square. And that's almost at old Horsetown about five minutes by canoe down the river. It was all on the Apalachicola Reservation. But the river changed course, and that put Horsetown on Old River. And that created an island called Fanning Island between Old River and where the new channel was."

Ramsey selected a copy of the 1831 J. D. Clements *Survey of Blunt's and Tuskigee's Reservation.* "Here's Fanning Island right here. This was the Clements survey when they sold the reservation, but they didn't remove. All these people were gone by 1838. Tuskie Haco [also Tuskihajo] died in 1832. Haco [is] a title that means 'Zealous Warrior' or 'Crazy Warrior.'

"My ancestors lived at Cochranetown here," Ramsey continued. "And you see it's right on the edge of the reservation? They wanted all the Indians on that reservation—and they used his house to make sure it was on the reservation.

"You know, when they sold this reservation," Ramsey added, "the Polly Parot band, or the Bogot people—Bogot means place of last refuge; last people and their last refuge. They went to Boggs Pond, which is on the other side of the Chipola River, right inside Jackson County. And this band hid out there. The reason why it came back: timber. They opened this country to timber.

"There's still a group of Creek Indians that live unto themselves in Jackson County," said Wisa, "and they do not associate with other Creeks or the whites. Except whatever they have to do to earn a living or buy groceries."

"And the McClellans, which were war Indians from Mossy Head in Walton County, moved here, and then this became an Indian town, and their daughter married my granddaddy, and that's how the Apalachicolas got back to Bloutstown.

"Polly Parot and them did not go [West]. Polly Parot was a bought wife. But you could only have a second wife with permission of your principal wife, and [Tuskie Haco's] principal wife was old Chief Blount's sister. Wives

Fig. 2.1b. Chief Ramsey and wife, Wisa, at a Tallahassee reception. Chief Ramsey is both Miccosukee and Apalachicola Creek. Photo by permission of the Ramseys.

that were bought were lower social standing. So why would they live out there [in Texas] to [be ill-treated]?

"The only way Polly is mentioned in the archives is that when the Seminoles captured John Blount's wife and children, Polly was with him. They found out she was from Horsetown [and] let her go, but they killed Blount's wife and children.

"Now, why did they let [her] go? Because we are really the Miccosukee clan that was left behind. My great-great-grandmother [Mary Musgroove] was Miccosukee, and Andrew Jackson destroyed Miccosukee in 1817. And they fled over [here]. And she married John Boggs. He was born here in 1810.

"This was hunting grounds back then. The first permanent [Creek] settlement here was 1815. The result of that being a refuge town [was that] when they found out she was from Horsetown they let her go."

Chief Ramsey presented copies of census papers. "My great-grandfather was born here in 1840 [and] died in 1917. [The form] said: 'Who was your father?' 'John Boggs.' They weren't schooled, and they didn't speak English. So down here when it said, 'Who was his mother?' he thought they were talking about his daddy's mother, so my great-great-great-grandmother Polly Parot's name is on that death certificate.

"The river was the lifeline and the highway. And you know where Montgomery, Alabama, is today? That's where the Apalachicolas originally came from. And the Indian town there was Tukabahtchee. The Apalachicolas were chased out of their homes.

The river was the life- line and the highway.

"There was a little town outside of Tukabahtchee called Peach Tree. Dalofa Bagana. And when they moved to Texas, they called them the Bagana Muskogees. [In Texas it's] the Alabama Cosetta Reservation. One of them married a Frenchman, and he moved the whole group out on that ranch.

"The reason why [Chief Blount] went to the Alabama Cosetta Reservation to start with is that Red Shoes, chief of the Alabama Cosetta, was John Blount's uncle. But their dialect was so different they didn't understand each other.

"Most of the Seminoles down south, except for those around Okeechobee, are Hitchiti people, and they don't even speak Muskogee; they speak Miccosukee. Miccosukee is a Hitchiti language. You take verbs and you make nouns out of them," Ramsey explained. "Like 'Wewahitchka.' 'Wewa' is the Apalachicola name for water. 'Hitch' is 'see.' 'Ka' makes place. So it's a place where you see water.

"They call it 'Stiff-n-ugly' right there in Liberty County, but it's 'este-een-funga.' 'Este' is 'person'; and 'een' is 'his' or 'her'; 'funga' is 'skeleton.' 'Ga' on the end makes that a place, a place where human bones were found. Ramsey touched the shell medallions around his neck. "These are the Muskogee nation in Florida. [It] has one renowned artist [Dan Townsend in Crawford-ville]. And these are old Creek designs out of Lake Jackson mounds. Mangazeit," he said, referring to a carved humming bird.

Patchwork is sewn with diamond shapes for Seminoles, rounded shapes for Creeks. A photo showed Ramsey in head dress and blue and red patchwork outfit. "That's kind of a pow-wow type thing, which is white in origin. We don't use drums. Creek dancing is what you call stomp. And it's always [with] singing."

"[Wisa's] family lived on the Aucilla River when the white people burned it," Ramsey said. "They didn't keep up with their history like we did. In 1853,

[After removal], the only way you could live here as an Indian was to live as white people.

Florida passed a law saying the only way you could live here as an Indian was to live as white people.

"Now my great-grandfather on my daddy's side, name was Letga Hajo [Letkv Haco]. And when they had to make livings, he just picked out of the air 'Honest John Ramsey' and started a rolling store, on a wagon. A lot of Indians say, 'You can't use Ramsey; that's not Indian.' But the name *Ramsey* here means Haco. In my Indian society, I'll introduce myself as 'Ndola [Vntold] Haco.' 'Ndola' means Andrew."

Indians did not achieve civil rights until 1964, Ramsey said. "Essentially right out here, my grandfather established [Boggs Cemetery] so Indians would have a place to be buried. There's a lot of white people in it now. The white cemetery was up at Meadow Ridge.

"Indians were slaves too. Did you know that when they first imported slaves into this country, they had Indians in slavery already?

"Now, going back to the river—Leedja Hajo's wife was named Cedar Woman. The Creeks had fertility people, and she was that person. Cedar tea was a fertility drink. And there used to be a lily that grew on the Apalachicola River that she made into a tea and that would keep you from getting pregnant. It doesn't grow around here anymore.

"Wisa had tumors, and the doctor told her she most likely would never have any children. And we came home [from] school [where we taught]— and Wisa had the cramps. And my grandmother [Boggs] said, 'I can stop those cramps.' And she steeped a tea out of cedar bark, and those cramps went away just like that.

"And Wisa said, 'Thank you, Granny. That's the most wonderful drink I ever took.' [Grandmother] laughed, and she said: 'I don't know if you're gonna think it's so wonderful. You're gonna be pregnant in four to six weeks.' And Wisa laughed and said, 'Granny, the doctor said I can't have any children.' In four weeks, we were expecting our first child."

Wisa added, "That's his picture up at the top on the wall." Two more sons followed; the youngest would commit suicide at age thirty-four, tortured by alienation and the pain of not belonging perfectly anywhere.

The biggest tragedy of the modern-day Indian is suicide.

"The biggest tragedy of the modern-day Indian is suicide," said Ramsey. "My wife's granddaddy committed suicide, and my wife's daddy committed suicide, and then we had our son commit suicide. It seems that people don't realize how bad depression can be and especially if you don't fit in your [culture]. I had two uncles that ruined themselves with alcohol, so I suffered from that; saw my grandmother suffer from it. And obesity. You look, I'm suffering from obesity and diabetes. We all have diabetes. We call it the beginning of death. In the olden times, we went through periods of starvation, and so Indian people's metabolism is more efficient than Nordic metabolism. So it really takes less food for us. We live in two cultures.

"We live in two cultures," Ramsey added. "When we're around white people, we live white culture; when we're around Indian people, we live Indian culture. Partly the two cultures don't overlap. They're too separate.

"When I was a boy, my grandmothers used to meet—and each would carry a piece of wood. Because you always had a fire. It could be 100 degrees and you'd have a fire. 'Cause you had your coffeepot and your [food].

"Most [living, quilting, meeting] was outside," Ramsey said. "It's just according to how much Indian you have in you; what part of you lived more a white lifestyle and Indian lifestyle.

"The Seminole chairman is trying to help us with federalization," Ramsey added, explaining that he wants the tribe recognized to receive federal subsidies. "The Creeks are not federalized in north Florida, though they are recognized. I've been working on this for twenty-three years. It's slow. There's a lack of unity."

Andrew was grand marshal in the 1995 Springtime Tallahassee parade, where he was assailed by those protesting the prominent figure dressed as Andrew Jackson accompanying him in the parade. "That's the first time I knew what it was like to be called a name," said Ramsey sadly.

Yet he has sixteen Florida pioneer certificates. "If you had ancestors that lived in Florida before it became a state, then you could get a Florida pioneer certificate. All [twenty] of my ancestors were born and reared and died in Florida.

"That's a picture of the square ground," Ramsey added, selecting a picture of a cleared square of ground with benches on four sides, shaded by thatched roofs. "We have a four-arbor town. That's me; the chief and head people sit in the west. That's the west arbor. And the east arbor, you have the women, children, and visitors. And then all the old warriors are in the north, and the young warriors are in the south."

When Shaman Charles Daniels-Sakim established Pine Arbor Square Grounds, Ramsey added, "it was very similar to what I remembered [from boyhood], except we always kept a pot of the black drink there. And it's really for our time of purification. It's made out of evergreen yaupon leaves, and it's really high in caffeine.

"Tribes from the interior traveled to the river each spring to partake of this tonic. It grows wild here. The children gather the leaves, [and] you parch [them].

"Sakim is a maker of medicine," Ramsey added, indicating a bottle of colored liquid. "It's a redbone. It's really good for arthritis. It was made from the medicine plant. There isn't anyone in the United States that has more knowledge than Sakim. You can believe him.

"But our cultures, until the civil rights law, you know—you really kept them separate. I was the first in the state that listed Indian in the position of supervisor. I was training teachers here in Calhoun County.

"I started wearing shoes and underwear at twelve," Ramsey added. "I mean, I had a pair of Sunday school shoes. But we always went barefoot. I could walk on a hot pavement in midsummer and not feel it. Now I can hardly walk across the floor over the rug.

"After I got my [Ph.D.], I bagged groceries and I served gas. I worked at the Piggly Wiggly for sixty-four years. And you know how I got my first [professional] job? One of [my customers] that worked for the superintendent said, 'They're closing down the Calhoun Adult School today.' And I said, 'If I get me up a class will you all maybe not close it down and let me have a job?' The superintendent said, 'If you have a classload of people there, and you keep them, then you can have that job.'

"So the next night I had all my kinfolk there, and they stayed for six months. [No one else wanted] 'an old Indian teaching my child.' I had to have a higher degree than most people to get a job, to get promotions.

"My grandmother never went to school. Indian people weren't allowed to go to school back then. My grandfather was smart enough that he taught himself to read and write English. And then he taught her to read and write English.

"The Indian religion is positive. You take what is, and you make something good out of it. You don't hold a grudge; you don't lose your temper. If you upset anything, you go to the quicken post and you beat the post and you throw it in the fire and you forgive. And according to the old Creek religion, you forgive like the Bible says, seven times seven times seven. It's just unlimited. And so when you find that people have any big, bad grudges, you know right off the bat that they were not reared Indian."

Wisa—which means "sassafras"—called Ramsey and me to a lunch of chicken, boiled potatoes, corn, and okra. Chief Ramsey sang a prayer in Muskogee that seemed to unite religious traditions: "Our creator who lives above all things, but you're everywhere all the time; our creator, you made the earth and everything that we need on it. We thank you for this food. In Jesus Christ's name we pray. Amen.

"See, all my great uncles were killed," Ramsey said, passing the chicken. "The last ones were killed at Sweetwater Creek over in Liberty County 'cause Liberty County was the empty spot, and they were workin' themselves south. And if you go to Sycamore, just north of Bristol—there's a grave in the back

The Indian religion is positive. . . . You don't hold a grudge.

of the cemetery says, 'These are the last three people killed by Creek Indians.' And I don't know for sure, but [those Creeks were] prob'ly the Haco people coming down. But that was the time of the war when people are trying to 'spel [expel] you from your home.

"My first memory," Ramsey said, "was crawling on [Granny's shoulders]. Mother would drop them off at [her friend] Rena's house, and you would have to walk 4 or 5 miles to get where they fished in the swamp. And I'd crawl up on her shoulders. And they'd come across a slough [and] just wade right on through. And I can still see Granny's nose just above the water and me on her shoulders. And we'd fish, and my job was to clean [fish]. No matter how young you were, Creek children had responsibilities. And they'd always carry cheesecloth with coffee in it. I'd just dip the water out of the river or sloughs, right here off the Apalachicola River. I wouldn't do it today," Ramsey added. "And then we'd wash the fish in river water," Ramsey laughed. "I wouldn't wash fish in river water now."

"And the last time those two women went fishing, I carried [Granny] in piggyback. She was eighty-one when she died," Ramsey added. "She converted to Christian Science. Christian Science and Creek has a lot alike. Mind over body. But it killed her because she was diabetic.

"We always caught a lot of fish," Ramsey added. "Like during December, January, February, and March is when redhorse suckers ran. And you'd fence in part of the creek, and then you'd go gig 'em out and slash those bones. And then sometimes at the old square ground at Creek Bend they would net gar fish, but they wouldn't scale them. They would cut them open and take the entrails out. They would start a smoldering fire, and then they'd put those gar fish and cover [them] with leaves and dirt. After a pretty good while, they would dig 'em up, and they'd use the scales as a bowl, and they would dip the meat out.

"I have some jewelry that have gar fish scales, and they give you power. They used them most on jewelry and to cut with; they're real sharp. As a warrior, you had to have something like gar fish scales.

"My first job in the grocery store was to keep the pigs and the cows out of the grocery store. I was six," Ramsey said. "When I was a boy, pigs and cows roamed down the street. [Not] until Fuller Warren, you know, became governor in '48 did he outlaw animals from roaming on the road. Going to Tallahassee, you stopped fifteen times to get the cows out of the road.

"There was a big change from the time I was little. You had a ferry that crossed this river, and it'd take you about an hour and a half to get to Bristol. You'd go down to the landing, and you'd wait for the ferry, and then it would hold three cars. The road from there to Bristol was just a rut for each tire. So if you got all the way to Bristol and you met a car, one of you was going to have to back up for a mile.

"I should be embarrassed to tell this. I was in the honor society. And you know Maclay Gardens [Tallahassee]? Miss Maclay invited us over, and she served hot water with tea bags. We had never seen a tea bag in our lives.

"A cousin whispered, 'I bet you tear that tea bag open.' So everybody tore their tea bag open, and Ms. Maclay came: 'Oh, my goodness, I must have bought a box of defective tea bags.'

"She was a short Scottish woman, and she was not a little woman, and she said, 'Let me give you another one and you just put it in the cup, and it'll suck out.'

"Listen, I misspelled one word in my school career," said Ramsey, "and that was 'separate.' I was in third grade, and I just cried. Even when my mother went to school, [taught by] a Cherokee Indian, now, they swept all the schools in Calhoun County free of Creek Indians and sent 'em to the black school. Except for my granddaddy's children—my mother and them—because my granddaddy cashed [teachers' pay] vouchers.

"When you're in the minority like that, it's important for you to do better. But even then, when I was in school here, your worst group of students were your Creek Indian students. That was the worst-achieving group," Ramsey said. "It's because the values were different. They're not used to sitting still in a restricted [space], and one of the things I had to learn to do was to have high eye contact. In our culture, it was an insult to even look anybody right straight in the eye.

"I have white characteristics; I could adapt to white society, but none of my three children could. Creek Indian people are not very talkative. When you first meet Indian people you say, 'Those are the most unfriendly people I've ever seen.' They take being silent for being sullen.

"But the river was a highway, and it was a place where you got food. Indian people would travel great distances at times, but they would travel so far, and they would stay there a month or so. Because Polly Parot's husband, John Boggs Jr., was Cherokee. They were on the Tahlequah Land Payments [Oklahoma]. So they had to be up there sometime, even though she was Creek.

"When I was growing, we were isolated here. I mean, we had nowhere to go. In fact, we all look alike. Of the Miccosukee group that was left behind, there's only about forty of us. We have a lot more kinfolks than that, but a lot of people don't want to be Indian. That's the reason why Indian populations are shrinking so, and it's because they marry white, and the children get

> They swept all the schools in Calhoun County free of Creek Indians.

lighter, and they want to be white. 'Cause all the important people are white. And you want to be part of what's important.

That fire is continuous. It never goes out.

"I belong to the church I was born into, which is the First Baptist here. But I am a Square Ground Creek too. I attend all the religious ceremonies out at the square. You have a lead singer, and the ones following it are the chorus, and that's part of the stomp dancing.

"Usually you start off around the fire; the fire is like an altar in the church. A lot of people think Creek worship fire, but they don't. But the [mound] out here begins with the bird world. See, you have different levels scattered underneath. And this is the only mound out here that has a Bible in it. Yes, my grandmother's Bible. Sakim thought it was important for me to have it in.

"And that fire is continuous. It never goes out. You take that fire with you in a lantern, and you have a fire keeper, and then he lights the next fire.

"My *minia* (grandmother) out here and my *anida* [great-grandmother], they used to attend a square ground at Boggs Pond [west of the Chipola River in Jackson County]. People would come in at Boggs Pond and stay two months in the fall, and that ended up with Harvest Busk. They'd gather the [wild Spanish] cows up and the hogs out of the woods, and they'd cure the beef jerky and cure that pork, and my granddaddy would divide it out among the different families.

"Creek Indian women do all the work. Those men get out and gather [game] up, and they would kill it. Then the women would take over. The women would skin it and everything else. And there'd be one group that'd go down to Port St. Joe and stay a month getting a year's supply of salt. And it'd take a week getting to Port St. Joe; wagon and walking.

"And they took muck out of the bottom of Boggs Pond and spread it over that sand, to be able to grow anything. Those are sand ridges on that side of Chipola River.

When they dredged the river, they blocked those [fishing] sloughs.

"When they dredged the river, they blocked those [fishing] sloughs. So where we used to fish, you can't even fish anymore. [The sand] filled them up. And that's where a lot of the fish beds were. And now there're no fish down here 'cause 'bout the time the fish get on a bed, the water drops out and leaves all the beds. We've not had good fishing since that dam went in [at] Chattahoochee. They have wonderful fishing behind the dam, but they ruined all of it down here. You have to work at it," Ramsey said. "I love to fish.

"I like big fish, and it takes eight big fish for me and my wife, and I have to spend all afternoon catching [them]. I put the rest back. But you have to be real careful; you have to wet your hands. We never heard of this disease when

I was young, but now they have a fungus that will attack those scales and make sores on the fish. And I've caught warmouths with sores that big around." The size of a saucer. "And when you touch them with dry hands, it [disrupts] the slime, and that disease can get 'em. You had that same thing up the river about two years ago—where they were catching fish with sores on them. It always happens sometime when the water was very low and stagnant.

"When I was a boy, I'd never think about trying to walk across the Apalachicola, and in recent years, it's been so dry you could walk across. It's awfully hard down here for any of the natural systems to keep going.

"Why does [Atlanta] want to get so large? I never have decided that. I've always ranged chickens. But I've put a few chickens in a pen. They just get along so well and lay and everything. But I don't crowd that pen, or they'd start eating each other, and I feel that's the way people are. Everybody has to have a certain amount of space.

"All this land used to be open. You could go hunting anywhere you wanted to. You could go fishing anywhere you wanted to. But now somebody from Ohio comes here and they buy land; the first thing they do is put a fence as high as this house and just dare you to put one toe in it. And hunting clubs rent all this river land, and you can't even hunt or get into the river except for public ramps. I grew up with the forest being everybody's, the river being everybody's.

"And I don't believe in gambling. I think there're too many other things that Indian people could go into to make money. You don't see the reservations putting up grocery stores; they have Safeway or Krogers come in."

Chief Ramsey led me past two larger-than-life paintings of himself, first in Muskogee, then in Miccosukee ceremonial dress, as he ushered me out to the bird yard. Chickens clucked in a roomy pen; geese, peacocks, and a large black swan ranged under hanging baskets of vibrant pink and purple impatiens. There was no person better suited to welcome me to this basin that had once been everybody's.

Sakim: Muskogee Medicine Maker and Webmaster

Charles Daniel Randall Andrew Daniels-Sakim shortened his name to Sakim for good reason. Sakim is a Creek language and culture teacher in north central Florida, founder of a Creek archive collection, and webmaster of the Creek Culture Web site (www.tfn.net/Museum). He and his family are subjects of numerous Muskogee-Creek language studies. Creek communi-

> I grew up with the forest being everybody's, the river being everybody's.

Fig. 2.2. Muskogee
medicine maker
Sakim. Photo by
Faith Eidse.

ties up and down the Apalachicola, from Eastpoint to Blountstown, have invited Sakim to help them revive language, culture, and ritual.

Sakim has studied ancient and modern medicines and is a maker of medicine, or shaman, one who is "with the invisible worlds," he said. He has driven 500 miles to deliver medicine, sing a prayer, or hold a hand. He is also a ceremonial leader, following a family tradition and line of succession. For Christian Creeks, who are the majority, Sakim has joined with full-blood Florida Seminole Mary Johns to provide Creek songbooks and translations of favorite hymns, as well as scriptures in the Creek language. Sakim was featured in a flute workshop at the annual Common Ground on the Hill festival at McDaniel College in Westminster, Maryland. Near his Tallahassee home on August 7, 2001, he told his story, sitting straight-backed, white-haired, blue-eyed, and intense.

"The Maker of Medicine: one may be the healer, usually a ceremonial leader; another is the pharmacist or herbalist. And one of them—the psychiatrist equivalent—we might call the diagnostician—his or her job is to ascertain the cause of the illness and then send you to the right person to correct it, which might be with herbs or with some psychological prescription involving fasting and other things. So it's a whole hospital staff rolled into one.

"But see, a lot of people look at me, and of course I look like my European half, which is not unlike many of the early southeastern peoples. The darkening of the Native American population actually didn't get started in full until the early 1800s and the beginning of the removals. If you check the very earliest descriptions, you'll find that the East Coast Native Americans ranged widely in size and feature. Whole groups had green or hazel eyes. Some groups have blue eyes. For instance, Neamathla from Florida was tall, of medium complexion and blue eyes.

"But many of the Creek kids were also already mixed-blood, and the population was very mixed in its complexion when they were rounded up. Any family that could [pass for white] either hid out or parceled their children out.

"And the government was the primary force behind removal, especially from south Georgia and north Florida. It was an economic decision based on land use. Number one, all of the tribes making up the Creek confederacy already had cleared, plowed land. They were in a good, rich location, usually in a river plain. Get rid of the people because the land is all ready to use.

"And here in north Florida from the Apalachicola River in both directions Andrew Jackson had formed a land company in Nashville and then came on down to Georgia and recruited some of his acquaintanceship and kinfolk, and they basically divided the land up before they ever crossed the Spanish frontier. And Native Americans were caught in the middle.

"Many of the southern families had no problems with their Indian neighbors. They depended on them. When these families couldn't make it, their local Indian neighbors showed them what they could eat, how to process it, how to hunt.

"[My family] held their ground right outside of Jacksonville on Amelia Island, the same land that they have occupied for probably one thousand years. The oldest written records go back to 1705.

"The tribal community covers the whole Apalachicola group. The map merely shows where they were the day that their location was recorded. These people were river travelers. And the Apalachicolas were in the South before the rest of the Creeks came. They are the founding town. And I have relatives from the Atlantic Ocean all the way across to the Mississippi River [and to California].

"Now the Creek communities knew who was of Creek descent and who wasn't, and we had our own list, which was pretty accurate. And provisions were made anyway for people that may have been lost or misplaced, but the government decided, 'There'll be more people.' And so, back in the seventies, the [government] began publishing notices in local newspapers. They announced the Creek descendants were going to receive payments. Suddenly everybody was part Indian. And for a short while, white people just about disappeared from the Deep South, and overnight whole tribes were formed.

"People who had no interest, no knowledge, no anything, suddenly became Indian. And what did they do? They got the Ben Hunt—*The Complete Book of Indian Crafts and Lore*. One of these so-called west Florida chiefs had—a Iroquois beaded dance apron over his shoulders. And he's got a Navajo velveteen shirt on, and he's got, oh, Navajo high-top moccasins, which he got from Tandy Leather Company. And he's got a silver concho belt on, which he bought from American Handicraft Stores, and there's rug fringe.

"And these people looked ridiculous, but they dressed up in feathers and beadwork and fancy clothing and hooted and hollered, and they held little rallies in shopping centers and [faked] authentic Indian dances. And one little dance team copied the Hopi snake dance, and I keep hoping that some Hopi elder is gonna come along, because they're messing around with a sacrament.

"But they really can't adopt a worldview without a thorough knowledge of the language, and you don't change your whole worldview [overnight]. You can't relate to the [Native American] sense of living entity.

"Our original [ceremonial] grounds is right up here [near Havana]— I-10 went right over the middle of it. When Mr. Ramsey's group asked us to relocate [in Blountstown], there were no Indian tribes in west Florida. There were Indian citizens, families who had a fair knowledge of their genealogy and their background. To be truthful, they had no [cohesive] culture, no language. They were just people of Indian descent living in the close-knit community of a small rural town.

"Well, when the docket monies became available, these people turned to the Panhandle Area Educational Consortium, PAEC. In about 1980–81, [they] asked, would I teach a class in the Indian language?

"And so I began going over once a month to the little town of Bruce, and these people showed up in war bonnets and feathers, straight out of John Wayne movies. And what I've tried to do over the last twenty years is to teach them Muskogee culture and dress and some of the language and the music. "Cultural revivification" is what PAEC called it.

"And so, honestly, there were small little bits of surviving mechanisms,

> They really can't adopt a worldview without a thorough knowledge of the language.

> I've tried . . . to teach them Muskogee culture and dress and some of the language and the music.

the way Mama did something is the way Grandma and Great-grandma did it. The so-called folk cures were shared by [everyone], and so it's hard to tell the origin of who got what from whom.

"For instance, in Dr. Ramsey's family, they have been church people from well before the early 1900s, and, in fact, the record will show that the vast majority of the Indians who were removed to the West were already Christians. Something like 80 percent of the Cherokee on the removal were already Christians, and they were in their second generation of Native Christianity.

"Record keeping, order, is an extremely important part of the Muskogee universe [represented by the square ground mound]. That's the key of our whole worldview.

"[Former FSU professor J. Leitch Wright] got a history grant to write *Creeks and Seminoles*. And everywhere he went people would refer him to me or my records. So, quite reluctantly, Leitch Wright came down to our museum, which used to be at Wakulla Springs.

"As a serendipitous act, my mother was on her way back from Oklahoma. And so [Dr. Wright] saw her outside throwing peanuts to some of the squirrels and said, 'Oh I bet you're a Native American.'

"And she said, 'Yes. My son has moved our family museum to the Springs.' And Mother said that his jaw dropped all the way to his knee. That if he had been a mule, she could have put six feed buckets on him.

"So Dr. Wright [said], 'You don't mean that man named Sakim in there? He doesn't look Indian.'

"My mother and I spent several days explaining language one way or the other. And I read his manuscript, and it was just excellent.

"But he still wasn't sure. So he took everything that I had told him about language and mailed it off to Dr. Crawford at University of Georgia, Athens, and had him verify. And he also sent it to John Attinasi, a linguist at Columbia [now at California State University].

"And Crawford sent back and said, 'Yes, not only is this very accurate, I am glad to finally learn what the word 'stinkard' means [conquered Indian][6] and where it came from.' And John Attinasi said, 'I've been doing linguistic work with Sakim for several years now, studying the Apalachicola language.'

"[After the state bought Wakulla Springs], we went to Blountstown in the old courthouse downtown until we got kicked out of there. They thought they could just take over the collection. See, they had no idea, now, this is an [established] nonprofit. We're an old museum. We go back to the fifties. We just aren't fortunate enough to own our own building.

"We're in boxes and crates, and we are mildewing and molding. And I've got nine thousand books, many of them two hundred years old, going to ruin. I have one hundred years of Creek clothing that I'm sure is just molded.

"We got all these people across the river over there. For twenty years [I taught] them language, culture, shepherded them to Oklahoma. I've had the chiefs of many of the Indian nations to visit there.

"Now, half of my family, or two-thirds, became Christian about 1887–88. But they made a mass decision to join a church for the simple reason, unbeknownst to a lot of people, the government was still removing Indians.

"They were sending people back from Oklahoma to visit their kinfolks and induce them— they weren't using the troops any more—because the remaining Creeks do hold on to some good farmland. Naval stores were coming into importance, and some of these [pine] lands were held in Creek hands. Plus the government had an early payout to people of Cherokee descent. And then the [1887] Dawes Commission came into being, and members of my family were afraid that this man gathering information about who's Indian [was putting them] on a list to be shipped west.

"There were a limited number of people where the language continued to be spoken, and my family happened to be one of them. Muskogee is the name of the language family, and Creek is the most common name in English. But the Creek language changed considerably on the other side of the river in Indian Territory. When I've been over, old people would sometimes bring their children or their grandchildren and ask me to say something. And they would say, 'That's the way my grandparents used to talk.' So people have said I am literally maybe the Shakespeare of Muskogee. My vocabulary is very antiquated.

"I have fifty thousand words typed up sitting on the Web site. And Dr. Rob MacLaury, who is now a linguist—I guess it's [at the University of Pennsylvania,] Philadelphia—came to spend time with me, and he discovered that our color system is really quite involved and that we have a green-yellow focus. But then he discovered, by listening to me and my kids and some of our relatives, that by our enunciation of our word for "red" that we could actually indicate the shade and intensity of red, a phenomenon that hadn't been discovered before.

"All during the seventies I went to Eastpoint, I think every other Tuesday night. We had language classes, culture classes. We sang and we danced. Because just getting together one to four times a year for a ceremony was not helping the kids because they no longer had Indian or mixed-blood playmates. And so that's why we began our community schools."

"[Bill Adler, a staff writer for the Florida Department of Commerce in 1974–75 and, before that, for the *Tallahassee Democrat*,] interviewed a fish-

For twenty years [I taught] them language, culture, shepherded them to Oklahoma.

People have said I am literally maybe the Shakespeare of Muskogee.

erman who was out there singing the old Creek fishing songs. And he always came back with a boat full of oysters. It must have worked. And out of that Mr. Adler wrote a small article for *Southern Living*. Then he wrote another one for [*Access*] called 'Technology Heals the Body but Tradition Heals the Soul.'" Adler's April 1975 *Southern Living* feature reports that Muskogee chief Edward Evans of Eastpoint asked Sakim to teach them language, music, garment design, basket weaving, and to revive the Green Corn Busk, as well as build a permanent council house.

"And then this [FSU music] anthropologist visited, and he wrote [me] that he was amazed that Indian culture and language survived." Dale Olsen's June 1974 letter reads: "It is sometimes hard to believe that the Creek language is so foreign to descendents of such a one-time proud people. Chief Evans said that his father used to beat him whenever he repeated a few of the Creek words he had learned from his grandfather. By teaching the Indians the language of their forefathers, you are doing much to instill in them a feeling of pride, which is rightfully theirs."

Sakim said he used to play a traditional river reed flute with his father, which interested ethno-musicologists. "We've always been flute makers. See, I taught several people how to make flutes. The cane that you make flutes out of grows on the Apalachicola River. I'm very selective, and I only gather mature cane, *arundinaria*, that's the right age and that's not reproducing.

"And I and my family may be the last people who still gather wild rice off the Wakulla and other local rivers. Come August, it's all over our part of Florida. Go out in a boat with a big, nice, fresh-washed sheet, take dowels and shake the plants and get all the [seeds] off." Sakim also mentioned the early winter ceremony of *chthlo-nithkee*, or lightered knot fishing night.

"I have lots of articles [on the Web]. But we have our own little newspaper. It's been around for decades. That's what the west Florida people have tied into. They just didn't have anything, and they've gotten what they needed. Hundreds now know some Creek language, many learned finger weaving, buckskin making, herbal remedies. [I taught] two sisters how to do traditional native basketry designs, trained many to be ceremonial leaders. Taught [people] how to sew traditional clothing, and they made a good living with it for years. [I] recorded music, vocabulary, and stories for numerous researchers over the years. Now I can go do something else."

These days Sakim volunteers for Tallahassee Freenet, signing up new accounts behind a desk at Leroy Collins Leon County Public Library. He appears at home in a Florida shaped variously by General Jackson's Seminole Wars and defeat of the British, colonist settlement, and the eventual revival of Seminole and Creek cultures.

Fig. 2.3. Retired judge David Taunton on his dock in Roberts Slough. Photo by Faith Eidse.

Judge Taunton: "Robin Hood" Defender of Swamp Dwellers

David Taunton was elected Gulf County judge five times by people who didn't want a lawyer for the job. A school principal with a doctorate in education, Taunton had such compassion for swamp dwellers that he earned the title "Robin Hood Judge" from several Florida newspapers and *Time*. In Taunton's courtroom, "the rule of law has been compassion for the poor," *Time* wrote in September 1978.

Though Florida's Judicial Qualifications Commission sought to have Taunton removed for "conduct unbecoming a member of the judiciary," the Florida Supreme Court let him off with a reprimand, saying his compassion verged on bias, but that his motives were "wholesome and unselfish."[7]

Taunton ran for the job, he said, to protect people like his widowed grandmother, who lost the family home because she was unaware of a $200 lien against it. And while he was judge, "I just saw a lot of kids that needed a place to live." David and his wife, Abigail, founded the Taunton Family Children's Homes, which house minors whose parents are serving jail terms or are otherwise unavailable.

For their initiative, the *Oprah* television show awarded the Tauntons a "Use Your Life Award," sponsored by actor Paul Newman and Amazon.com's chief executive officer, Jeff Bazos. The show visited secluded Wewahitchka and gave $100,000 to the Children's Homes, which have sheltered hundreds of children over several decades.

The donation helped the Tauntons build a new kitchen, renovate a third children's home, take in fifteen more children, and fund several college scholarships. They no longer face foreclosure, and the children live in a virtual paradise with outdoor pool, gymnasium, and fishing dock on Roberts Slough.

Taunton also owned the *Gulf County Breeze*, a monthly newspaper full of local history, features on women's contributions, and editorials replete with such folk wisdom as, "Eat what you can, can what you can't, and what you can't can, turn the hogs in on and then eat the hogs."

Taunton's mother sewed clothes from flour sacks, and his father built a new house with planks and nails from a leaky old one. Taunton was one of thirteen children raised in the river swamp. He still lives near Old Fort Place, where the first white settlers, some of them his ancestors, took part in Indian removal and died in retaliatory raids.

In an airy gazebo overlooking an aquamarine pool, he recorded his oral history on February 15, 2002.

"We built [our home] twenty-two years ago," Taunton said. "We've taken in between two hundred and three hundred kids over the last twenty-two years. Some are here for a few days and gone; some stay here the rest of their lives. We have seven in college, ten in college next year. We have five that work in the truss plant up there that are grown." Taunton Truss, Inc., owned by Abigail, is expanding to $10 million annual production capacity from $2 million.

"My dad loved children, and he really wanted to start a children's home. He had a third-grade education; my mom had an eighth-grade education. Four [of their thirteen children] died early on, but they sent nine of us to college. I was the first one to finish college, and I ran for judge and was elected, mostly out of respect for my family. I served as county judge for twenty years, and we built this house and just started taking kids in. We're not part of the state system at all. It's private."

In the *Gulf County Breeze*, Taunton is gradually recording a history of the area. "You've gotta tell the story of how this area was settled, how it's evolved over the years. [The paper] was established in 1925, same year the county was established. It's really prospered. Circulation is between two thousand and three thousand right now.

"This area is on the verge of growth. St. Joe has subdivisions on the drawing board that have 2,000 units in this one, 1,500 in that one. Over the next

Eat what you can, can what you can't, and what you can't can, turn the hogs in on and then eat the hogs.

ten years, this and Bay County are projected as the two fastest-growing counties in the state.

"The first white settlers that came to this area were soldiers during the War of 1812 under the direction of General Andrew Jackson. They were so fascinated by the beauty they found in this area around Wewahitchka, Blountstown—the Apalachicola basin river swamp—that they got their families and brought them back here. Meanwhile the Territory of Florida was originated, and General Andrew Jackson was governor of the territory, territorial Florida.

"He assigned Thomas Richards, one of the original white families in this area, to be his Indian agent. There was a bill passed by territorial Florida called 'The Indian Removal Act,' and it was Thomas Richards's job to remove the Indians from this area [to] west of the Mississippi River. 'Course that didn't go very well.

"The Richards family settled on the banks of the Dead Lakes, 4 miles north of here, originally. But there was a massacre [by Indians]. And the house was burned; several people were killed.

"There's several old graveyards, [such as] Jehu. Jehu was one of Richards's sons. He was the kid, one of the two children that escaped that massacre. That's where Jehu Cemetery got its name and Jehu Landing got its name. He hid in the swamps and escaped. He and his sister fled to a neighbor's house.

"This particular area right here is called Honeyville. The white settlers that survived that attack fled south, and 100 yards from where we're sitting, there was a 2-acre compound with a fort built within that compound.

"They have a historical marker up on the highway, says 'Old Fort Place.' It later was burned down. But as the Indians were moved out or intermarried or peaceably intermingled with the white settlers, eventually the Fort Place was abandoned. Several families lived in that Old Fort Place, including my great-grandfather Jeremiah Roberts and his wife, Sally Scott. They had twenty-two kids; only ten of 'em lived 'cause those were tough, tough times.

"My grandfather actually came down the river; the river has such an intricate role in the early-on settlement of this area 'cause it was the only reasonable access. And he, of course, married one of those twenty-two kids, my grandmother Carrie Roberts.

"And when Gulf County was carved out of Calhoun County in 1925, he was on the initial Board of County Commissioners. His name was Saul Van Horne. He came all the way from New York but found his way here only because of the Apalachicola River, 'cause this was just a jewel, [and] there was no road access to it. There was no way across what's called Scott's Ferry now, the Chipola River.

"And my daddy, he came from Phenix City, Alabama; Tallassee, Alabama, which is part of this same river swamp basin. This was back in the 1920s, early thirties. 'Course, he and his buddies just fished along the river, and then they would barter their fish for provisions and keep fishin'. Then [they would] get all the way to Apalachicola, and they would load their paddle boats on a steamboat, hitch a ride back up to south Alabama, south Georgia, and start the whole thing all over again. So the river was just the spinal cord of civilization in this area.

"But when my dad got here, the old fort was abandoned at the time, and he moved in it with his two or three buddies. By then it had been pretty well ransacked. It had been taken off the pilings; the timbers that made up the 2-acre compound had been used to build homes. One of the homes is partially still here, where my grandmother was raised. But 'bout all that was left was actually the port house, which had the portholes where they shot the muskets through.

"What made this such an attractive spot was this is not only fed by the river, but, in low water, this is fed by some huge springs. So it's fresh springwater here no matter how low the river gets. Normally, this was fed by backwater from the river and six months by the spring. But now, hardly ever does river water get in here, so it's mostly fed by the springs.

"We are about a mile or so west of the Chipola River, and then across the Chipola River there would be what is called Cutoff Island. That's formed by the Chipola River and the Apalachicola River converging. It's about an 11-mile-long island.

"The original trail—the route that all the early-on settlers used—was right along the curvature of this swamp. Starting at Blue Gator, which is north, is bounded by the Dead Lakes, and going all the way to Willis Landing, which is down in the Dalkeith area, it would be about 17 miles as it wound along the slough.

"Fifty different clans of Indians lived along this swamp basin from Blountstown to Apalachicola. One of these Indians was John Blount. He was befriended by General Andrew Jackson, and he served as an informant. He had to be removed because of the hostility.

"I'm writing a book right now," Taunton added. "The name of it is *Buck*, but it has to do with early-on vagabonds that were partially Indians, partially black. Some were totally Indian but had been abandoned by their side of the family and by the white settlers because they had intermarried. There is considerable documentation that there were several of these families that for years lived in this river swamp.

"The swamp was their livelihood. They were the best preservationists in the world. Without any laws written on the books, they took better care of nature and its bounty than we civilized folks.

"Back then [Indians and early white settlers] basically cleared out little garden spots here and there. Most of their meat came from the wild turkeys, fish, deer, and the river swamp—loggerhead turtles, ducks. There's just an abundance of wild game all throughout that era.

"For the next century, settlers moved here [and] lived very much like the Indians. The first jobs would have been logging the huge primitive cypress swamps, and that would have been in the latter part of the nineteenth century. Mr. William Lawson Whitfield moved here in 1850 with his own personal slave, John Henry Roberson. And they got a job logging in the Dead Lakes.

"Whitfields have been in the honey business over the years. Now the Laniers are primary, but the Lanier family and the Whitfields are intermarried from way, way back. My great-grandfather was one of the original honey producers here too. That's why this is called Honeyville, 'cause this is the first area that tupelo honey was actually produced. Ninety percent of what you saw [in Roberts Slough] was tupelo.

"That [tupelo] was logged in the 1950s, 1960s during the heyday of early-on ply board. Made a fine cabinetry ply board out of white tupelo gum. They refuse to die. And they still blossom, and there's still an abundance of tupelo blossoms and honey.

"[The first tree to be logged in this swamp] was cypress. There was a huge cypress sawmill in Apalachicola . . . when I was a young boy. My great-grandfather was a cypress logger, my grandfather was a cypress logger.

"But I do remember when the loggers would come through in the summer and early winter. The girdling crew chopped huge rings around these magnificent trees. Sometimes it would take almost all day to girdle one tree. Then in the spring when the sap tried to rise, it couldn't do so because of the girdle. It made the tree lighter. So then the saw crew would come through with these huge gator tail saws, and they would saw the tree down and saw it into log lengths.

"And then the floating crew would come, and they got paid so much for each tree they floated. And they would literally ride on top of the trees with a spike pole. And they would thrust that spike pole out ahead of 'em and then pull the log, and they could fairly get those logs trotting comin' out through there.

"In the main slough they were rafted into what's called billies. Then they were pulled by primitive motorboats, called 'pitty-pats' by the sound [of the] 1- or 2-cylinder engines.

"They bound them into huge, huge rafts, so big that the loggers would actually live on top of the rafts goin' down the river. They would shovel dirt up on some of the sturdier logs and make them a campfire. In Apalachicola, they sawed the logs into what's called cants, and they were shipped to England and France and all over the world.

"There were a lot of these trees; whenever they were sawed originally, they floated. But it would get stuck in the trees and the limbs. Since [the logger] was getting paid so much a log, he would abandon that one and jump on an easier one. Then that log that was stuck would absorb water and eventually sink into the mud. And those deadhead logs, I'm sure there's layers of 'em, 30 to 40 foot deep under some of the mud out there now.

"There's a statute that empowers the loggers to brand their logs just as it allowed them to brand their cows and mark their hogs. You had to register your brand in the county seat at the courthouse. Nobody could bother your log or your cows or your hogs.

"We're not in favor of [having to get a permit to deadhead] at all. The same laws should apply that apply to the bottoms of the bays and govern the oysters, and it's [hard work], opened to the public.

"In the last several years, there was two or three cases made, leading to the provision where you have to get a permit," which costs $5,000, Taunton added. "People did it to raise Christmas money. They supplemented their income; when the paper mill was down, you saw a lot of it.

"During the twenty years that I was county judge, there were cases made that involved a conflict in culture. The person who was charged was carryin' on a lifelong way of life. One was a gentleman by the name of Durden Hall, who's deceased now. He was raised on this river swamp, and he lived off loggerhead turtles [and] 'coons. He never wore shoes. In fact, he came to court barefooted.

"[His conviction] was a violation of his culture, his livelihood. And I wrote [an] opinion on that and suspended the fine. What he'd done all his life was all of a sudden wrong because of a change in culture. Loggerhead turtles were placed on the endangered species [list]. 'Course he probably felt like he was [an] endangered species too.

"I probably should have recused myself. [I had] some knowledge and some sympathy of his way of life from very early on.

"In the forties, there was a huge camp on [Virginia Cut Slough], also served as a bee apiary. And it was owned by the local sheriff, Byrd Parker. And that Virginia Cut Slough was so huge that he was able to barge those bees in and out. In fact, I found recently [a] remnant of one of the barges.

The size of that barge causes you to realize how magnificent that slough was at one time.

"Anyway, in 1958, when the initial dredging was to take place, pumping up a mountain of sand in the mouth of that centuries-old slough, the Corps gave Sheriff Parker notice. So he tore his camp down and moved his bees out to the River Styx on the Apalachicola River. But he left his lighthouse . . . where he had his generator. And he gave that to our family for our personal camp.

"Back then camping season customarily started the second Saturday of November. And that river was just buzzing with activity. You could almost see one campsite from the other, goin' down the river.

"As kids, we were raised looking forward to camping season, what we called hunting season. Very little hunting done, mostly camping, more so than any other vacation or holiday of the year. It was such a tradition.

"During hunting season, we would load our boats up, and back then, we'd head to Virginia Cut until it got stopped where we couldn't. And even after that we would park our boat at the mountain of sand and carry our provisions for a mile down that Virginia Cut on our backs.

"We'd take all the children in the neighborhood that wanted to go with us. Sometime we'd have forty to fifty. We continue that tradition even to this day. This past camping season we had seventeen tents; we're still allowed to camp in tents [on the Northwest Florida Water Management District property]. And I think we had about fifty kids.

"My first camping trip was when I was eight years old. I'm sixty-two now, so that's how many consecutive camping trips I've gone on the second Saturday in November.

"We explore a lot. The kids learn to walk logs. We take 'em out and we do a scavenger hunt: snails, clams, five-pointed leaves, on and on it goes. We teach some how to find their way in a natural setting. You'll always find the drift from the water on the north side of the trees.

"Lots of times [I've been lost on this river swamp]. It used to be scary when I was a little kid. But it's kinda pleasant now. I know I can find my way out by using all the techniques. 'Course if the sun's out, it's easy to get a direction, and generally we're on the Cutoff Island, so if you walk very far on a certain path you'll come to a river.

"The entire time I was growing up [this swamp] was so mucky that there were areas that you'd actually almost have to swim in the mud. Just rich, rich top soil, decayed leaves, and vegetation. This river swamp is what feeds those oyster bars.

"We're probably 35 miles upstream from the oyster bars in Apalachicola

Each year that same mucky swamp . . . has gotten firmer and firmer, largely from the mechanical dredging operation.

Bay, but we have seen this coming since 1958. Gradually each year that same mucky swamp that you would bog down knee-deep . . . tryin' to get across, has gotten firmer and firmer, largely from the mechanical dredging operation. A longtime practice of the Corps [was], when they would pump these sand mountains at these deposit areas, then on high water take bulldozers and push the sand back in so they could pump more in there next season.

"That sand has found its way across these swamps, and where there were sloughs when I was growing up, now there are no sloughs. Gum Drift Slough was a major slough. Maddox Slough was another major slough that feeds this. Those two are the main arteries of this several-thousand-acre tupelo swamp south of Wewa all the way to Burgess Creek. Both have been completely destroyed. Some areas, you can't even tell where the slough bed was 'cause it's right level across with sand, with trees, now, fifteen-year-old trees growin' right where it used to be the main drift of the slough.

"At first we didn't know what was happening. We would go to fishing holes that used to be 10 feet deep, marked on a measuring tree, and it would be only 8 feet deep. The next year it would only be 7 feet deep and then 4 feet. Then the fishing holes disappeared because they were [being filled in]. We wondered, 'Is the bottom growing up?' The water wasn't falling, the land was rising.

"But in the process, all the river swamp that was fed by those two major arteries and the rich nutrients that went on down to feed those oysters now is sealed beneath a layer of sand. And you can walk across those same areas now the biggest part of the year without getting your feet muddy. And that's why the oystermen are complaining about the waters being clear. I can see unstopping the sloughs, but what's it gonna ever take to get this thick layer of sand off the top of those nutrients?

"Some of the tupelo trees are dying in areas because tupelo depends on that same rich nutrient. The ironwood tree is taking over the swamp. It used to be just a minority species, and it has absolutely no use. It grows crooked, can't be used for lumber, does not have a blossom that could be used for making honey. It just covers an area.

"This formerly was filled with bream and shellcracker and trout. Now just as the cypress and gum trees are being replaced by the ironwood, the shellcracker and bream and bass are being replaced by the gar and the blackfish and the jackfish—the trash fish. And that's kinda sad.

"This last two years [are] the first two years in the history of our family that we haven't been able to catch game fish behind our house. And that's such a tragedy. You know we built this children's home here primarily be-

> The water wasn't falling, the land was rising.

> What's it gonna ever take to get this thick layer of sand off the top of those nutrients?

cause of the allurement of this swamp and bein' able to take little kids out there and fish right off that dock.

"Maybe if we got rid of the dam our problems would be solved. I think even more so there are a couple of other culprits. One has been the navigational window, which has served to scatter the fish across the swamp and allow them to lay their eggs, and then the dam gates are closed, and the fish are stranded and their eggs are destroyed.

"But I think the biggest culprit is when those major arteries were clogged, then the capillaries had no supply of energy, and then the body dies, just as would the human body. And what we are looking at is a dying and a dead swamp.

What we are looking at is a dying and a dead swamp.

"[Virginia Cut] was the shortcut route for the Indians. They made their way from the River Styx area of Liberty County, where there's major Indian clans, to the citrus groves that were rich along this area of the swamp.

"I've found that there was a fella by the name of Dr. Keys that brought citrus here right after the Civil War and planted those along this same two trail road that served as the main travel artery for the early-on settlers. This, in fact, was the first commercial citrus operation in the state of Florida as far as can be determined. It revived the steamboat industry for some while here. There was a major freeze early on in the twentieth century that destroyed lots of 'em.

"Those Indians could make that, about a 3-mile trip, in a couple of hours on canoes. But on horseback and foot it was about a 60-mile trip. It still is today, from the Telogia area [on] modern-day roadways.

"To me it was sad that just some guy sittin' behind a desk in Mobile or Washington could sign a document—they never had seen this swamp—and say, 'Let's pump a mountain of sand right here 'cause we need this water to go down the river.'

"The [Corps] is scheduled maybe to do a little work in the very mouth of [Virginia Cut]. The fact is, it's stopped up for miles. It has trees, you know, huge trees growing right in what used to be the slough bed. The only part of it that's not filled up with sand is filled with stagnant water. So we've taken what was a natural paradise, for our Indians and for game, and we've turned it into a graveyard, a dying place for the fish and for the game.

"You would [fish] in the river, not in the sloughs anymore 'cause there's no access for the fish. Occasionally when we have a river reading of 15 to 18 feet (at Blountstown), then we get a few fish flushed back in here. But that is so rarely true anymore that you have a river that floods the backwater.

"Central to [river restoration] is looking at some of these main tributaries. Otherwise it's like trying to revive a body without having blood goin' through it.

"We had hogs in some river swamp, as did about five or six other families. Any given day we could come back with a wild hog. Sometimes we'd only take one bullet with us. We had hunting dogs, we had a half bird [dog]/half hound dog that would find the hogs; the bulldogs would catch 'em. The bulldogs would follow along the trail behind us until the hound dog/bird dog bayed up the hogs. They wouldn't even track 'em down. But once they heard that ol' bird dog/hound dog barking, they would zero in, and the hog would customarily back himself up against what's called a tussock. That's a blown-over tree with the roots sticking up. And he would defend himself the best he could.

"Usually you'd have three catch dogs. One would get at one ear, one would get at the other, one would get directly in front of the hog. If the hog diverted even slightly toward the left, then the one on the right would catch. Just fascinating to see them work as a team.

"A dog would get cut, and my dad would take ether and put the dog to sleep, and then he'd take fishin' line and sew him up. The dogs would be, I mean, within inches, inches of the hog, and he would sit there like he was petrified, you know, not lookin' one way or the other. Then all of a sudden [the hog] would dart. The hog would have long tusks that came out either side. They would sling their head, and if they caught [a dog], then they cut them pretty substantially.

"[One local character] had this donkey called Blue Moon, and this donkey actually would ride in his boat with him. The donkey would never move, never turned the boat over. And the donkey would help chase the hogs down, actually help catch the hogs just like the dogs would. Then he'd have a way to get the hog out once it was killed. He'd put it on the donkey's back. 'Course then he was prone to drink, as was the donkey," Taunton laughed.

"I was born in 1939. The Depression supposedly was over, but it wasn't for our family. We depended on the swamps in lots of ways; fish, wild hogs, turkey, deer. Now, here in 2002, we've got a new generation of people movin' in, and 90 percent of them never even give any thought to that swamp out there, and that's kinda sad.

"We were survivors, you know, whatever it took to have food on the table. The swamp we looked at as our life's blood, really.

"My dad was a welder in the St. Joe paper mill. [It] was built in 1938. It was big-time money back then, $1 an hour or so, then $2 an hour. Every year and a half [Momma] had a baby. We supplemented our income by the swamp; either by logging or fishin' or hunting. We never went hungry. Be-

The swamp we looked at as our life's blood, really.

tween the swamp and what it offered and the garden and what it offered, we ate very well.

"[Clothes are] a story within itself. We would go to the feed store, and my mom would make the gentleman there go through a stack of [patterned] feed sacks until she [found a match with] what she'd already had. The clothes that we wore to school, Momma would always get out of [the] Sears Roebuck catalog, but she would sew one patch on top of another for my dad, who, as a welder, was continuously burning holes in his dungarees.

"When my baby brother was the last of us to graduate from junior college, they stopped the ceremony and called my mom and dad up on the stage and gave them an honorary degree.

"About 1952, the rural co-op first brought electricity into this area. We had an outhouse for a toilet; we had a smokehouse where we cured meat. But my dad had come downriver from where they had long had indoor plumbing and electricity. So he was driven by the goal that his children would have a better life.

"This land that we are sitting on was homesteaded by my great-grandfather. My grandfather was educated. He came down the river from New York. But when he died, he had a $200 bank note secured by this acreage and 100 head of cows. The bank foreclosed on that land and got it on a default judgment.

"[My grandma] never knew what happened, and I saw, in fact, that's how a lot of land transferred from the older families to the families that were moving in that were well-educated. By default judgments, small amounts of money owed, mortgages on the land, death in the family.

"Not only blacks, the poor whites lost their land in the same way. And I determined that some day, out of gratitude for my dad giving me a chance to get a good education, I might try to stop some of that. And I was elected judge by the common people and probably over-reacted for the first couple of years. There was a move on to have me thrown out of office early on because I was determined to protect the undefended, the underdog.

"The [Florida] Supreme Court voted seven to nothin' to leave me in office because a lot of local newspapers came to my defense. In other words, I was supposed to sign those same default judgments that always had been signed, transferring property, no questions asked.

"Surely my grandma would have come up with $200 and paid that off. All she knew was the sheriff comes one day and says, 'This is not your property anymore.' She had to relocate from the west side of State Road 71 to where I was raised. But she lost this tract of property.

"The poor people would buy from the appliance store because that's the

Fig. 2.4. Preacher and community icon Joseph McMillan Sr., ninety-three, told his story in his garden while mending a broken leg in March 2003, a year before he died on June 21, 2004. He was born to sharecroppers in Selma, Alabama, and came to Florida during the Depression to lay tracks for Apalachicola Northern Railroad, a member of the "Gandy Dancer Crew."[8] He endured two days firing the boiler at St. Joe mill before escaping to Tate's Hell, where he "cut more logs than anybody" and lived in a floating house. On weekends, he built his home at 242 Twelfth Street, where he and his Sumatra bride raised four children. Photo by Faith Eidse.

only place would give them credit. Just before they'd get their washing machine paid off, [the store] would talk 'em into buying something else. They'd add the washing machine onto that note. So that, in effect, they would never pay anything off, even though they'd paid thousands and thousands of dollars. [The store] would foreclose on it and take everything they had. It was just a disgrace. The [businesses] were right legally; there was a clause in the contract. But they were wrong morally and every other way.

"Eventually this guy with cancer was brought to court; this was one of the cases they took me before the Supreme Court on. Peg-legged man. In fact, I had learned to pulp wood with him years earlier. I admire him very much 'cause he's not on welfare. He had cancer and was dying.

"I said, 'How much does he owe on the washing machine?' The man's name was Alto, and he said: 'Judge, don't worry. They've already cut my electricity off anyway; let 'em have the washing machine back.' So I said, 'No, I got it.' I pulled the money out of my pocket, and I went and paid the electricity bill. But a judge can't get involved in a case before him. He can only rule.

"This was another thing they had filed against me, for example, about having to take a defendant to court in the county where he lived. There was a company locally that would bring families to court in Gulf County even though the bill occurred in Gadsden County. They would get default judgments because maybe [the defendant] couldn't get here. And I resisted that to the point that the Supreme Court drew up new rules and required that the defendant be taken to court in the county where he resided if the bill occurred in that county. So, I won some and I lost some. I survived twenty years and never was seriously contested in any election in five terms. That's the longest in the history of this county."

I resisted . . . to the point that the Supreme Court drew up new rules.

3

From Steamboat "Elation" to Rail and Road

Now and then we had a hope that, if we lived and were good, God would permit us to be pirates . . . but the ambition to be a steamboatman always remained.
Mark Twain

The first journeys by steamboat occurred on the Apalachicola River in the 1820s. Lush, lavish, and electrified is how passengers described their voyages. In this chapter, Neel Yent describes his first encounter with electricity aboard a steamboat, when he tried to extinguish a flaming tungsten wire by blowing on a light bulb. Lavernor (L. L.) Lanier was agog at cigars, cigarettes, and candy sitting out for the taking in the steamboat saloon. John Hentz's family piled into the Model T when they heard the steamboat whistle and raced several miles to meet the lighted princess as she landed—once to receive a new pump organ they'd ordered. Hentz also remembers that the electric lights on the *Callahan* or *Chipola* were the first he'd ever seen. Tungsten was mined in Liberty County thirty years before the first bulb blazed in its houses.

But three decades after the steamboats arrived, a drought dropped the river stage to extreme lows and exposed snags that sank paddle wheel steamboats. Cotton agents began seeking a more reliable way to get their product to market. Railroads arrived by 1853, connecting the Gulf states, through Columbus, Georgia, to Savannah on the Atlantic Ocean. This cut in half the cotton shipped through Apalachicola.[1] When the Union blockaded Apalachicola in 1861, just $1 million worth of cotton was defended with two 34-pound cannons.

Apalachicola's cotton economy ended with the war. By 1882, cotton was shipped off the river by the less weather-dependent rail at River Junction. Apalachicola declined after suffering two devastating downtown fires in the 1890s, and its population of five thousand shrank by half.[2]

Then, as the century turned, so did the city, revived by logging, sponging, fishing, and river travelers.[3] Gilded steamboats arrived, carrying shopping parties to tony Apalachicola department stores. For several decades the plush boats carried musicians and dance parties up and down a mostly rustic river.

But transportation shifted ever more to rail and road with the advent of trucks and clay surface roads from 1901 to 1920. Industrialists changed their use of the river increasingly to hydroelectricity.[4] Hydro lit the first bulb in Columbus in 1882, powered a trolley line by 1895, provided long-distance electrical transmission by 1912.

Despite the Apalachicola's record of extreme flows, the U.S. Army Corps of Engineers tried to keep transportation viable, adding the river to the proposed Intracoastal Waterway endorsed by President Woodrow Wilson. A series of devastating floods between 1901 and 1918 caused poet F. W. Nash to lament clear-cutting in the Chattahoochee basin, but leaders continued to respond with dams and levees that couldn't hold back the floods of 1936, '48, and '61.[5] As dredging and "wing dams" (opposing spoil banks postulated to narrow and scour the channel) shoaled the river,[6] commercial traffic turned to trucking. The Victory Bridge at Chattahoochee was built in 1922 and was followed by the paving of U.S. 90. The 6-mile John Gorrie Memorial Bridge linking Apalachicola and Eastpoint was opened in 1935.[7]

After World War II, James W. Woodruff Sr., a river developer, envisioned the Chattahoochee joining the Intracoastal Waterway with four additional locks and dams, by dredging the Apalachicola and cutting a channel through St. George Island. The Three Rivers Development Association was formed in 1950 from seventy-two counties bordering the Chattahoochee and Apalachicola rivers. Its mission was to promote a new industrial frontier through construction of the Woodruff, Buford, George, and Andrews dams from 1955 to 1963. Georgia Power Company added the Oliver Dam in 1959 to its four at the Falls of Chattahoochee.[8]

In 1960, Apalachicola mayor Jimmie Nichols presented Atlanta mayor William B. Hartsfield with a 2-ton anchor in support of a channel all the way to Atlanta. Hartsfield, backed by West Point flood survivors, asked for "a few million measly dollars." The flood of 1961, 5.67 inches of rain in a day, washed out eight bridges and seemed to prove his point.[9]

Many members of the Florida fishing community have largely opposed development as they seek to preserve one of the last local economies. The river communities that in 1974 defeated a proposed series of dams in the upper Apalachicola have deplored disposal of dredge material on point bars within the riverbank to maintain a barge channel. Sediment has reportedly covered a quarter of the river's banks, destroying habitat, endangering floodplain trees, and blocking sloughs and tributaries. These impacts were

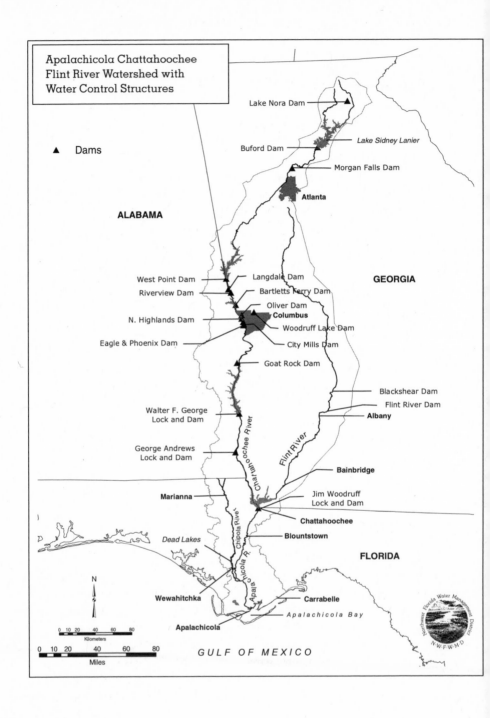

Apalachicola Chattahoochee
Flint River Watershed with
Water Control Structures

▲   Dams

Lake Nora Dam

Lake Sidney Lanier

Buford Dam

Morgan Falls Dam

Atlanta

ALABAMA

West Point Dam
Riverview Dam

Langdale Dam
Bartletts Ferry Dam
Oliver Dam

GEORGIA

Columbus

N. Highlands Dam

Woodruff Lake Dam

Eagle & Phoenix Dam

City Mills Dam

Goat Rock Dam

Blackshear Dam
Flint River Dam
Albany

Walter F. George
Lock and Dam

George Andrews
Lock and Dam

Bainbridge

Jim Woodruff
Lock and Dam

Marianna

Chattahoochee

Dead Lakes

Blountstown

FLORIDA

Chattahoochee River

Flint River

Chipola River

N

Wewahitchka

Apalachicola R.

Carrabelle

Apalachicola Bay

Apalachicola

0 10 20   40   60   80
Kilometers

0 10 20   40   60   80
Miles

GULF OF MEXICO

blamed for a 75 percent decline in game fish on newly spoiled habitat within one year.[10]

In 2002, American Rivers (a nonprofit conservation group) listed the Apalachicola River as the nation's eleventh-most ecologically endangered, due to repeated dredging and drastic flow manipulation. The "Corps periodically opens upstream dams to create 'navigation windows' that allow barges to travel upstream, [but] disrupts natural spawning cycles." It called on Congress to de-authorize channel maintenance.[11] In 2003, the Apalachicola did not make the endangered list.

The Florida Department of Environmental Protection (DEP) calculated that, at $3 million a year spent dredging, only forty cents on each dollar was returned for the $20 million in taxes spent.[12] Assistant Secretary of the Army Joseph Westphal wrote on August 9, 2000, that maintaining navigation "is not economically justified or environmentally defensible." The George W. Bush administration has proposed slashing or eliminating federal funding for dredging.

In this chapter, we hear from four men: the system's last steamboat pilot; a history buff who remembers crossing the river by ferry on horse-drawn wagon; a transportation consultant; and a Corps area supervisor for the tri-state region.

Tom Corley: Last Steamboat Pilot

The moment that boat was under way in the river, she was under the sole . . . control of the pilot.
Mark Twain

During the 1918 flu epidemic, the late Captain Tom Corley was distraught at having to operate a forty-head dairy alone. He was only ten years old when he ran away to the Chattahoochee River and boarded the *W. C. Bradley* in the waning steamboat years.

Aboard the *W. C. Bradley*, he served as captain's boy and soon was promoted to striker pilot. Before his fourteenth birthday, Corley piloted the 202-ton *John W. Callahan* from Columbus to Apalachicola. He received a pilot's license at seventeen, having completed twenty round trips, five at night. He also accurately filled in an outline of the river, noting rocks, snags, height and width of crossings, and pipelines.

"Corley is the last first-class pilot of the Apalachicola River," said his son Ric, who inherited his father's marine surveyor business in Panama City. The Society of Marine Surveyors honored Corley as the oldest and longest-prac-

Fig. 3.1a. Captain Tom Corley, the last first-class steamboat pilot on the Apalachicola River. Photo by permission of his son Ric Corley.

ticing marine surveyor, or inspector, with more than fifty-two years of service, twelve thousand boats surveyed.

Corley, of Cherokee descent, became an Unlimited Master of "any steam vessels, any gross tons on any ocean." During World War II, as a commissioned officer, he chased submarines in the North Sea, the Gulf of Mexico, and the Caribbean Sea. In 1954, he built the oldest business on Grand Lagoon, in Panama City, now Lighthouse Marina.

In April 1969, Corley purchased the sternwheeler *Louise* and ran it on the Apalachicola, Chattahoochee, and Flint rivers for several years, making it one of the most widely traveled diesel sternwheelers anywhere.

Captain Corley recorded his story at his modest home in Panama City on November 30, 2000. He died of natural causes on March 18, 2001, two months shy of turning ninety-three.

"My parents separated when I was six years old. Now, we were all on the farm right there where Fort Benning [Georgia] proper is now. Arthur Bussy owned the plantation, and it reached from the Upatoi Creek at the county line to Jamestown, about 14 miles.

"Now, when my mother and father separated—and I never knew why— my mother went back to her people there east of Columbus in Muscogee County, on a dairy farm. When I reached eight years old, I was put to work like the rest of the labor. And we were milking some forty-odd cows twice a day and all the other chores that accompanied.

"And besides that they did truck farming—vegetable farming. We used to be up early—do the milking [and] get tomatoes, cucumbers, squash, pepper, in continuous baskets set out at the edge of the road. The peddlers would come by and get what they wanted and leave the money and go on about their business. You couldn't do it like that now.

"Then you'd go back and clean up the barn and everything, and the older ones, of course, would go to the plow, the rakes, mowers—or whatever they was using—and work. Well, during school time, I'd go to school.

"But it come along in 1918, the flu epidemic. And everybody in my family, but me, got down with the flu. And we los' my great-grandmother, an uncle, and a first cousin. People were dying like sheep with a rot. And the neighbors would come in. I'd get me four, five over here and four or five over there. Well, I was the only one up, and it fell on me to tell them grown people what to do, and back then children didn't do that.

"About the time my folks were getting up, where they could get out of bed and could get back to their chores, I was so stressed-out I hardly knew who I was.

"Well, my father had two brothers that were on the steamboat, and that was in April. And I thought one evenin': 'I'm gonna get me some stuff together and I'm gonna go on and get one of them boats. I can't take no more of this.' Of course, I was too young to know it was all stress.

"But I had me some stuff together. In place of getting up at three thirty to four o'clock, I got up about a little before three thirty, I got my bag, and I went to the river.

"At that time [Tenth Avenue] was the eastern boundary of the city of Columbus, and we were about three blocks distance from the city limit. So I went down there and I waited 'til daylight before I went to the boat. I didn't tell my uncle nothing about why I was there. But I think the good Lord was working for me—still does.

"But the cabin boy that served the cap'n didn't show up that morning. And I understood he was about fourteen years old, and I was three weeks of being eleven years old. And this cap'n asked my uncle, 'Let [this] guy serve as the cabin boy.'

"I said, 'I'll do anything wants done.' So, that started my career right there.

"The captain at that time was Cap'n Magruder. [The boat] was the *W. C. Bradley*. [My uncles], Frank and Charlie Corley, were engineers on that boat.

"My first trip—it was an elation. I was working. I was gonna get $10 a month. It was the first time I'd been paid to work.

My first trip—it was an elation.

"[A cabin boy] just carried messages around to the passengers—messages that you'd been given. And you cleaned up the captain's quarters. You sent messages between the cap'n and the engine room, anything you don't want spread out all over the boat.

"Sometimes they were written messages, and sometimes they'd tell some message to watch for something on the bank. Back then there were a considerable number of wild animals . . . wildcats, black bear, deer.

"I had been aboard the boat several times by then, but I had never sailed on it. That was my first trip. We went into Apalachicola. And I remember there was buildings, buildings, buildings. There' nothin' down there now. They tore all them brick warehouses down.

"But I remember Wefing's Marine Hardware Store there on the corner of Water Street. I come to know Mr. Wefing well and his son who just sold the business—George Wefing. He lives over there on the island now. We were good friends; I was their oldest customer they had—still.

"When I run away, I was gone three months before they ever found me. We didn't have the communications that we have today, and I stayed right on that boat.

"Finally, when they come to get me—my mother and my grandfather came down, and they were nice. I think they were scared I'd go with my dad and be gone.

"Well, Granddad needed all the help he could get. I told my granddad, 'Grandpop, I'll go back home wi' y'all, but I ain't pullin' no more teats.' And that's the way I never milked another cow. I went back home then. I went on and went to school every winter—and worked on the boat all summer.

"It was fifty-one hours from Columbus to Apalachicola if you didn't have too many stops or if you didn't have any problems. It was a lot of landings

[The two captains on strike] said, "Now, son, this is your chance."

that you picked up a lot of stuff.

"Sometimes we picked up two, three bales of cotton. They'd get it down to the river, and we'd pick it up and carry it on to Apalach. Some were 450 pounds, some were 500, some were 525.

"Oh, I used to know a world of [stevedores]. They had an initiation procedure for the new ones coming in. I'd get 'em to Apalachicola, and they'd get all their work done. Waitin' to reload, they'd take the new member an' put 'im on a wheelbarrow and all, into the river. And he better not come out of that wheelbarrow.

"One-and-a-half years I was a cabin boy. There was a striker pilot, some'll recall Captain Cameron 'n' Tom Dudley. [Dudley] could run it in the blackest night, the thickest fog. He [later] fell off the boat, and they found him drowned at Chattahoochee, Florida. He [had] bought and owned the steamship the *Beulah Ray* and the *Barbara Hunt*. Fortunately those men saw my interest and how I emulated their experience.

"You couldn't stand in front of the wheel and turn it like today. It was a big wheel. A striker pilot helped spot and turn the wheel. There was one pilot who turned from port and the other from starboard.

"Mr. Bradley owned boats then—and two captains [on another boat] wanted to strike. Mr. Bradley said: 'Let 'em strike. We don't need 'em. We can run boats without 'em.'

"[We carried] general commodities. Railroad and trucks were already taking over this activity. The two captains I was with kept saying, 'We better make the best of this, 'cause the end is not far away.'

"The captains' strike was in '22 or early '23. Henry Snyder was one of the pilots. And the other pilots were Cap'n Cameron and Cap'n Dudley. And I think Cap'n Wilson was one. The captains I was working with struck with them; they were colleagues. Today I despise the . . . union.

"I was sittin' down there on the dock, the boat sittin' idle. Mr. Bradley drove up in a big old Lincoln with his chauffeur. He got out and came up to me, 'Democrat, can't you take that boat to Apalachicola?'

"I said, 'I think I can.'

"'[Will] you carry that boat?'

"I said, 'I'll talk to Captain Cameron.'

"I think [Mr. Bradley] knew what their answer would be. He said, 'Meet me back here at two o'clock this afternoon.'

"It was the Prohibition, and I knew the captains were at a bootleg joint on Brittenham Street. So I walk up to the bridge, crossed. My cousin was running the bootleg joint on what you call Silk Shirt Alley. And the reason for that, all a' the bootleggers wore silk shirts. They was the only ones wha' could afford it.

"I opened that door, I'm lookin' at them sittin' at a table with a bottle and glasses. Well, ol' Cap'n Tom Dudley was lookin' right at me. I started walkin' acrosst there.

"'What are you doing in this place?'

"I said, 'Mr. Bradley was down a while ago, talked to me.' So they told me to sit down between them.

"'What did Mr. Bradley say to you?'

"'He wanted to know if I can carry the boat to Apalachicola.'

"'What did you say?'

"'I said, 'I think I can.' He said he wanted to know if I *would* carry it.' I said, 'I'll have to go talk to Captain Dudley and Captain Cameron.'

"I saw 'em look one to the other. They said: 'Now, son, this is your chance. These boats aren't gonna be running much longer. You go back out there and tell 'im you will carry it, but you tell 'im to keep Magruder off your back.'

"I went out there, and it was a jubilation. I said: '[Mr.] Bradley, I can carry it, but tell Mr. Magruder to stay off my back. He can tell me when to go and when to quit. But it's my judgment when I'm running.

"He said, 'All right,' and he trooped me down there and told Magruder, 'Now, I want you to leave the running of the boat to his judgment.' Next mornin' they had that jewel loaded and ready to go. And we went. And I had no trouble.

"Now mind you, I didn't have nuthin' but a striker with me. I didn't have no pilot relief. I had that boat from the time it left Columbus 'til it got to Apalachicola.

"That took days, if you didn't stop, and . . . we stopped a lotta little landings. But I had to stay right there at that wheel from the time we left 'til we got there.

"Captain Magruder was just skipping the boat. You look alive with everything else that had to be tended. The master of the boat didn't do no steering.

"We'd go through the cutoff and go up the [Chipola] River a ways. We'd go up to Iola and a big hotel up there. No sign of it there now. And a lot of people went down and stayed a week and fished all in the Dead Lakes.

"But anyway, late in the afternoon, and come time to go, 'tween sunset and dark, and I couldn't tell the stumps from the shallows. I didn't turn around, I just backed up 'bout 3 miles down the river—it was crooked—and backed into the cutoff and headed out.

"Ol' Captain was up there on the roof. He walked from one end of the boat to the other and pulled his hair. He never said nuthin' to me.

"Next mornin' at breakfast in Apalachicola, he says, 'How come you backed this boat down all the way from Iola to the cutoff yestaday evenin'?'

"I said, 'I'll tell ya, I was scared right of one of them stumps.' Later it dawned on me that was the craziest thing I'd ever done. I coulda torn the boat all to pieces . . . but I got away with it.

"The river didn't fluctuate then like it fluctuates now. They didn't have but two dams on the river. They had Goat Rock Dam up there in Columbus, but they didn't have Bartlett's Ferry Dam, and they didn't have the North Highlands power plant dam. All they had was City Mills and Eagle & Phenix mill [dams]. They didn't impound the water and stop the flow like these big dams they got today. See, they got two of 'em above West Point. Big, big fellas." Those are Buford Dam and Morgan Falls Dam.

"Now then, they got a dam or two at West Point [the private Langdale and Riverview dams]. Then you get down [below Columbus] and you got Walter George Lock; then you got George Andrews Lock and Dam. And then the next thing is the Jim Woodruff.

"I spent most of my time there in the pilothouse. But I did this too: I spent enough time in the engine room to get an engineer's license as well. I was one of the few that was referred to as a 'double-ender.' I could work in the engine room; I could work in the pilothouse.

"In the engine room, you start and stop the machinery by the bells. Now, if you ring the bell one tap, that's move ahead. If the boat was standin' still, and they jingled you, you was gonna go astern. And if you start backing when you should be going ahead, you'd create calamity in a hurry.

"The boilers were forward. You have to balance the boat between the machinery in the stern and up forward. And back then [the 1920s] it was cordwood racks on each side of the boat, and you fired with cordwood. Old dried pine lighters. Make the blackest smoke. It'd take ten cords at least to bring it from Apalachicola. That wouldn't take quite as much going down 'cause, you see, the current was steering.

"I had the good fortune to be liked and respected and encouraged by the fellows all through the union. And I told 'em, 'I would like to get a license, but it will be another two years.' You had to be nineteen before you could get a second-class license.

"One of [the captains] said: 'Hell, go on over there and tell 'em you're nineteen. They don't know the difference.'

"Well, I didn't know no different than to do what he said so I went over there [to] the steamboat inspectors. One of 'em says, 'How old are you?'

"I said, 'Nineteen.'

"One of 'em said, 'Hell, we got boats at this dock that you couldn't even begin to try to start up.'

"They said, 'Well, we'll set 'im and see.'

"So they set me down, and I worked them papers out.

"One of 'em said, 'Well,' he said, 'he did know enough to write about it.' And next thing I know they come and handed me my [license].

"Well, I was on a boat that burned, blowed up, and sunk. Lifted me about 100 feet over the stern of it out in the river.

"Yeah, that was the *Mist*. Well, we were goin' up the river, and Captain Sam Cameron was asleep. [Someone] discovered the fire and [began] hollerin'. I was up on the roof. I smoked cigarettes then. When this old feller hollered, I grabbed a fire extinguisher—2 gallons. You had to turn the bottom up. And I ran in there, and there was [another] one just inside the aft door of the engine room, and I reached in there and I got it. And I done turn the other one down and hold the stream, and I got that [other] one and turned it up and started spraying it, and a big fuel tank busted. I saw the flash and threw that arm up, and it busted."

I was on a
boat that
burned,
blowed up,
and sunk.

Fig. 3.1b. During the captain's strike of 1923—and before he turned four-teen—Corley piloted the 202-ton *John W. Callahan* from Columbus to Apa-lachicola. Photo courtesy of Florida State Archives.

Corley revealed a wrist still scarred and bent. "There're three stitches over that eye." He pointed to a white scar in his left eyebrow. "But anyway, it lifted me over the stern of the boat and blew the shirt off of me—and didn't burn me. It's the force, I reckon.

"A little boat comin' down the river—called *Midnight*, belonged to the Florida Gravel Company—and they come 'n' picked me out of the water. I was knocked out.

"The *Mist* was destroyed. It burned to the waterline, and the rest of it sunk. I was the only one that was hurt to any degree. Captain Cameron jumped off the bow and ran into a big old bramblin' bush and tore himself up.

"We'd make anywhere from $60 to $80 [a month] in the engine room, $90 in the pilothouse. And then if you happened to be on a boat that was carrying a good many passengers, you got paid a little more.

"Every once in a while [we hit a snag], especially after a freshet. Freshet is a high water comin' down that washes out stuff. Trees at night. But they wouldn't anymore because the government marks [the channel] now. When I was runnin' it, there was only natural markings. If you didn't know what you was lookin' at and where you was lookin' at it, you didn't have much to do with yo'se'f. But we managed, and the fellows I was fortunate enough to work with, they knew every twig.

"Sam Cameron could tell you where you were at night. He must have had 'coon's eyes. But he'd go into a landing, and he wouldn't miss it that far from when he did it the last time when he could see. It was miraculous.

"Nobody had ever measured that river way back there, and one old fellow went up there to Congress, and he told them it was 750 miles. And someone corrected him, and he said, 'Well, I'm talking about the round trip.'

"But anyway, the river now is 106 miles from the Jim Woodruff Dam to the Water Street dock in Apalachicola. Well, it's 156 miles from the lock to the Parallel Walk there at Columbus. That's 262 miles, isn't it? And they know, 5,280 feet to the mile. I've been on every foot of it. I' been all up to the lake above Bartlett's Ferry.

"There was mixed freight. Lord, you'd be surprised how many tons of plow points [went] one way from Columbus Ironworks. A lot of farm equipment went overseas, and there was all kinds of plow equipment and the shirt pans, kettles, and then there'd be groceries no end.

"[After piloting the *Callahan*], I stayed their striker with [Tri-State Navigation], as long as they run. I didn't make the last trip. That was June of '25. I'd a' had to walk back. Cap'n George Lapham was the last captain on there. The *Callahan Jr.* was the last boat. The *Sr.* come before it, and they come out of Bainbridge—the Callahans.

"I stood on the dock and watched it back down, turn around, and head out, and I'm sure I had tears in my eyes. I thought my world had come to an end. That's what I loved, and I had an affection for it no end. But they went on, and that September I went to Sweeny Institute of Technology, Kansas City, Missouri. Went over there 'til the money give out.

> I watched [the boat] back down, turn around, and head out. . . . I thought my world had come to an end.

"Now, before I forget, I'll tell you this so you'll remind me. The last ones to own the packet boat that run was Mr. Fred Schellenberg, Mr. Fred Hume, and Mr. Jack Knight. They sold it when Mr. Bradley wouldn't give 'em short hauls.

"I come out of [Sweeny Institute] in '27, come back home to Columbus, and I met a little gal there, and the love bug bit me, and we got married, November 11, 1927. Yeah, Armistice Day, but we declared war," Corley grinned.

Corley's World War II service portrait shows a clean-cut man with deep, dark, ruminating eyes. In 1941, he was the oldest man on his ship at age thirty-three and was immediately promoted to a senior. They hunted Nazi subs in the North Sea, and "In October '42, we took a hit in the house that rendered us inoperable."

Corley later took command of a submarine patrol craft in the Caribbean and Gulf of Mexico. "They were sinkin' ships over at St. Joe when we were there, the *Empire Mica*. The propeller on those is down at the Anderson's Restaurant now. Huge thing."

Legally blind due to degenerated retinas, Corley pointed to a framed picture of a bright red, white, and blue sternwheel boat. "That's the last boat I built. Finished that May [1] of '95. It's at Columbus now, powered by one 671 GM diesel.

"I named it the *Cherokee Princess* for my grandmother. And the fellow I sold it to, he changed the name to *Chattahoochee Princess*. I was the only one that she gave any family secrets to about [Indian removal], and she was always apprehensive. Anyone in a uniform, she was afraid they was comin' to carry her to Oklahoma. They carried some of our people to Oklahoma in the March of Tears. I've been through it, all the way to Oklahoma.

"I had a chief—during his time—come here and stay with me about three or four weeks. Eugene Irons. My grandmother's name was Irons back there. They had only had a surname for about three generations. My grandmother's immediate family were renegades. They wouldn't go. And there's some people named Sweatt took 'em in. They had favored these people when they first come to north Georgia, and, in time, they favored my grandmother's people by hiding them out. And they were dark-complected, too, and it worked.

"And a little after that, my grandmother's people moved down to Fayette County, Wolsey, Georgia, just below Atlanta. They got away from the activity [of Indian removal]."

Corley fetched a hand-lettered genealogy from a dining room hutch. "I had one uncle, foreman at Eagle and Phenix Mill, where they finish the cloth, had the most beautiful handwritin'." In calligraphy it read: "Old family Bible, Transcription of family record of James W. and Elizabeth A Sweatt." She was born in 1854 and died in 1923. "That was my great-grandparents. This is done by [her son] Tom Sweatt." The record also shows that Corley's grandmother Sara Ann lived from 1881 to 1937.

"I started [building the *Cherokee Princess*] in October '93, and I went through twenty-five helpers, one at a time. They couldn't stand the pressure, 'cause I was working, and it took something to one-man build that in two years. I built it out here at a local boatyard [Queen Craft], and I asked [the manager], I said, 'Grover, what am I gonna owe you for this?'

"'Owe me?' he said, 'What can I pay you? [I] seen you push these boys. They're learnin' something about hard work.'

"The boat is 73 foot long, 16 foot wide, and the depth of the hull is 4 foot. I used mainly heart cypress cut out here at Creamer's Sawmill.

"Now it runs excursions and dinner trips in Columbus, Georgia. I was up there . . . oh, three, four months ago. They said, 'We want you to come up here, and we're going on that boat of yours tonight.'

"We had an enjoyable time. They cater the dinners—and they had fun on there. It sat about fifty. I sold it to an infantry captain at Fort Benning, and he sold it to a boy named Woodham. Now, I built two or three boats for the Columbus Transportation Co.—Jim Woodruff is one of the stockholders— [for] $135,000 to $150,000.

"Mr. Woodham's daughter is managing the boat. And she said, 'I wish you'd give me some pointers about this.' So I talked to her a bit. She's doing a good job."

John Hentz: Bristol Native, River Defender

"You know what a little town Bristol is," John Hentz said. He was born south of Bristol in 1911. As a lad, he heard the steamboats blow as they came into Bristol and Blountstown landings.

Hentz took the first 4-H courses offered in the late 1920s and won a $100 scholarship to the University of Florida, where he worked his way through, majoring in agriculture. "I caught a ride out of the sticks," he said. Hentz became the first assistant county agent in Walton County, county agent in Bay and Okaloosa counties, and head agent in Walton County during the eight years following graduation. He then bought a dairy and tripled its production before the pasture became part of Panama City. He also forged alliances with another dairy family, that of Senator Bob Graham.

Hentz's dairy supported his extended family, including a niece who married Grady Leavins of Leavins Seafood, Apalachicola, and returned a branch of the family to the ancestral river.

Hentz is a fly fisherman, raconteur, and letter writer to governors, senators, and newspapers since 1993. He's addressed dredging, spoil bank practices, and navigation windows. He's joined with Marilyn Blackwell and L. L. Lanier to form Help Save the Apalachicola River Group. They want to open Battle Bend, Double Points, Oxbow, and Virginia Cut sloughs and Point Poll-Away. He shared his oral history on February 12, 2002.

"Beginning about 1807, 1811, was when the steamboats were being experimented with and developed, and in the next thirty years they got to be a way of life on these waterways. Our little town of Bristol was one that de-

Fig. 3.2a. River chronicler John Hentz grew up farming in Lake Mystic, south of Bristol. Photo by Faith Eidse.

pended on steamboat traffic for its livelihood. 'Course for a hundred years the steamboats were the main movers of people and freight.

"You know, for years after the Civil War, my people lived in the south end of Liberty County and logged on the lower Apalachicola River, rafted logs into the mill there at Cypress Lumber Company in Apalachicola. Apalachicola was town to my people, and it'd take 'em several days to go shoppin'. Go to Apalach on the steamboat. Every community, or just the family, had their dock, and they'd catch the boat, and it was about the only way they could travel, either that or horseback or walk, 'cause there wadn't any roads.

"When I was a small child, before they even started gradin' up roads, it was nothin' uncommon to come to a set of ruts that went around a clump of gallberries or palmettos one way and the same set go around the other way.

"At one time, my mother had typhoid fever, and we had . . . a vaccine that was developed along 'bout that time. I was big enough to go to town with my daddy and my granddaddy, and I loved to 'cause they would buy me a box of popcorn [with] a prize, a snapping beetle or somethin'.

"Just as we got to that clump of palmettos, we met the Doc comin' to give all the family shots. I guess they saw how terribly disappointed I was, and they finally let me go on to town, and then he went on home to give my sisters and mother the shot. And the way he had to sterilize his needle was he'd put it in a tablespoon and heat it on the cookstove.

"The year we went to fourth grade we saw our first moving-picture show. The boys brought a tent and bleachers [down the river] from up there around Bainbridge. So it was black-and-white and silent, of course. Well, the picture was a western with all the cows and the cowboys; the good guys and the bad guys. Shoot 'em up, bang, bang.

"Well, Mr. Bill [Summers] looked up suddenly, and here come that bunch of cows running across that screen. He jumped up, snatched off his hat, and [tried] to head them up. 'Whoa here, Whoa here.' He thought they were gonna run over him.

"I had an older sister graduating over in Blountstown on or about the first day of June 1927. The sermon from Job [was], 'And what is man that thou are mindful of him?'

"The reason I recall it so well, Charles A. Lindbergh was flying across the Atlantic Ocean that morning, and we hadn't heard whether he had successfully landed. And just look at what has happened since that time—hundreds of thousands of people flying every direction over oceans every day.

"They used to grow their own rice in the low, wet places on the farm and then processed it themselves. They made everything they could outta wood back then. Take a big wooden block about twice as tall as a man and bury one end in the ground and then hollow out a bowl in the top. They had this pestle; it was set in the ground, and it curved, and the end bumped down on the grain, cracked the dry husks off. The wind would blow the husks away, and after 'while you've got nothin' but the pure shiny white rice. They did that for barley [too].

"As time went on and money became more plentiful, farmers got to where they specialized, and, to live, they go to the grocery store. The only thing we ever bought from the grocery store was sugar and coffee. We grew our meat and sausage. Now'days it isn't sausage at all. They quit putting sage in it 'long about the early thirties.

"Old man Pat Schuler, he was the head of all the Mormons in that part of the country. He was a very good friend of my daddy's, but they differed on religion. [He] lived just south of Hosford. He raised a big family; some of

They used to grow their own rice in the low, wet places.

them got to be multimillionaires, but raised just as poor as people could be. He always had that woods full of hogs, and we always grew a lot of hog feed. So my daddy would furnish 'em produce, and they'd furnish him hogs.

"We didn't have any refrigeration, so we had to butcher our year's supply of hogs on a cold spell. We didn't have any weather reports either. But if my daddy got up at two or three o'clock in the morning and it was real cold, we would kill twenty-nine or thirty head of great big fat hogs. We scalded 'em in our sugar kettle, scraped the hair off, butchered 'em out, and stayed up till twelve or one cuttin' up that meat, hangin' it up to get all the animal heat out of it.

"Then it was hung up in a smokehouse [over] a great big earthen bowl. Up overhead between the joists of the smokehouse we had the meat on gamblin' sticks and the fire underneath smokin'. [To hang it] we stuck a hole through the meat. The skin was always left on it. My daddy would send me over to the sandy oak ridges to get what we called bear grass. Bear grass [was like] Spanish bayonets, blades three feet long, real tough natural fibers. You can use it for string.

Now, '28 was one of the highest freshets I ever remember.

"The Ramseys were one of the old families. Old granddaddy Brozz owned a good bit of land, but he always thought he was going to starve. His son [Louis Joe] owned [a] grocery store in Bristol. He pedaled okra around on the sidewalks, a nickel for so many pods. Everybody in the country knew him.

"I remember the old streets in Bristol. That ol' sand was [a foot] deep, churned by the oxen hooves and the mules and the wagons. We bought our first car about the time everybody started usin' cars commonly. It was 1918, January.

"Then the county commissioners, they got an idea that ol' sand needed hard surfacin'. So they put clay on the street of Bristol, just one street with a row of stores on the north side facin' south. On the south side, there was the old hotel, a barber shop, a part-time café, [and] the old post office.

"Now, my daddy had two buggies. One was a single-seated buggy, [and] he had a surrey, [a] two-seated buggy. I had four sisters, so when we all went, it took two seats. We lived in the Lake Mystic community, and then my daddy had a younger brother who lived over in Blountstown.

"To get to Blountstown we had to go to Bristol, then we went on by the ol' courthouse, on the hill to the ol' river landings. There were two landings down there. The Henndon Landing, which was the Bristol Landin', and the Bo Ramsey Landin'. Then we turn to the left and went to a two-rut road down 4 miles to the old Charlie Cayson ferry. And we crossed the sloughs on little wooden bridges that were tied to the trees with wire to keep them from floatin' off durin' high river.

"We passed the old Indian mound just 'fore we got to Charlie Cayson Ferry. There was nothin' at the ol' ferry 'cept the ferryman and a little shack or two. There the river is about at the widest and most shallow. It was known as the Blountstown Bar, and it [was] where steamboats would hang up.

"I can still remember in 1927. The only time I ever knew the river to get low enough where it cleared up pretty good, it looked blue. And I was told that people could wade the river there at Blountstown. Of course, before we had the impoundments, we [usually] had yellow water [from] mud in the river.

"And we didn't fish for scale fish directly in the river. Only in '27 did I know of it clearin' up enough that we fished for scale fish. Now catfish, they'd catch catfish in that yellow water.

"I can remember when high rivers were very common. Now'days they are very unusual. Now, '28 was one of the highest freshets I ever remember. Albert Cayson had a big pasture where his daddy [Charlie]'s old ferry took off on the Liberty County side. He had a big Hereford cattle ranch, and that high river deposited white sand all over it. Albert was the Standard Oil dealer there in Blountstown.

[The ferry man said], "We'll throw the children in."

"Back in the early days we'd get to the old Charlie Cayson Ferry, and I remember the ferry man tellin' my parents that the fare was so much a piece for the grown folks, 'and we'll throw the children in.' I took a look at that landing, I took a look at that river, and it like to have scared me to death. I was greatly relieved when my parents explained that he wasn't gonna charge for the children.

"The twentieth of December 1916 my daddy and older sister were going to [a] funeral in Blountstown, driving [Dobbin], a young horse we had raised, and a buggy. They got out there in the river, and luckily he was loose from the buggy. One of the boys on the flat, just bein' friendly, came by and slapped him on the back, and he jumped in the river. Dobbin did the right thing; he circled around and headed back to the Liberty County side.

"My daddy had on his tie, coat, suit, and shoes, but he knew if that horse got up that hill he'd go home 8 miles. So he jumped in the river after him, and he was able to get hold of the lines. And Papa and Clara didn't get to the funeral; they came back home. Papa was sopping wet, and it was cold too.

"Nobody is more to the credit for us getting this bridge across this river [than Governor Fuller Warren]. He ran for representative for Calhoun County before he was twenty-one. 'Course, the man running against him

Fig. 3.2b. The old Victory Bridge frames a new span and the Jim Woodruff Lock and Dam. Photo by John Crowe.

used that very much. Fuller replied, 'Folks, I got here just as soon as I could.' Highway 20 wadn't built until 1938, when they built the first bridge across from Bristol to Blountstown.

"When I left here in September of 1931, there wasn't one foot of pavement in Liberty County. In wet weather, we just stayed at home. I remember when [the old Bristol-Telogia road] was just two ruts through the sand ridges, when everyone rode a horse or had mules, wagon, or buggy. When they first started to improvin' the roads, that was done with convicts.

"Then they started clearing that right of way, and they got just below our house, and they'd dig a hole down by the stump, and they'd set that charge of dynamite. And the blowin' was done by a convict. He had set a charge, and they all run. For some reason, it didn't go off, so he started back there. Just as he looked over that big pile of dirt, that thing went off. Well, it blinded him, blew all the skin off his face. Mr. Hunt, who lived about a mile south of [Bristol] and drove a team of mules for the county, put a red bandana over his face and hauled him to the doctor.

"A few years later, the county decided some roads needed hard surfacing. The quandary was to improve the road east out of here, the 12 miles or so from here to Hosford, or come down into the Lake Mystic community and around to Telogia and then over to Hosford.

"So my daddy and the neighbors all come up before the board and offered the use of their farm mules and wagons to haul that clay if they would bring the road through the Lake Mystic community. And all the county had to do was to furnish the convicts. And that's the way we got what is now [State Roads] 12 and 67 from here to Telogia.

"Mr. Bub Schuler—he lived about 6 or 7 miles south of Bristol. He stayed on his horse most all the time. The county had decided they needed a new bridge across Telogia Creek there at Hosford. For economy's sake, they built a little narrow, single-laned bridge, but they widened it in the center—where the first fella could come to the center and go over to one side. And the other one could pass him.

"So Mr. Bub come up on the south end of that bridge. He'd gotten a good ways on it, and here come one of them cars from the north end. He was thinking to himself: 'Now I was on this bridge first. That man is gonna have to back off.' He said that car just kept a comin' and got to the middle of the bridge and stopped. He said he was a settin' lookin' at that fella, and that fella stuck his head outta that car, and he yelled, 'Well, if you're comin' by me, come on.' He said that's the way he found out what that bow was in that bridge for.

"Telogia was pretty much the most central town in Liberty County, and that is where we had our picnics—Fourth of July, special occasions. And the ladies would just out-do themselves with all their cooking and have a great long table, and we'd have a party program.

"The mill was operating out of Hosford, and Dr. Ben Smart, the mill doctor, had him a recipe for a Brunswick stew. He would be located at the end of that long table [with] a great big ladle and his chef's cap and his apron. One time, Greensboro had a little brass band, and they all came down and played for us. Lee Mercer was quite an athlete. Lee and some of his buddies would put on a boxing bout. We actually had a baseball game one afternoon.

"Telogia was on the railroad, and the ticket agent had to stay on duty pretty much around the clock. His friends would come down. They were grown men. They'd crawl around on the ground and play marbles just like a bunch of kids.

"My uncle, J. I. Hentz, had the first Ford franchise in Blountstown. Over in Liberty County, where we lived, ol' Mr. W. P. Shelly had the Ford franchise. Papa's brother being the dealer there in Blountstown, he bought the car from him. They went on a big huntin' trip in January of 1918, and one of the grown nephews drove it down to our home.

"The next day Papa was afraid to try and drive the car in the buggy house 'cause he'd done heard of some of the neighbors that forgot how to stop it and knocked the back end out. So he goes and puts the harness on one of the mules and got a singletree off a plow and took a trace chain and tied it to the

"When
better auto-
mobiles are
built, Buick
will build
them."

front of the car, and he hooked the mule to the car," Hentz laughed, "and drug the car in the buggy house.

"Now he had a older brother that owned a 1908 Buick. Ol' Uncle Frank died when I was a year old, and that old Buick sit out close to the Johnson Grist Mill until it just rusted away. It had the crank came out the left-hand side, right out from under the driver's seat, and apparently it was chain-driven, had sprockets on the back axle. Do you know what [Buick's] slogan was all durin' their developing years? 'When better automobiles are built, Buick will build them.'

"The first cars had cloth tops, and it had side curtains that you would haul out and put up. But that's too much trouble, so seldom did the cars use the side curtains.

"My family went to the Victory Bridge [opening] on U.S. 90 there in Chattahoochee, July 22, 1922. It rained on us all day. In those days, a person [would] see if somebody else was gonna make the same trip in order to help each other. There'd be awful slick, greasy hills if it was rainin', deep sand if it was normal, and no roads.

"We got with the Louis Joe Ramsey family. So my dad and mother and sisters, took her and the baby in the car 'cause they had a top. And Louis Joe, he had a little old cut-down T-Model roadster truck. So I rode back there. We got to Crooked Creek Hill on the Gadsden-Liberty county line and tried to push Daddy's car up the hill. We finally had to turn it around and back it up.

"We parked in this old field, and then we had to walk down to where they were having the celebration under the bridge. And back then U.S. 90 was just a dirt road. We'd go to Gainesville, [and] there was no pavin' until you got to Lake City.

"In the early days of Model T cars, if we went 10 miles and we didn't bog down or have a blowout or breakdown, we'd had good luck. The first cars [had] little wooden wheels and high-pressure tires, 65 or 70 pounds. They had patch kits of all sizes and shapes. Heat 'em up and melt the stick'em and seal up the patch on the tire. Then you'd get down and pump—had a cross handle and plunger, and you just pumped it up.

"In the late twenties, along come low-pressure tires, big wide tires. We didn't have near as many blowouts, and they rode better, and they traveled over the sand better.

"Did you know that the first cars that came out that were sold in this country was what they call wide gauge? About 4½ to 5 inches wider than the normal cars today. And the wagons that were sold in the South were big enough that that bale of cotton would lay down flat sideways, and that deter-

Fig. 3.2c. Hentz was in the crowd at the dedication of the Victory Bridge, Chattahoochee, in 1922. Photo courtesy of Florida State Archives.

mined the width of the wagon. And then wagons and buggies determined the roads. So all the cars that were sold in the South, originally, were wide gauge.

"Now the Yankees had more money than we did, so the Yankees had the big powerful cars. A lot of them were custom built. So as time went on, though, and they hard-surfaced the roads, everything finally became narrow gauge.

That whole bunch [of car thieves was] gonna mob us.

"That was rough, rough country, and my daddy was pretty rough himself. Papa had been foreman of a grand jury that had indicted three women and eight men. They had a regular car thieving ring that they run the cars from Blackshear, Georgia, to Perry and Hosford, Florida. Hid 'em out and changed the numbers and sold 'em.

"So the sheriff and his deputy tried to arrest 'em, and they beat up the sheriff, gouged his eyes with scissors, and got away. Well, [some local farmers] went and rounded 'em all up and threw them in the jail there in Bristol.

"In the spring when it came to the trial, it rained enough that afternoon to stop us [planting]. Papa said, 'Let's go up to Bristol and listen at the trial.' Old [Circuit] Judge Love [from Quincy] was there, and all the defendants were sitting up at the rail. One of the girls sent out and had ice cream brought in to serve all the defendants. Yeah, just as ugly and arrogant toward the court as they could be.

"Well, come night we had to go home. All we had was the kerosene lamp on the table. Well, all of a sudden lights flashed all over our house, and somebody yelled 'Brim, Brim, Brim.' They knew my daddy would recognize that name 'cause that was one of the names involved. They had bought their way out. The jury had turned 'em loose. That whole bunch had come down there, gonna mob us.

"My daddy, he had a double-barrel 12-gauge shotgun. He came out with that shotgun, and they ran in the dark. We had a big hole in front of the house, and we had quit diggin' clay out of it, but we used it for a garbage dump—broken glass and tin cans and barrel hoops and hay wire. One of them jokers fell in it. I mean those tin cans didn't quit ringin' 'fore he was up and gone. They went toward the car, one ol' boy sayin': 'I'm goin' down there and get him. He's the cause of my daddy bein' in that jail tonight.' Another said: 'No, you're not. That man'll kill you.'" Hentz laughed.

No part of the United States has more history than the Southeast.

"[My father] took his shotgun and sat out in front of our house and just rolled that shotgun across his lap. Tuesday night, those local farmers down there got that ringleader named Brim. They carried him out in the woods and held him across a log, and they beat the devil out of him. And they told that fella not to never be seen back in Liberty County again. That bunch down there in Liberty County, they cleaned them up.

"No part of the United States has more history than the Southeast, and this part of the country was mighty important. There's just a lot of history down here around the old Fort Gadsden area.

"The steamboat operat[ed] up and down this river here for about a hundred years, from 1828 to 1928. Jack Wingate, [who runs a lodge on Lake Seminole in Georgia], two of his ancestors were steamboat masters or captains that piloted on this river. One of 'em was Hezekiah Wingate, and Hez was killed in a steamboat accident down here at Ricco's Bluff. The steamboat was backing out and hit a snag.

"'Stiff-'n'-Ugly' Bluff was the highest bluff on the river between Apalachicola and Bristol. A friend of mine operated a fish camp [there, and in] less than twenty years, that bluff had eaten in 13 feet. Now, we have seen these barges gouging out these deep bends for years, doin' a lot of damage. The barges have rolled that mud back up in the mouth of all the creeks and sloughs that make it to the river. Beginning with Owl Creek, Ft. Gadsden, and they have completely stopped up the end of the outlet on Virginia Cut. The mouth of the River Styx, the mouth at Kennedy Creek is near about stopped up at low water and Dog Slough and Iamonia Lake. [Navigation has] created about 24 miles of dead water that we used to have live fish in.

"You know the little town of Altha over here? Back in the early days my mother was teaching school there, and she boarded with [the] Richards. Mrs. Richards kept the post office in her home [and] wanted to upgrade it. So they had to come up with a name. Beautiful purple althea trees grew profusely in that area, good clay foundation. So [my mother] suggested they call [it] Althea. Well, whenever it came through, it was approved A-l-t-h-a.

"My daddy was raised on Kennedy Creek 'til he was about sixteen, and he had a sister just older than he was that died [at sixteen], and she's buried close to White Oak Landing. There's only two graves in that whole graveyard that has any information at all: Seaborn Larkins and my aunt Louisa.

"One time the [steamboat] pulled into the Hathcock landing on Bushy Creek, and my great-great-aunt Kelly, who lived 'til she was just about a hundred years old (she was born in 1815 and died in 1915), saw a man kill another one with a hatchet there on the deck of the boat, knocked him in the river, and run into the swamp and got away.

"The next little creek on the Liberty County side is Scott Creek, named for Tom Scott, who was killed there. He was foreman for Cypress Lumber Company. He was standing by the campfire, and he was shot from the bushes. Some of the people living in the area resented the timber being cut. [My father] had just been foreman of that same crew the year before, and some mysterious people were running his timber workers out of the woods. He told the Cypress Company that he wouldn't go back in there; it was too dangerous. The next year they ordered him back, [and] he quit, and Tom Scott took the job."

At Pinhooks, Hentz said, the current gave out, and lumber mills had to send tugs up to haul in the rafted logs. North of Brothers River, Brickyard Cutoff used to be called Logjam until the Corps opened the channel.

"Tom Johnson used to butcher and carry some meat to Apalachicola. He had a catch dog, and one day he went on the steamboat to tend to some business. He got off the boat and went back to the house, and the dog stayed on the boat. So Mr. Fanning, clerk on the boat, put a sign on this dog's collar said: 'I'm Tom Johnson's dog. Whose dog are you?' He said the dog went on to Apalachicola, got off and stayed around town for several days, and when the boat went back up the river, he caught the boat and went on home."

Hentz also spoke about his lifelong passion for fishing. "That was our [family] recreation, to go fishing and have a fish fry and a picnic all day. My mother had a big ol' iron skillet that fit inside the engine in the T Model.

"We were down on Gregory's Mill Creek; it went into Florida River and Apalachicola River, and she was up on the bank, cookin'. One of her [grown] pupils came along; he was the game warden," Hentz laughed. "We had a limit on the size of the bass you could catch, and they called 'em trout. He looked over there, 'Mrs. Hentz these look like mighty little trout you got here.' She said, 'Yeah, when they hit that hot grease they sure do draw up.' [The warden] laughed and went on.

"[Back then] you just put a worm on that hook and dropped it in there. The fish would bite, and we'd pull 'em out. The only thing that we'd carry from home would be corn bread. You always ate bread with fish—and pies."

Videotapes of Hentz's storytelling are archived at the Maxwell and Evelyn Herald Library, Bristol.

Homer B. Hirt: Lured by Shipping

For a Chattahoochee boy weakened by polio, life along the Apalachicola River became a seagoing fantasy. Not only did Homer Hirt's father take him to the river to talk with ship's mates, but while Homer's legs were paralyzed for weeks and months on end, Hirt read maritime adventures. His father ran the Ford dealership in town, but Hirt enlisted in the U.S. Navy and became a commissioned officer. Homer Hirt took over the family business but finally sold it to become a field engineering supervisor. His firm designed a port near Sneads, and Hirt became Jackson County port director for fourteen years, until lack of water and commerce closed the port in 1990.

He hopes to one day see the return of barge transport, noting that "barge transportation moves 16 percent of the nation's freight for 2 percent of the cost. It does this with less air pollution than rail or truck. There are 24,000 miles of waterways, most connecting through the Gulf Intracoastal. Any section of the country that does not provide this connection does its citizens a disservice."

Hirt is president of H. B. Hirt, Inc., which runs a 500-acre turf farm in Jackson County, as well as a grain terminal in Campbellton. "I am active but not fully in charge," he joked. He conveyed his oral history at the Homeplace Restaurant in Chattahoochee on September 6, 2001.

"My father came here in 1923, and driving up one day from River Junction, which is where the railroads are, he met my mother walking up the hill—a hot day—and he stopped and picked her up. A few days later he sold her a Model T, but he had to teach her how to drive. Two years later they got married, and then I was born in 1929.

Fig. 3.3. Shipping consultant Homer Hirt grew up playing on old steamship wrecks like the one in this Chattahoochee mural. Photo by Faith Eidse.

There were
times when
Chattahoo-
chee . . . was
the second-
busiest rail
freight port
in the state
of Florida,
next to Jack-
sonville.

"There were four railroads that terminated here. Now, the Apalachicola Northern came from the coast at Port St. Joe. One that went north out of here no longer exists. And, of course, the east-west and west-east, which have combined and are now owned by CSX. Even into the forties and fifties, there were times when Chattahoochee, so far as freight goes, was the second-busiest rail freight port in the state of Florida, next to Jacksonville.

"Back in the thirties there were a few smaller towboats moving, and our recreation centered around the river. There was an old hulk of a steamboat, the *J. W. Callahan Jr.* It was up on high ground down at the river and not much left except the pilothouse. Now, we kids would go down there and pretend to pilot that.

"When I was about five years old, my father and I would, on Sunday afternoon, walk from our house, which was over here on this Morgan Avenue, down to the river. Sundays this town didn't do anything that was not church-connected. You sat around on the porch, you visited. And we would walk down to the river.

"And one day there was a fairly good-sized towboat there, and we went aboard. The only man there was the cook, who was an old sea dog. His name was Scotty, and he had just cooked up a batch of cookies, so we ate cookies, and Scotty started telling sea stories.

"If he hadn't been all over the world, he'd come close to it. And I heard a lot of good sea stories that day. I think, if anything, my desire to go into the navy goes to that time. And I did see some of [the world]—six years.

"I did retire from the reserves as a lieutenant commander. I'm a member of about five different regional or national waterways associations, and I've been officers in all of them. When I was the president of the Tri Rivers Waterway [Development] Association several years ago, I presented testimony before the House Subcommittee on Water Resources, the ones that actually allot the money to the Corps of Engineers.

"[The Chattahoochee] is the border between Alabama and Georgia. But the border is not down the middle of the river; it goes to the west bank. And the reason is, after the Revolution, the treaty said, 'to the west bank of the Chattahoochee River from thence to its intersection with the Flint and thence across the 31st parallel to the St. Mary's River.'

"In 1969, I was appointed to the Jackson County Port Authority by Governor Kirk, the first Republican governor we had in that century. And in 1971, I sold my dealership. A few months later, an engineering firm contacted me about working as a field engineering supervisor. The first project was to set up the Jackson County Port on the river.

"I stayed with that for fourteen years, operating the port. The river dried up in the nineties, almost like it is now. We had to make our own way, even though we were set up by an act of the Legislature. So we decided to lock the doors, and I went out as a consultant then.

"We had six months of good water, six months when we didn't have any. What we handled, primarily, was bulk fertilizer . . . 50,000 tons or so a year. We handled coal for Gulf Power plant, and that was usually 100,000 to 200,000 tons a year. [Then] the river got to the point where we could not count on moving year-round.

"Atlanta's about to make a water grab, and we need to stop it."

"There was no [water allocation] at that time. See, . . . ten years ago is when the water compact concept came on.

"[Atlanta was] trying for more water to be allocated . . . out of the Chattahoochee River. I was waiting to go into the [congressional] subcommittee hearing for my testimony [when] a staffer got me and says, 'Homer, Atlanta's about to make a water grab, and we need to stop it.'

"And Congressman Tom Bevill of Alabama was the chairman of the subcommittee, probably the most powerful man in the House, other than the speaker, so I said, 'Mr. Chairman, I have something very important to bring up,' and he looked at me like, 'how dare you?' And I brought up about the Atlanta water grab. And I said, 'And it's going to be very bad for the downstream interests for them to get this.' And he says: 'Mr. Hirt, I don't think they will get it. Because we're going to stop them here, and we're going to start a study.' And he set aside, I think, $3 million to begin the study for the compact. But that's where it started, eleven years ago.

"The three governors [were] the commission members, and each one of them set up a mechanism so that stakeholders could have some input. And Florida set up a stakeholders committee through the Northwest Water Management District so that we could have an input from the six counties directly affected.

"Now, in Georgia they [had] an advisory committee clustered up there around Atlanta. And then Alabama has one that's probably more oriented toward power companies. Each state has a different opinion on what is essential.

"Georgia naturally is controlled by the Atlanta folks. You know, on 6 percent of the land area in Georgia, they'll have 35 percent, probably, of the population. And their water, most of it, comes out of the Chattahoochee River, and that's a finite amount. If they'd get it from anywhere else, they'd need a pipeline. You can't drill a well in Atlanta. It sits on a granite dome. So you've got to drill a well 20 or 30 or 50 miles away.

"They've talked about going to the Tennessee River, and the Tennessee governor says, 'Not out of my river.' So others've talked about desalinization at the Atlantic coast, pipe it over. That's costly. So they will take all they can out of the Chattahoochee River.

"Ninety-nine percent of [Florida's] reasoning is, we need to support the bay. I think it's good, but we also need to support the river itself up here for recreation, for example.

"Lake Seminole was the first impoundment on this system. This lake is almost a run of the river lake. It probably averages about 2 feet deep. There are some deep holes, but there's a lot of 3-inch water too. It's the same size on top as Lake Lanier, 38,000 acres, give or take. But Lake Lanier averages 40 feet deep. [That's where] the majority of the reserve water on the system [is].

"Five or six years ago there were about seventy-five homes [on Lake Lanier] that cost $1 million or more. Which lake are they going to draw down for us? They'll even draw Seminole down some to help navigation, hydropower, all the downstream interests of any kind. So that has, in essence, taken Lanier out of the equation for flood control, for hydropower, for navigation, for releases into Florida. In fact, there [was] a movement to take it completely out of the project.

"Atlanta draws a lot of water out of Lake Lanier. Georgia says, 'We want to maintain the level at Lake Lanier as though a drought is imminent.' Let's take a flood. If they can't control Lanier, they don't have a control there. They haven't the drawdown capacity for spring rains. It goes down to West Point Lake, and it floods. It only has a foot of holding power. Blountstown was flooded.

"You can't control a massive 500-year flood, but you can help it. Take the use of the river, which is environmental, primarily in the bay, flood control, hydropower, municipal and industrial water. The easiest thing to quantify is navigation.

"I can tell 'em what flow I need under any condition at Jim Woodruff 'cause that's the only place we have a problem, because it spews water. I can tell 'em what flow we need, with or without the dredging, or the proper dredging. I can tell 'em, within a few cfs [cubic feet per second], what we need for those barges. Find out how deep we have to be.

"Hydropower's next. I can tell you pretty close to what they'll need to fulfill their contracts. See, Jim Woodruff Dam supplies power to the City of Chattahoochee. Okay now, the next thing, municipal and industrial. You can come pretty close. At least for today," Hirt shrugged.

"Three Rivers State Park is owned by the Corps of Engineers, and it's leased to the state for maybe $1 a year. This last year, the state said: 'We're not gonna fund it anymore. We'll let it revert to the Corps of Engineers.' That meant they were padlocked.

"A group of us went to see about getting it funded one more year. But that only gives us time to [decide]—either the county takes it over, or it goes into a public-private [sale]. There's 660-some-odd acres that has been used for some camping, a little bit of fishing, boat launching. A major part [could] be retained and some other things added.

"For example, Columbus, Georgia, has just spent $10 million to build a marina on the Chattahoochee River. That is for luxury craft that will come down the Intracoastal and up the Chattahoochee River.

"When I met with the mayor there and the chamber of commerce, I said, 'It just happens that we may have an opportunity to put in a small marina at Sneads.' I would like to see that as a public-private type of relationship where the major lodging is farmed out.

"Georgia uses theirs a lot better than we do. Bainbridge has six or seven fishing tournaments a year. It took us three to four years to get a fishing tournament here on the lake. And we had two of them. One of them was very successful.

"Sneads and the east end of Jackson County is our population center. Everything's centered around there . . . like tourists. They bring money, leave it, go home. You don't have to build a school for them.

"We opened [a grain terminal] last week up in Campbellton. It's connected to the railroad, [so] we're servicing a lot of farmers when fuel costs are high. If we didn't open up, they would have to haul their grain 50 to 70 miles one way. And it goes out to the world market. We're almost out of the corn season right now. First part of October, we pick up soybeans, and then early spring, the winter wheat crop will start coming in.

"When we started [roadside mowing] six years ago, [my son-in-law] worked for DEP. The next year we had three contracts; he had to quit [at DEP]. And now we have a total of nine mowing contracts; we're mowing eleven counties, and we've done some marine repair, the fender system on the bridges.

"Oh, I'm still consulting too. I work with Georgia Ports Authority. I do the marketing for their two inland offices (Bainbridge and Columbus). I go to [the] deepwater port in Brunswick, [where] they do a lot of dry bulk cargo. We bring in grains out of Scandinavia and ship it out by rail.

"A company calls up, says, 'I want to move a cargo of clay from the mines up in Georgia to the Midwest.' I look at rail versus water. Trucks really don't come into play on that because it costs so much. I mean, you're looking at 1,500 tons times seventy truckloads or one barge load. So I put together what it would cost to the Mississippi and upriver, say, to Kansas City.

"I'd say 90 percent of our contacts don't know anything about barges, or don't know anything about the possibility of trucks moving things. Right now, truck rates are pretty good, but they're not competitive with barge. Rails have been deregulated. Ten years ago there were about twenty major railroads in the United States; today there're six in the whole United States. That's not the ones that run Port St. Joe up to Chattahoochee, 100 miles. We're talking about the CSX. Rio Grande–Union Southern Pacific combination went together five years ago and almost stopped all rail transportation.

"Barges have always been competitive if it's the same distance or the same area. The Intracoastal Waterway—this is the waterway that goes from St. Marks Port over to Brownsville, Texas, up there to Mobile, goes over to New Orleans, then on out to Houston. Last year they moved 112 million tons of cargo. Truck couldn't handle it. Divide 100 into it, and you see how many rail cars it would take. A barge is slower, except barges usually don't get lost, and rail cars do.

"A study I did for the Corps of Engineers shows 1.5 million tons could be on this river. These are direct inquiries where I had to tell the people, 'No, we have a drought, or we are not dredging, otherwise you could come up here, or you could ship your product.' And this is a wide variety of products— lumber and logs, steel, scrap iron, municipal solid waste bales. We say in the barge business that we move the big, the bad, and the ugly. The big is machinery: generators for the power plant over at Gordon, $120 million worth. The bad can be chemicals—moved safer that way than any other. The ugly would be coal or rocks or [solid waste].

"I think there can be a solution to the dredging that everyone could live with. Now your Water Management District did a good study on [spoil reuse]. It was $8.50 a ton. But that was what they called a high mobilization cost, which meant bringing in the equipment, a small amount going out, and no end use of any value. They were just going to put it on the road. [Why not] look at splitting the fine white sand, which can be used for beach renourishment? Then taking what's left and using that on your roads. If they pay me $5 million to get rid of the sand and some kind of vitamin to rejuvenate me—" Hirt smiled.

"What was it, $52 million they spent on the dam? And a lot of that centered around Chattahoochee. They had a huge concrete mixing plant across the river." The basin was so porous that dirt was excavated and used as fill, Hirt said. "There is some seepage, and they went down very deep. There's water flowing longitudinally through there. They allowed for that."

"The whole economy [in Chattahoochee] was keyed to the Florida State Hospital. I met many a man [during the Depression] that came to work at the state hospital to get three meals a day and a place to stay. In return for $30 a month, [five thousand employees] worked twelve hours a day, seven days a week, except for one Sunday per month, when they took the patients to the church service, and then they could have the rest of the day off.

"I worked there one summer in 1946. I was in the first group to earn $100 a month eight hours, five days a week.

"Maybe I had it a little better than others. We did run barefoot in the summertime, and we played in the swamps of the woods. I learned to swim in the river, and we didn't care that there was a dead cow floatin' down spring of the year, flushed out [of] the farms. It wasn't beautiful and pristine and clean, but we'd fix us an old boat up that we'd find drifting down and play in it. And sometimes hitch a ride with a boat up the river and swim back down. And we fished," Hirt said.

"I had polio when I was about seven years old. I was paralyzed from the waist down for about six weeks. The doctor knew; my parents knew. And they didn't tell me because they didn't want me to have that fear [that I] might not ever walk. They didn't know how to prevent it then, how to treat it. Now, just think what's happened with the polio vaccine.

"Seems like if there was one case of polio around in the thirties, nobody went swimming, nobody went to the movies. They just didn't know how it spread.

I learned to swim in the river, and we didn't care that there was a dead cow floatin' down spring of the year, flushed out [of] the farms.

"But boy, did I learn how to read. *Robinson Crusoe*, Mark Twain, his *Life on the Mississippi*. I remember taking that one book out of the library called *The Sea Devil*. This is [by a] German officer, Count Von Luckner, in World War I. He had a converted merchant ship, [and] he raided Allied ships. I thought that was one of the most wonderful books I ever read.

"I gradually started getting my ability to walk back. I do have post-polio syndrome, the result, late in life, of nerve damage from the polio I had when I was young. The nerves that took over functions, from those polio over-loaded, are troubling me now. Dr. Peach up in Georgia said, 'There's nothing we can do except prescribe some light exercises.'

"I can't walk far. I have to take it fairly slow. I remember before that hit I could run like the wind." Hirt and his wife, Theresa, have three grown children, all adopted. "My son was born with one hand. I think he was maybe thirteen, and he wanted to take a computer course. They said, 'You can't do touch typing.' I said, 'Let him take the computer course; if I need to go see the gov.' I'll go see the gov.' Well, in three months time he was programming the school computers."

Alton Colvin: Navigation Channel Engineer

Alton Colvin served as the U.S. Army Corps of Engineers area supervisor for the tri-state region from 1973 to 1992. His duties included maintaining the navigation channel on the Apalachicola, Chattahoochee, and Flint rivers. On March 26, 2002, he spoke candidly about efforts to reduce environmental impacts while trying to maintain a difficult channel.

"My dad was master of the U.S. snagboat *Montgomery* and [Cleve Flemming Sr., of Blountstown,] was the pilot on there. The *Montgomery* is now part of a marine museum at the Tennessee Tombigbee Waterway Visitor's Center in Aliceville, Alabama. Prior to the arrival of the *Montgomery*, he was a captain of the U.S. snagboat *Albany*. The *Albany* was one of the early snag-boats on the Apalachicola, Chattahoochee, and Flint rivers.

"He was also master of the U.S. dredge *Guthrie*, before he retired. He was born in 1909. When the Corps began looking at improvements on the ACF, my dad operated the survey launch *Arrow*.

"I was born in '36, but I began visiting the boats with him back in the forties and fifties. I remember the system prior to Jim Woodruff Dam. I began working with the Corps in November of '54.

"I worked on the Apalachicola River in the survey party while attending Auburn University. My schedule included working three months and school three months. We did surveys and navigation channel layouts for the Chatta-

Fig. 3.4a. U.S. Army Corps of Engineers tri-state supervisor Alton Colvin opened and maintained the navigation channel on the Apalachicola River from 1973 to 1992. Photo by Faith Eidse.

hoochee River. The navigation projects on the Chattahoochee and Flint rivers included three navigation locks—Jim Woodruff, George W. Andrews, and Walter F. George."

Without dams, the navigation channel would've never been developed, Colvin said, "because it would not have been feasible to maintain the channel. Initially they attempted water releases and dredging, and the channel would shoal because the area between Woodruff and the mouth of the Apalachicola River is a pretty good fall. The river is an alluvial river. There are suspended solids that move along the water column. The river flow scours in the curves, and when the river velocity recedes in the straightaways, the solids are deposited, which creates shoaling. It was determined in the early dredging cycles that training works would be necessary in the straightaways.

"The training works, or dike fields, were placed to restrict the flow, thus increasing the velocity. This method allowed the river solids to remain in suspension.

"When the 9-foot-[deep] project began, the dredged material was placed

Fig. 3.4b. The U.S. Army Corps of Engineers transfers sand from spoil site 40 to replenish beaches. Photo by John Crowe.

along the riverbanks in the floodplains. The 'return water' [seeping from the dredged material] would cause the banks to sluff and destroy much of the vegetation.

"I witnessed this procedure in my earlier years with the Corps. When I became area engineer in '73, this methodology was continuing. Due to cost restriction it was not transported outside the floodplain.

"After returning to the area, I recommended we put the material within banks, and during flooding, the river would recover that material. This procedure would also help in alleviating bank erosion and snagging. It worked well until the drought years, when the high water did not recover the dredged material.

"So I developed the idea of 'mechanical redistribution,' which was nothing but to put 'dozers in the disposal areas along the riverbanks and push the material back on the edge of the water for the river flow to recover it.

"This is the manner we worked throughout the navigation project on the Apalachicola River. Except for the areas around Corley Slough, Sand Mountain, this method was used to eliminate future 'sand mountains.' Of course there has been a lot of statements that there's a lot more sandbars. But if you go to the Choctawhatchee River and other rivers where there's no dredging, you will find sandbars.

"The major reason we did not use within-bank disposal in the Corley Slough area was the lack of space along the riverbanks.

"While traveling the river in later years with the Corps, it was interesting to note that when people fished, they liked Battle Bend, which is nothing but an oxbow created by dredging. A lot of the fishermen use the dike fields because of the rock structure, which attracts critters. The recreational improvement created by the reservoirs is difficult to estimate because of low river levels in their natural state.

"There's pluses and minuses, but the reservoir northeast of Atlanta, Lake Lanier, has brought billions of dollars to the region. It was nothing but just a hilly country with a small stream. This small stream is the headwaters of the Chattahoochee River. In '92, Lake Lanier had approximately 17 million visitors a year. Eufaula was a ghost town, and look at it today because of Walter F. George Reservoir. It is also one of the best bass and crappie fishing spots there is in the world.

"Until we got into the drought conditions, there was never a problem. Many times the Apalachicola River, too, flooded the Howard Creek area along the river and caused havoc. It has flooded homes and businesses in Apalachicola, Blountstown, Columbia, Alabama, and Bainbridge, Georgia. Of course, too much water in Apalachicola Bay closes the bay to oystering.

"The Corps developed the depth from 'low-water profile.' It's from an imaginary fall line you establish through years of flow data. In many instances, we would shoot for 6½, 7 feet, whatever we could establish by dredging critical areas rather than just trying to begin at the mouth of the river and work all the way up.

"Before my tour, we removed all snags and debris from the river. We cleared the river and placed them along the bank. To build fish habitat, 'selective snagging' was begun. Selective snagging was a technique where only the snags in the navigation channel posing imminent danger to vessels were removed. The ones deeply submerged in the river bends were not disturbed. The hazards were removed and placed within the river stream to improve fish habitat, rather than placing them on the bank.

"In Apalachicola Bay, before [Sikes Cut], West Pass was used by fishing vessels entering the Gulf through Apalachicola. When you have a natural channel, it is difficult to mark. Because of the shifting channel, Bob Sikes Channel was constructed. The new channel allowed safe passage to shrimping grounds in the Gulf.

"I was a member in the survey party when the first channel was made through St. George Island. The first channel did not have jetties to protect the channel. After a nor'wester came through, the channel shoaled so badly that the dredging vessel was stranded in the Gulf.

"The [Vulcan Materials] dredge *Greenville* was one of the dredges. They had the contract on the original dredging for the 9-foot-deep project on the Apalachicola River.

"Through the years, the river bottom has scoured. The scouring allowed the sandy bottom to move material, but where the bottom was rock, there was no scouring. This phenomenon resulted in rock ledges less than 9 feet. In some instances, dredging to 12 feet was necessary to maintain the low-water profile. This is a natural process similar to the bottom degradation in the Grand Canyon. We had to dredge the rock bottom more than one time because of the lowering profile.

We had to dredge the rock bottom more than one time because of the lowering profile.

"The drought cycle would change everything. Before the drought, we were able to maintain 9 feet around 80 to 85 percent of the time. To improve channel availability and to reduce dredging, low-level dams were planned for the Apalachicola River. The Corps had a public hearing on the idea. I was the new area engineer in '73, and the hearing was held in Marianna. This is when opposition was discovered; maybe fifty or sixty [spoke].

"But there were people that [were] also in favor of it—Jim Woodruff Jr. from Columbus, Georgia, whose dad the dam was named after." Dams were supposed to "alleviate dredging," Colvin said, "through the pooling effect. It would be a lake effect like Jim Woodruff or Andrews Lock or any of [those].

The Corps found out that there was a few opposed to dams.

"But of course, through the years there would be some accretion behind these dams because of high water. They would flood out during the high water. There would be some dredging in future years. But it would eliminate a lot of the erosion that was occurring along the river.

"The Corps should have been prepared to meet with the local opposition and explain the plans in detail rather than catching them on the cold. Then they would not have any opposition.

"See, I grew up essentially on the river. And of course, a lot of the people that worked for the Corps were from those areas—Wewa, Apalachicola, Blountstown, Chattahoochee. They would come and explain to me, and I would explain it to the Corps, but they said they had a handle on it. It was a great awakening. It's called public relations.

"Oh, I did a lot of contacts with the local entities, city, county governments throughout Georgia, Alabama, Florida. [I needed a] local sponsor [for spoil disposal]," Colvin said. "The political arena was changing constantly. [Every two to] four years there would be new county commissioners. You talk to them one day and they're goin' in one direction, and the next day they're goin' in a different direction, so you have to continue to communicate with them because they'll surprise you. So the position was quite a public relations venture.

"When low flows occurred on the river, they had very low flows," Colvin said. "You couldn't even operate a skiff boat in some areas. You could walk across Blountstown Bar. In earlier years, there was no augmentation of the flows upstream. After creation of the upstream reservoirs, recreation began great demands for water. Water releases were greatly reduced from these other reservoirs during the summer. Overall, training works did reduce dredging and improved navigation.

"But of course, some people view [Sand Mountain] as . . . scenic, because it is a break in the landscape. I myself see it as a mistake because we should've constructed a series of cutoffs and revetments. When they started looking at improvements in later years, of course, then the environmental agencies did not want any structural solutions. They want a natural system, and . . . if you want navigation, you can't have both.

"That's the reason they came up with the '56 River and Harbor Act. The river in its natural state was not suitable for barge traffic. One of the keys [was] building five dams for water storage. They were: Jim Woodruff Dam; George W. Andrews [at] Columbia, Alabama; Walter F. George at Ft. Gaines, Georgia; West Point; and Lake Lanier at Buford Dam. Justification for all the construction included flood control, navigation, and hydropower.

"Except for navigation, the results were tremendous. That water was used for recreation as well. Recreation was not one of the original purposes. It has now become a major one because of the political scenarios at Lake Lanier.

"[With] recreation as a primary player throughout the system, land values have skyrocketed. However, without navigation, these reservoirs would have never evolved. Prob'ly all the oysters would've died in Apalachicola Bay because there would've been no releases from these dams. The oyster industry and navigation was kinda tied together. But we've been in a drought cycle, essentially, for the last twenty years.

"We've had some record high floods, but they would come, and then they'd chop off. The reservoirs would be full, and of course, it would not rain again for a month or so. But everybody had too much water, and then all of a sudden that flood hydrograph disappeared.

Sediment collects behind dams, and eventually they lose their storage capacity.

"A dam is designed for certain flows. If you design it for a hundred-year flood, you go out and buy x amount of property to be flooded. But when flows exceed its design, the dam will not operate within its parameters. When record flood waves approach a dam, the dam can only handle so much. The excess goes over fixed crest and gated spillways.

"There are many more campsites [than when I was a boy], more access, more boat ramps, more recreation. Some days you might never see another boat. And now there's power boats up and down the river all day long. And the fishing load on it is prob'ly a thousandfold because, with all these new ramps, access is so easy now.

"They've been letting out fingerlings both upstream and downstream for years. I caught five bass with red worms [on Johnson's Slough recently].

"The low-level dams would've been a key [to maintaining navigation], but of course, eventually, they silt up. Sediment collects behind dams and eventually they lose their storage capacity. Any navigational river system requires some structural solutions. There's very few natural channels in the world, other than open oceans," he laughed softly.

"I loved the people I worked with. I met a lot of characters, a lot of different personalities, and it was always a challenge to turn their thoughts around.

"And you know, there were the users, and a lot of those users were conservationists as well. There were environmentalists, which you could work with, and then there were preservationists. And this is my own interpretation: they were sent down by God to protect that area, and only they, and they alone, could use it. A lot of these people lived on the river, had camps on the river, built structures on the river, enjoyed the dams at Dead Lakes, had cabins on that dam, and then they weren't willin' to remove it. If the dam would've been anywhere's else, it'd've been a great idea.

"The local people along the river, all the way from Apalachicola to Columbus, Georgia, to Atlanta, Georgia, wanted a navigable waterway. Congress tasked the Corps of Engineers to develop the project.

"They said, 'Do it in a cost-effective manner.' So the benefit-to-cost ratio had to be feasible. They utilized these dams, which stored the water for navigation, for power generation and flood control. At that time, recreation wasn't a benefit.

"Much later, environmental concerns arose, which changed the [navigation] concept. We got into droughts, and you had different groups clamoring for the water. With all the differing water needs, we tried to satisfy each need.

"[In] the tri-state area, some wanted navigation, some did not. Some wanted just total recreation, some did not. Some wanted municipal water, some agricultural. Some didn't want water releases for the Apalachicola Bay; some . . . people in Atlanta wanted to keep all the water up there. Some fishermen wanted the lake levels at certain levels. Then the Game and Fish Commission, they wanted the levels to be maintained during fish spawning. So you got all the balls you're juggling, and you're gonna drop one every now and then.

"And of course you have Sprewell Bluff [proposed dam project] on the Flint River. That was really s'posed to [have gone] through, but then Jimmy Carter, of Georgia, removed his support. Some say his rejection came after his canoe capsized. [The idea resurfaced] because of the drought cycle and because farmers won. And people [need] drinking water, sanitation water, and that's really first priority, potable water."

His first memory on the Apalachicola, Colvin said, "was when I was four or five years old. I'm on the old snagboat, *Albany*. They let me blow the steam whistle. It was a tremendous whistle on the *Albany*.

"My dad, he was the pilot on there then, and the gentleman that he was with, his name was Hezekiah Tant. And the chief engineer on there was from Apalachicola, and his grandson is a lawyer there. Anyway he chewed tobacco all his adult life, and crew members always laughed that the Beechnut Tobacco Company gave him a pair of dentures because he bought so many packs of their product. I'd look at him, you know, and only see his teeth, the ones the tobacco company gave him.

"Ever since I can remember, [my dad] was the captain of some Corps boat. [The Corps] had their own floating plant, dredges, snagboats, tugboats, survey boats, quarter boats and barges. That's the way it used to be. Now you contract everything out. When you're a kid, you always think your dad's so big," Colvin added with a hearty laugh. "And he was just a boat captain, but to me he was a giant."

4

Fishing a Sandy River

"It Is Filled Up"

Because I drink these waters they are bitter.
Kathleen Reine

River courses, floodplain sloughs, and forests are subject to near-constant natural changes. But it is likely that recent changes in the Apalachicola River main channel and floodplain are exacerbated by construction of the Jim Woodruff Dam and the engineering and maintenance of a 100-foot-wide by 9-foot-deep navigation channel.[1] Enough sand is dredged from the Apalachicola River each year, under typical flow conditions, to fill a football field twice the height of the twenty-three-story Florida Capitol. This sand is thrown up on point bars, and sometimes creates sand mountains in the floodplain.

The Corps dredges the thalweg part of the river, which is the deepest and fastest-flowing. Often soils and snags block flow in floodplain sloughs, creeks, and tributaries, restricting access to diverse backwater habitats and suffocating fish nurseries. As mitigation for environmental degradation, the Corps began opening some of these blocked sloughs under a dredging permit issued by the state in 1999.

To help determine restoration priorities for hydrology and floodplain habitat, the Northwest Florida Water Management District, in cooperation with the United States Geological Survey (USGS) and others, digitized bank line changes from 1941–42 to 1999.

As GIS analysts aligned backwater features, it became clear that the large, alluvial river has scoured deeper into its bends and cut closer to some backwater streams. Some smaller water courses have become drier and almost disappeared as distinct floodplain features in aerial photos.

Environmentalists want to see dredging stopped, restoration accomplished, and locks operated for recreation only, said Dan Tonsmeire, with the Apalachicola Bay and Riverkeeper group.

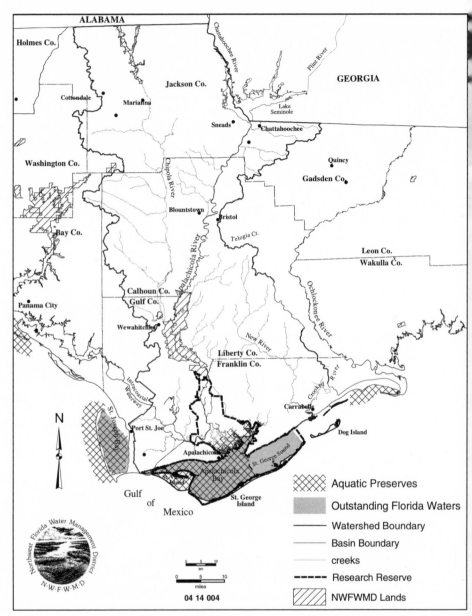

Map 4.1. Apalachicola River Basin Management Designations

Fig. 4.1. Riverkeeper Dan Tonsmeire, then district project manager, investigates restoring Virginia Cut Slough, which was once the main river channel. Photo by John Crowe.

Virginia Cut, too, is substantially blocked, a significant river meander that no longer provides the long-term ecological benefits it once did for plants and animals. Only during high flows does this major slough connect the main channel of the Apalachicola with the Chipola River. Yet a portion of it was once the main channel of the Apalachicola River, which, during the Civil War, was obstructed by rock fill and defended by gun emplacements. Steamboat trade began using the adjacent swift and narrow Moccasin Creek as a bypass in 1863;[2] the creek was later dredged open as the new channel.

By cutting out several river bends, the Corps had reduced river length by 2 miles during the period 1955–75. Measurements revealed that the 1941–42 river length was 107.9 miles. Yet by 1979, the river had regained the channel length lost and gained 1.3 more miles. By 1999, it had increased another .8 miles, so that the river is now 110 miles long. The net result is a 2.1-mile lengthening of the river.[3]

USGS investigators have suggested that causes of increasing length include both natural processes and river entrenchment below the Jim Woodruff Lock and Dam. Decreasing river slope could cause more meander. Also, the increasing height of within-bank disposal on point bars may exacerbate erosion of opposite banks as the river is forced into the outer bank, picking up velocity and, subsequently, more sand.

Thalweg dredging also changes the location of the deepest and swiftest scour and may exacerbate channel movement. Other causes may be increased erosion from boat wakes and increased volumes of river water being held back in upstream reservoirs, which lower river levels for longer periods, causing more collapse of banks.

Such navigation maintenance practices, plus natural shoaling and scouring processes, will determine the lifespan of restoration benefits. Three basic types of sites have been proposed for restoration: large within-bank disposal areas; floodplain forest disposal areas that have not revegetated; and floodplain sloughs, streams, or lakes.

Florida's battle for a natural river system was enhanced with a successful application for a National Estuarine Research Reserve in the 1970s. The designation allowed navigation projects to continue, however, and Florida leaders lobbied through 2005 to end dredging, which continues to imperil the system and the local economy.[4] In this chapter, lifelong riverside residents Lavere and Thelma Walker and Jimmy Mosconis, and biologist James Barkuloo, give their experiential accounts of how a once-plentiful resource became stressed.

The Walkers: Catfish Trap Makers

At his home on the banks of the Apalachicola River, the late Lavere Walker spoke on January 12, 2001, of a life so tough he worked a crosscut saw all day with only a half piece of corn bread for lunch. Born at Brickyard Landing in 1910, Walker fished, ran supply boats, turpentined, collected honey, worked in a sawmill, and lost a leg in a timbering accident—all before he was fifty.

Disabled, with six children to feed, he and his wife, Thelma, designed and patented sturdy catfish traps out of deadhead cypress. They sold both the Walker Baskets and the fresh channel catfish they trapped.

A Walker Basket is on exhibit at the John Gorrie State Museum in Apalachicola, a memento of "Gatorman," so named because Walker told tall tales about losing his leg to an alligator. Walker died of cancer at his home on May 3, 2003, at age ninety-three. He had just celebrated his birthday on April 8 with his family gathered around him. He is survived by his wife of fifty-eight years, one son, five daughters, eleven grandchildren, and twenty great-grandchildren.

For decades the Walkers also worked half-time as sentry and groundskeeper at Fort Gadsden Historic Site, a mile away. Under Lt. James Gadsden, the fort became a supply base for Andrew Jackson in the First Seminole War.[5]

Walker used crutches and was often accompanied by his wife, Thelma,

Fig. 4.2a. Thelma and Lavere Walker with a Walker Basket fish trap they designed and built. Photo by Faith Eidse.

who cleaned bathrooms, mowed grounds, and raked leaves, gratis. She is tall and active, despite a slightly disabling stroke. But she doesn't dwell much on herself, preferring to promote her husband's heroic survival and his love of storytelling.

Walker had the searing recall of someone who never learned to read or write. He delivered precise dialogue in the tones of authoritative doctors, experienced secretaries, and remorseful bosses. He strained to see through clouded, hazel eyes and, though nearly deaf, struggled to hear responses to his stories.

Walker recalled the weighted, paperwood barges that floated downriver during his boyhood. "They would bring two hundred cords of paperwood on barges from up yonder in Georgia, down this river, and carried it to Panama City. I helped cut wood here, and they loaded it up on barges.

"And now then, you can't hardly run a motorboat up the river. It is filled up. I can show you places when I catfished that I had a 36-foot line on my basket. The basket was 4 foot long and would stand on its end, the water was so deep, and now then, you can walk out there.

"And right up here—it ain't over half a mile up there to Brickyard Creek along this side the river—the steamboats would land up there. Now then,

> I can show you places when I catfished that I had a 36-foot line on my basket. . . . [It] would stand on its end, the water was so deep.

you can't get a bass boat up there. They pumped sand up there, and it's filled down here. When I moved here in '59, right out in front of my house, that water was 45 foot deep, and I hadn't over 8 foot out there now—or 9.

"It's a shame the way they do it. They want to cut it just like a string goin' down there. Being raised on this river, and the way they have cut it up, there's places I don't even know no more."

Thelma added, "And Bushy Creek, Kennedy Creek—you can't get in them to go fishing; the sand has filled it up."

"I have towed logs out of Kennedy Creek up there with a tugboat," Walker added. "I'm a boat man, same as they are. You can walk all the way in there.

"And I was talking to the captain on a dredge, and I asked him, 'Why are you all pumping that sand back in the river?' He said that was to shallow the river up, to slow the current of the river.

"They said they weren't allowed to pump it on the hill. But they pumped so much of it in here, it got everywhere on the bank, and they had to go back and pump it back out in the river. And the boat had to pump so much sand that they couldn't back out with the pumps on it. They had to get a dredge to go down there and pump the boat off of the hill.

"Back in the thirties," Walker continued, "they pumped sand out here at Bloody Bluff and right up here at Brickyard. There wasn't but about three places they pumped that sand. And they was bringing those barges down here, as big as these same barges they're pushing up here.

"Right here below my house, we used to tie baskets to the woods there, and they pumped sand to the other side of the river. That's aught for you to see."

"You can't even get any bream fish now," Thelma said.

"Pump the sand, and keep the river open," Walker said. "Haul that sand out in the Gulf somewheres. Don't fill up the river to keep people from travelin' on the river.

"There's a place up the river here where they have pumped that sand up higher than the tops of the trees. My son-in-law [took] me around there, and his motor would drag the ground.

"I have waded the river right over here—where this ol' rock dam was [a Confederate defense at the Narrows, 15 miles north of Fort Gadsden] back in the thirties, and they were bringing paperwood down at the same time. That river was deep then," Walker said. "There wasn't but just a few places where they had to pump sand.

"[I worked] in these woods all through there and up here at Wewa over that [Cutoff] Island there—sawed logs, run boats, anything—anything that

Fig. 4.2b. Walker worked at this lumber mill after Jerome H. Sheip bought it from Cypress Lumber Company during Apalachicola's lumber boom in the early 1900s. Photo courtesy of Florida State Archives.

come to hand. We didn't have no certain jobs. Whatever they wanted you to do, that's what you done."

After they sawed trees down, they'd "take caterpillars and pull it to the river," Walker added. "They'd cut a ditch [in] a 'V,' and they'd take a cable and hook it to [a] tree, and when they pulled that log across there, they'd attach it to [a] cable and roll it in the river. And they had men rafting and picking those deadheads up. I worked at that too.

"They had a block up there in the tree; when the caterpillar would turn these logs loose, well, they'd stop the logs on [a ramp]. They'd go up there and get a hold on that cable, they'd pick [the ramp] up, and them logs would roll in the river.

"There was a barge here and a barge here, and they had pieces coming across. We called them strongbacks. And then they'd pick these logs up and put wire around them.

"When we picked up the sinking logs, they was on pontoons," Walker explained. "[Jerome H.] Sheip came there [from Alabama], and he opened that mill in '28."

Next door to the Walkers a small electric sawmill now operates, supplied by navigation barges that snag sunken logs, some of them over a hundred years old, Walker said. Deadheads tend to be virgin pine or cypress trees, dense and strong from centuries of undisturbed growth, and resistant to rot by water and oxygen.

Walker described how foresters used to girdle cypresses so they'd float.

"They'd cut into the heart. They'd start in September, and the sap starts down the trees. And whenever the leaves would fall off them, they'd raft them.

"And in the creeks, they'd take a log and they'd fasten it, and they'd take another one and fasten to that one—and [the rafts would] reach across the creek there. And back in [the Apalachicola National Forest, the clear-cut] was just like a pasture where you put your cows. They'd run 'em down in there, due to the high water. Well, when the water'd get so [high] they could run 'em outta the swamp into the creek, they'd raft 'em up and drift them to Apalachicola. I seen as many as five and six rafts at a time, up and down this river, one right back o' the other."

"They came on down the river here to what they call Hurricane Reach [8 miles above Apalachicola at Hoffman Creek]. The boat from the mill would come up, measure 'em up, [and] pay the people for rafting them up."

"Oh, there were about two or three people that I worked for, Milledge Philips was one. And Orin Revells was the other one. And then I worked some for Brock. He was down at Buckeye, but he turpentined up here.

"I dipped out the still. I'd fill out the still, and then I'd make rosin barrels. You'd take your head, and you'd put [rosin] around that groove, and you'd push [the hoop] down, and you'd take your hammer, and you'd drive that hoop down. And then I'd take the hammer and put some rivets through there and brad them.

"And they had a windlass, like a steering wheel on a boat, with spokes in it? It was a big outfit and had a cable comin' round there. And the bench here had a circle in it, and you'd push that barrel in there where it couldn't jump out, and you'd tighten them spokes, and then you'd put the hoops on and drive them down. You name it, I've done a little bit of everything. I guess that's the reason I'm as old as I am."

"And they called him Waterboy," Thelma added.

"I pumped water. You know the old pitcher pump? [I used that] to get water to the mill," Walker said. "I fired the boiler, pumped water. There was a feller, and he told me, 'I can fire that boiler.' And Charles Kenney, who owned the mill, put him up there to fire the boiler. Mac couldn't keep steam in it. He'd take them green slabs, now, and he'd just bank 'em in there one on top of the other. Charles Kenney asked me, 'Waterboy, do you know how to fire that boiler?' I said, 'Yes, sir.' I wasn't but 'bout seventeen years old.

"Well, I got the old fire poker, and I shook that stuff up and got [the wood] kinda crossed up, you know, where it'd burn. And it wa'n't but just a few minutes, I had steam on that outfit. And I was pumpin' water too. And he told that fellow, 'You see that?' He says, 'You ain't never fired a boiler with green slabs.' I done that for about two weeks and I quit. The next week they shut the whole works down."

"We ran trotlines when we first moved in this house," said Thelma. "We had bush hooks to help us. And I hated the trotline. It would just cut your hands. It's a tight line right across the river, put bush hooks in them bushes and take a dip net and dip [the fish] up. We have gotten trout that weighed 15 pounds off of them net lines," she added. "He caught a bass on a bush hook sometime."

"He weighed 9 pounds," Walker said.

"And I dressed him and cooked him right here in this kitchen, and my babies sat down and et it. It was our dinner. I called it supper, but they called it dinner that night," Thelma said.

"I'd go on to Apalachicola with my daddy and his brother on a little old boat," Walker said. "Just be paddlin'. There were no outboard motors then. If you went anywhere, you had to take that stick and get on. It'll take you a good day and a little over. There was no other way to go [except] on the steamboat. There were no outboard motors until the 1930s. That's when they came out with the Johnson motors. Even then it took three hours by motorboat to Apalachicola.

"It wasn't a thing but flat woods just like you see going out through yonder. A wagon road. There was no bridges across these creeks nor anything. Wasn't nothing but a railroad. They put that railroad through there before I was born. It was rough. Oooh, it was rough."

Even then, his family didn't stay in Apalachicola over night, Walker said. "Did I go down there and get what I had to and head back. Sometimes we'd leave before daylight, me and my daddy, and I paddled that boat by myself. Until my daddy died, the twenty-ninth day of September of 1925.

"He died in Apalachicola [of hemorrhage]. See, there wasn't no hospital. I was the oldest boy. I had to look after my mother and eight kids, and when I worked I wasn't gettin' but $1 a day."

"Scrapin' turpentine," Thelma said.

"You could get more with $1 then than you can get for $50 now."

"Get 'im a sack of flour 'n' some meal 'n' some rice, some grease, and that's about what they lived off of—and the fish out of the river," Thelma said.

"I have worked in this river-swamp, livin' on one piece of corn bread about like that." Walker measured half of his small, stained hand. "That's what I had in my lunch for my dinner. Runnin' a crosscut saw, and the water would be up, and that swamp would be froze over. You'd have to break that ice to get up close enough to pull that crosscut saw.

"We'd cut 4-foot wood, loaded it on barges up there, to fire up them [steamboat] boilers with. And I cut crossties; snaked crossties with an old ox," Walker added.

"And right up here at Brickyard Landing," said Walker, "they used to have a post office there, and there's a big oak tree [10 feet around]. And the name of that post office was Lone Oak. The steamboat would bring the mail down from Wewa and then to Apalachicola, I reckon. And they had an old mule and wagon up there. They'd just hang the mail bag on the horn of the saddle, and take it up to Sumatra. They'd pick up the mail there and bring it back to the post office down here, and when the steamboat came back up, it'd go back on the steamboat.

"When I was about big enough to know anything, we had a fellow living up there in Sumatra," Walker continued, "name was George Branch. He had a big place there, and he got my daddy to clean it up. [His sons, about age twelve,] walked from Sumatra up here and tell my daddy that their daddy want him to come. My daddy'd walk up to Sumatra, through the woods—there wasn't no road, nothin' but a wagon road—wadin' in water waist deep, for 50¢ a day.

"And when [Herbert] Hoover [U.S. president, 1929–33] got into office, I couldn't get a job nowhere at anything. I would catfish, I would deer hunt, I would frog hunt.

"You might say, well, you just tellin' me something ain't in the books. I'm tellin' you the actual fact. If you went somewhere tryin' to get a job, the people was standin' in line just like your hand over there [fingers pressed together] waitin' for one to be dropped out 'fore he could get a job.

"One night, fellow come up the river. It was one o'clock in the mornin'. He come out and called me, 'Hey, Lavere, this is Jack Tillman.'"

"He was a camp cook," Thelma interjected.

"He said, 'I want you to take your motor and go up the river with me.' I got me a little motor—it wasn't but a horse-and-a-half—and I put it on my shoulder, and I hooked it up on his boat. And it seemed like I run it for hours just getting up there to Brickyard Landing.

"He said: 'You take this flashlight. You lay down up there on the bow of the boat. You hold that flashlight right up there.' I holed up there, and we went close to the head of Cutoff Island up there above Wewa.

"And next day, comin' back, he says, 'Did you ever run one of these motors? It's a big one, 22-horse Johnson.' I said, 'No, sir, I never have.' He said: 'Get back here. You might get you a job runnin' this motor.' I couldn't believe it. That was on Sunday. He says, 'You come down the river, down Smith Bend [17 miles above Apalachicola] in the morning.'

"He says, 'You know how to mix the oil and gas?' I says, 'Yeah, if you tell me how much it will be.' He says, 'I want a quart to 5 gallons.' He said, 'Now crank it up; we're going up the river.'

"And I worked for him, I reckon, a year. I went from one camp to another, and he'd write up a whole rasher—I couldn't write. I'd go to Apalachicola and get it.

"And then they put me on a tug," Walker said. "I worked with the Sheips 'til the mill shut down. I was workin' in the mill and in the swamp. Gettin' it logged out, and they was cleanin' up the mill pond and everything. I seed it when it sawed its last line."

"He saw the last log go through," Thelma explained.

"In President [Franklin D.] Roosevelt's days [1933–45]," Walker added, "I was working at the Sheip's Mill then. Jerome H. Sheip. People there in Wewa worked [for] the mill, worked in the woods up there, and I worked with them. But they all might be dead now."

"He's the oldest Walker that ever was," Thelma said.

"I thank the old man up yonder for letting me live," Walker said. "You see, I got a tree cut on me in '58. The twenty-ninth day of July '58, a boy cut a tree on me's how come I'm one-legged."

"He drove a school bus," Thelma said. "School was out, and he had to have a job 'cause we had six children, and the baby wasn't but nine months old. So he went to work cuttin' paperwood."

"When you got kids, you got to reach up and scratch that head when it don't itch. When I lost my leg and I couldn't get nuttin' to do—[social services] wouldn't let me have nothin' at all—my kids went hungry."

Thelma added, "'Bout how long was it before we started to work piecin' fish baskets?"

"Just took as I got able to go."

"He was four months in the hospital," Thelma said, "and I built this house here. Me and my brother built it."

"That was '58 when I lost my leg—and in '59 we were moved in this house here. I built me some fish baskets, and we started to fishin'. I had a' old piece of boat, but we went. And the game wardener, I told him I want two fishing licenses. And he wrote 'em out for me. I could get enough bread for the kids. And the next time I went to get my license, he says, 'I ain't got no more [forms].'"

"That was Seab Larkins," Thelma said, "the [sheriff's deputy] and game warden's [brother]."

"And he said, 'Just go on, go fishing.' I said, 'They'll catch me.' He says, 'They got to come to me first.' He still bought my fishing license after he retired. And just two or three days before he died, he asked me, 'Can you make it by fishing now?' And I said, 'Yes, I can.'

"Well, we built baskets then," Thelma said.

We got nigh 65 pounds of fresh fish out of one basket.

"The game wardeners would come down the river and see him 'n' her pullin' them baskets," Walker said. "They might wave at us and go on. I didn't try to hide nothin' from 'em. Noo-oo, I don't believe in that."

"Oh, it was good fishing then," Walker said.

"We had woods to tie our baskets to," Thelma said. "Now ain't no willows out. It's sand."

"You'd go out 'ere to those baskets. It would be just as full as one could get it," Walker said. "We got nigh 65 pounds of fresh fish out of one basket. God is my witness, them tails were stickin' out the cracks."

"I would have to holler: 'Lavere, you're gonna have to help me. I can't hold it.' So he crawled over the seat and got a hook to it, and by us havin' round baskets, we were able to twist it and pull 'em out."

"I would have to brace that foot there," Walker said, "and get a hold of that rope [rigged] over my head, and me and her pull 'em in that boat."

"Just channel cat would go in that trap," Thelma said. "If we got another kind of fish, we turned it loose."

"I tell you what," Walker said, "I've sat on that brick walk where I could get light from the house and worked on fish baskets. Built one, and then I'd go 'cross the river and put it out. Go back next mornin' and would have a fishin' rope about that long left on the limb."

"Build one, and then them take it," Thelma said. "And you know what he said? 'Well, Mama, they wanted it worse than we did.' I said, 'Yeah, but if I come along I'll just paddle after him and beat him where he can't get up.'"

"I won't tell you [who took it]," Lavere said. "There were so many on the river, but there was one man on the river—I won't call no names—but he could win a basket like a dog winnin' a deer. And there would be nobody in the world on the river that we seen. And I hate a thief," Walker said. "Lord 'a' mercy, a liar and a thief."

Thelma fetched a cone basket made of wooden slats. "The catfish comes through here [putting her hand into the narrow end where an outer cone leads into an inner cone] and passes to here," the wide end. "When they go on through; they can't turn around and come back."

She unhooked a thick rubber band and lifted a gate to show how the fish were lifted out. The sturdy, reddish slats are "Deadhead cypress. We hauled it from Apalachicola too, from Cairo Ingram" (see chapter 5).

"We made a lot of them for $25 a piece," Thelma said. "And we built one for a man [from] Pennsylvania. He said, 'I ain't gonna give you a penny over $60, and I ain't gonna give you a penny under. And don't you ever make another one without charging $60 for it.'"

"It's worth every penny of it when you go to start building," Walker said.

"It takes a lot of nails and a lot of time . . . because you have to brad all the nails, see?" Thelma showed how the nail heads were neatly buried in the wood.

"I fishin' right by myself when she had to go to Gainesville with my baby daughter for open heart surgery," Walker said. "[With one leg] I had to sit down on the seat of the boat—I couldn't get up and get in the boat—I had to go from one seat to the other. And after I got that rope, I'd get on that seat— I had a stick there with a rope on it.

"And I'd put [fish] in a tub. And I'd take me a rope and tie it to the handle of that tub, and I'd make a step and pull that tub until I'd get my fish up there in that little old [shed] down there, and I'd sit right there and skin fish and dress 'em out. Nobody ever offered to help me."

"I took in washing," Thelma said. "'cause I didn't leave home—'til my young'uns was all grown. I didn't work off . . . and I'd go fish baskets. I got up in the mornin', I fixed their breakfast, and then when they came in at night, their supper was ready.

"But I'd go sell [catfish] to Georgia and Alabama to restaurants. Some people that sell seafood down here—tell 'em if they want that freshwater catfish—that the Walkers had 'em. And that's the way we got [the business]. Do you remember how much a pound we got for channel cat when we first started selling?"

"25¢," Walker said.

"And he'd stay down at [Gadsden] Park [as watchman]. On Saturday we'd have a full day [of fishing], and then in the evenings when he'd get off from work.

"Then when I quit building baskets so much. I cleaned [Cairo Ingram's] house," Thelma said. "Then I had the stroke, and I never did clean no more." Thelma walks with a slight limp. "February of '91 my pressure, I guess, went so high. But I cleaned houses, a lot of 'em [on the coast]. Comin' home I couldn't get this hand off the steering wheel. I took my left hand and pulled my fingers off and fell out on the ground. And [my grandson] went to screamin', 'Come on, Poppa, there's something wrong with Nanny.' So they got me in the bed of the truck. He said, 'We're not takin' her to that first aid in Apalach; we're takin' her to Tallahassee.' It was three days before I even knew I was in there.

"That's when Lavere was workin' at the park, and my granddaughter would come out every morning and help him 'til I got back. They say it took me about six months."

"[My sister Agnes was born] just a month after Daddy died," Walker added. "She's eatin' up with cancer. That's what killed my mother [and] two of my sisters. Three of my sisters died from childbirth."

"Toxic poisoning business that women get," Thelma said, "and they livin' way up here not going to a doctor while they were pregnant. They're buried right here [in Sumatra] in Walker-Brown Cemetery with their babies in their arms. They had 'em, but they died." Lavere Walker was also buried there on May 6, 2003.

"I'm a diabetic," Walker said. "I worked down here in Fort Gadsden State Park thirty years. They kept me on that OPS sixteen years. They shouldn't have done it."

"And I cleaned bathrooms, swept, raked, and made it look better," Thelma said. "Lavere worked two-and-a-half days a week as a watchman. Eddie Nesmith was the ranger who asked him to watch down there when he lost his leg. Take me back to the day you lost your leg," Thelma prompted.

Walker bowed his head. "I worked, and the boy was cuttin' the tree, and I was trimmin' the trees, you know, measurin' them up. I says, 'Which way is that tree going?' He says, 'It ain't goin' toward you.'

"And I just started to step over a log—and a nail where they hang that turpentine cup on it?—caught my britches' leg, and I heard that thing comin'. It fell right up and down me."

"Smashed it just like hamburger meat," Thelma said.

"I lay there in the woods about an hour or longer. That happened at nine o'clock. They got me in the [old Weems Hospital in Apalachicola] at quarter to twelve."

"Broke his back four times," Thelma added. "Tore his leg clean off except some [outer] thigh held it."

"It even mashed my entrails out. And I'm sufferin' from it right now. I'm never eased," Walker said. "I knew I was going to die," said Walker. "I seed the devil. And the night they amputated my leg, five doctors all givin' me up not to live through the night.

"Abraham picked me up in his arms," Walker continued. "He carried me to heaven. He carried me to hell, and if I keep my right mind, I ain't going to hell."

"There's a room—I ain't makin' this up," Walker paused. "Some folks say, 'You were dreamin'.' A dead person can't dream. There's one door to that place, and they's lined up just like your fingers. They're dumpin' them in that fire, and there's all the screamin' and hollerin' you ever heard. And it's burnt black as far as 'tis from here to that door. Abraham had me in his arms.

"I seen the rich man; I seen Lazarus. Abraham still had me in his arms; the rich man asked Lazarus to dip his finger in some water there and stick it to his parching tongue. And Lazarus started and Abraham pulled him back—he sure did.

"And I could see the good Lord just like I'm lookin' at you—but the devil was standin' between me and him." Walker's voice rose, anguished. "But that devil moved, and I'm living today." A long pause followed.

"Abraham had me in his arms, and I saw three moons. I asked what the three moons were. Abraham said, 'That's not the moon. That's the Father, Son, and Holy Ghost. You just stay in the rim of lights.'"

When Mr. Walker was released from Apalachicola, he was sent to Dr. Murphy in Thomasville, Georgia, for a checkup. The doctor said, "Mr. Walker? No, that was a dead man when I left there." Dr. Murphy dressed his leg, Walker said, and told him, "You won't have to come up here no more."

"And you know, I wasn't old enough to draw Social Security," Walker said. "And I went to the social [services] board right here in Apalachicola, and a lady in there said, 'Well, Mr. Walker, you have to lose weight to draw [disability].'

"I said, 'Lady, they didn't tell me I have to fatten up to pay it.'"

"He didn't get it, either," said Thelma.

"That is how come me to work down here in this park."

Walker later gave up his Social Security for disability payments, but for the most part, fishing has sustained the Walkers.

"Any time you went, you could catch a mess of fish," Thelma said. "You could sit on the dock and catch bream and shellfish. Now there are flatheads," a red meat catfish that cannibalizes other fish. "They got bream that big in their paunch." Thelma measured 4 inches with thumb and forefinger. "You can be catching fish, and one of them flatheads will eat 'em up right off the line. That's what's eatin' up all those fish. And those dredge boats—that's another thing."

Thelma said she typically cleans the fish, boils it, and fries onions and flour for gravy. When the meat comes off the bones, she mixes the fish with gravy and serves it over hoecakes (a cornmeal cake once cooked in the field on a hoe). To make salt mullet, the Walkers spread alternate layers of salt and cleaned fish; they'd freeze them and eat them for a breakfast of mullet, hot biscuits, and syrup.

Fig. 4.3a. Marine biologist James Barkuloo at his home on North Bay, Panama City. Photo by Faith Eidse.

James M. Barkuloo: Counting the Disappearing Fish

James Barkuloo came to the Apalachicola River first as a student, then as a graduate student, and finally as a professional. He is wiry and soft-spoken with a perpetual tan, glasses, a master's in biology, and a fisheries history dating to 1951. He was assigned to the Lake and Stream Survey at the Florida Game and Fresh Water Fish Commission in 1955 after he graduated from Florida State University and became project leader of the Florida striped bass project full-time in 1958.

Straighten-
ing the river
channel and
cutting off
bends, low-
ers the river
upstream
and reduces
critical
habitat.

He witnessed the decline in anadromous fish (marine fish that enter freshwater to spawn) when the Jim Woodruff Lock and Dam impounded Lake Seminole. It interrupted critical spawning habitat and destroyed nurseries for striped bass, Alabama shad, and Gulf sturgeon.

Barkuloo continues to work with the Gulf States Marine Fisheries Commission to revise the striped bass management plan for the Gulf and is on the board of the St. Andrew Bay Environmental Study Team. He recorded his story on December 13, 2001, overlooking his dock on North Bay in Panama City.

"I was born in 1929, Tifton, Georgia; went to the Abraham Baldwin Agricultural College there for two years; then went to Auburn for two years; and went to Florida to get fisheries credit at Auburn. I met a lady, married her, and finished at FSU. I went back to work with the Florida Game and Fish Commission and got my master's at Stetson.

"I worked with the Lake and Stream Survey on the Apalachicola for about a year before we went to south Florida." A year later, "we came back to the Apalachicola, and at that time, we started in Marianna and worked the upper river and Lake Seminole, which had [just] been impounded. The dam was there, partly, but it had only been raised about halfway so they could get in the cofferdams and get all the holes in the dam filled. Evidently it was like a honeycomb of holes in the lime rock there. They had to accommodate all the springs and so forth that were coming out of those areas.

"When I was diving in the dam, I could see a lot of water coming through grates in the bottom. They had grated areas, and it was real clear water, so I suspected it was the springs that were flowing out, back in the sixties.

So we know exactly how much the river [below the dam] has fallen ... about 5 feet.

"Anyway, as the lake was rising, it left a lot of islands, and you could see rattlesnakes crossin', tryin' to find higher land.

"There hadn't been any major improvements to the navigation channel below the dam, and mainly what we saw 'em do was surveying the depth from the dam on down. So they did establish an excellent baseline for the

Fig. 4.3b. Aerial view of Jim Woodruff Lock and Dam. NWFWMD archives.

Fishing a Sandy River: "It Is Filled Up"   97

river stage at that time. So we know exactly how much the river stage has fallen since then. I think it's about 5 feet.

"That was a pretty interesting time. Mr. Pringle, manager of the dam, asked me if I could dive into the dam to find out why they couldn't de-water one of their gates. We had to climb down a ladder in the concrete shaft all the way down through the dam. It came out just above the gate where the water is released. The water was surprisingly clear, and I was fairly heavily weighted so I could walk pretty much where I needed to. I walked over to where the gate was dropped, and there was a big piece of metal [gate], so I brought it back.

"While I was down there, I was amazed at the number of eels that were assembled around these grates. I assume that's the way they accommodated all those springs is to vent the water out through those grates. Now with the massive water withdrawals for agriculture usage or municipal, that may be greatly reduced.

"[On the surface], you could see a pretty definite line where the Chattahoochee and Flint meet. The Flint was much clearer than the Chattahoochee. But the muddy color can fool you 'cause it can still be very diveable—visibility up to 6 feet, even though it's real brown. It's not as turbid as it looks from the surface. And you get around those springs that come up from the bottom or edge of the channel, you can actually see pretty good.

"We didn't start to look at [the springs] carefully until I started work on the striped bass in 1958. The creeks were totally in their natural state, and you could actually run your boat up into the mouth of the creek in most cases, especially on the east side. On the west side, it was hard to see exactly where the spring was. In fact, in some cases, it was several hundred feet from the river, through the floodplain, to where the spring actually rose.

"Flat Creek came in on the east side, and it turned out to be a major cool-water habitat for the striped bass because it was deep enough they could go up several feet. We collected a sturgeon once in a while, but we didn't really target sturgeon until much later, probably in the seventies.

"Their biology is quite different, but the fact they need cool-water habitat is very real. If you lose your cool-water habitat, you've lost the species, essentially. Especially your large striped bass; your small striped bass can tolerate up to 30 degrees centigrade. But once [they're] four years old, they have to have 24 degrees or less, or they probably won't survive.

"Any creek that is not cleared up to the bank, and which had a good overstory and deep enough water for the striped bass to go in, that established a cool-water habitat. Selman's Ditch (Red's Landing) was one of the better

> If you lose your cool-water habitat, you've lost the species.

habitats at that time. That's not far from Blountstown on the west side. [It] had been dredged—probably for [logging] boats—and it was about 8 feet deep for about 300 or 400 yards. Normal water, without a rain, was probably 3 feet wide and maybe 5 or 6 inches deep. There was plenty of oxygen in it.

"We [strung] a gill net across the mouth of it. There was a very harsh thunderstorm that night. Lightning you wouldn't believe. We were camped up on the bank, and we all got drenched. So we went down to the net the next morning, and all we could see was white bellies. We had over 500 pounds of dead striped bass in the net, and I think the smallest one was about 25 pounds. One of them that was still alive in the net was the largest striped bass that I had ever seen at that time. He made a lunge and went and broke the net and went right through it. I would estimate that he was at least 40 or 50 pounds. They found one in the Flint River in the seventies; he was around 50 pounds. I found one in Wetappo Creek on the Intracoastal, caught him with a gill net in the sixties. He was 41 pounds. He was a down-stream migrant from the Apalachicola population.

"What we wanted to do [with the gill net] was put tags on them and turn them loose. But with the storm raging, we didn't go down and check it. We didn't expect that population of striped bass bein' in that little area either.

"I worked on other fisheries projects until we moved the project back to the Apalach. From '75 on we worked on striped bass. I was consulted a lot, and I'd go out with them quite a bit after '75.

"Probably in the seventies I started getting more aware of habitat changes, especially in the upper river when they started straightenin' the bends and making the cuts. It immediately dropped [the stage] probably 3 or 4 feet.

"One good instance is where the Chipola River met the Apalachicola used to be a dead end almost. It went right into the bank of the Apalachicola. There was a 50-some-odd-foot hole there all the time where the Chipola came in. It would, I guess, tend to back up the water every time it had a bend in the river. They made cuts so that it would come in at an angle to the Apalach, and that made a big difference. Those boats were comin' down at a pretty fast pace, and they had a hard time making the bend on the Apalach where the Chipola came in.

"The main thing you saw was that the whole river stage upstream was lowered. So what happened, the barges goin' up the river started hittin' the rocks up there. And they said: 'Oh we can't have that. It's getting lower and lower up there.' So they said, 'We gotta take the rocks out.' Actually it was like takin' a seal out. It made it even lower below the dam.

[Taking the rocks out] was like takin' a seal out. It made it even lower below the dam.

"'Course the [Corps] wanted to build a dam up above Blountstown, but everybody got together and stopped 'em on that. They didn't get together enough to stop them on takin' out the rock seals and things like that. In the first place, the cost of the navigation [project, compared] to the amount of river traffic they had, it just never could have been justified. I talked to some of the economists at the Mobile [Alabama] Corps as they were about to retire. They said they would take every fishing boat comin' in just as far as Apalachicola and [count] that as navigation on the river. He said they were being pressured by the congressmen at the time to make sure that it was better than a 1-to-1 ratio in favor of navigation. They would get $1.1 for every $1 spent.

"In the lower river, sand kept filling in the channels so they had to put it somewhere, and it was such a broad floodplain that they didn't want to pump it all the way through the floodplain and put it on uplands. So they put it right beside the river, and it just, in some cases, blocked off the creeks. They wouldn't necessarily put it right across the creek. But it would just wash down and fill in the creek, so many of the tributaries were completely destroyed.

"Upstream we had a problem of the river dropping down below the mouth of the creek [due to entrenchment]. So these fish couldn't go up without jumpin' a waterfall. And then down in the lower river they just completely closed 'em off. Also, the oxbow lakes would fill in where you couldn't navigate into 'em. Later on we got 'em to open some of those up. At first they wanted to cut everything off, so it was pretty bad.

"The biggest problem when they get authorization for navigation, they forget about every other use of the river. Gotta be navigation and nothin' else, and if it's [bad] for the fish, it don't matter. Fish and Wildlife Service and the Game and Fish Commission tried their best to get that turned around, but they just couldn't make any headway with the Mobile District.

"The main reason for that big [dredging] allocation [after the dam was completed] was because they had an authorization to dredge to 9 feet. Before it had a 6-foot channel. And when they go to a 9-foot channel, they can overdredge to 11 feet, so that means that they had a lot of dredging to do.

"You could hardly ever see a dredge in the river before the dam was put in. You could see this old paddlewheel dredge and it would get the hot spots or the deadheads, and trees.

"'Course, another thing, on Lake [Seminole] is all that sand that normally came down the river [is] comin' to the lake, and it's fillin' up relatively fast. There's large areas that used to be water that now is uplands. Areas that I had been to that were open water were covered in vegetation. Of course, the res-

When they get authorization for navigation, they forget about every other use of the river.

You could hardly ever see a dredge in the river before the dam was put in.

ervoir manager people, they know exactly what's happenin'. You can compare photographs pretty easily and see.

"Not long ago I came across [a] photograph of a big flood that showed all the gates opened across, and it didn't look like water was comin' very far down from the floodgates. It was really, really high. I think 72 feet."

"Within-banks spoiling built a dam between the river and the floodplain, and it didn't flood as quick, and in some cases, it didn't drain out as fast.

"Then later on when they started their navigation windows, it would leave a lot of fish high and dry, lost to the river. Fish would go out in [the floodplain], and all of a sudden the river would drop, and they would be caught. It didn't take long in the drought for [the fish] to disappear. The spoil policies could also change the [floodplain] vegetation types.

"I couldn't make an estimate like [20 percent of the water is in the swamp, down from 40 percent]. We set aside ten stations [for] fisheries surveys, mostly on sandbars for several purposes. One, to just get an idea of these species' composition, changes over the years, and to see how many striped bass and how many shad we could get in those areas. We were 'specially interested in striped bass and Alabama shad reproduction.

"Also, years ago the Corps had done a lot of spoiling along [Red's Landing], and somebody asked 'em to put the spoil where they could build a road right across the floodplain to Highway [69] north of Blountstown. That seriously [dammed] the area downstream from there.

"We wanted to try to keep the striped bass in the Apalachicola a viable population after the dam, knowing that probably a lot of its spawning area was cut off. We found out later that the Flint River was the major spawning area. Now that the dam is there, it cannot spawn properly because [fish can't move upriver freely, and] the eggs have to be suspended by current. They have to have three days of flowing water to hatch. When they get to the still waters of the lake, they settle out on the bottom and die. So, the State of Georgia did a study and found out that only about 4 percent of the ones spawned in the Flint River hatched before the lake. And we found very little spawning below the dam.

Now that the dam is there, [striped bass] cannot spawn properly because the eggs have to be suspended by current.

"There will be some striped bass going [up] through the dam. They go in through the locks; Alabama shad and maybe a sturgeon, once in a while. They're the three anadromous fish that we have in the river. But striped bass in the Apalachicola probably prefer the cooler waters of the river.

"Part of my master's thesis was about striped bass in the St. Johns and Apalachicola rivers. I wanted to give the taxonomic status, which I decided was a race. Now they're talkin' about makin' it a subspecies. At the time, it was just a race, and the biggest threat to it was the introduction of Atlantic striped bass. They learned how to produce the young [and] were stockin' them all over the country, and I threatened to go with endangered status, and the states [agreed to] produce only Gulf stripers for the Apalachicola River.

"I'm workin' with the Gulf States Marine Fisheries Commission, developing a revision to the striped bass management plan for the Gulf. They've been doin' a lot of DNA work on all these rivers lately [and] can tell there is little recent mix between the Gulf and the Atlantic fish, although most striped bass now in the Apalachicola probably have some Atlantic DNA characteristics.

"Right after the dam was built there was a good reproduction, and that was the last year of good reproduction that I remember. For two or three years there were some real big striped bass caught right below the dam. These fish can commonly live ten or twelve years, and they've been known to live up to twenty years.

"The Flint has some large striped bass in it, but, with the big reduction in the cool water refugia, they have been reduced quite a bit. Especially during this drought. But they've been stocked in Lake Blackshear.

"[I used to see Barbour's Map turtles] everywhere. All along the Chipola was always the stronghold of the Barbour's Map, although there were plenty of them in the Apalach. But in-bank spoiling would have a serious effect on them. You are eliminating some key elements of the fauna. Used to the guys would go up and down the rivers with their .22s poppin' 'em off the logs too. Just for sport, target practice.

"I used to go with the local game warden through areas I'm sure there's no way you could go through now. We had no problem gettin' in and out of Lake Iamonia when the river stage was quite a bit higher.

"See, we used to camp along the river when we were doin' the lake and stream survey. We had a little 10- or 12-horse motor and a big aluminum boat. We'd pile all our junk in there and go for miles and just camp on the creek bank. Hang all our groceries from the trees to keep the hogs from gettin' 'em. They'd tear up everything to get to your groceries.

"We didn't worry about bear [as] much as we did hogs. We got some bear meat from some of the ol'-timers, but there were plenty of hogs. They're not native; they're all feral. You can't get rid of 'em.

"We camped on the River Styx, Florida River, and all up and down up there doin' our samplin'. We'd camp sometimes two weeks out on the river. Come in, work on our paperwork for a week or so, and go back and camp for another two weeks. We got all our coffee water out of the river. Pete, the guy that I was with, was able to get shine, and he liked to do shine at night.

"The local sheriff got some from the guys he arrested and gave us a gallon of it [from] Wewahitchka, Gulf County. It was good. It was a nice gallon jug, and it didn't have but two or three flies in it, and we just strained [them] out. Those flies died happy, I'm sure. Later on, I sampled some shine from up in Holmes County, and none of it was ever as good as that we got down in Wewa.

"I'd go up with [the pilot], and we'd fly over areas of Calhoun County, and he'd say, 'I can't go too low over here 'cause there's moonshiners; they'll start shootin.' He would never turn moonshiners in 'cause he knew if he did, he wouldn't be able to do his job as a wildlife officer.

"Used to be striped bass came up in Blue Spring Creek, a tributary to the Chipola River, there below the power company dam. They'd usually come up at night. They could catch them early in the morning. That was before the Dead Lakes dam was built. When it was built that pretty well blocked most of [the striped bass]. Now [that the dam is gone] they go back up and use those thermal refuges up there.

"I testified at the administrative hearing when they challenged removal of the dam. But I was there before the dam, and I did a field survey on what the public was feeling. It was right after the drought of 1955, [which left] all their piers in Dead Lakes high and dry. And their tax collector had a fish camp there so he was able to get a move started to dam the lake; I argued with him all the time.

"When they put the dam in at Dead Lakes, we—the Game and Fish Commission—got them to put a drawdown structure in the center of it. It amounted to stop-logs that could be pulled out by draglines. 'Bout a year later there was a flood that washed those out. When they went back, they made it solid. During high water, fish could actually go over the dam. Most of your anadromous fish, though, won't do that. The shad would, but your striped bass and sturgeon come up to the dam on the bottom.

"After several years, the water quality started goin' down in the lake, and a lot of the fishermen changed their minds. I did what I could to promote dam removal.

"[Go] back to a riverine situation [and] you would restore the striped bass and it would be better for the sturgeon. They'd have more access to cool-water habitats. You do have some springs that come up in the lake itself. All in all, I think it would be better for the public to [take the dam] out of there.

"Albany is on the Flint River, where Lake Worth is. If you go north of there, Cordele is where Lake Blackshear is. Those are the two reservoirs on the Flint River. A little creek coming out of Macon is the head. The fall line is below there. It's almost rock rapids all along through there. It's really nice, and that's probably where they're going to put the dam if they ever [do]. They had plans to put three dams on the Flint River. When [former president] Jimmy Carter was [governor], he nixed all of it. Now it could be resurrected, especially with Atlanta takin' all the water.

"They need to learn how to reuse water. You can't make more rain, and you can't keep getting more out of the Chattahoochee because you gotta have some goin' downstream other than sewage water. If you're goin' to AWT [Advanced Wastewater Treatment], why not use that water? Especially if they use ultraviolet light. It leaves chlorine out.

"Mussels [were] everywhere along the natural bars [and can live a hundred years]. When they started dredging, the natural bars disappeared so we didn't see the mussels. Toward the end of our work there, the Asian clams (*Corbicula*) were takin' over. And they were not there durin' the early days. The *Corbicula* [are] fast growin', and where you had a depression, it'd be full of these *Corbicula* shells, just thousands of 'em.

Here we had to spend all this money and destroy all this riverine habitat and wildlife to accommodate these few barges.

"They're talkin' about the Corps doin' the [slough] restoration. That's an oxymoron right there. [The spoil] should go back into the river where it came from. Economically, when you consider what has to be paid for the navigation, there's no comparison. Tupelo, used in honey production [whose sprouts struggle against sand fill], was noninvasive. It probably helped the area because of pollination and everything else, whereas navigation didn't do anything but destroy for private interests, subsidizin' a transportation industry that could have been easily handled by pipeline or by train. So they helped kill the train freight to subsidize the navigation interests.

"In several hearings, railroads would send people there to protest the navigation developments. Here we had to spend all this money and destroy all this riverine habitat and wildlife to accommodate these few barges. If the public saw just how bad the economics of barges were on the Apalachicola, how expensive it was to the taxpayer, there would be some changes."

Jimmy Mosconis: Greek Fishing Heir

Ghosts of Native Americans and early loggers haunt Bay City Lodge just north of Apalachicola. Mussel shell middens and artifacts dot the grounds from Creek settlements of centuries ago. Flanking the fishing lodge is the cement foundation of the 1909 Bay City Saw Mill Company's steam-driven log skidder. There are remnants, too, of a narrow-gauge rail line that operated until the 1930s.

Fig. 4.4. Franklin county commissioner Jimmy Mosconis is dwarfed by the foundation of a steam-driven log skidder at Bay City Lodge, his fishing resort on the Apalachicola River. The skidder used a dragline to pull logs from the woods to the Bay City Saw Mill until the 1930s. Photo by Faith Eidse.

Jimmy Mosconis's house is built on the spoil site where Poorhouse Creek and an adjacent canal were dredged for logging. Pilings jut at the creek mouth on the Apalachicola River, where a large loading dock once stood.

Recent dredging operations in the canal turned up a sunken log with a brand mark and two wooden pegs pounded into it, an eighteenth-century method of joining logs to be floated downstream.

Mosconis also displays the hull piece of a small steamship that was pulled from the river nearby. The remains may be part of *Eva*, named for the mother of Bay City Saw Mill's owner. It barged log rafts downriver during a lumber boom that fizzled with the 1929 stock market crash. The unique engine assembly drove a propeller, not a paddle wheel. At Apalachicola, cargo was loaded aboard shallow-draft schooners, or "lighters," and sailed to deepwater vessels anchored off Carrabelle for points abroad.

Mosconis, a twenty-year Franklin county commissioner, bought the lodge in 1974 after returning from Vietnam, a decorated veteran. Born in Apalachicola on March 28, 1944, Mosconis also headed a $1.5-million drive to place in town a replica of the Three Servicemen Statue memorial in tribute to the Southeast region, which is most represented by U.S. soldiers.

His grandfather was a Greek sponger who came to Apalachicola in 1907, drawn by cousins who were established spongers. He saved his money and sent for his pregnant wife, Aspacia. Together they raised six children and buried two in Apalachicola. Tragedy struck again when Aspacia died in 1923, when her youngest, Jimmy's father, was only six months old; the nearest hospital at the time was in Thomasville. Jimmy's father was raised by a neighbor and his older sisters.

"He worked for me as a fishing guide," said Mosconis, of his father, who was sixty-three when he died of a stroke.

"The main thing is the river," said Mosconis. "This is a dynamic resource. Nature is putting this together, and when you get a low river system, we suffer. In 1976, we had a bad drought, and what I've discovered is that rainfall varies from 30 to 100 inches a year. That's a big swing. Our biggest concern is the flow of the river."

Mosconis told his story while running the hundred-bed lodge on February 12, 2002. "Tugboat traffic is hazardous, with its potential spills," he added. "Our guys, when they go fishin', they bring the garbage in. Most people that use the outdoors, whether hunting or fishing, they have a genuine concern about keeping the resource renewing itself.

They tell me all the time: 'Junior, you keep this place like it is. We don't want no development down here.' 'Course, [much of] this river is in stewardship by the [state and feds] now. Some of the right things have been put in place to give us long-term protection.

"Long time ago [I ran a dry dock]," Mosconis added. "Well, [boat builder] Mr. Glass retired about ten years ago. But that was interesting work. Those ol' shipwrights that worked on those ol' wood boats, those were a real horror to be working on and cuttin' the boards right. There were a lot of boats then [that] we would work on that was eighty or ninety years old. Built in 1800s, 1900s.

"But you see, because of fiberglass, that art is being lost in this part of the world. We did build some small skiff boats for fishin' out of, some 16-footers. But the larger boats we just worked on.

"When the [Greek spongers] came to Tarpon Springs [in 1905],[6] they also brought boat builders with them, and they built what was called a divin' boat. Well, my granddaddy, my uncle, and my daddy—all three of 'em had those type boats. They're gone now, but they were built in the early 1900s.

"They actually used 'em for sailin'. Before they came out with diesel power, that style boat was around. Anyway, I went over to Greece, tryin' to find some of my ancestors, and there was that same boat. The bow's got a special curve to it that makes it real distinctive. It was a deep-draft boat. It had a tiller like a sailboat. The boat didn't have any superstructure on the top. The little cabin in the front just stuck up 3 or 4 feet. Everything was down below deck. So it was built very much like a modern sailboat is today. They were [a] real durable boat.

"When I was ten years old, I spent five days out there with my daddy on a fishing trip. There were five or six men on the boat. Back in those days they caught a lot of fish. They were snapper fishin' before the shrimpin' got to be a big deal. When the shrimpin' got to be more popular, they didn't have to go as far, and they could make a livin' doin' that. Another thing they used, they came out with a LORAN, which is a [Long-Range Aid to Navigation using pulsed signals from paired radio towers for positioning].

"Now they got GPS [Global Positioning System]. When they came out with that, it took all the guesswork out of fishin'. Prior to that, they used a soundin' lead. It was a [1-foot] cylinder-shaped piece of lead probably 2-1/2 inches in diameter, and in the [hollow] bottom of it, they put Octagon soap. And then they dropped [it], and it'd pick up a sample of the bottom.

"And they could see if it was live coral bottom or dead bottom. Also, it [marked] how deep the water was, so they actually sounded out the depth by hand. If you'll read some of those adventures of Mark Twain on the Mississippi River, they talk about that. 'Mark Twain' is two fathoms of water, which is 12 feet.

"If they were just getting sand, for example, they wouldn't even stop. But I can remember the guy who was throwin' the soundin' lead, callin' out things, how deep it was and what it felt like. If it was hard or soft, if it was mud. And when they got what they were lookin' for, they would stop and start catchin' fish.

"It was adventurous. I can see where Mark Twain was wantin' to be a pilot of the [steam]boat because nobody tells him where to go or when to get there or when to be back. He's got his own deal goin'. I thought that was really good. Untethered.

"[My father's boat] was about 40 feet. He had pretty good crews on 'em. They had like four bunks in the front, and down in the engine room they had two or three down there. They used to talk more in terms of their adventure, catchin' a lot of fish. And even though there weren't that many people doin' it then, there was a lot of competition.

There was a group out of Panama City, a group out of Pensacola, and you had these guys fishin' outta here. My daddy and my granddaddy's family and two or three more. They'd run across each other in the Gulf. They were real competitive; see who could catch the most fish and who can get here first.

"[They] told a story about my Uncle Nick one time. There was a storm comin' up, and they were catchin' fish, and these guys from Panama City were there catchin' fish. And neither one of 'em would leave. The storm caught both of 'em out there. My granddaddy was mad when Uncle Nick came in because he thought they had all drowned.

"They didn't have radios back then. They had no communication, and I know this lady in town, [Miss Kelly], that was an ol' widow woman. Her husband was lost out there. They never found a trace of the boat. They just didn't have the forecasting.

"Their barometer was their weather station. [When it dropped], they went in. Uncle Nick was a real good weatherman. And it was all those years of bein' out there with nothin' but a compass and your barometer, and watchin' the weather and knowin' the time of the year, and knowin' how to figure out the weather when it blew a certain way for a couple of days.

"It was a seasonal thing. When you get bad blows in the wintertime, they couldn't go. Their standard procedure was, they would go out until they filled the boat up with fish, if it took three days or seven days. They would take enough provisions to probably stay out a week.

"Now, they had [ice] in the thirties," Mosconis said. "I think my granddaddy had a couple of trucks, and he shipped fish up to [the] Atlanta fish market. Then some of it left here on the railroad and went even further, to New York maybe. Ice opened up a whole new rail market.

"They brought [a few tons of] ice with 'em, but they would just take the guts out of 'em and ice 'em down. And that's how they shipped 'em, too. They shipped 'em whole.

. "[Fishing], that's all they ever did—my daddy and my uncles and my granddaddy—and they loved it. It's hard to describe, but they just couldn't get enough of it.

"[When my] granddaddy died, everything kinda went, business-wise. He was the kingpin, and, well, my daddy and my uncle didn't really take a keen interest in trying to keep the family business goin'. But by then they'd gotten into shrimpin', and that's primarily [in the bay]. My daddy was one of 'em that started fishin' off of Carrabelle back in the early fifties.

"And Carrabelle, twenty years ago, had a bunch of senior citizens in it, and every one of 'em knew my granddaddy, every single one. A lot of 'em had worked with him on the boats, you know. He was a legend down in Carrabelle. They spent their summers down there 'cause they had the natural pass at East Pass out into the Gulf. I think in the fall and the spring they would fish outta here.

"Yeah, I guess I was lucky growin' up and listenin' to all those tales from those old people. They were different than people are today. They reminded me of, like the ol' WW II greatest-generation crowd. They were good people, and they looked out after each other and [were] hardworkin'. They were fearless. There were a lot of unknowns then because you didn't have modern technology. I mean the first thing they figured out was they'd take a car radio with 'em and listen to the radio news, weather, or whatever.

"My granddaddy used to speak Greek to Daddy and Uncle Nick, and I guess they hated it so bad; when he died there were no more Greek words spoken in our house. The friction between their daddy and them—neither one of 'em had any interest in maintaining their past, at all.

"'Course, Tarpon Springs was all Greeks then and [tops the nation in percentage claiming Greek ancestry].[7] There was a movie called *Beneath the 12-Mile Reef*. It was made in the early fifties; Robert Wagner is in it. He wasn't but about nineteen or twenty years old, and it was mainly filmed in Tarpon Springs. It was about these Greek sponge fishermen. They even had the [story] in there about the cross [that boys dive for each Epiphany], and when they got the cross.[8]

"Here's my granddaddy here." In a close shot, a craggy man in jacket, work boots, and camouflage hat holds a fishing rod, looking alert at the helm of a boat.

"He was one of the pioneers. Started snapper fishin' cause snapper was the [big fish]. They couldn't even give grouper away then, much less sell 'em."

Mosconis pulled out a navigation chart. "Now, my Daddy told me the first time that my granddaddy went out here to what is called the Florida Middle Grounds, they just about sank the boat they caught so many fish. In those days, before they had these treaties, the Cubans would fish up in here in the north Gulf too. And they didn't have refrigeration, and what they had was pens with water in 'em, and they brought 'em back to Cuba alive.

"[The Middle Grounds] is just a big natural coral area, and the water is 50 or 60 feet shallower there. It's just a big live bottom, big coral area. There's Tarpon Springs right here [adjacent to the Middle Grounds].

"They did a lot of their sponge fishin' in here, and they may have got a lot

The first time that my granddaddy went ... to ... the Florida Middle Grounds, they just about sank the boat they caught so many fish.

of sponges off the Middle Ground, I really don't know. My granddaddy never did care anything about the sponge.

"I just bought a boat last year, and I've been deep sea fishing. I've been goin' about 20, 30 miles out, which is [also an] area where [my dad] fished. If they could do away with the LORAN and the GPS, where you have to go do it the old-fashioned way, fishing would be a lot better 'cause people wouldn't catch as many," Mosconis laughed.

"Fishing is not like it was back then. When my granddaddy started fishing, there was no dams on the river. There was no industry in the Southeast. The paper mill wasn't built at St. Joe. Everything was just about as natural as it could be and stocked up because nobody had fooled with 'em ever to that point in time.

"I understand [commercial fishermen's] fears [that sport fishermen are pushing them out]. I was raised in a commercial family. Been around, represented these people for years, but that's not true. The net ban was a horrible thing they did to 'em. I blame that on, primarily, the State of Florida through the Marine Fisheries Commission. And I fought the Marine Fisheries Commission since they've been in business, tryin' to keep our livelihood. They've got us whittled down so much on these quotas and these bag limits, it's totally ridiculous.

"If we're gonna have a low-density development in Franklin County, a low height restriction (35 feet), protect the environment—the river's bein' protected through [land conservation]. If we want to do all that and then we gonna have all these resources, then why are we bein' penalized? Why can't we harvest these resources, not deplete 'em but harvest 'em in more reasonable numbers than what they're allowin' us to do?

"They're puttin' us in the same boat as Tampa Bay or Florida Bay; they've ruined 'em 'cause there's too many people there. I did convince [Marine Fisheries], at one point, to do some regional rulings. Instead of lookin' out after the fishin' industry in terms of havin' American fishermen supply protein to the citizens, [it's] comin' from Japan or China, and who knows what kind of child labor laws they have, much less sanitation—but here we are eatin' their food instead of our food. So the Marine Fisheries did a real injustice to the American and the Florida fishin' folk. Instead of workin' with 'em."

5

Oystering, Shrimping, Fishing, Sponging the Bay

We're not against progress; we're just against pollution.
Steve Davis

The 1994 net ban amendment to the Florida Constitution did not end gill netting in the waters around Franklin and Wakulla counties. So said Lt. Jeff Schremser a decade later from his Florida Fish and Wildlife Conservation Commission office in Carrabelle. Fishermen were briefly permitted to use the small, Pringle-Crum cross between a gill and seine net due to a February 2002 ruling by Judge N. Sanders Sauls. But the ruling was stayed on appeal to the Florida Supreme Court.[1]

Schremser's office retrieves an estimated half dozen abandoned gill nets per month, some of them huge, 500 yards long, and made of outlawed monofilament. Most violators defy all four legal criteria, he said. First, gill nets can only be used 3 miles off shore; second, they must be made of nylon; and third, the mesh area cannot exceed 500 feet square. Also, each bar of the diamond mesh may be no longer than an inch.

The penalty for getting caught is a $500 fine and sixty days in jail. But Franklin County judges "don't fine much," and the fishermen get good defense attorneys, Schremser said. The punishment is nothing compared to the loss of the net, which can run $2,000 to $3,000, he added. Fish and Wildlife officers seek judge's orders to burn nets, which usually go unclaimed.

The net ban may be enacted to protect fishing resources for the public, some fishermen acknowledge, but our seafood appetites haven't changed, and seafood imported from less-monitored waters may present its own health risks. Moreover, recreational catches in 2002 outstripped commercial landings among populations of concern in the United States, rising to 64 percent in the Gulf of Mexico, an FSU study found.[2]

Fisherman Joe Nichols also notes in this chapter that the absence of nets in the bay permits larger fish with bigger appetites to take over, and a smaller mesh merely gills juvenile fish.[3]

The state provided $30 million in net buy-back and reeducation funds in 1994, but in many cases it was not enough to offset lost homes, trucks, and livelihoods. The fishing community considers the net amendment a civil rights issue since it limits access to fishing resources.

Fishermen continue to challenge the constitutionality of the net ban under the provision prohibiting "any law which abridges the privileges or immunities of citizens . . . ; nor deprive any person of life, liberty, or property, without due process of law and equal protection of the laws."[4]

During the drought cycle, the Apalachicola Bay fishing community has also contended with diminished river flows, historical red tide events, increased sedimentation from dredging, and development pressure that is expelling fishermen from waterfront property.[5] They remember brimful rivers before the Woodruff Dam was completed and a bay "chocolate" with detritus during storms.[6]

Fifteen percent of the national oyster harvest was considered threatened by reduced freshwater flows during the late 1990s, including a diverse fishery with breeding and nursery for 90 percent of Florida's oyster landings.[7] The bay also supports seventy species of mollusks, of which six bivalve species are rare and endangered, requiring federal agencies to conserve critical habitat.[8]

Fishermen praise government efforts to preserve natural floodplain and marine habitats. Two protected zones in the Gulf off of Apalachicola are the Madison-Swanson Experimental Preserve, 115 square miles closed to bottom fishing since 2000, and the Florida Middle Grounds Habitat Area of Particular Concern, 348 square miles closed to bottom longlining, trawls, and fish traps since 1984.[9]

In this chapter, commercial fishermen, net-makers, seafood dealers, and a conservationist discuss development pressures on historic ways of life.

Buddy Ward: Commercial Fishing Survivor

Buddy Ward is tall, broad-shouldered, lean, a commercial fisherman in his mid-sixties who's survived lung cancer. Ward breathes through a tracheotomy, his voice a whisper. The man who was tough No. 75 on the Apalachicola High School football team, was so thoroughly irradiated that healthy tissue died and had to be reconstructed with skin grafts. Ward is generous and congenial, welcoming visitors to his spotless, dockside seafood plant.

Ward started plying Apalachicola waters when he was just six years old, the son of a tug captain. As a lad he oystered and shrimped down "the Miles" of St. Vincent Sound, west of Apalachicola. Here he discusses the importance

Fig. 5.1. Seafood merchant Buddy Ward at his dockside plant in February 2001, with the boat his late fishing partner, Bud Seymour, built for him and his three sons. Photo by Faith Eidse.

of wetlands and rainfall cycles to seafood production; the necessary Gulf access provided through St. George Island by Bob Sikes Cut; oyster leases; and the loss of commercial dock space to the tourist industry.

Record low-flow durations in recent years have impacted oyster harvests, despite oyster growth being faster in the moderate temperatures of the Apalachicola estuary—at 4 inches in thirty-one days—than in any other part of the country. Their harvesting waters have also been more sanitary,[10] another factor Ward is concerned about.

Ward remembers a river so full that it took an hour to chug to the Pinhook above Apalachicola. They never had to worry about an average stage of less than 3 to 4 feet a year, which increases salinity and allows predation of growing oysters—by stone crabs and oyster drills—thus impacting harvests two and three years later.

A long drought was one reason Ward bought his in-laws' oyster business in 1957 after Franklin County landings had hovered at less than 1 million pounds of oyster meats for seven years. Production rose to nearly 2 million by 1960 and has seldom dropped below since. Spikes of over 4 to 6 million pounds were harvested cyclically in 1962, 1968, and 1978–80.[11] Production cycled downward to 3.7 million pounds in 1985 and 1.4 million in 1990.

Shrimp, however, increased in value eight times over the same thirty-year period, even when harvests fluctuated.[12]

Ward operates Buddy Ward and Sons Seafood, continuing his wife's family business with son Walter as part owner and operations manager, sons Joey and George working as fisherman, and son Thomas operating Buddy Ward and Sons Seafood and Trucking, Incorporated, and Thirteen Mile Oyster Company. Sales range from $2.5 to $4 million a year, and Ward operates five boats from Mexico to North Carolina. His story unfolded at his dockside office on February 27, 2001.

"I was born in Apalachicola. My father was a tugboat captain for Sheip. I went on the tugboat when I was quite small, pulling logs up and down the Apalachicola River.

"The river is very important for the Apalachicola Bay. It provides the freshwater and nutrients for the bay. And nature can do certain things, but it can't do it all, and it can't correct what man may also do to nature. In 1946, the first time I was really involved in makin' a living out of Apalachicola Bay, our father started oystering and shrimping. I remember goin' back and forth to St. Vincent, oystering down in the Miles. I was around ten years old.

"Back then we were tonging the oysters and the mussels and all, and every time it slowed down, we shrimped in summertime and so on, to make it up. And sometime nature would be nice to us, sometime it wouldn't.

"Then they had another small mill out here—Stem Red. They cut red timber [cypress and juniper]. And [my father] run the tugboat for them, up and down to Huckleberry Creek, toward the rock dam there, up to the mill. The other tugboat would bring 'em to the mouth of the creek, and he'd bring 'em to the mill. And he used to tow ash and juniper over to Panama City's deepwater port over there to be loaded on a ship, but most of it was cypress, and it went to the mill in Scipio Creek. They made cigar boxes out of it. And they took a lot of juniper too.

"I left Apalachicola in 1954, to Panama City working for International Paper until 1957. I came back to Franklin County to what we referred to as Thirteen Mile, west of Apalachicola, and my wife's family had been in the oyster business several years. So we bought them out. We had a big drought [during the period 1950–57]; the oyster business had been bad. Some years you have a lot of rain, and some years you have drought, and there's not very much we can do to compensate that.

"But I think what upsets me more than anything in the seafood industry is the way that our uplands are being rearranged. Our wetlands are being destroyed by this whole extension [of] streets, pavement, yards. I realize we have to have development, but development destroys the output producing the food for the resource, which we have to have for the shrimp, oysters—or any seafood in our bay. And that's one of the main things, I think, that's affecting the seafood industry. It's our upland changing our habitat completely. It takes that freshwater and nutrients coming down that river to supply the food for this bay down here.

"When I purchased Thirteen Mile, we had two small shrimp boats, 35-foot boats to operate more efficiently. We moved uptown here where we got better access to the shrimp boats, and we started buying some larger boats to go offshore. We started buying shrimp from seafood producers in other states. We just separated the two businesses and had the oyster business from Thirteen Mile right on and trucking business and shrimping business up here.

"The fishing fleet got older. They used to have those sleek wood boats, some fiberglass boats. But as the fleet got older, the people started graduatin' to larger, more powered, deeper drafting boats, which cannot come and go in Apalachicola Bay due to the fact of Bob Sikes Cut not being maintained.

"I think Bob Sikes Cut is a very essential part of our external seafood industry, as well as the sport fishing industry, our charter boats. And I feel like it's an asset to the river as a more frequent flowing area where we can get a boat fishing in and out of the bay.

"When you don't have the deep water here, the [alternate] East Pass has deep water, but you're talkin' about three hours off Carrabelle from Apalachicola. West Pass is just not maintained. They don't maintain Bob Sikes as well as they *claim*.

"In 1993 to 1999, they were going to try to close off Bob Sikes Cut. The salt was reachin' a peak. They come by with the water intrusion [issue]. But I got information to warn everybody in Apalachicola. The seafood industry's not dead," Ward said, even if some oyster bars were affected. "It's been changed, and we better change with it.

"[The cut needs to be] maintained on a regular basis. And it's very essential to the economy of Apalachicola and Franklin County. Now if you have to go out through St. Joe, you're talking about five hours, plus getting back in. Especially if you can get to the fishing grounds out here in an hour, an hour and a half, two hours. And safety—the worst thing that can happen to a vessel is not having water to make it mobile.

"And we can't keep filling out here and turning all the waterfront into boardwalks for the tourists. We need areas for commercial fishermen to tie their boats up. It irritates me when they say that the seafood industry here is not willing to change with the times. Try to figure that out.

"We got out of the oyster business [temporarily, but] I had to take it back over, and one of my sons operates it now. And we got oyster leases and it's perpetual. One of them was leased out to Dewey Miller in 1940, the other lease was in 1950, to Dewey Miller, and I bought from his heirs. I bought those in an agreement in 1957. The one was up at least in 1950 and [regulators] probably thought they were making some mistake doing it by re-leasing.

"Now you have no problem with outside people [oystering] as long as nature provides enough on the natural bars out here. But the minute you have a disaster, a storm, or high salinity, or a big freshet, they then say, 'Well, we going to sell oysters,' and they come out on these oyster leases, and that's the problem," Ward said.

"Back in 1965, '67, [we had] what they called grants. A commissioner from the state granted these people this area to grow oysters on. And they just laid out there, so some people decided, 'We gonna pick these grants up, and we gonna get people to work them in the summer months.' At that time, you could oyster leases, but we agreed that we'd close our oyster leases down if we could get something done through grants. So we went in, and they gave the people with the grants [permission] to survey them off and take them up as a lease, and if I 'member right, it's an acre, and they would have a certain time to do that. Well, there was one company that did manage to [mark] a part of their leases, and the rest of them went back to the state. Now, since that time, the [leases] had not been operating in the summer months until the state opened summer bars."

[Woody Miley, then director of Apalachicola National Estuarine Research Reserve, explained that perpetual leases meant that Ward could sell his lease as though he had deed ownership to it, and that questions arose about conveying state land to private companies in this way. There are 610 acres of leased bottom and about 7,000 acres of public bars open to individual tongers. Commercial leasers, such as Buddy Ward, wanted to use mechanical harvesters and scrapes, and tempers flared. Individual tongers feared the leasers would take their machines to public bars. The courts ruled that private leasers could use mechanical means on their own property.

Miley added that ANERR tried later, with Harbor Branch Aquaculture Training program, to mark off 1-acre grants to public tongers using PVC pipes to mark intersecting corners. But the private leasers worried that an oysterman would buy up the leases and they'd have to say "sir" to someone else. State representative Al Lawson wrote a bill giving a county commission veto power over leases in open waters of the county. As a result, there will be leases only for private leasers.]

"Oh I don't know if I believe in [a seafood boom that may be over]," Ward said. "At one time you had a lot of people like sealin'-packin' companies, sending products throughout [the Southeast], plus all the development destroying the habitat.

"But the DEP is doing a very decent job trying to protect the uplands, as [is] the [Northwest Florida Water Management District]. And this is something that I think really wants doing to further resources that have dropped. And we can't be taking away the habitat, the marshes, the drainage, and so forth. But Mother Nature determines it. I've always submitted, you have about a seven-year cycle of rain and droughts.

"[The years that we had semi-trailers supplying Georgia and Alabama], the boys didn't know it was a boom. What you consider a boom year, we were just expanding a much larger operation than we [have] now. We improved the operation by narrowing it, by getting rid of a lot of liabilities.

"Back when we bought fresh shrimp all up and down the coast and all different kinds of ocean products every day, and you'd do $7, $8 million worth of business, you just get to the point where you look at the overall profit margin, and you start turnin' back to where you made the same amount of profit with a lot smaller operation. At that time, the funds that you had to operate with wasn't that big, and you had to turn a product fast, and you just had to keep your capital turnin', and that's the reason I used to handle so much product [that] I was in trouble. We had our trucks all up and down the road [with] $70,000–$80,000 load of shrimp, doing it five days a week—then your liabilities are awful high. And then, if you do dip into your insurance, how long do you think your insurance lasts like that?

"We don't ship as much fresh seafood as we used to. We usually process and freeze it all right here, ship it out that way in refrigerated trucks all through the United States. Oysters are a different situation, now. If you have them in fresh brine, you have a shorter shelf life you have to deal with.

"It's a fact that we need our nursery areas for every species of shrimp, fish. And I think you have to have the marshes and the wetlands to filter out all the toxins, which flow in this bay. If you didn't filter out all the water that's coming out of town right now in the bay—well, you get me. I like to be optimistic. But I realize we've got to have development, we got people. But we got a unique situation in Apalachicola Bay and surrounding areas, St. Marks.

"When my dad used to get me up to get on the tugboat, I remember the way the water flowed down that river. That was all marsh from right there at that marina, from that creek right on down to Fourth Street railroad. And it's gone forever. All to this point out here, you could cross that area on a boat. It amazes me.

"But I actually remember when the water rose, we'd chug down on one of

Now, you had a real drought after they put the dam in.

those tugs, and it'd take us about half a day to make that turn to [the Pinhook]. It would tear out that bridge; it just rolled that thing. But that river was red.

"Never in my life, back when I was younger, did I remember the Apalachicola River being down to where it's been in the last few years. If it ever got down to 3 or 4 feet, we worried. Now, you had a real drought after they put the dam in up there. But the last few years are the lowest I have remembered—and then staying that way [it affects the nursery areas].

"Once in a while, with the ancient trade winds, you'd be surprised what kind of effect it has on the Apalachicola Bay, pushing the water, mixing the water, and aerating the basin. And that determines whether the oyster spats or your drills, your starfish, your conchs—all that stuff comes in—your red drum, the other species of fish. But your freshwater directly determines how this thing does.

You have got to go demand the water to come down that river.

"You got Atlanta and all those towns up the river. You have got to go demand the water to come down that river. I do know that the relative population of Georgia and Alabama make demands on our ecosystem. Now, how you fix that is way beyond my ability—but it does need to be done. Atlanta up there, for instance, dumping their sewers. But then, too, Bainbridge, Georgia. I mean they gotta stop puttin' their pollutants in there because it works its way down here. A filtering system would clear it up.

"Now, I'm really an environmentalist, not a biologist, but I do have knowledge, and I know how oysters grow as much or more than anyone in Franklin County. And I sure do know what it takes to grow oysters. Same way with shrimp. Shrimp has to have that freshwater coming in to eat.

"I can remember floods where the river stage was 26 feet for six weeks. The oysters used to get so fat they could not close their shells. You've got to have that for the reproductive cycle. Leave the shells there for the spat to attach to. Nature controls what I'm speaking about. We've destroyed what nature has put there.

"[Apalachicola] could have record-breaking weather conditions by another two years [2003]. This year I'm afraid it's gonna be [dry]—but I mean you're stuck. And we hope we have enough expansion to overcome it. We have five shrimp boats now. We operate from Key West, and we even operate on the east coast.

"We have a seafood truck at Thirteen Mile, runnin' a regular truck all the way up to the edge of North Carolina, and we buy shrimp all over the East Coast certain times of the year—bring 'em back here and process them. We buy from other producers, process here. We're also in the [ocean] scallop business. We used to just catch 'em; now we have a plant, and we process those, too. You have to have your assembly ready.

"You just try to diversify, but now you've got so many different people in seafood houses down the strip. I can remember when the railroad train ran and picked up stuff out here. Where the seafood processing plant is now, that was an ice house. Next door right here was a Texaco distributor, and we use that as a warehouse, and we've moved down to the other side of the bridge, which has no one over there.

"You just pushed back Scipio Creek up here, you've got Sea Quest Seafood, you've got Quality Seafood, you've got Taranto Joe and Son Seafood, which is right there where Bruce's [Seafood Trucking] is right now. You used to have riverboats come in 'n' out here, but primarily they do that at Carrabelle because they have better access to the tugboats.

"We have had six years of using these two city docks, for which we pay a monthly fee. But now they're talkin' about chasing away commercial boats as well as charter boats or general packin' boats. They're trying to make another boardwalk like they have down in the tug basin. Now that's bad for fishing. [A] commercial fisherman does not have an access to use that marina down there. And ever'time you see anything on TV—the 'Forgotten Coast'—they charge that, well, we're going out of business. And it irritates me.

Ever'time you see anything on TV—the "Forgotten Coast"—they charge that . . . we're going out of business. And it irritates me.

"We're just as big as we were except we diversified. At one time we used to do $8 million worth of shrimp. It was not produced here in Apalachicola; it was from Alabama, Texas—fresh and we'd process it, carry 'em down to Tampa Ocean Products. Now we do—frozen—$2.5 to $4 million of business a year. We process everything, most of it. We buy most of it off these boats out here. Half of it, two-thirds of it, is produced—and loaded—right here in Apalachicola. This is one business. See what I mean? You're talking about the way they treat the fish business.

"[Bud Seymour built my first boat,] *Buddy's Boys*. Bud Seymour and I go back a long way—even to the first time I ever moved to Thirteen Mile. I had an old boat, and Bud Seymour was runnin' for me, so we decided we'd get rid of it and he would build this boat here. [It's a] 55-foot wooden, oceangoing boat. He built it in '70, '71.

"This boat is framed out of cypress. But the keel was always out of hardwood, of heart pine, and your decks are usually pine. But your frame is usually out of cypress. Cypress is a soft wood—and so you have more flotation with juniper. It's less absorbent than cypress is. Bud Seymour is a real man about town. And he's a talker; he'll talk your ear slam off. [Seymour died within months of this interview.]

"We have a family operation here, and we hope to keep it that way. Since my illness, I'm very restricted in what I can do. I'm drawing my disability because I have a respiratory problem, as well as a bad communication problem," Ward laughed. He pulled his collar aside to reveal skin grafts on his throat. "[They] took the skin off my leg, at Shands [Hospital]. The first [of three] operations was September twenty-second. I got home a few days before Halloween '87. Nobody gave me a chance at all except my wife and my friends." Ward escorted me over a weathered dock to show off his freshly painted legacy, *Buddy's Boys*.

James Golden: Nothing but Net-Making

James Golden builds nets in his old Eastpoint bedroom, a splash of sunshine warming the wooden floor of what is now his net shop. "Build" is a curious verb, but as Golden pointed out on November 28, 2001, what he does is construction. The nylon mesh comes in bales, ready-made from a factory. He designs, cuts, and binds reinforced nets that will last several seasons. It's a skill he learned from his father, Buford, and a craft he's practiced for nearly thirty years. Only since recently—when his friend Charles Thompson opened a net supply store in Apalachicola—has he had any competition.

Golden is dark-haired, stocky, and deliberate in speech and action. He shrimps with his own nets and hunts in the Apalachicola National Forest and Tate's Hell State Forest, grateful for District and Division of Forestry preservation.

Years ago Golden knocked the back wall out of the old shotgun-style home he was raised in and extended it 60 feet. Bales of netting line the open walls, and block-and-snatch hardware and wooden net doors hang from a rail running down the center aisle. Nearby his nephew, Michael Holt, stitched a Turtle Excluder Device (TED) into a shrimp trawl neck. A TED is a metal bar platform that slides turtles through a hole in the net.

Golden acknowledged that the 1994 state-mandated TEDs have brought him new business and that they may save several turtles each year. But he believes beachfront development is a bigger culprit in turtle deaths.

Still, numbers of nests counted on St. George Island increased steadily over ten years, through 1998, according to Marine Turtle Permit holder and retired park ranger Bruce Drye. He credits improved skill in identifying park nests (about a hundred per summer, or half the island total), as well as fewer drowned turtles. "I used to bury five carcasses each nesting season." Second-row homes, not covered by the beachfront lighting rules, do lure hatchlings,

Fig. 5.2. James Golden and his nephew Michael Holton stitch a mandated Turtle Excluder Device (TED) into a net. Turtles hit the metal platform and slide out through a hole in the net. Photo by Faith Eidse.

he said, as do flashlights not filtered by theater-grade red plastic. A new campaign to increase TED size to accommodate a 6-by-12-foot leatherback turtle is controversial, Drye acknowledged, especially since the turtle is an infrequent nester here. "But the duration that a turtle can hold its breath decreases under stress."

Golden, in his interview, discusses the net-making legacy he inherited; the advent of turtle excluder devices; and development impacts on fisheries that the net ban amendment didn't address.

"I was born in Carrabelle, Florida, in 1964," Golden said, and have been making nets, "basically since I was old enough to do it, about ten or twelve.

"[My father] learned from a guy named Billy Burbanks in Tampa, Florida, probably in the early '60s. He had moved to get away from oysterin' and crabbin'.

"In a way we are [connected to the ancient Mediterranean], but back then they done it basically for food. In Apalach during the Depression they would trade fish for other supplies. There wasn't no money."

Golden massaged his fingers but shrugged off the pain. "Usually in the wintertime our fingers get cramped, and we just flex them to get the blood back. [We tie the nets] with an overhand, or half hitch, knot. I could tie three or four thousand if I started in the morning and didn't stop. A lot of my time, though, I have to answer the phone, wait on customers. This is just a bad, slow part of the season.

[The net ban] was just too drastic of a move.

"The busy season, we could sell five or six. But there's nets that we can build two a day, and then there's some that take two days to build, [such as] a [50-foot] commercial shrimp net. It's probably $5,000 or $6,000 from start to finish, like your [80-foot] commercial shrimp boats use. The new nets that I build, we repair them.

"We cut [our material] out in patterns, basically [in] triangles, rectangles. Our net is just basically a funnel, and it just consists of a bunch of triangles." He drew a trapezoid. Binding the edges together "is what we call 'seines.' Basically a net consists of two bodies, four corners, and two wings. That's what you would call a 'four-seine net.'

"We use these to sew"—Golden held up a 4-inch plastic disk, both ends pointed, and wrapped with green thread—"and then a larger one to tie it to the rope or cable. It's called 'combination cable.'

"[My father put in] a lot of hard work and dedication. He was pretty strict, and a lot of people respected him. He would put in his ten hours a day, and some people would call him late and he'd come back. He'd work six days a week.

"My father was on the school board for twelve years. I remember a guy telling him he wasn't a very good politician, and it sort of made my daddy mad. He said, 'Why is that?' He said, 'You're too honest.' If you told him to vote 'no' on this 'cause of this and this, he wouldn't do it just as a favor.

"He was willing to go that extra mile to help somebody if they needed it. But now, if you missed a day or two of work and then come down here needing something, he wouldn't help you at all. If you was workin' hard and tryin' your best to feed your family and weren't quite making it, he'd break his back trying to help you, even after he got sick. We told him he didn't need to be down here, but he'd come anyway. He died of prostate cancer. He was sixty-eight.

"I tried to avoid [the net-making business] 'cause I growed up in it. But I tried construction work, and I just came back to [net-making]. Back then the business was real good, and he more or less asked me. I was just making better money then than I could anywhere else.

"The net ban was probably the biggest change [in this business]. There's fewer boats, fewer people doing it now. And of course we've gone through three bad seasons."

Golden didn't vote for the net ban, he said, but some people in the region did. "There was some fish that was overfished. During the old days, they closed mullet season during roe season. And if you kill off all your juveniles, they're not going to be able to continue. I think [the net ban] was just too drastic of a move.

"There's other laws they could've [invoked]. The shrimpin' [rule] has hurt the big boats on the beach. It's this time of year they're normally inside the [net-prohibited] 3 miles 'cause the weather gets bad. So basically what everybody's done is bought bigger boats so they can stay offshore during the bad weather. A lot of your bigger boats now are company-owned. There's fewer privately owned big boats.

"[My business is] probably a third of what it was ten years ago. But I don't attribute that all to the net ban. I'd say 30 percent maybe. But it's the mullet fisherman that's really [affected]. It about cleaned them out.

"I done some bay shrimping. [A small mesh net] would be used for what they call a 'cod end.' We call it 'bag.' The [mesh size] would be an inch and an eighth. Now the universal way of measuring a stretch mesh would be from here to here [across the center of one diamond]. That's called 'stretch mesh.' If you were measuring like this now," along one side of the diamond, "it would be called 'bar.'"

A small mesh is for "live bait. We build what you call roller frame nets. We don't make the frames. They're basically 2 foot high by 12 to 16 foot wide. We can build or design a net, and they tie it to the frame theirselves. The frame is attached to a piece of cable or rope, which they lower down in the water. That's how it's pulled. But ours up here have what you call 'doors,' and that's how it spreads and the net opens. It's called an 'auto-trawl.'"

Golden added that the University of Georgia Marine Extension Service designed the turtle exclusion devices. "Basically it hurt the business. There were a lot of people fightin' it to start with, and then once they got used to using the TEDs, they learned to live with them. But certain times of the season when the sponges are bad, it actually helped maybe to a certain extent. But they still lose maybe 15 to 20 percent of the shrimp.

"A majority of [TEDs] do [work]. They've got a big debate on that now.

But I've got to be careful what I say on that part 'cause I wouldn't want to upset some shrimper. I think it's in litigation now, making them pull bigger TEDs because of the big leatherbacks on the east coast. [They're] actually bigger than the TEDs we're using, and that's going to hurt even more.

"The bigger problem is pollution and development. They know that themselves, but how can they stop development? Maybe they are tryin' better on the pollution.

"A lot of these old oyster houses, you know, they paid probably over $100,000, $150,000 for 'em; it's just sittin' idle. You ride through. Every one of these old houses [is] just waitin' [for] condos.

"I can 'member when there was just one store [on St. George Island]. We used to ride our bicycles across the causeway. My father, he'd probably kill me if he knew it," Golden laughed. "We used to go over and go fishin'. But now it's three-story houses and condominiums. Financially it's probably helped. But as far as helpin' the environment, it hurt it.

"A lot of people's turnin' over to tourism. I mean a lot of people are being forced out because of the new laws and regulations. The decline in oysterin' I think goes back to regulation. They're a lot stricter on the bay now. 'Course, ya know, they've got to. Any time somebody gets sick [from eating oysters] somebody is liable. You're more likely to get sued now than you was twenty years ago. I guess Texas and Louisiana, they're not as strict on the laws 'cause there's a lot more oysters shipped in than what there used to be.

"I don't eat oysters shipped in. I don't know how old they are. I don't know how long they've been sittin' out in the sun. You can double underline 'I don't.' My Granny died at eighty-nine years old, and she ate them once or twicet a week, probably, if I'd shuck 'em for her. When they ship from here to Jacksonville—there's no tellin' how long they sat in the coolers; that's how people get sick. Cooked oysters they don't have a problem with.

"I have UPS service [for my nets]. And [I supply] mainly on the west coast of Florida. I have one person in Miami that orders a couple of times a year. I think he's just got a couple boats. But mainly it's from New Port Richey—the Tampa area—up to Cedar Key or Perry—the roller frame. But most of my door nets are made for local people. Now there's probably five different styles of door nets.

"You start with flat net. Well, I guess the oldest would be box net. Basically them two styles are the same. They're made for brownies and hoppers, which is shrimp that stay close to the bottom.

"Then you've got western jibs, a flat net, but they're mainly used out west. They get grass real bad out there. The only difference between a western jib and a flat net is the corners. Once you pull a flat net maybe six or eight months, these [corners] get distorted, and we have to redo the corners. When a guy came up with the western jib, the corners are cut a little different, and they hold the shape better.

"This one, being basically a box net, [would] be the same way 'cept it doesn't have the corners. The body comes all the way out to the end of the wing, which fastens to the doors. When you're draggin' it in the water, it puts all the pressure out here, and it causes the net to rip out. Corners are designed to relieve pressure on the net.

"But the last two seasons business has been bad; it comes in cycles," Golden said. "Basically I start out with an hourly rate. Sometimes I spend more time than what I can charge for. If a man brings a net in that's tore up, once I reach the point, labor-wise, to build a net, I cap it. Ten or fifteen years ago it was just as bad, and I had to oyster in the off-season.

"I do donate my labor and part of the material [for] baseball cages to local schools, Carrabelle, Apalach, and here in Eastpoint, Little League. I've made golf ball stops. One time we shipped one to California. A guy was here vacationing and stopped in. I sent one to—I think Pennsylvania. Kinda gives me something to do in wintertime. But I look for it to pick back up. Seems like there will be three or four bad years, and then it will gradually get better for two or three years. It's just a roller coaster.

"I'm a firm believer in the droughts having a lot to do with it. For instance, I think it was '97 we had them big floods up North; we had a bumper crop of shrimp. Alberto, it stalled out around Atlanta, Georgia. They've got to have water to drink, but it's been a drought for them too.

"How do they think they can control [river water]?" Golden asked. "I mean how? Are they going to set up a committee? Do they care what goes on down here?

"What they do up there affects us, [but] we have no control over [it]. We're on the bottom of the ladder. If they spill paint, it falls on us, and if we spill paint, it hits the ground.

"But like four years ago we had more water than we knew what to do with. And I think part of the flooding problem was them holding the water back too long.

"That flood I'm talkin' about, it set an all-time record in Columbus. The year after, we actually had water [that] got higher in the Blountstown area than it did then. It flooded houses in Apalach. And [one] poor lady said she done been through two 100-year floods in two years.

"Well, we've got to have rain up there [in Georgia] to affect us," Golden continued. "It can rain 30, 40 inches today and tomorrow here, and in a couple days it's gone. It don't even affect the rivers. We got to have the rain above Woodruff Dam.

The Goldens "originated out [of] Banks, Alabama. There was nothing goin' on up there in the forties. They moved to Apalachicola. There was eight kids. Granddaddy had done passed away. [My dad] was forced [to fish].

"He'd always talk about leavin' before daylight and be home after dark, six days a week. But the man [he worked for] firmly believed in takin' Sundays off—George Kervin. [He] died probably five or six years ago. There was probably twelve to twenty men fished for him at one time. See back then everthin' was done by hand. They would literally catch thousands of pounds at a time.

"Then [Dad] got a job at the paper mill. When he started this business, actually, he started it for a couple of friends as a favor on the back porch. And we never worked here on Sundays, never hardly.

"Oystermen go out on Sundays and catch oysters so their wives can start to work Mondays. But the wives got to work Fridays when the men don't. But most of the year the bay's not open on Sundays anymore either. They go oysterin' whenever they can. It's been off and on so much. The sales are down on oysters, up until the red tide anyway."

During the first red tide event, Florida declared a disaster and received federal aid. The Corps released water from upstream reservoirs to flush the bay.

"Daddy never would take charity at all, not even food stamps; didn't matter how bad things were at the house. I'm a lot better off than my dad was when we first started. My dad raised five kids in a 24-by-30-foot house. I was like thirteen years old before we had a air conditioner. Probably in '75 it was converted entirely to a net shop.

"[At first my dad worked] making nets on his off time and on the weekends. He did shift work [at the] paper mill. It always shuts down for maintenance. That's how [the net business] got started. I was a teenager at the time. He started in the seventies full-time.

"It's hard to learn net-making. Lots of people can repair little holes. It's hard to teach someone to build nets. You have to spend eight or nine hours a day on your feet. It's just like a crochet; it's one little knot at a time.

"A lot of times you get someone trained to where you can turn your back and not worry about them making a mistake; they usually get tired of it. In the many years I've been working here there's been my brother [John], me, my uncle Danny, Bill, probably been seven people. I just bought [John] out more or less. Sometimes I wish I had done other things, but I like the work and working with the people in the summertime.

"There's people that know us from Texas to Albany, Georgia. Word's already out. If I went into sports nets, like golf ball nets, I'd have to advertise then. But as far as the shrimpin' industry, you can probably go anywhere on the Gulf coast and they know of Golden's Net Shop."

Golden answered the phone, hung up, and said, "Mr. Thompson . . . , the other net shop. He asked me for different ideas on how to make nets. Right now there's changes. Fishermen are learning to make their own nets to save money.

"The problem about repairing a net someone else made is you don't know exactly how they made it. It takes longer for me to go back and see how they made it. When a net that I made comes in, I don't have to count and see how it's made. I know there are no mistakes in it. I don't let a net go out with a mistake in it, if it takes me an hour to cut it back open and resew it.

"Usually the [mistakes] are cut tapers. Tapers are what makes it triangle shape. That's the hardest thing to do. As you cut it, you have to count so many tapers and then it'll be straight. When you cut the taper, you cut one point, four bars. That would be like a 4-and-1 taper.

"I just wish more emphasis would be put on the pollution and the development. Turtles aren't goin' to come on the beach to lay eggs with a bunch of lights on. But he still has nests on Little St. George where there's no lights. And over on Eglin Air Force Base, where there aren't a bunch of lights, Tyndall Air Force Base, they still have nesting. But on Panama City Beach, out there where them condos are, they don't have nesting. So you've gotta preserve more beaches and wetlands up above us. That's another reason I'm glad the State of Florida bought all that [river acreage].

"We make money off of [TEDs], but I'd rather build a new net than a new TED 'cause a TED can foul up a three- or four-hour drag. It can ruin 'em out easy."

Davis Family: Saving the Resource for Someone Else

Steve Davis built three of his own fishing boats. The first took two years, the second took six months, and the third took forty-five days. The first supplied his father's seafood retail business, Lloyd's Fish Market, 455 Highway 98, which he inherited with his wife, Earlean. For twenty-three years, the Davises have run the business with their two sons. But Davis believes his grandchildren will have to find other careers, thanks to the net ban. Com-

Fig. 5.3a. Earlean and Steve Davis inherited his father Lloyd's seafood business at Thirteen Mile. Photo by Faith Eidse.

mercial fishing is being phased out with the development boom, and working fishermen, opposed to development, have been silenced by high-rolling growth interests. On January 23, 2002, he spoke about his life.

"I'll be sixty-three in a month, and I was just thinking. Back when I was about sixteen, they had a Sheip sawmill located up here on the river where the boat basin is now. Two-story, and they tore all the buildings down, and then somebody tore the vaults down. The papers was scattered all over the ground. It would tell who the captain was on the vessel, tell when he left Cuba with a load of rum, stopped in here to pick up a load of lumber, and go to New York to pick up a load of ice to carry back to Cuba.

"Well, I got married in '60, and we oystered, and of course my wife, Earlean, shucked 'em when I caught 'em. And then we gillnetted for a while, and she went with me. Then I built the first boat, the *Family Affair*, 40 foot by 13 wide with a 371 engine in it. It took two years. We put it in the water in '79. 'Course, I was workin', and we was payin' for it as we went. And me and her started runnin' that boat. And so, within four or five years, I started buildin' my own product through here. The second [boat] took six months; the third one took forty-five days.

"[For the first one] we dove the lumber for the ribs out of the river and sawed it at the sawmill. Then we used half-inch AC plywood for the plankin' around it. We only built it [to last] five years, and the boat is twenty-two or twenty-three years old now. That's the boat I was on yesterday.

Fig. 5.3b. Davis built three fishing boats, the last one in forty-five days. Photo by Faith Eidse.

"No, [I didn't wrap it with fiberglass]. Wrapped it with paint," he laughed. "All the oyster boats in this area were built out of AC plywood. You take a 150 Evinrude on the stern of a 24-foot oyster boat built out of half-inch AC, run it against a so'wester, and it holds up. I didn't figure I'd have no problem with a 40-foot boat not makin' but about 7 or 8 knots, so we built it out of half-inch AC plywood.

"We haul 'em out every nine months; used to, give 'em a new paint job. Now we're lucky if they get hauled every two years on account of everthin' being different. I've got a steel hull downtown tied at the millpond. It's 64 foot. We bought it, but I got three [homemade] out here [cost about] $6,000 [each], not countin' the labor.

"The last one I built, I bought the lumber, and we used juniper. From the time the sawmill dropped the juniper off 'til the day it made its first trip shrimpin' was forty-five days. I knew where every bolt went; I knew where every nail went. The most time-consuming part of buildin' anything is havin' the material on hand. I didn't have to go hunt it.

"I had a boom truck that was strong enough that we could turn the boat upside down. I never did no overhead nailin'. When I got ready, I built the sides, put the decks on it, turned it over, put the bottom on it, rolled it back over with the boom truck. You rigged it up, and there'll always be a little slack in your rope—you can't help it. If it snaps and the boat hits the ground, you can just throw a match to it; you're through with it," he laughed.

"I've been studyin' about [the fishing livelihood], and all my life I have heard, 'Save the resources for your grand-young'uns.' I don't think we done too bad a job in this bay at savin'. But whose grand-young'uns did we save the resource for? It's not ours. They voted us out in the net ban election. The feelin' in this state is to do away with commercial fishin'. I've been told that from the governor's office down, and I was real involved in tryin' to keep this business goin'. But there's no future in commercial fishin' for the grand-young'uns.

"I've got two boys, and they're both commercial fishermen. One of them is thirty-six, and one of them's forty. But their kids will not be commercial fishermen. They'll be somethin' else. We're raisin' one of our grand-young'uns, and from the looks of it, he'll probably be a computer whiz 'cause that's what he's doin'. He can tear one down and put it back together.

"To start off with, we had an island over here, St. George Island, that was tryin' to develop. In 1965, [the workin' people] started havin' to meet at the courthouse to hold the development down. On this side of the courtroom sat the unpaid people, which was the commercial fisherman. He had worked all day that day and had to work tomorrow, but he was setting in the courtroom being unpaid.

"On this side of the courtroom sat all the lawyers, all the big wheels that were tryin' to develop that island, and the man that got up and spoke for that side was getting $100 an hour. And it continues to be that same way today.

"You've got to have people to buy your product, but at the same time, people cause pollution, and pollution causes your bay to be shut down, and you can't get your product. And the biggest problem we had, the reason we were scared of St. George Island, was the amount of density that was goin' to be over there. And some of our natural bars are located on the shores of these islands. We held it down, but it's gone now. I hate to think what it would be like over there right now if we hadn't'a held it down some.

"I've seen [red tide] two times in my lifetime hit Apalachicola. This last time was the worst I've ever seen it. They say it's an algae bloom. But you can't walk on the beaches for it because it burns your eyes and your skin gets to itching. But in the bays, it don't affect the oysters, and it don't affect the

You've got to have people to buy your product, but at the same time, people cause pollution.

I hate to think what it would be like [on St. George Island] right now if we hadn't'a held [development] down some.

shrimp. It kills all the fish. But the health department is scared to let people eat the oysters, so the bay was closed down I think about ten or twelve weeks.

"Yeah, and these people couldn't draw a dime. And they were bringin' food in, but I don't think anybody's ever starved to death in Apalachicola. What the people needed was money. They probably lost a lot of stuff, you know, went back to the finance companies.

"Now we were shrimpin', and we didn't have a good year, but we were makin' a little money. This business could go every day 'cause [red tide] don't affect the shrimp. Somehow or another they were just scared of the oyster, which they say [red tide]'s not transmitted to humans [as gastrointestinal illness]; that you can even eat the fish. And you can see signs of the dead fish, but we never seen no sign of no dead shrimp.

"[Red tide] was offshore, several years ago, and it never came in the bay. We never were shut down on it. This is the first time. Now they've always had red tide in Tampa and off to the south and probably several times up off the coast of Panama City. But this particular year the tide came inside and stayed.

"A lot of people got different ideas on that Bob Sikes channel, but it wasn't cut for the commercial fisherman. It was cut for the tugboat traffic to come down the river, but they never had the tugboats.

"There's been a lot of people wanted to close Bob Sikes channel to put the bay back like it normally was. But now in a normal year when you have rainfall, you have bay closure 'cause of freshwater—which you didn't have twenty years ago. We made our money in freshwater; oysters get fatter, you get a better yield. But now when you get a certain amount of freshwater, you get a bay closure. I believe if Bob Sikes channel wasn't there, this bay wouldn't drain out as quick and the closure would be extended longer than what they are. I do know that Bob Sikes channel takes a lot of the nutrients, and a lot of the pressure off these other passes around here, and they're shoaling up.

> In certain tides . . . there ain't a bit of movement in the Pinhook . . . 'cause there ain't enough pressure in the river.

But still 'n' all, you don't have the pressure comin' down from the river at the same time 'cause we have no flow from the river at all. Because there's no rain and because Atlanta's drinkin' the water.

"I have never seen 'til the last couple of years, [the] water still [at Pinhook]. It has always run, and it always run hard, and you can go up there now in certain tides and there ain't a bit of movement in the Pinhook location 'cause there ain't enough pressure in the river.

"And if you was to have 25 inches of rain, you probably still wouldn't get no water down the river 'cause you got 'bout nineteen dams up there that's got to be filled before you get any water down. And Jim Woodruff flood stage is 62 foot, and I think it's about 46 up there or somethin' like that. And every dam behind it's down.

"I seen somethin' this year I never seen in this bay. Comin' back in West Pass, comin' home, you can see bottom all the way from what we call the Dry Bar, which is 6 miles across the bay.

"'Cause we have no flow comin' down the river. This bay depends on that river for the mud. I've oystered in clear water, but it was in 2, 3, 4 foot of water that you could go along 'nippin'' oysters. See a little bur here and a bur over yonder, you could take your tongs and 'nip' 'em up and throw 'em up on the cull board. But I have never seen it where you could see bottom all the way across this bay.

"It ain't gonna take but 25 inches to finish [the drought]," Davis laughed. "I don't believe that 8 or 10 inches will put the water back. [The river stage] is 1.8 [feet] at Blountstown. Fifteen foot, I think, they consider flood stage. It takes 17 foot to put it over the banks down here in our river system. And that happens every year until the last three or four years, it hadn't happened.

"[During low flows] you're not getting the nutrients down; the other side of it is, you're not getting the pollution down either, comin' out of Atlanta and different farm systems up this river. But the pollution, in my belief, don't outweigh the nutrients comin' down with the mud.

"Now they'll shut the bay down to oysterin' when the bay gets 13 foot, I believe. They say 13 foot is flood stage, and it can run off four or five days, and they'll open the bay back up.

"People don't realize that [the net ban] affected the shrimpin' as much. We fought it. This bunch right here that worked for me gathered up enough money, besides the money that was donated to the lawyer. We put four bill-boards up across the state that said 'Don't ban the nets.' I think it ran about $500 per billboard.

"North Florida, where we put the [billboards] up, voted in favor of the commercial fishermen. The people were a different class of people than what lives south of the Mason-Dixon Line, which everybody used to think was north of us, but it's south of us. The Mason-Dixon Line stretches north of Tampa, Orlando and Cape Canaveral," Davis laughed. "They had more votes in Miami and Dade County than we have in all of northwest Florida. There hadn't been any gill net fishin' in Dade County in twenty-five years. They were votin' on a moot situation.

"I want to tell you what the score was. A Texas-based operation started with us on the net ban. The Gulf Coast Conservation Association became Florida Conservation Association—sports fishin' money, and they used it. I was at a Marine Fisheries meetin' when the man got up and told 'em, 'If y'all don't do like we tell you, we're goin' to vote to outlaw the net; we're goin' to get a constitution amendment.'

"I will say this, if the Marine Fisheries 'a had the guts to say, 'All right we gonna make it 300 yards, we gonna make it 500 yards,' whatever, we'd'a fought it. If a man told you you couldn't drive your car, you'd fight it. Ten years down the road, you might see, 'Well heck, I'd'a been better off if he'd'a put his foot down and not let me drive my car.' But you'd'a fought it, and we fought it.

"I used to have the figures on it, how many commercial fisherman, how many licenses were issued, and everything against the rest of the state. It don't make no difference what your profession is, if you take a rod and reel and cast out and catch a trout or a redfish, you're a sport fisherman. And the net ban had the sport fishermen against the commercial fisherman. And all the people on the Marine Fisheries were sport fishermen. And we had doctors up there, and we had lawyers, and we had a farmer. He was a pretty good fella, but they were all sport fishermen.

"There wasn't no conservation in it. They got us now where we got to pull two nets. We can't pull a tri-net. With the net ban law, we can pull two 25-foot nets across the cork line. A tri-net is a 8- or 10-foot net, smaller version of the same two nets that we're pullin'. You set down on the bottom, pull it five or ten minutes, snatch it up, see if you're in fish, if you're in grass, or if there's any shrimp, you're catchin'. It's against the law to pull that tri-net if we got the two rigs out. If we had the rigs hangin' up and not fishin', we can pull the tri-nets. Well, that tells us at that particular moment whether there's any shrimp.

"But when you set them two rigs out and go to pullin', you pullin' 2.1, 2.8 miles per hour. In an hour you can be almost 3 miles down the beach. You don't know whether you pulled through fish, grass, or no shrimp or shrimp until you take up. If you take a three-hour tow, you could be coverin' 6 to 9 miles of bottom. You can't pull the tri-net, and they're hollerin' conservation. And you come along there, and you hit a bunch of fish. You don't know you in fish 'til you take up.

"We've got turtle excluder devices, and we've got fish shooters. We have to shoot the fish too. All my life I was taught to patch a hole in the net. Now they cut a 36-inch hole in it. So we don't patch no webbing no more," Davis laughed.

"The most selective type of fishing there is, is the gill net, and they've outlawed it. In other words, if you were mullet fishin', you targeted mullet; if you were trout fishin', you targeted trout. You didn't have no by-catch with a gill net. But they outlawed it. The reason why they give 'em 100-foot net is because one of the Marine Fisheries Commission gentlemen from Jacksonville stood up and said he enjoyed goin' down to the beach with his 100-foot seine and his family, and he wasn't gonna let them take that away.

"Well, you wasn't even supposed to have that when it started out. Don't get me wrong, we were allowed two 500-square-feet net shrimpin'. And we had to take it to court to get the length. If you build a net that's 24 foot wide at the throat, it can only be so many feet long to the bag. And they don't fish in the white shrimp fishery. Now you can catch hoppers and pink shrimp with 'em. So we had to go get a lawyer, and we got it where it was 25 foot, which was 66 foot around the throat of the net, and it could be any length you wanted it to be to the bag, but only in this county.

"When it first come up, the governor and cabinet said, 'We don't see where the length of the net makes any difference.' We paid a lot of money for lawyer [fees], and he done a good job, but it's only in this county and Wakulla County. And the [State of Florida] didn't like it.

"Well, if it wasn't for the county judge that we got, a lot of people would be shut down quickly. Now I support this county judge, Van Russell. A county judge is more locally oriented than a supreme court judge. If it wasn't for the county judges, the commercial fishermen couldn't survive. It's a felony to get caught with an oversized net; that's serious business.

"We used to be in the mullet business. I have not had a mullet in that fish house since the net ban. In the shrimp industry, which I'm in, we've had maybe two or three cases of oversized shrimp nets in this county and a couple or three in Gulf County. Somehow or 'nother they come out all right."

Shrimper Jimmy Kelly Cameron, born in 1944 and raised in Apalachicola, entered the office after working on Davis's truck. "When we were comin' up we didn't hardly ever buy groceries or nothin'," Kelly said. "'Cause we hunted and fished; maybe buy grease and flour."

"Used to could buy you a mobile home, put it out in your yard and move in it," Davis said. "Dig a hole, put a 55-gallon drum down for a septic tank. Now the septic tank costs you $3,500 to install."

"When my granddaddy first come here down at Eleven Mile," Kelly said, "they'd catch fish. They would salt the fish down in boats. They had a man come from Blountstown. He'd swap 'em grease and honey and flour for the fish. There never would be no money exchanged."

"Daddy moved down here in 1940 to Thirteen Mile," Davis said. "He got a dollar and a dime a bag for oysters. And he could catch twenty to forty bags a day. All right, five days a week. [That's] $150, in 1940, 1945 during the war.

Didn't have no light bill, no car payment, no rent, no TV. The house was supplied. He had plenty of money. Him and momma'd walk around town huntin' somethin' to buy.

"When Earlean and I got married," Davis continued, "we had a three-month closed season on oysterin', any month didn't have r's. Now we did work May. If I had my bills caught up at the last of May and $500 in my pocket, I could just mess around. I didn't have to work June, July, and August. If you had $5,000 now, you couldn't make it three months."

"All these young boys, every one of them's got $1,500, $2,000 a month [in] bills," Kelly said. "They got to make $40,000 a year just to buy groceries."

"They'll finance you a trailer for $500 a month for thirty years," Davis said. "Give you a lot of land to go with it, $180,000. Your light bill'll cost you $200 a month. If you're driving any kind of vehicle, it's $400 a month. I don't see how they make it."

"They just broke all the time," Kelly added. "The way we always come up, if we seen somethin' we want, we'd just save a little money and pay for it and not be stuck with all them bills."

"He raised his self," Davis said about Kelly. "He was raised on this river and this bay. He was building nets to catch shrimp with when he was ten years old. And people were buying his nets 'cause they were catchin' nets. Every net you build don't catch, and you got to be a pretty good man, build a pretty good net. You talk about streetwise people in New York City; now he's street-baywise.

If we'd'a' been sorry fishermen, we'd'a' been doin' somethin' else, but we were good at it.'

"Earlean and I got two sons that work here, and one or two more boys workin' here. Other than the forty-year-old generation now, there's no young generation comin' on. The state coulda said, 'We gonna issue license; when you die out, your license can't be transferred.' But they done it through the net ban; we don't have no young generation interested in commercial fishin'.

"The funny thing about commercial fishin' is the people that were no good at it have went on to other jobs [and] have got retirement and insurance comin'. And we still don't have anything, so we're the unfortunate ones. We the ones, we were good enough to stay in the business, but we just aren't good enough to survive. If we'd'a' been sorry fishermen, we'd'a' been doin' somethin' else, but we were good at it.

"In oysterin', you gotta be fast," Davis added. "You got to be strong. I wouldn't say strong 'cause a lot of women oyster. But you got to be fast, and you gotta have a knowledge of the bay, where you want to go and what tide you wanna go on.

"In shrimpin', you got to have the knowledge to build your own nets,"

Davis continued, "work on your own engine. In my case, we do our own weldin'; I do my own refrigeration. Everything that keeps this business goin', I do. Then, when you go out on the boat, you hafta have enough responsibility to either know if your engine is workin' right, your oil pressure, your water temperature, your navigation. Then you hafta have an idea in your mind where there's goin' to be a product that day to catch.

"You've got enough knowledge that this hunch is not totally wrong, the wind direction, the tide effect. Three things in this world that I found out you don't predict. One of 'em's a woman, the other one's a hurricane. Women, her-icanes, or shrimp you don't predict," Davis laughed.

"I think they've realized that these fishermen are a lot smarter than they thought they was when they signed the net bomb. Don't you?" Kelly asked.

"Used to you could put a net on the stern, on your doors," Davis said. "The trawl doors are what spread your net. You could put a net on it and go out, and if that net wasn't catchin', then you'd go back, and you'd set this, and you had a chance of makin' it work. Now you go back there, and you put this net on them doors, and it's not fishin', you don't know whether turtle shooter or the fish shooters affectin' the outcome of your net. Used'ta be, when my daddy was shrimpin' in the forties, he went down to the beach, and if his boat wasn't sunk and if his engine cranked up, he could go shrimpin'. Now, 'cause he was hand-rigged, everythin' he done was by hand.

"Now the engine's got to crank, the clutch has got to work, your winch's got to work, your radar's got to work, your LORAN—any one of these things I'm namin' off'll stop you from goin' off today. Your generator on your boat that supplies your power for your lights—if it don't work, you don't go. I had a feller told me the other day, 'Hoover days was better.' So he just about had that down pat.

"We used to count a lot of money. Didn't none of it stay. When you're workin', you see a lot of it go and come. Well, I've got four boats, and a feller told me one day, 'I can't ever find you.' I said, 'There ain't but two places you need to be, that's either down in the engine room of one of them boats or down at Wefin' [marine supply store], where I'm payin' a bill. You can sure find me at one of them two places. But yeah, we do all of our own mechanican'.

"I'm the oldest [in my family]," Davis said. "[The other boy's] sixteen years younger. He's a flounder man. He makes a livin' flounderin' in these bays. [To flounder] you take a gig and a boat and a underwater light. When I was workin' for $6 an hour on some of these summertime jobs, he was

He's a flounder man; he makes a livin' flounderin' in these bays.

makin' $20,000 a year flounderin'. Now they're runnin' the motor, but they used to pole along 'til you see a flounder. Then you'd gig 'em and throw 'em in the boat.

"[They used to use] lightered knots. You stuck a lightered knot in the bow, and you pole along and the whole time the tar is drippin' on your toe. Ten or twelve flounders for most people is a good night's work; he'll have 400 pounds. Yeah, he'll catch two hundred fish. He's the best."

Earlean appeared at the office door in sweats and tee shirt, looking tanned, fit, and natural with short white hair. She was born in St. Joe to an oystering family in 1944. "[Steve's grandma] come to this country from Georgia in a covered wagon," Earlean said. "She never went nowhere in no vehicle that she didn't pack a blanket, kindlin' wood, and drinkin' water in case they broke down. Even after the regular cars got on the road, you still had to have that blanket and that water."

"We're not against progress," Davis said. "It's somethin' that's comin'. We're just against pollution 'cause we know that pollution comes with people. Our jobs is gone. We slowed it down, though, but we can't stop it. This bay is 210 miles of waterfront property. The commercial fishin' industry has less than a mile in Eastpoint and less than a mile over here. That's includin' the bay line on this side, the line comin' down the island side, and the line goin' down the outside . . . in the Gulf. You could stand by and let 'em change the zonin'. But we gonna fight it. We have fought it and we will fight it."

Franklin County commissioners may not know how to spell progress, Davis said, "but they do know how to spell . . . loyalty. Unless they doin' it under the table, they haven't turned too much of this stuff aloose.

"Somethin's got to give somewhere," Earlean said, "because there has to be something for the kids to do, . . . 'cause they can't go out in the bay much more."

"I know this," Davis said. "You get more population, you get more tax money comin' in, you pay out more fire department, you pay out more sewer, you pay out more police. And when you get down to the side and look at it, you're no better off than you was when you didn't have just a handful of people against a bunch of people.

"Me and her is the employees in this business, and I couldn't even meet payroll this last week," Davis laughed. "I'm thinkin' I'm gonna have to lay her off."

"Since I got paid so well before, ya know," Earlean said drily.

> This bay is 210 miles of waterfront property. The commercial fishin' industry has less than a mile in Eastpoint and less than a mile over here.

"Commercial fishin' always been up and down," Davis said. "We don't go to church, but the book says seven years lean, seven years fat. We just waitin' on the seven years fat to come. They'll be here. It'll come."

"Maybe after a while the commercial fishermen will get back in favor with the public," Earlean said.

"You know how to make rules and regulations?" Davis asked. "In the seven lean years. In the fat years, there ain't nobody goin' to support ya. It takes the lean years to get your regulations passed.

"They tried to get me involved in [tri-state negotiations], and I had a lot of people come out and talk to me," Davis said. "But I'm gettin' too . . . old. I don't think that any . . . deal is gonna work if you can't get the water. It's got to rain. And they not goin' to stop Atlanta from growin'. And I read somewhere that there's never no more or no less water in the world. That means that when it's dry here, it's wet somewhere. It don't make no difference what kind of regulations; if you don't have water, it ain't gonna do you no good no way.

"I feel good about what they're tryin' to do. They're tryin' to make more water to come down the river and I hope they're right.

"[But] there's no water, when this river flows back'ards, and that's what it's doin' now. Go downtown in a rising tide. Get around a buoy and see if the water ain't runnin' that way. Now that's normal, don't get me wrong. But when, like about Pinhook, where the water don't run anymore, then you know there ain't no water comin' down Apalach."

"My dad, he oystered all his life," Earlean said. "He died when he was eighty. I do a little bit of everything."

"Boss," said Davis. "We used to load boxes, 100-pound boxes, by hand. We got a forklift now, but we done it for years by hand. And the reason I bought the forklift is 'cause she got too old to throw them 100-pound boxes up on the back of that truck by herself."

"I done that a lot," Earlean said. "I hadn't by myself, but I've been on the other end a lot of times."

"This was a co-deal," Davis said. "If I'm workin' on the boat, she's takin' care of this [seafood store]. [My father] built a buildin' here where this trailer is now, and we was in the live shrimp business, live bait. I was about fourteen years old, and we supplied these camps with live shrimp. Had the juke at one end and the live bait business at the other end of it. And the bait business went haywire there. He extended the juke out big enough to hold a dance hall, and he did that for years. Then he built this building over here and went back to mullet fishin', and he sold mullet . . . up 'til the net ban.

"In the meantime, I started movin' my products over here too. The small shrimp eventually wind up in Alabama at the peelin' plant. I've sold some to Buddy Ward down here to his peelin' plant. The bigger shrimp—peddlers come in and buy them and peddle them around. I don't have any what you'd say big trucks comin' in takin' excess amounts. Just what few we get, we peddle out. But the small shrimp—we went one summer there handlin' a hundred boxes a day.

"We're here seven days a week, 'cept the days we ain't here," Davis said. "I don't know how to tell you. We're here twenty-four hours. We use to be 24–7. We've unloaded boats at two o'clock in the morning. But things is changin' up.

"I don't see no chance [of retiring]," Davis said. "I don't have no retirement. They's a little bit of Social Security, but it won't make the payment on the truck out there. The commercial fisherman pays minimal income tax; that means he pays minimum Social Security in, and I got a lot of goose eggs where I didn't pay anything that year. So I don't draw any Social Security, ain't no chance.

"I got two things workin' for me: I got the lotto goin' and got an invention. I got a 'pat pending' on it. That's a piece of colored Plexiglas with two suction cups on it. You drivin' down a four-lane highway. Don't nobody ever dim their lights on the other side. You stick this up in the corner of your windshield. That shields them two lanes through this colored Plexiglas. Yeah, and you can move it. If the sun's burnin' your ear and your sun visor won't come over far enough, you just snap that up there.

"And before you can open your door," Davis explained, "you got to remove the sun visor and get it out of the way; you don't ever have to move this. And you buy one for $19.95, and if you order before ten o'clock tonight, I'll send you two. I don't have the money to [produce] it . . . , and it wouldn't cost nothin' to produce. And now you could sell it through the Internet."

Earlean brought out a picture of a boat loaded with round, gray scallops, and another of the same boat ablaze.

"That's the *Little Lady*," Davis said. It was his only boat big enough to fish outside the 3-mile net ban limit.

"My youngest son and his buddy was [offshore] in the water, Friday, December 13, 1996. [When the fire started] the boys had worked all night and they had laid down and went to sleep, and one of 'em woke up, and it was on fire. They jumped overboard.

"We didn't get nothin' back. The boys stayed in the water, and they didn't even have life jackets. They were several miles offshore of the Crystal River Light Plant. They didn't even know there was hypothermia. They couldn't even crawl up on the boat when they come picked 'em up."

"The first thing the Coast Guard told 'em was, 'Do you know what day it is?'" Earlean said. "'No what?' 'Friday the thirteenth.' They would tread water for a little while and then grab hold of one of those crab buoys. And they were beginning to argue about which way was the hill."

The *Little Lady* had reaped a record 300-gallon scallop haul before she burned, Earlean said. "Did we get $9 a gallon for them?" she asked.

"Started out," Davis said. "Winded up at $6 before it was over. A thousand dollars is a working day on one of them big boats," Davis said, "and we were getting about $1,800, $1,900 worth a day."

There is a lingering suspicion that, a year and a half after the net ban, someone desperate took the boat's new nets and stainless steel gas tanks before setting fire to it. The boat was uninsured, and the new steel-hulled vessel Davis replaced it with hasn't made up the loss.

"[We use a] scallop net," Davis said. "I'm beginnin' to think it's when El Niño comes, when the Gulf warms up, the water temperature warms up. About every five years we have a scallop season—or seven years. I think it's got to do with El Niño. I think if you had a graph to find out when you had El Niño and a graph to find out when you had scallops, they'd correspond.

> If you had a graph [of El Niño] and a graph to find out when you had scallops, they'd correspond.

Stories of Davis's hunting for buried pirate treasure along the Gulf coast have been published in the *Panama City News Herald*. "You know Billy Bowlegs?" Davis said. "William [Augustus Bowles], he retired in Mary Esther [60 miles west] when they gave him amnesty. He buried several million dollars of treasures up and down this beach. He had a camp on Dog Island.

"You look for markings on trees. Did you know that if you mark a cabbage tree at eye level, 200 years from now that eye level will be the same spot? 'Cause a cabbage tree grows from the top. We've found 'em where they had [an] eye carved in it. I'm talkin' about a natural eye carved in the cabbage tree with a hole drilled through it, lookin' at another cabbage tree with an eye on it, lookin' another direction, and that tree's gone.

"We even went down [to Indian Pass] after a hurricane, and some of the cabbage trees' lower trunk showed up, and there was the markings. Lined the markings up, walked across it with a metal detector, and it said, 'Zing!' Lot of people walkin' up and down the beach fishin'.

"Had an iron rod with us and stuck the iron rod down, went down about a foot and a half, and hit the top of the chest. Rotten wood—we punched it, and it went on through. We could hear the coins rattle against that iron rod. Hit the bottom of the chest, rotten, punched on through. Said, 'We'll come here tonight and dig this up.'

"[Daddy] says, 'I ain't leavin'.' So we built a fire, put the coffeepot on. Was crabbin' with [some commercial fishermen], and they wouldn't leave; two in the morning they was still fishin'. My brother said, 'I'm gonna go up there and dig it anyway.' So he slipped up there and dug it up, and it was a [Styrofoam cooler] full of beer cans.

"During the net ban, this [*Panama City News Herald* reporter] Brent Unger come down here," Davis said. "And he talked to Daddy. And then when he found out he died, then he wrote this up for him." The article, "Death in the Morning," compared Lloyd's death with the beginning of the net ban, when, "on that strangely beautiful July 1 morning these tough and resourceful men all sort of woke up dead."[13]

Davis introduced his brother, a muscled man in sunglasses. "This is Johnny Davis. He floundered all his life," Davis dead-panned.

"You could gillnet at night down at the beaches of this island in the summertime, and the mosquitoes some years would be so bad that the deer would be standin' out in the water," Davis added. "It happened a lot of times. There'd be herds, all filin' out chest-deep.

"We workin' a sea bob; he's a shrimp. He don't get real big. He only comes to the beaches mostly in the wintertime, Indian Pass beach. Now other shrimpin', lot of time we like it to blow 'cause it muddies the water up. White shrimp are hoppers. If you get muddy water, you can catch a few of 'em.

"I wrote to the Marine Fisheries on this turtle excluder device, and in a ten-year period, we caught four sea turtles. All of 'em went back overboard alive, and two of 'em was the same turtle. Now I'm talkin' bay rigs; I'm not talkin' offshore fishin' 'cause it's a little different. But I've never seen a dead sea turtle—unless we had steak that night," Davis laughed.

Capt. Joseph Barber: Aided Torpedoed Sailors

Joseph Barber was among the Apalachicola citizens who, on June 29, 1942, rescued survivors of the *Empire Mica*, an English tanker torpedoed by a German U-boat "about 20 miles off of Cape San Blas," he said. Grandson of the St. George Lighthouse keeper, he was raised on the water and retired from the Florida State University Marine Laboratory as marine mechanist and research boat captain in 1992. He was interviewed at his home in Carrabelle in the fall of 2002 and again on March 22, 2003.

He discussed St. George Island's role as one of the largest amphibious training bases during World War II; his uncle Herbert Marshall's accidental boating death; his life from an island boyhood to fisherman and captain; and his part in rescuing British sailors.

"I was working for the Corps of Engineers, building the airfield at Apalachicola for the government, and I was on the late shift that day. I got up

Fig. 5.4a. Captain Joseph Barber, a lighthouse keeper's grandson, helped rescue survivors of a torpedoed World War II tanker. Photo by Faith Eidse.

late, and I went down by [James Carol McCloud's] house, who lived close to where the boat basin is now. I hadn't heard about the [the *Empire Mica*] being torpedoed. This guy said, 'You could've heard it if you'd been still about one o'clock in the morning.' He said, 'Well, they're bringing the survivors in now.' He and a buddy had a little fast, about 25-foot boat. He said, 'Why don't we run out into the bay and see if we can meet 'em?'

"About the middle of Apalachicola Bay, the *Sea Dream*—belonged to Mr. Randolph—gave out of fuel 'cause it wasn't designed to go way out and back. So we towed 'em back to the dock. Actually, I helped pull the survivors in, some of them were hurt, some of 'em just had their underclothes on, they had to abandon the ship so quick. Some of 'em had jumped down in their lifeboats and hurt their legs and ankles.

"They stayed in Apalach several weeks. I think the paper mill had a branch about 6 miles out of town, and they stayed out there. They did find one of the lifeboats and brought it in later on.

"They're real young guys. I think there was forty-eight on crew, and I think thirteen got out of there. [They were] carrying fuel, maybe high-octane gas or something, 'cause we were supplying Britain with almost everything back at that time. The ship was coming from Texas. Back then we had almost no defense against the German U-boats in the Gulf or on the Atlantic coast either.

"We had one PBY Flying Boat [marine patrol plane] that came down in the morning and went back to Pensacola in the afternoon. And other than these auxiliary vessels like the *Sea Dream*, that weren't really assigned to fighting service, they were just mostly for survivors.

"The Germans first came after [the] supply lines; stopped all the fuel and all the food and all the guns and ammunition. 'Course, in the end they lost six hundred submarines. The British were the first with radar, and they would catch these German U-boats on the surface. They had to surface to recharge their batteries. [The British] depth-charged 'em before they even knew they were there. It got to be if a submarine left, they knew they wasn't coming back, the British and us had gotten so good at killing them.

"During [the 1940s], the army held maneuvers [at Little St. George Island]. Had all these amphibious vehicles, and they were practicing invasions all up and down the coast [at] night. They dug the pond, and they also built the road across the island, and there's a road that goes diagonally across the island; comes out east of the lighthouse. They did all this with the machinery, practicing.

"They would leave here [on amphibious vessels], go on board right here at the boat basin, and go all the way to the island. They were called Ducks, amphibious vessels, that go on land and go in the water too. Well, they had a lot, and great big vehicles.

"Camp Gordon Johnson was one of the biggest amphibious training bases in the country. Lanark Village all the way over to the Ochlockonee River was taken over by the army.

"They had this gunnery school at Apalachicola, part of Tyndall. That's the reason the barracks and all were built. But it was a gunnery school for Tyndall Field in Panama City, and those were swivel gunners, like on bombers. They used to shoot all up and down the island. I have several 50-caliber bullets that were found over there. You weren't allowed to go on the island other than the lighthouse keeper and the Coast Guard.

"During the war, they put a Coast Guard unit over there. I went in the navy in January of '43. We captured a German U-boat during the war. The U-boat skipper seemed a real nice guy; he was forced into the war. I felt real sorry for him 'cause his family lived in Hamburg; we devastated Hamburg; twelve days around the clock [the Allies] bombed it.

"One time I was coming home on leave on the Greyhound bus; it was cold as the dickens. At the Carrabelle beach, they were having invasion training that morning. They were wet and laying out there in the sand hills, so it was pretty rugged.

"[On Little St. George], if you go straight across from the Marshall House [built from army barracks by Herbert Marshall], when you get on beyond my grandmother's house, you'll see some clearings, and that's where they put their tents.

"When they wound [the training] up, they had open house. They flew people over to the island in helicopters. They raked up the shells and made little walkways into the tent.

"My granddaddy, Edward G. Porter, was a lighthouse keeper on St. George. He bought the whole island for $500, and my mother and all the kids were mostly raised over there.

"You come up on a ridge, and on the right-hand side there is the pump pipe for the Hammock House, the house that my granddaddy built. The island has burned several times during the years. Lightning, and fishermen would stop and build a fire and wouldn't put it out. There's been several pretty bad fires on the island during my lifetime.

"Granddaddy built the little schoolhouse, and it's on the same ridge as the Hammock House. It was also a storm house, 'cause the lighthouse sat right out on the open beach. If they had a tidal surge, they couldn't get out. You don't wait in a storm 'til the wind gets up around 80 miles an hour. I think there's five diagonal ridges that run across the island. The road went straight across to the Government Dock, over to the lighthouse and that little schoolhouse, or storm house.

"We lived over there in the Hammock House, two or three summers. My dad worked on the bay, and we went over to the lighthouse almost every Sunday and had dinner. Then about eleven or twelve o'clock we would borrow the horse and wagon and go back over to our house, which was up in the middle of the island. That [was] during the Depression, a bad time all over the country.

"I used to work over at the FSU [Florida State University] Marine Lab, and it's been thirty years ago [that my uncle Herbert died]. I was at work when they called. Herbert was a real do-or-die kind of guy. Something didn't work, he was going to make it work. He was over there [at his house] with two fellas, and he had that little enclosed slip over there.

"Well, he backed into the bottom and bent the rudder. He didn't realize it, and when he was trying to come out of there, it was blowing from the northeast about 25 miles an hour, which was broadside to him. The wind kept blowing him ashore, and finally they turned the boat around and were goin'

Fig. 5.4b. Wefing's Marine Supplies, established on Apalachicola's Water Street in 1909, moved to Eastpoint and has expanded to commercial fishing and recreational boating supplies, sales, service, and rentals. Photo by John Crowe.

to spend the night. Herbert and J. B. Gander were overboard pushing the boat around with their backs. The other guy, George Wefing—that used to own Wefing's store—was inside the boat. They'd holler, 'Put it in gear.' It would go a little ways, and it would blow back on shore.

"The mud had settled in there, and it was real soft. I was mullet fishin' down there one day, and I stepped off from hard bottom and almost went up to my waist. The boat went over him and the propeller hit him. He had a real bad cut, and I think he bled to death. The other two guys had to feel around in the water. He was already dead when they found him.

"He had a radio on the boat, but it didn't work. There was a phone on the island; it went to the lighthouse, and when those big shrimp boats started working out in the bay, they cut the line. They couldn't communicate to tell anybody what had happened, so they had to stay there with him all night. Next morning, Gander walked down to Bob Sikes Cut and had someone fishing down there to put him across. He walked up to a house and called.

"I was getting ready to go down to my aunt's house; the Coast Guard were coming in through the 2-mile channel here past my house [in Carrabelle] with Herbert. My aunt gave me the boat; a 36-foot wooden boat with a diesel engine.

"I had the house down there for two years, took care of it, [and] she still had some stock. There were still a few hogs on the island. There used to be a lot of goats, but I guess with the sanctuary's blessing, they had the Fort Rucker helicopter outfit shoot the goats at what we call Sand Dollar, where that old grave is.

"I was walking across the island when here come this [FSU professor] with like a Frank Buck hat on. So I said: 'Why in the world do they want all the hogs off the island? It used to be a source of food for people here in hard times.'

"Well, this guy said, 'Oh, they're eating up all the [native] plants on the island.' 'Course, my granddaddy had cows over there at the lighthouse. He had a big corral there, and there's an old dippin' vat just east of the lighthouse. We had the screw worm fly, and if a cow or a pig scratched himself, this fly would lay an egg in the wound and kill the animal.

"You walk in on the Government Dock, you can't get down off of it now, it's eroded away so bad. There's a foundation in the water, four pillars, and that was the oil house. That sat about 40 or 50 feet up on the beach at one time. That's how much the island has eroded away through the years.

"I fished ten years [out of Pensacola]. During those years the average man made a dollar an hour working. Me and my boat together very seldom come in under $150 dollars a week. The boat paid for itself. My wife thought it was a lowly way to make [a] living, but I did well at it, and it was about to break us up. 'Course, we had two kids, and I came from a busted-up family, and I didn't want that for my kids. So I sold my boat, and we moved back to Apalach.

"You know, the fishing—they tell me—that you may have five, six, seven years of good production; five, six, seven years of bad production. It seems to work that same way with your game. There's still quite a few trout and redfish. A friend of mine still living in Apalach caught 600 pounds of trout by himself here.

"Yeah, my uncle and my neighbor there where I lived [in Apalachicola], they used to fish in the fall. They had a job; my uncle worked in the post office, but he had the time off. He made his Christmas money every year catching trout and so did my neighbor there, Mr. Jenkins. Mr. Jenkins worked over at Tyndall as a fireman, but every year near the fall, when the fishing was good, he'd fish and paid for his Christmas.

"'Course, the snapper we considered our money fish. But even back then—it's unusual to do this—but I have made $600 in a day's time, me and my boat. The harder I worked, the more money I could make. I used to make two trips a week. I ordinarily went out about dark Sunday afternoon, run all night to get out to where we fished, and would stay out the next two or three days. But if I hit it good in two days—it took three days come back in and unload—and right back out the same week.

"Wintertime, you couldn't depend on the weather long enough to make the trip. I used to get me a job on the hill and work January, February and

March for $1 an hour. Sometimes I'd catch a good weekend and make more money on the two-day fishing trip than I'd made all week working for a plumbing company.

"I was sunk one time, lost the two men. I rode the bottom of the boat for 9½ hours. I think what hit me was a nor'wester. It created a lot of freakish weather, and I think a tornado hit my boat. 'Course it all happened at nine minutes after twelve at night, and it all happened so fast you don't have much time to think. They never did even recover the two men. But we dumped out about 1,500 pounds of fish when my boat was sunk, so it's a possibility that the sharks got 'em.

"I rode the bottom of the boat 'til about nine o'clock in the morning when the pilot boat picked me up. He'd come out to put a pilot on a German [merchant] ship, and on his way back in he came close enough that I could get his attention.

"We had a coastal steamer, the *Tarpon*. It came in [to Apalachicola] about noon time on Thursday. You could almost set your watch by it. Captain Barrett blew for the bridge after it was built in 1935. They had to open the bridge for it to get through. The riverboat came in [too], from Columbus on Thursday.

"The train came in every night of the week about dark. There was also a little tanker that came in bringing oil to the Gulf dock out there. It came in on Thursday, so I guess Thursday was our most important part of the week. People used to go down to the train every night to see who came in or who went out, because they carried passengers as well as freight.

"In this [steamboat] pamphlet that my friend had, from Columbus down to Apalachicola, it took three days 'cause they stopped at every pig trail along the river, and they had to get firewood. The fare was $7, and that included your meals and your room. And they were pretty elaborate boats. Sam Johnson [of Apalachicola] did a lot of the fancy work on them, probably in the pilothouse, in the kitchen, dining room. I understand he actually built two of the boats. He was an amazing old man. His son was married to my Daddy's sister, so it was kinda in the family, but we enjoyed goin' around there and seeing what he was doing.

"I worked in the Sheip's Lumber Company that was still operating where the workboat basin is up there. I was just a kid; it was production work. I ran a saw for 'em, and I made $13 a week, forty hours.

"One thing we could do back then as kids, we could fish; catch flounder and speckled trout, and 'specially in the fall we caught the speckled trout. But we always got 25¢ a pound for those two fish. Mullet you couldn't hardly give away. I cast-netted a lot for pleasure. I'd come in Sunday afternoon I'd have maybe twenty, thirty, forty mullet, and I'd go around try to give 'em away, and people'd say: 'Are they mullet? Are they trout? Are they clean?'

"Even in the Depression around Apalachicola, if anybody went hungry, it was just because he was too lazy to get out and get it. Because you can go down and catch a mess of crabs; go down on the dock, anybody'd give you a mess of fish or a mess of shrimp. I can remember when shrimp, to the catcher, brought a cent a pound.

"We had a canning plant there in Apalachicola at one time, Acme Packing Company. They tell me people have seen shrimp from Apalachicola in places like China. My momma worked there some. It eventually burned; they never did rebuild it.

"You could walk out in the woods and pick up palmetto cabbage. You pull the center out of a small one, and people used to go get it, even cut the big ones. It's kinda like cabbage you grow, a little bit different taste, but you could eat it just raw. We used to do that as kids, not 'cause we was hungry but just something to do. You can walk around, lots of places around the bay in Apalach, and pick up oysters right off the shoreline.

"My earliest connection with the river, my dad ran a turpentine still up on Howard's Creek. This was in the late twenties, early thirties. We lived there for two or three years. At that time, there wasn't any road out to the highway from Howard's Creek. We went back and forth by river, and we would pass the river boat. Me bein' young, when one of those old paddle wheelers goes by you, it leaves a wake for a long time behind it, kinda a rollin' swell. My dad had a small launch, I'd say 35 feet. Boats back then were built long and narrow 'cause they didn't have much power.

"The loggin' was still goin' on the river. Well, anytime you're up in that river, you could hear this whistle goin' all day long for a 'pull boat.' It was a great big steam engine on a barge that pulled any log they cut out of the swamp. One guy stood out where they were attachin' their logs onto the log that carried it out to the river, and he blew the whistle wire goin' back to the pull boat to tell the man runnin' the winch what to do. You know, 'back up, stop, go ahead.'

"What they would do was take a cable way out in the swamp and around a tree and back to the pull boat. It had dangle lines to attach to each log, and they would hook ten or twelve logs at a time, and when he give the signal to take it to the river. The thing was really powerful, and they would pull these logs butt first, which was the big end. When they would hit the creek it would knock water 40 or 50 feet in the air. There are still, to this day, up in that swamp land, pull hulls where they dug a trench pullin' those logs out to the river.

"Those tugboats only had about 60 horsepower. When you think about your car or outboard motors with 200, 250, 300 horsepower now, it's kinda' amazing. 'Course, during this time of year when the river's high, they lost a lot of the rafts; they'd lose control of 'em, and they'd break up. If there was any green cypress, it'd go to the bottom, and the best cypress that we've had for quite a few years came off of the bottom.

"You know, the way a cypress tree grows, it takes about two [to] three hundred years for a cypress tree to get great big. Kinda like the redwoods. You can see some of the old stumps up there. The limbs were way up high; back when they had plenty of timber, they'd just take what we called the first cut—maybe the first 20 or 30 feet—and leave all of the top. In the later years, they went back and recovered that log that's been buried in the ground those many years. All that is left is the heart, which is the good part of a cypress tree.

"You could take a piece of good heart cypress, put it up on the outside of your house, and don't put any paint or anything on it. In a hundred years later it'd be right there.

"I can show you wooden crosses and headboards stuck in the ground that have been [in the Apalachicola cemetery] ever since I can remember, out of cypress, good heart cypress. 'Course, the ships came in from all over the world to pick up the cypress lumber because it is such a good, durable lumber. 'Course, they brought people too."

The continuing influx has raised property values, and Barber sold his house in Apalachicola for a considerable sum. He and his wife retired to Carrabelle, where he continues to fish and hunt, often with his son, whenever his heart desires.

Mike Millender: Oyster Kid to Seafood Dealer

Mike Millender is a wiry, red-haired seafood retailer. He had expanded Island View Seafood, adding a room of seashells to catch tourists. In July 2005, Hurricane Dennis swells knocked the back room out, requiring Millender to rebuild.

On March 22, 2002, Millender told of falling in love with oystering as a boy, earning credit accounts with local merchants as a teenager, and becoming his family's retailer as a young man. He also talked about the impacts on the community of fishing regulations and of losing family members to storm. As he talked, a shrimper arrived with a full fish locker, and Millender paid him cash from a roll in his pocket. Community goodwill is important to him. Millender fillets fish free for sports fishermen, shucks oysters, and

Fig. 5.5. Michael Millender repairing his ice machine atop Island View Seafood, Eastpoint, March 2002. The waterfront oyster house beside him has gone out of business. Photo by Faith Eidse.

pinches heads from fresh shrimp while customers wait. He packs their selections in ice and adds a souvenir. Millender is a tourist's retailer and a fisherman's friend.

I reckon I must have fell in love with it.

"I was born in 1954, and by the time I was five, six years old, I went to work with my father on the weekends. I reckon I must have fell in love with it and wanted to go, so he didn't turn me down. As I got older, I started learning more how to do oysterin' and all. And on weekends I went to work with him, and then it got to where I di'n want to miss a day.

"But it paid off, and I'm proud and I'm happy that it made me work 'cause I learned how to do it. 'Time I was fifteen years old, I had my own boat, I had my own motor, and after school, I'd get off the bus and go to work and made my own money. And I was happy with my rewards, to be able to buy things with and even had a credit account at that age.

"I didn't have a bank account; I just had credit. Up here at Taylor's was my first credit account. And my uncle had a grocery store, a gas store, where I got my stuff to go oysterin'. And I had a credit account with him. So that was my two first credit accounts I had.

"Plus the first year I had an old motor my father gave me, but then I had a credit account with Jimmy Mosconis and Ronnie Gray on a 20-horse Mercury. I had a new motor I could really crank up besides that old Evinrude Johnson, which you had to pull. Then in my graduation year I didn't have to go but half a year. So I took my father's car and drove to school, and I'd go to work then, oysterin'.

"Durin' them times of the year, then, you could go seven days a week oysterin', weather permittin'. Pretty well the demand for oysters was full demand.

"All of a sudden it started gettin' more Lou'siana oysters in. The semis got more comin' in here. The shuckers fell in love with them. They was bigger oysters than our oysters, and they was fatter at times. They got a better turnout where they made more money. Our bay just produces a smaller oyster compared to a lot of them out in Lou'siana.

"I would say twenty-two years [ago] in the 1980s started more comin' in. The Department of Natural Resources [DNR] got so rough on the trucks comin' from Georgia and Alabama that they put the squeeze on 'em. You had peddlers from all over Georgia and Alabama comin' in here, buyin' oysters. Before the sixties and the seventies most of these people with seafood business in here didn't have no trucks. People was comin' and buyin' all the oysters you could get. Then the Department of Natural Resources started confiscatin' the [little] oysters off the trucks. Where they should have been on the water, but they would check the trucks and turn 'em back, and that put the hurtin' on them.

A lot of people believe that we come from the water.

"When DNR got more overzealous, thinkin' more of people workin' in the seafood industry as a criminal more than a truant, all the seafood houses had to start buyin' trucks in order to get it outta here and take the gamble of takin' it to the markets up there.

"Then you had them hurricanes. The hurricane of '84 and '85 hit and destroyed the bay, and then they come in with the check stations. And they was tight. They didn't care about you or didn't have feelings. It was more, 'You do this.' You was under a dictatorship.

"Even with your Marine Fisheries under the State of Florida they're 'solidatin' it to be under one rule. I guess that could be called dictatorship too. Instead of saying what each county is eligible to production, it's more statewide production. If you go by statewide, then you check on how many redfish is in this area here, and you go by that and make the rest of us that got more go by the leastest. So they put it to one-a-day. So that goes even if you have an abundant amount up here, you see?

"[I] went from bein' on my oyster [bar] with my father and my uncle. My uncle, he had two son-in-laws that was in [the] soft-shell crab business. He said they was doin' good at it, and he kept tellin' me that 'You need to try it.'

This building here that we' in now was abandoned fer prob'ly about seven years. We wind up havin' to pay the taxes on it, and we had to do somethin' with it, and my uncle talked me into gettin' in some soft-shell crab business. And while we was here doin' it, several people pulled in and wan'ed to know if we had anything for sale.

"So the next thing we said, 'Hey, we might need to start sellin' some of these crabs out here.' So we started buildin' these tray boxes to put ice chests in, and we went and bought the $25 license. We already had electricity [and] water, so we went on doin' some remodelin'.

"So I started off with this little room right here and a few ice chests sellin' seafood to the public. Then as we got more people comin' in, we expanded, and I'm still expanding today to the back. Then we got the front for show 'n' tell and selling. In the back's gonna be more your shells and ornaments that tourists love to buy, take home with them for memory's sake.

"When I was comin' up, you didn't see that many tourists. And ever since St. George Island has been founded, prob'ly two-thirds of the people here in the county is not homegrown. I imagine two-thirds of the oystermen wasn't born and raised here. It's people travelin', or gypsies, you might say. People and all have moved here. So as far as the original people that should'a been, there'd be plenty of land for us to expand all over the place, you know what I mean?

"But another ten years there the ancestry people won't have a place to buy or a place—I won't have a place—to work. Prob'ly won't have a job on the water; they'll slowly be pushed on the hill. I guess that's the way a lot of people believe, that we come from the water, but slowly everybody's makin' it to the hill. Instead of self-employed, it'll be employees. Cleanin' houses up for these rich people, or cuttin' their grass or paintin' their houses or workin' for the state or county. Cleanin' the streets, haulin' garbage.

"We used to cuss the dams up here. We'd cuss Bob Sikes when it was comin' up. I heard the old-timers. Before the cut, used to get a lot of freshwater comin' down those rivers, and it was the clay water and its nutrients and all to the bay system. And all of a sudden they started puttin' in the dams, and we got top water. Prob'ly bug spray and everything else come over, and then the cut would let the freshwater out so fast the oysters wa'n't growin' big enough even, so the more Lou'siana oysters. But now today we don't cuss the dams, and we don't cuss the cut because of pollution.

"When I was comin' up, my father would have workers that would come off the grouper fishing boat, and he'd take 'em oyster'n,' work 'em for a few months [during] their bad season, and when they went back to work, he'd ask them for scamp. They'd bring him scamp to eat. It was the best grouper.

You got different types of groupers like you got different types of redfish or snappers. Every now and then we get some of it, and a lot of our customers fell in love with it.

"[I ice up people's coolers] as long as they're buyin' seafood. You got to accommodate the customers. They come buy seafood from you all week. Then they goin' home, and they wanna buy enough to take home, and so you got to ice it up good enough where they can make it home. And that's good for business.

You gotta keep a certain amount of oystermen, shrimpers, seafood workers.

"It's hard to put the barrel between [saving the resource and making a living off it]. But I always said, 'How many hunting dogs are in the county?' How many months does he hunt, and how many months he just sit in the cage and eat? But they keep 'im in the backyard, don't they?

"You gotta keep a certain amount of oystermen, shrimpers, seafood workers. You gotta keep a number of them goin'. Who knows where [we'd get seafood if] we go into a nuclear war or some'm, and your Gulf is still okay and people wantin' to eat food? They love to forget about rules and regulations and say, 'Go catch it because we up here in Washington is starvin' to death.'

"People come here from Georgia, Indiana, Iowa, Arkansas, Connecticut, Vermont, all over. Great Britain, Australia, and that's [why we're] open seven days a week. If you're not open, wherever they go to first is prob'ly where they gonna spend the rest of their money that week or two weeks they're here."

The year before, Millender was asleep one night when the phone rang with news that two of his cousins, Eastpoint fishermen, were missing. "They hadn't made it in yet, and I didn't have no boat, no motor, or nothin', and it was blowin' a roar; I reckon a nor'wester, the strongest one. It was howlin' across the roof in here, and so I called and looked at the map. And my concern, they might be in the water.

It was blowin' a roar.

"But by my experience [of] saving some people, you can't leave your motor running. You gotta cut it off and holler and listen for that faint little voice. Because they could hear a motor a mile away.

"The next mornin' [my brother] Pat come in to go back, and I showed him a map and told him if the current's runnin' this way so many yards, if they float and didn't drown, they would be in this vicinity in so many hours. But they wound up drownin'. I don't know how many marine patrol made it out there and what time they made it out there. But my worriation was my experience with the [Florida] Marine Patrol when I found some people, they was goin' all the wrong direction.

"[The drowned men were] my second cousin Ray Hatfield and my third cousin Bruce Keith," Millender added. "They were both professional oystermen. They worked in the bay all their lives, and tragedies happen, you know. They didn't last long in the water. If they floated long enough, I figured that wind blowin' would blow 'em to Little St. George Island. But they found Ray not too far from where the boat went down.

"They found him on the flat, but he still had a life jacket strapped to the side of him. So it's a possibility that they both was hangin' onto it together. My belief is that Bruce might've drownded or died of hypothermia, first, and he might've had to turn him loose from the other side of the life jacket. 'Cause you'd think Ray would've had it on like a full vest.

"I lost about two [family members] in twenty-five years. It ain't an every-day thing, and if the family loses somethin' professional [it's a hardship]. Accidents do happen, though. I could've done drownded a dozen times. Maybe [the boat] went down just as fast as that weather come out. Or maybe they stayed a little bit too much longer tryin' to make Christmas money or something.

"You know, you got First Responders," Millender added. "You got Fire Department, you got Marine Patrol, but you don't have a rescue organiza-tion for the water. And right now they got Cat Point closed off. If some'm happened on Cat Point, there's no way for a family to get in touch with people because they're out building that bridge, and they don't have it fixed up where people can get on the beach for an emergency response. You can't get an ambulance on the beach down there right today."

Joe Nichols: Suing to Retrieve a Livelihood

Joe Nichols is middle-aged, tall, tanned, and grizzled. He came to Island View Seafood on March 22, 2002, to ice his fish locker, and told this story.

"I' been a fisherman all my life. I was born and raised in Wakulla County, but I've worked here for about forty-five years.

"The state owns it all, and they control it. And they tryin' to knock the commercial fisherman and the commercial workers out where their tourist industry can come in. That's what they're doin'. If they can get us out of the way, then they can sell the land around here for a big price.

"Also the fish that they're savin' is destroyin' the bay. The redfish is eatin' the crabs up. Sheepshead and redfish has took over since they took the nets. You can't go to the market and buy trout and redfish no more. Not in the state of Florida. The big fish that they're saving is what's killing the bay. The little bitty mash nets they give us, they're catchin' the baby fish before they grow up," he added.

"I mullet fish; it's the best. It's one of the finest fish you got. A mullet's a

The fish that they're savin' is destroyin' the bay. The redfish is eatin' the crabs up.

The little bitty mash nets they give us, they're catchin' the baby fish.

good eatin' fish, but people can't afford it. It's costin' too much to get out there to catch 'em.

"That's right," Nichols said. "Well, when they come down they can't even afford to catch but so many, you know. They even limited what they can catch. We got a meetin' tomorrow, [in] Panacea, talkin' about the nets and all and what's goin' on our little waterfront. We gonna have two lawyers up there, and they gonna be talkin' about the fishin' and the Florida coast here all along the beach line, what we can do if we don't get our nets back. We're planning a lawsuit if we don't get our livelihood back. Fishermen are turning into the criminals. We been fightin' it five years, tryin' to get us a piece of net to make a living with. We don't want the length of net we used to have because we're not tryin' to rob the bay like they're talkin' about.

"We look out for the bay, a whole lot more than the state and environmental [protection] does. They highly educated, but they don't even know where the roe at. See mullet roe all along as they come, see? A little bit of eggs here and a little bit of eggs there. They go in canals and creeks and sloughs and lay their eggs. It's not even in the books what I'm talkin' about.

"[Ditritus] is what raises the oyster, see? Right this whole muddy bay out here. It's the silt that comes from Georgia. And [Georgia's] just about stopped us up, you know. They got the rivers all dammed up all along, and that keeps a lot of our water from coming down, see? State just keeps interferin.'

"The consumers is hurtin' too 'cause they can't pay the price on the fish. You can hardly get a crab. They used to be 3¢ when everybody was catching them, see? Now what are they—$1.75 or $1.50?

"If they gonna save our bay—and just keep this crowd that we got now workin' and [the haul] would dilute its own self if they can get a better job on the hill.

"They better stop listenin' to book knowledge and get somebody born and raised around the bay that knows what's goin' on," Nichols concluded. "See, we know what's happenin' in that bay. See, now chemicals come down, we can be hurt. But far as nets, nets help the bay.

"They spend billions of dollars protectin' the sea turtles. And the sea turtles go right over across the country yonder, and they ship 'em back to us in cans, turtle soup and stuff like that, after we raised it for 'em. And the places they used to nest over here on our land? There' condominiums and motels where the turtles can't live.

"Commercial fisherman ain't gonna waste his time tryin' to butcher out some'm like that. And we respect the porpoise and the dolphin.

"See, harbor fish don't stay. They come through and they feed, then they travel on. But when they come here in great big herds and eat the crabs and the shrimp, we have to charge a big price for what little bit's left."

Nichols's concerns about the net ban reallocating a resource from one group to another were reiterated by Woody Miley, outgoing director of the Apalachicola National Estuarine Research Reserve.

Woody Miley: Let's Not Love Our Resource to Death

Woody Miley's cinder-block office walls were as bare as his feet on February 25, 2003. His belongings were in boxes as he prepared to retire after almost twenty-four years as director of the Apalachicola National Estuarine Research Reserve (ANERR). ANERR was established in September 1979 as a cooperative effort among Franklin County, the State of Florida, and the National Oceanic and Atmospheric Administration. It is administered by the Florida Department of Environmental Protection and managed for long-term research, environmental education, and resource management.

"The Apalach Reserve is different than the other twenty-five reserves around the nation," he said, "in that Franklin County is also a partner. Franklin County was dubious of a federal-state program here, so the deal was that Franklin County represented half of a policy-making management board. The Apalach Reserve was larger than all the other reserves combined [until] Kachemak in Alaska was designated."

Fig. 5.6. Woody Miley on his last day as director of the Apalachicola National Estuarine Research Reserve, February 25, 2003. Photo by Faith Eidse.

"My first office was a folding table in the courthouse. Then I went through 57 Market Street, a little two-room office. Then we built the Apalachicola facility, and by the time we moved in, we had outgrown it. So it is now the Environmental Education Center, and we built the facility here in Eastpoint and moved research, resource management, administration, and maintenance over here. We've gone to eighteen full-time people, and we double that with temporaries.

"Our job is resource protection through research, education, and resource management. After a few years, Franklin County gave us just exceptional support. I was most proud of $20,000 a year that we used to match environmental education grants. We're not regulatory, we're not enforcement.

"We have a small contingency of [Florida Marine Research Institute] staff that share this building and do most of the fisheries work. We do some in Apalachicola Bay, and it works well. That's information we need.

"I was a Senior Fisheries Research Biologist for the University of Florida [when I applied for this job]. I had hunted and fished here for years, and I was already in love with Apalachicola Bay. The management board—three people from Franklin County and three people from the state—interviewed the finalists.

"Bobby Howell was on the board. At the time he was officially the clerk of the court for Franklin County. Unofficially and unchallenged, he was the king of Franklin County. He said: 'I never met a redhead I liked. I've run three out of Franklin County, and I busted fifteen in the army.'

"I thought, oh geez. I said, 'Well, sir, I'd like a chance to change that opinion,' and Bobby and I have been friends ever since.

"I won the position on a four-to-two vote, but the important thing is I got all three Franklin County votes. Bobby Howell said he was 'going to vote for that redhead because he was the only one that could live more than two hours past dark in Franklin County.'

"The Apalachicola River and Bay system is the most amazing natural area I've ever seen and arguably the best system from a function [and] productivity standpoint left in, at least, the United States. We have 308 species of birds, 21 nest here, 7 of those are listed. We've documented 1,162 species of vascular plants within the reserve; about 1,300 in the basin; 107 of those are listed species. We have 57 species of mammals. Listed mammals include the black bear, probably the Florida panther. We have about 200 species of fish; at least 4 of those are listed species. We have the highest species density of amphibians and reptiles in all of North America north of Mexico.

"It is a most magnificent place, and the seafood industry has always been the backbone of the economy. We have a growing ecotourism industry here, but as long as we can keep the bay productive and worth money, then we have a chance of saving all the critters. If we keep the conditions good enough that the oysters are edible, and we produce shrimp and crabs and fish, then the assumption is, all the other critters are doin' fine.

"So this program has always been in full support of the commercial seafood industry and the recreational fishing in the bay. That doesn't mean that we always got along. The seafood industry has been mad at me several times.

"I came out against the net ban and published a little article in our newsletter called, 'The Down Side of the Net Ban,' and all it did was get me in trouble with my own department. But the net ban, in my opinion, should not have happened. It was unnecessary, and what we did with the net ban was reallocate a declining resource from one user-group to another. And if we think we can regulate a fisheries back into existence and continue not to pay attention to the reasons that the resource was declining—water quality and habitat loss—then we didn't pay attention in Biology 101.

> What we did with the net ban was reallocate a declining resource from one user-group to another.

"When we reduced our commercial catch, we didn't reduce our appetite for seafood. What we did was import more, and the places we imported it from, typically, have [few enforced] environmental regulations. So, globally, we didn't do marine life any favors at all. It's a false assumption that we saved whales and turtles.

"What we do is monitor water quality. Our biggest project in the water wars with Georgia and the Corps of Engineers, [was] data loggers [who took] water-quality readings every thirty minutes. Then the Water Management District put out some additional stations, and establish[ed] that three-dimensional model that [was used in] negotiations.

"So now when freshwater comes down the river we know the effects on the bay, based on the volume of water and the direction and wind speed. So we've got better science now than ever before.

"The [critters] we have the best data on, of course, are the commercial species, and while we have good years and bad years, Apalachicola Bay is still quite productive. The laws of supply and demand make it a fairly stable economic base.

"[I'm a] critter hugger; I'm also a hunter—a dichotomy, I guess. But I love all of 'em, especially snakes. Snakes and people don't mix, so in areas like St. George Island there are far, far fewer snakes. But if you go up in Tate's Hell, or you go up in the river swamp, there's still healthy populations of snakes. But when development occurs, you can notice a marked decline.

"If we took all the snakes out, we would have more rats and more roaches. And the option there is pesticides; well, pesticides offer a greater threat to humans than all the poisonous snakes in the world. And that's where we go when we lose the natural balance of predator-prey relationships. Pesticides have a domino effect, and larval forms [of fish] are much, much more susceptible.

"The Apalachicola basin has a really good chance of maintaining the functional relationships and the dynamics of productivity here. Without a doubt the best tool in resource management is Florida's aggressive land acquisition program. If we can put the key habitats in public ownership, then we can maintain the functional relationships forever.

"That's not to say that Apalach doesn't have some problems. We have hot spots. There's no such thing as a clean marina, for example. The pollution and sediments in the water are at bad levels, but they're very small areas. Typically the open waters and the open sediments of the bay are still in good shape, especially relative to other estuarine systems.

"I had a group of adults from FSU hikin' on Forbes Island. It never got shallower than knee-deep water. I was talkin' about the role of the floods [and] floodplains relative to the productivity of the bay, and every time I'd pause, they'd start talkin' about water moccasins. I had this beautiful buttressed cypress tree to my back and was tellin' them about buttressing and why it occurs. There was a limb just a couple of inches over the water, and it had a 4-foot brown water snake on it. And why people don't see snakes has always puzzled me. I love 'em so much they may as well be a neon light.

"I reached down and grabbed this big ol' female brown water snake right in the middle and she turned around and just started bitin' me. It gets pretty impressive because I'm a free bleeder. So I'm holdin' this snake, and blood's drippin' in the water. I said, 'You think this is one of them ol' moccasins?' I said, 'Nah, it doesn't look like it.' And I threw it down in the water, and she went under. Well, it took thirty minutes to put that class back together 'cause they scattered all over Forbes Island.

"One of the main reasons [this is the biggest preserve for amphibians and reptiles north of Mexico] is the ravine system. Especially in the upper river, the steephead and ravine systems that's very similar to the Blue Ridge Mountains. We have a similar habitat, a disjunct habitat, and then we had this river for all these species to move up and down. So in those ravine systems, we have the same salamanders that they have in the Blue Ridge Mountains. Only lizards are a depauperate group for us. Every other type of amphibian and reptile we have large numbers of.

"Then [there's] our avifauna list. We're part of the Mississippi flyway and part of the Atlantic flyway so we get lots and lots of birds. We list 308 species, but the next time we put out the list it will be higher than that.

"Birding here is just phenomenal, especially springtime because we're first landfall for the trans-Gulf migrants, the neotropical birds. So by the time they get here, they're more tired and hungry than they are afraid [of birders]. Scarlet tanagers and the summer tanagers come through, all the buntings and the warblers.

"I've seen several bear here. Matter of fact, bear come into downtown Apalach and downtown Eastpoint sometimes. But on the floodplain, especially when the river is low, you can see bear tracks. And up in Tate's Hell and south of Sopchoppy, you frequently see bears. The population is increasing.

"Bear hunting is no longer legal. They are still killed occasionally 'cause they just devastate beehives. But most of the [beekeepers put] electric fences around their hives. If they taste that tupelo honey, they don't want to leave, and FWC will trap 'em. There have to be a few hundred here 'cause they're seen frequently. We had one get treed in downtown Apalach by a dog.

"The official story is that panthers were extirpated from this area and that if one exists, it's probably a puma. Most of the old-timers are convinced that there are real Florida panthers here. The puma and the Florida panther are the same species, so I don't care whether it's a puma or a Florida panther. That just adds more credibility to the wild conditions of the Apalachicola basin.

"[Seven or eight] years ago, Dr. Loran Anderson, working on a grant through the research reserve, described a new species of vascular plant in the basin, the Apalachicola daisy. It tells you something about the wild, pristine conditions of the area, 'cause most everything has been found and described. [The daisy was] up in the floodplain in the northern part of the research reserve. It grows right on the banks and hangs over—beautiful flower.

"[The future of the ANERR] program [is] bigger and better. There's still room in environmental education for additional programs, reaching additional people. From a visitor's center/environmental education standpoint, ANERR is the only show for many counties. Our education program covers preschool to graduate credit marine biology, taught at least in part by the staff. We do a lot of coastal management decision-maker workshops and training.

"The education staff has written and installed the [grade school through high school] marine science curriculum in most of northwest Florida. It's understaffed, and so is our research program. The researchers' jobs here are as much to facilitate research as to conduct it. One day they'll tote a bucket for a university professor, and the next day they're a principal investigator on a program of equal scientific merit. As additional lands are purchased by the state, some of those are assigned to ANERR for management. So our prescribed fire, our hydrologic restoration programs will grow.

"[The Turkey Point FSU Marine Laboratory] is a good place for marine biologist training. It produces a lot of good information and a lot of good management information. But if it served the sole purpose of a field lab for training marine science students, it would certainly be worth the state expenditures to keep that lab open. And the St. Joe development [has] decided that's not the best place for a marina; they have another place. So other than politics and money, the marine lab's in good shape.

"If it were staffed and funded better, they could have more students going through, and that's a very unique system over there. The estuarine systems along this coast are just totally different. Apalachicola Bay is a lagoon and barrier island system that is dominated by the river.

"Alligator Harbor and St. Joe Bay don't have freshwater inflow, and that's termed a 'negative estuarine system.' They actually go hypersaline. They get saltier than the open Gulf. But because of the lack of freshwater inflow, their water clarity [promotes] vast sea grass beds, unlike the Apalachicola Bay.

"I worked with the [lab] some [after] we tried to get oyster aquaculture going here. The fear of the seafood industry was that some big company would come in here and lease the whole bay. The way the law was written that Al Lawson got passed, that would not have happened. A person could only have one acre.

"Alligator Harbor [has] clam aquaculture. Some of the leases are already let. We need to find areas where there's bare bottom and allow those areas to go into clam aquaculture. And that gets tricky because the sea grasses move. But clams do well in Alligator Harbor and help the economy. We're a society based on short-term profit motivations, so if we can show the resource is worth money, then we have a better chance of managing and protecting the resources.

"It gets even more absurd. Florida's economic base is tourism so we get our money for resource protection from the biggest threat to the environment. So we rely on our nemesis for financial support.

"The only thing that's going to save us is the land acquisition program. If we can tie the functional habitats together in a protected way, we can maintain both. And the public has every right to access except that we can't have [so much] access that we destroy the resource. You can love a resource to death just as easily as you can bulldoze it, and to the victim it doesn't matter whether it was manslaughter or murder one—he's dead.

6

Turpentine, Timber, and Restoring Tate's Hell

When we found the dwarf cypress, that was a beautiful thing.
Billy Kersey

"I carried Tate's grandchildren through Tate's Hell two summers ago," road builder Billy Kersey said with a wry smile. There was little chance they would get lost or snake-bitten—as their grandfather had—with Kersey at the wheel. For thirty-four years he had slogged through the swamp with machete and dragline, "breaking the country open" for Buckeye Cellulose Corporation's pine plantations.

"[Tate's] an old man that lived over there in Sumatra," Kersey continued. "And according to the tale, he went off into the swamp huntin'. Got lost. Got rattlesnake-bitten. He stumbled out on the highway just the other side of the lighthouse down here. [Wagon] come along, and he raised up and said, 'I just been through hell.'"

Kersey was also at the wheel when the Northwest Florida Water Management District investigated restoring the area to its natural state, haunt of Florida panthers and snakes that in 1873 preyed on Cebe Tate and his dogs and cattle.

Restoration specialists can only hope for such returns. The land was so thoroughly ditched and drained for pulpwood production that wiregrass died, and silty rainwater coursed from large clear-cut areas of bedded pine forests to tributaries and the upper bay, smothering roe and tadpoles. Titi thickets choked open grasslands. Named and numbered roads gridded wild habitat like a cityscape.

To restore the area requires that water flow and plants be returned to their original composition. Non-native pine stands must be logged; underbrush must be chopped and burned. Roads must be removed to reconnect and restore former wetlands, and culverts that siphon seepage water must be blocked. As tracts are restored, native wiregrasses return, river otters, deer,

Fig. 6.1a. Restoring Tate's Hell has required removing logging roads that dammed some sections and drained others and reflooding the unique dwarf cypress. A raised walkway permits visitors to stroll among hoary, hat-rack canopies. Photo by Faith Eidse.

and raccoons scamper, leaving tracks in the soft black mud. Hawks fly overhead again, able to hunt scurrying prey.

Recently restoration planners strolled a canopy boardwalk through a revived dwarf cypress stand off North Road. The logging road that bisected the unique community had been removed, the 150- to 300-year-old trees were reflooded, and their gnarled flat tops were greening with new life. The boardwalk was named for the late Ralph Kendrick, Buckeye Cellulose dragline operator and mechanic who became county commissioner from 1980 to 1984.

"You go along in the environmental field, and most times the best you can do is break even," said Riverkeeper Dan Tonsmeire, then restoration project coordinator for the District. "But here we actually gained ground in restoring a significant number of wetland acres." Culverts running under raised roadways have reconnected upper and lower basins on a natural grade. Culverts that once drained the lower basin directly into the bay have been plugged.

The first large ditches carved to drain Tate's Hell Swamp were evident in 1953 aerial photos. Intensive bedding, planting, fertilizing, logging, and road-building continued through the sixties and seventies.

In the late eighties, convinced that the landscape could not produce an economic product and concerned for impacts to fishery resources, Proctor and Gamble forestry interests decided to sell 215,000 acres. At first, a lack of funds and local support prevented the state from quickly developing an acceptable acquisition proposal at the $47-million asking price. Local opposition to state ownership held sway, and a real estate agent from Georgia, acting as intermediary, optioned the land. He sold six parcels as private hunting plantations. Residents of Franklin and Liberty counties soon called for public protection.

At that point, the Northwest Florida Water Management District sought to purchase buffers to protect water quality and quantity in the upper reaches of Apalachicola Bay, one of the nation's most productive fisheries. Preserving wetland functions and freshwater flows to East Bay were vital to the fish and shellfish nursery.

In 1992 and following, the District, the Florida Game and Fresh Water Fish Commission (now Florida Fish and Wildlife Conservation Commission or FWC), and the Florida Conservation and Recreation Lands (CARL program) designed a 214,000-acre preservation project, and the first 30,000-acre parcel was acquired. Management was split among the Division of Forestry (DOF) as Tate's Hell State Forest and FWC.

The first restoration parcel was a 28,000-acre purchase through Florida's Preservation 2000 program for about $8.5 million. The District and Florida Department of Environmental Protection (DEP) each contributed $3.5 million. The FWC added $1.5 million for its share of the land that bordered the Apalachicola River on Bloody Bluff.

Tonsmeire consulted local residents about historic flows and indigenous vegetation. He coordinated with federal and state agencies, District hydrologists, and local botanists to plan rehydration.

Tonsmeire can drive through Tate's Hell State Forest today and see that ten years of restoration efforts have raised the water table 2 feet on certain restored tracts. The unique dwarf cypress, a bonsailike variant, has been reflooded after forty dry years. Dense thickets of pine and titi are being cut, burned back, and returned to wiregrass habitat.

Federally endangered red cockaded woodpeckers are active in twenty-nine clusters, and threatened eagles nest again. Wildlife biologist Dan Sullivan identifies woodpecker nests from a helicopter, looking for cavities they excavate for years, releasing sticky sap to discourage climbing snakes and raccoons. Overhead osprey, turkey, great blue and little blue heron fly.

The District's restoration model was recently accepted as management

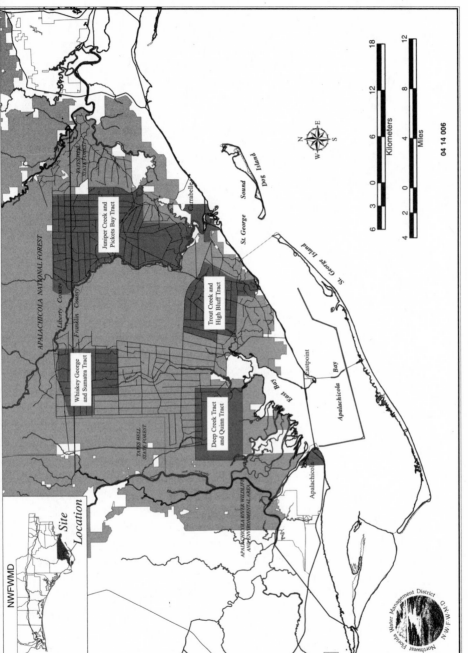

Map 6.1. East Bay/Tates Hell Swamp Restoration

Fig. 6.1b. Dan Tonsmeire discusses removing a road segment with forester Ace Haddock. Photo by Faith Eidse.

practice throughout Tate's Hell by the Division of Forestry as its first restoration mandate.

Certain natural ridges persist, such as the natural levee along the tree-covered banks of the New River. As floodwater left the river, it deposited sediment over the floodplain. Floods still spread 3 miles to Road 3, another natural ridge.

Near New River, planted pines were thinned three years ago and burned twice last spring. The land is gradually returning to a grass savanna. A tract across the road has been under restoration for over ten years and is now dominated by transitional bluestem grasses. Repeated burns have brought back the native wiregrass. Carnivorous sundew burst from the restored wet savanna. "If the soil is so poor that plants have to eat bugs to survive, there aren't going to be a lot of trees," Haddock said.

"If you continue to burn, more wiregrass and less bluestem grasses and woody shrubs will come back." Longleaf pines were struggling out of grass stage, and the tall, tanned Haddock studied their tender needles. In Tate's Hell, the "DOF doesn't bed," he said. It prefers to keep swamp elevations natural.

On the northern border of the restoration area, a machine with a bladed drum roller-chopped acres of thick titi. The brush would be burned in spring, just in time for the new wiregrass flowering season.

Tonsmeire and Haddock want to reconnect the wetlands, where roads hinder sheet flow and natural drainage courses. They have spanned wetlands with 60-foot bridges and reconnected them with low-water crossings. "The culverts aren't moving the water," Haddock said. "We want to get sheet flow across tracts that were once natural low areas." The University of Florida recently demonstrated laser elevation surveying by flying over a small area and plotting a point every 4 feet to help map natural hydrology.

Tonsmeire would like to see sediment wash reduced into streams and wetlands by crowning roads with vegetated slopes, he said as he crossed Warren Bluff Creek. Bees swarmed on blossoms along the creek that was gently babbling again.

Neel Yent: Panther Flight Memories

In October 1984, eighty-eight-year-old Neel S. Yent completed a rollicking memoir of panther pursuits and Union attacks on Tate's Hell. The oral histories he set down reached back to the lives of his father, Rufus M. Yent, born in Sopchoppy in 1851, and Grandfather DeYent, who dropped the "De" when he emigrated from France. Neel Yent was a Franklin County native, born on October 7, 1896, at the confluence of Whiskey George Creek and East Bay. Selected stories are reprinted here by permission of the Yent heirs, who each year award an Apalachicola High School academic scholarship in his name.

"Papa told of the night the family was sitting on their front porch, enjoying the enchantment of the bay sparkling [under] a beautiful full moon, when all of a sudden their cattle began to bellow and bawl. The entire family tore out for the cow pen, [where] a large panther [was] trying to drag a small calf over the rail fence. Their yelling and screaming scared the panther off, [and] the little calf was not killed.

"The next morning Grandpa loaded his muzzle-loading rifle, and he, the boys, and dogs went panther hunting. The dogs struck trail where the panther crossed the fence. They trailed him to a swamp about a mile away and treed him. Grandpa, with one shot, knocked him from his perch.

"A tragic event in the Yent home was the War between the States—known as the Civil War—which began in 1861. Papa was eleven years old [when] his two older brothers, Robert and Samuel, rode off on horseback to join the Confederate Army.

"Early one afternoon a Union gunboat came in sight, entering the bay through East Pass near Dog Island. A landing crew of several men came ashore in a small boat and burned their house down. They claimed that this was in retaliation for Grandpa shipping large quantities of fish to feed the Confederate Army.

Early one afternoon a Union gunboat came in sight, entering the bay through East Pass near Dog Island.

"My mother, Martha Agnes Neel, was born October 30, 1860, in the community then known as Ricco Bluff, near the little town of Bristol. Her father, William B. Neel, owned a large plantation and many cattle. Grandma Neel died when Mamma was five years old and her sister, Seanie, was three years old. Grandpa was a commissioned officer in the Confederate Army, and he didn't learn of this until he returned home riding a beautiful black horse. During this time Mamma and her sister were well taken care [of] by their grandfather, William Cox.

"Grandpa Neel owned a flourishing orange grove where today no one would plant an orange tree. [He] shipped his oranges by river steamboat to Columbus, to a wholesale broker named Hochstrasser in homemade [hickory] crates fashioned from logs taken from nearby swamps.

"Later Grandpa married a wonderful lady named Sophronia Prather. They had five children: Dan, Bill, Bob, Cleve, and Clara. Also they adopted a child, Susie Whittle. Mamma lived with her Grandfather Cox until she was fourteen years old. In the meantime, Grandpa had moved his family to Apalachicola, where he purchased a large parcel at the western border of the town on which he built a large, two-story home. [Mamma] moved to Apalachicola, saddened that she must leave her grandfather's home.

"Soon Grandpa became prominent throughout Franklin County. Apalachicola was a thriving and prosperous community with its large lumber industry and busy seaport. Grandpa established a large livery stable, which he outfitted with beautiful saddle and buggy horses, buggies (one seat), and surreys (two seats), forerunner of our present-day taxi and car rental enterprises.

"[He had two] fast-stepping solid black [horses]; one was named Black Satin, and the other, Midnight. The two, hitched together, always pulled the hearse, which was used by the local undertaking establishment, Cotter and Sangaree. It was a custom strictly adhered to that, as the procession started, church bells [tolled], and all store owners closed their front doors, claiming it was bad luck for the front door to be open when a funeral procession passed by.

"It wasn't long after that [Grandpa] was elected sheriff of Franklin County, a position he held for twenty-five years.

"Mamma and Papa were married at Mamma's grandfather's home at Bristol, October 18, 1876. Over three hundred guests attended by horseback, buggy, ox cart, and some afoot. Mamma was only sixteen and Papa, twenty-five. [Our family consisted] of nine devoted children [and] two orphans—A. A. (Buddy) Core and a girl named Mymie.

"In my earlier years, I would follow Papa to the field and toddle along behind him, barefoot, as he plowed. I loved the feel of the cool earth beneath my feet.

"It was my job to hold [the calf], which I would turn loose after [Mamma] finished milking. [One] morning the calf ran between my legs, and I was sitting backwards astride the calf and he began to bleat, run, kick, and squirm, and as he passed [a] pile of manure he kicked high, throwing me head first right into [it]. When I got to my feet, there stood Mamma [and] Papa almost in hysterics. Mamma said, 'Papa, I believe it would be easier to have another one than to clean him up.'

"Papa was given a contract to furnish a large quantity of cord wood for the electric light plant in Apalachicola. On the occasions Papa took me to town, he would give me a nickel. I would head for Mr. Jack Zingarelli's store, who sold the best roasted peanuts and the biggest bag for a nickel. He always took time to be nice to me. I was shocked and saddened when Jack Zingarelli was murdered in his store by a robber.

"Papa served as county commissioner in Franklin County for many years. It was on these trips, crossing the bay, that Papa taught me to maneuver a sailboat by snubbing the end of the halyard around the end of the tiller, which I could hold to keep the boat properly aligned with the wind's direction. Papa always knew how much sail a boat could take in any wind [and] when to reef the sail.

"One day Papa took me to town, and by the time we got to the dock, it was pitch-dark. The *Delia* was under full sail and splitting the water as she surged from a strong westerly wind. Sitting there watching the phosphorus spray, I said, 'Papa, it's so dark out here, how do you know which way we're going?'

"He said: 'Son, do you see that bright star right above the top of the mast? Well, I'm steering the *Delia* toward that star.'

"Then I asked, 'Suppose it was cloudy all over the sky and you couldn't see the stars?'

"He reached under the seat and brought [out] a little square box in which was a compass. He explained that God created only one spot at the top of the earth to which the needle of the compass would always point, and that spot was called 'North.' It would be impossible, without a compass, to steer a proper course at night if the stars were not shining.

"Papa was chosen as a delegate to attend the annual Methodist Conference in Tallahassee. So he and Mamma decided that I could go with him. The way to Tallahassee was by boat and train. The boat, a beautiful side wheeler, *Crescent City*, made daily trips from Apalachicola to Carrabelle. Every morning the train ran from Carrabelle through Tallahassee [to] Cuthbert, Georgia.

"I can well remember the thrill of boarding this great big boat and watching as Captain Andy [Wing] sidled her away from the dock. Papa took me up to the pilothouse and let me watch Captain Andy steer the boat with the large pilot wheel. Then he took me down to the engine room, where I first saw how a ship was propelled. Two engines pulsate[d] as they turned the two large side paddle wheels.

"In Carrabelle, we were standing by the train station when all of a sudden came the loud blast of a whistle [and] from around a curve came this huge monster approaching on the rails, black smoke billowing from its stack, bell ringing, steam hissing, and brakes screeching. If Papa had not had me by the hand, I'm sure I would have headed for the woods.

"The trip to Tallahassee was memorable, especially the speed of the train, which was perhaps 40 to 45 miles per hour. Papa explained how the train's wheels were made to stay on the steel rails and the train steered itself.

"Papa took me through the Capitol Building, and the thing that impressed me most was the old Civil War cannon perched on the front veranda. The return trip we went by train to Bainbridge, Georgia, and boarded the sternwheel river steamer *Callahan* and spent the night on her. The next morning we were met at a river landing called Bloody Bluff by Buddy Core with the horse and buggy.

"I was with Papa on a trip to Pensacola to visit my older sister Seanie. We traveled by the steamer *Tarpon*, mastered by Captain Barrow. The *Tarpon* plied between Apalachicola and Mobile, carrying passengers and freight.

"After Papa got me ready for bed, he held me up and told me to blow out the light. I blew and blew, and Papa was laughing all this time. He showed me how to click the light off and explained electricity.

"Papa designed a [two-story] building that would completely shelter the cane-grinding process. The building was supported only by long, stout columns on its outer perimeter. The floor was about 10 feet from the ground, which gave the horse or mule plenty of head room to walk in circles, operating the mill in the floor above.

"Cane grinding and syrup making was anticipated as a happy get-together. There was just some enchantment watching the horse, or mule, go around pulling the mill's tongue, feeding cane into the mill rollers, and the juice coming out of the spout into a large vat. Feeding the cane into the mill was one of my boyhood pleasures, and Papa had no trouble getting me up to start the day's grinding by the light of a lantern. Someone, usually Papa, had to stand by and continuously skim off the dregs, which were emptied into a barrel and would quickly ferment. It was called cane buck.

"Two of my sisters and I one afternoon poured a bucketful of buck in the hog trough. Much to our glee, those hogs in their drunken state were squealing, running in circles and falling down.

"When dipping the cooked syrup from the boiler, [Papa] would vigorously stir the remainder until it turned into a thick mass, and the children would mix this with other ingredients to make taffy candy. Then we'd indulge in a taffy pull.

"One day Buddy suggested fishing at Sand Beach Bayou. Instead of getting a shovel to dig [worms], he got the axe and a stob and said, 'I'm going to show you a new and easy way to get the worms out of the ground.' Buddy drove the stob in[to] the ground, leaving about 6 inches exposed. He then began rubbing the face of the axe across the top of the stob, which made a grunting noise.

"To my bewilderment, worms were crawling out of the ground everywhere, at least 20 feet from the stob. He explained that [he had] caused a vibration that agitated the worms and [that] this effect was first observed by a man splitting cordwood, which jarred the ground.

"[With] the first calls of the whip-poor-wills, usually on the first moon in March, it was time to round up the cattle, which were scattered 20 miles from home. My brother Rufus and [I rounded] up several hundred head, including lots of calves, 'bunching' them up in one large herd to be driven home. We called it the 'drive-around,' and some of the neighbors would always help [since] the herd would 'string' out for almost a mile. [At] Whiskey George Creek several miles north of home, the calves would usually have to swim across.

"One time when we started out on the roundup, Rufus and I had to swim our horses across Cashes Creek Ford, due to a flood. I was instructed to not try to guide my horse with the reins [since] I'd pull his head under the water, to just sit easy and his instinct would guide him to the other side. It did.

"From early spring to early July, we penned the cattle every evening, mainly to fertilize the ground [since] we never heard of commercial fertilizer. In May, with the help of neighbors, we marked and branded the calves. [I tended] the fire and [kept] the brands hot, to pass to Papa.

"Each year Papa would give each child a calf, marked in each child's registered mark. It was always a heifer so our little herd could multiply. In early July we'd drive the herd back to the east range where there was better grazing.

"One morning Papa and I left before daybreak on horseback headed for Juniper Ridge, several miles from home, to round up some beef cattle. We reached Juniper Slough when the sun was about an hour high. Papa was leading the way when, all of a sudden, his horse snorted and shied sideways.

Fig. 6.2a. A turpentine worker uses a hack to cut a "cat face" into a pine tree sometime in the 1930s. Photo courtesy of Florida State Archives.

As far as we could see there were countless hundreds of cottonmouth moccasins of all sizes feasting on tadpoles. They were so thick, some were crawling over each other. Papa said, 'Son, there's no way we can ride over the trail; you follow me.' He then took to the swamp through thick underbrush. I was glad when we reach[ed] the ridge.

"It was quite a while before we found the cattle, and Papa relieved my anxiety by telling me that by the time we reached the slough, [the snakes] would have eaten all they wanted and crawled into the underbrush. He was right. We drove the cattle over that same trail and never saw a snake.

"One afternoon Buddy and I were fishing at the mouth of Indian Bayou, a tributary of Lake Wimico. I suddenly noticed, lying on the shore, what appeared to be a log, but I immediately discerned it to be a giant cottonmouth moccasin. Buddy handed me his .30-.30 rifle and told [me] to 'put a bullet through his neck,' which I did. The snake [was] 4 feet, 10 inches long.

"Mr. Buck made a deal with Papa to lease the turpentine rights of Papa's vast timber holdings. He then established [a] distillery on the bank of Whiskey George Creek, 2 miles north of our home. The facilities [were] the distillery to convert the raw gum to spirits of turpentine and rosin; a cooper's shed for making barrels; a commissary; [a] house for the officials; shacks for the laborers; and a barn and mule lot. The commissary provided us many necessities that otherwise would require a trip to town.

"The hands were not paid by the day but were allotted a specific area [where] they chipped the trees, dipped the gum, and were paid per barrel. Payday was once a month. It was my assignment to take a wagonload of farm produce to the still on payday and peddle it among the hands. I later chose [salesmanship] as my life's vocation.

"Mr. Buck sold this business to the Creel Brothers—Doc, Tom, and Moot Creel—and established another still on the border of Cashes Creek about 3 miles east of our home. Buddy Core [superintended] for Mr. Buck until [Core] was elected superintendent of schools in Franklin County, an office he held for almost thirty years. His signature is on my high school diploma.

"Papa reserved about 400 pine trees surrounding our home place. I made a deal with Mr. Doc Creel that I'd chip the trees, dip the gum, and he would pay me $2 a barrel. My deal with Papa was, I would have to do this during my spare time. It was hard work, chipping trees with a heavy hack, and a full gum bucket becomes heavy to lug through the woods. All of this passed into oblivion when payday arrived. My crop of trees produced three barrels of gum. For some reason, I asked Mr. Creel to pay me [the $6] in dimes. Perhaps the rattling money just sounded good in my pocket. When I got home, Mama made me put $3 in my savings jar. I thank her for instilling in me the wisdom of thrift. I turpentined those trees until we moved from East Bay.

Fig. 6.2b. Barrels of gum accumulate at a turpentine still in northern Florida around 1930. Photo courtesy of Florida State Archives.

"It was [to] Creel's still one morning that I was sent on horseback to get 10 pounds of sugar. When I arrived I heard music coming from Doc Creel's house. On a table sat this little box with a tin horn, and from within the horn came music, the likes of which I'd never heard before. The name of the piece was, 'Listen to the Mockingbird.' I stood there completely stupefied. In a few years, Santa Claus (my sister Lena) gave me a nice Edison graphophone with a large horn that played cylindrical records.

"Papa and Mama decided to build a much larger house—one with seven bedrooms, a large kitchen, and dining room. The family moved, and practically camped, in the sugar mill house while the old house was being demolished and the new one built. As incredible as it might seem, however, there was no such thing as wire screen to put over window and door openings. In mosquito season, we slept under nets hung on a frame. If we had company, a family member would fan the flies from the table with shreds of newspaper glued to a broom handle. But one day, Papa brought from town a large roll of [screen], and soon we had [it] installed. What a happy day for the Yent family.

"There was a large deer that ranged around the west border of Tate's Hell Swamp that had eluded everyone who had tried to kill him. He was given the name 'Old Slick.' When the dogs jumped him, he held fast to the same pattern. Circling, he'd head west, swim across East River into the swamp, where he'd stay a few days.

"One Sunday in October after preaching was over, [one man] said, 'I don't believe there's a hunter in this part of the country who can bring him in.'

"Buddy spoke up, 'Well, fellows, I've given all of you a whack at him; now, the first cold morning we have, I'll take Old June and go up there and get him.' Old June was a black and white slow-trail hound Buddy raised from a puppy.

"Late one afternoon, Buddy said, 'Son, do you want to go with me in the morning and watch me bring Old Slick down?' We were up early the next morning, horses saddled and on our way. Soon after we forded Graham Creek, Old June began to range back and forth, sniffing the air. Buddy, who was riding a fiery horse named Maude, said, 'I believe he's bedded down in those palmettos.'

"Just as we approached, Old Slick jumped up, scaring Maude. She reared up and wheeled around, throwing Buddy off. He landed on his shoulders, holding his rifle high in one hand. I yelled that the deer was coming by fast to the left. He scrambled to his knees and simultaneously injected a cartridge, jerked the gun to his shoulder, and fired.

"Old Slick's hind end [went] straight up in the air into a complete somer-sault. Buddy got to his feet, picked up his black hat, and I realized that I had seen the most unusual rifle shot made. We walked over where the deer lay, a beautiful ten-point buck. The bullet that Buddy fired hit the deer just back of his head and broke his neck."

"I was plowing corn in the hammock field, which was close to the bay, and I heard this strange popping sound coming from Sheep Point. I fastened the mule to a fence post and tore out across the woods. I was astonished to see a boat without a sail coming up the bay, blue smoke trailing behind.

"The boat belonged to Mr. Ben McCormick, and he came over to tow a raft of logs for Papa to the sawmill in town. As I sat, charmed by the magic of that [gasoline] engine with its spinning flywheel, I hoped that some day we would have a boat with an engine.

"One day after a terrific tropical hurricane, [we] saw a white boat that had been washed up in the marsh across the bay. Some of the planking had been damaged, and we surmised it washed overboard from one of the seven large schooners that the hurricane piled up on Dog Island. Unable to find its owner, we remodeled [it] for a gasoline engine.

"Eddie Dameron completely rebuilt it for a pretty bright red [engine] with brass fittings, which he purchased from H. Marks, a local engine dealer. When Eddie cranked the engine and we were heading down the bay, about 8 miles per hour, I felt the day of paradise had arrived.

"Sister Sue was standing at the rear and her underskirt got caught by a set-screw in the shaft coupling, winding it around the shaft, and before Eddie could stop the engine, her underskirt was pulled off completely. Sue wasn't hurt, but [it] provided everybody a good laugh. I was permitted to navigate [it] alone, carrying beef and produce to town.

"One afternoon in August 1912 [when I was almost sixteen], Papa told me that he and Mamma were going to sell the home place to the Creel Broth-ers and all the cattle to Clave Neel, and were going to buy Ben Gibson's dairy farm in Apalachicola. This dairy farm, comprised of a 40-acre farm and a sizeable herd of dairy cattle, supplied the town.

"He said, 'Son, you must realize that all the children except you and Jack are grown up, and there's just you and [me] left to take care of all the farmwork.'

"Shortly after noon, September 12, 1912, all of us walked toward the landing where Creel Brothers' large boat, the *Covington*, piled high with all our belongings, was ready to begin the journey to town. The Creels [had] sent two wagon teams and plenty of help to transport everything to the dockside, [including] crates of chickens, turkeys, geese, and guineas. My as-

Fig. 6.2c. Opal and Neel Yent, November 1, 1968. Photo by permission of Rhonda Yent, Verne Klintworth photographer.

signment was to bring along old Tige, our favorite hog dog. When Tige and I reached the end of the lane, I had the feeling of walking away from a cemetery in which a loved one had been interred. Papa and Angus Morrison led the two horses and the mule.

"The trip to town with the *Covington*'s two engines churning the water took about one- and-a-half hours, and our arrival drew a number of spectators who probably thought Noah's Ark had just docked. The dairy farm owned a large two-team wagon, and it was there waiting for our arrival.

"Naturally, I was excited by wonderment of what this new life would be like. I felt for sure that easier times were ahead for me. I'd never again have to bail out leaky boats nor traverse turbulent water to and from town.

"The dairy personnel included three men; one of them, Marvin Quin, drove the delivery wagon. The milk was bottled in quart and pint bottles, and all of this was performed by hand, there being no bottling machines.

"The first day Papa firmly awakened me at 1:30 a.m. and told me to come on out and help with the milking. By daylight the milking was over, the milk bottled, and the delivery man on his way. Then the real work began; cleaning and flushing the gutters, scalding bottles and bottling equipment, preparing feed and [filling] feed bins. This routine was necessary through every day of the year.

"May 22, 1914, [was] the day I received my high school diploma. But I'm sure that one of the happiest days of my life was the day Papa sold the dairy and we moved into town."

In 1923, Neel Yent married Opal Graham, whom he'd met through a World War I squadron mate. After achieving district manager at Mack Truck Corporation in Tampa, he retired in 1962. He returned to East Bay in 1984 and picked up some chimney bricks, all that remained of his boyhood home.

Boncyle Land: Turpentine Stories

Florida's storied turpentine history started long before the late Earl Boncyle Steward Land (born in 1903) married C. C. Land in 1942 and moved to Land Still near Eastpoint. In 1935, author Zora Neale Hurston published the tall tales of Polk County turpentine workers in *Mules and Men*, tales that echo the stories in this chapter.

For instance, Mrs. Land's account of a boiler exploding and killing six men recalls Hurston's tall tale of a straw boss so mean that "when the boiler burst and blowed some of the men up in the air, he docked 'em for de time they was off de job."[1]

Early in the twentieth century, before falling to the sawmill, longleaf and slash pine were tapped for their naturally occurring plastic, or oleoresin. Turpentine became Florida's largest industry, and Florida became the world's leading turpentine producer.[2]

When heated and distilled, its vapors were captured as turpentine and used in medicine, as a disinfectant, and as paint thinner. The pine gum, or resin, has been used since ancient times as tar and pitch to waterproof ropes, cloth, and ships' hulls. Glues and varnishes from resin products were used by carpenters. Clay pots were glazed and sealed with resin. Eventually, hair spray, facial powder, lipstick, synthetic rubber and flavors, and even crayons were manufactured from the resin. But a forty-year decline began after World War I, when paper mills produced pine-resin chemicals by an extraction process.[3]

By 1918, Florida had clear-cut or lost to wildfire, 17 million acres of pine. Turpentining diminished and loggers replanted fast growing loblolly and slash pine instead of longleaf.[4] But C. C. Land, whose heirs reminisce in this chapter, continued tapping pine trees on Apalachicola Bay well into the 1950s. Gradually the family switched to logging and cattle breeding.

Clifford C. Land founded his turpentine operations in Tate's Hell in 1931, starting at High Bluff and moving to Greenpoint two years later. His second wife, Boncyle, graduated from the Huntingdon College for Women in Montgomery, Alabama, painted fine porcelain, and was a colorful pianist. She worked in the Crawfordville and Apalachicola welfare offices during the

Fig. 6.3a. C. C. Land ran a turpentine still in Tate's Hell during the 1930s and 1940s. Photo courtesy of Jerry Allen.

Fig. 6.3b. Boncyle Allen Land, stylish wife of C. C. Land, played piano and taught him to grade lumber. Used by permission of her son, Jerry Allen.

Roosevelt administration, one of the first social workers to visit homes and hand out food vouchers.

Her oral history was taped by architect Mays Leroy Gray on July 4, 1993. Gray had designed a working turpentine still for St. Andrew State Park, where Mrs. Land's granddaughter worked as a park ranger, interpreter, and collector of turpentine paraphernalia. Mrs. Land's son, Jerry Allen, gave us permission to excerpt the interview, which described local history; turpentine operations; workers' daily lives in shantytowns; woodsriders on horseback who oversaw them; feuds among turpentine families; and industry changes after World War II. We also interviewed Jerry Allen in Apalachicola in May 2002, but start with excerpts of Mrs. Land's interview.

"When [Mr. Land] moved down here and bought this place—I think it was '33—it was the old Robbins's place. There were four or five turpentine stills around Carrabelle. There was Pope. There was Mr. Robertson, and then Clivverts came in, Land Turpentine Company, L. G. Buck, a [Mr.] Creel. He was our neighbor.

"You see, the woodsriders for the turpentine had to ride horses. We had a big pasture of horses because we had to have woodsriders to watch [the workers] because they'd lay down and take a nap.

"And the first cups he had were clay cups. In the wintertime they'd freeze and break. Then they went to tin cups. They looked like flowerpots. And that wasn't very successful 'cause it could rust. The better cup you had, the better grade of gum you made. And then they went to aluminum cups. And aluminum made beautiful gum.

"They used [turpentine] for face powder and talcum; they used it in all kinds of cosmetics; the medical world used it. In fact, we used to bottle some ourselves, and they wanted fire-stilled. They didn't want that gum to be made by electricity.

"[Mr. Land] leased [Little St. George Island] for turpentine and grazing rights for hogs and cows. He had the house first on the big St. George, and that was one island at that time. Right before they put the sliced cut there. It was the worst mistake they've ever made. It damaged both islands.

"We're at Greenpoint. Greenpoint and Catpoint was on the map long before Eastpoint. They had all kind of fisheries down [at Catpoint]. A lot of Indian villages were along here. I've picked up pottery right in front of the house. From here to Porter's Bar was a big Indian village. The seafood was good. You could wade out there a long way.

"[Mr. Land's father] Charlie Lee Land lived in Wewahitchka. He was a big powerful statesman and a turpentine man. He was in the courthouse doing some business one day, and as he got him a drink of water, a man shot him in the back of the head and killed him.

"[Mr. Land] had him locked up. And then the State of Florida sent the man to prison down below the Suwannee River. The man was never allowed to come back across the Suwannee River. They didn't execute him. They should have because that was cold-blooded murder. He was hired, and he knew the people that hired him. And now, there was a lot of conflict back in those days and a lot of contention between people. Old families were like the Hatfields and McCoys, feuding. Turpentine people, feuding.

"They had jooks in those days. They played blackjack, and they'd had something to drink. [Mr. Land] was a deputy sheriff. He always carried [a badge], but that was—for protection—had to have some kind of law out here.

"Anyway, they were at the jook that night, and this man came at him, cutting him. The next lick was for him. And he shot him. He never got over it, either. He didn't want to kill that man. He said there wasn't an excuse for it.

"Now, a turpentine man was issued a crop of boxes, which is 10,000 trees. Now, he could take a week, or he could take two weeks. If they got half of it, why, they were paid. Every two weeks. And they went in the office, and they had a commissary, and they could charge there what they wanted to. But it was held out of their time.

"A naval store took care of your gum and sold it and carried it to Valdosta, Georgia, by truck. But at first he came down here for Lurtin and Company in Pensacola. That was one of the biggest naval stores in the South.

"The only way you could get it out of here at first was on [the Georgia Florida and Alabama railroad to Carrabelle, and from there] on the old *Tarpon*. And it would be shipped into Pensacola.

"[W. J. Boynton in Tallahassee] had a still, [and Mr. Clifford], in the later years, sent his gum up there.

In World War II, the government "just took" St. George Island, Mrs. Land said. "We stayed in a lawsuit for years about that. [Also, Mr. Clifford] had just leased all that timber on that other side of Carrabelle, and we just don't know how much money we lost. Liquid gold it was, liquid gold raining on that ground. And they wouldn't let us get back and get our cups, wouldn't let us get our gum that was running on the ground. And they shot those cups. We lost every bit of that.

"I know [World War II soldiers] had a awful time [in Harbeson City]. They would take those men over [to] train, and they'd crawl on their stom-

Liquid gold it was, liquid gold raining on that ground.

achs, and they didn't know anything about snakes, and the [rattle]snakes bit 'em. It was terrible.

"I felt so sorry because those poor boys had barracks with dirt floors and hard to get [fresh]water. They would come here and beg [Mr. Land] to sell them some of the [half barrels] to bathe in. Clifford gave 'em to 'em.

"The best slash is right on the coast. Saltwater slash will outrun any tree in the world. It makes the best turpentine. It makes the best rosin. Beautiful rosin. There's four grades of rosin. One of 'em's waterglass. That's the whitest. And one of 'em is amber, and rose."

At Sopchoppy, Mrs. Land witnessed a sawmill explosion. "I saw this boiler go up in the air and explode. Six [workers] were killed. And they hauled 'em [away with] trucks. And 'course, fire set in. I think it was Roberts sawmill. I'd always been frightened; I knew they'd better watch those boilers. The scary thing was there's steam.

"Spirits of turpentine is steamed. We had one of those [gauges], and it would tell you [the steam pressure]. But [our] stiller couldn't read it. He listened with his ear. And thank God he never had a blow up."

Asked about her sawmill family, Boncyle Land said: "Mr. Harbeson came from DeFuniak. We lived 20 miles from DeFuniak Springs. So Mr. Harbeson wired my father and asked him to meet him to show him [Tate's Hell swamp] and to see the land and to see the timber and all. Mr. Harbeson owned the San Carlos Hotel in [downtown] Pensacola. He wanted to put up an electric mill. And there wasn't any such thing in this part of the country.

"I knew the people from Harbeson City. The Harbeson daughter was one of my best friends up in Florala where I lived. But Mr. Harbeson had a son, I think moved down here account of the stake in the mill. But my father brought a portable sawmill down and cut the timber for Harbeson City to build this sawmill."

She added that a lot of timber was cut around Crooked and East rivers and that tram roads were built. "In the olden days those trams were pulled by oxen. And then they were pulled by mules. Father had some pulled by mules.

"The tram roads were very essential. And they weren't hard to build. But, see, we were very advanced because we had skidders. And we had portable sawmills. We had several of the big sawmills. It wasn't electric, but it was a big sawmill, much larger than Harbeson.

"We had one here [at C. C. Land Still]. My husband didn't know a thing in the world about a sawmill, but I knew something about a sawmill. So he built a sawmill here because he didn't want anybody knocking down his young timber. So I knew how to grade the lumber. My mother knew how to grade

Saltwater slash will outrun any tree in the world. It makes the best turpentine.

lumber. We had a chart. And so he learned to do that himself and with a very good sawyer, which is the life of a sawmill.

"See, there was an old cypress mill [at Apalachicola]. And they had some of the finest cypress that's ever been made came out of that Apalachicola River. It'd be black, and the black cypress is one of the most valuable timbers you can get, besides pecky cypress. Pecky cypress is very expensive, too, and that was hard to get. But most of those houses have black cypress walls or wainscoting and plate rails.

"All of the real good timber in Florida has been cut over. But you don't have the same kind of timber that you do in Alabama and Georgia. That longleaf yellow pine is yellow as butter, and the rings are almost as small as a pinpoint. [It makes] the very best hardwood. But this down here is different. You have slash pine, saltwater slash, and they run good turpentine, but they're not as good for lumber.

"[Mr. Harbeson shipped] by rail. I'm sure he had a spur that went on down [to Carrabelle]. Harbeson City was about 7 miles out of Carrabelle. [His electric sawmill] was an experiment. I don't know whether he had to generate [electricity] himself or [if] it came from Carrabelle. Carrabelle was kinda advanced. Carrabelle was [a] very old and very respectable place, and there're some [Greek] people, and they used to pick sponges off of Carrabelle, too, as well as at Apalachicola. 'Fact, they wanted to use Carrabelle as a headquarters for sponge, but the people objected.

"And they did the same thing in Apalachicola, but they weren't as hostile to 'em as Carrabelle was, but they went on down then to Tarpon Springs, and that's the reason that most of the Greeks left here and Italians. Most Italians were fishermen.

"[Mr. Chapman, the famous botanist], took an oak tree [at C. C. Land Still] and grafted a hickory nut to it. I believe that's the way it was, or vice versa. But they were two hardy trees. He tried to teach people to graft."

With her first husband, Virgil Allen, Mrs. Land moved from Birmingham to Sopchoppy. "We brought a portable sawmill, and we brought a skidder, and people came from miles around like it had been just invented, 'cause that skidder would bring those logs out to the sawmill. Now, my father was already down there [with] the sawmill, and he died in Wakulla County."

Mrs. Land died shortly after giving this interview. Her daughter-in-law, Anne Allen, described her as "petite with short red hair, dressed like she had just come out of a band box. She wore suits, always with pumps and hose, makeup, earrings, and matching necklace. She was never unkempt." Jerry Allen later sold C. C. Land Still to be developed as Gramercy Plantation.

Fig. 6.3c. Jerry Allen with carved fishing lures. Photo by Faith Eidse.

The Allens: Guarding a Turpentine Legend

Jerry and Anne Allen have a rare turpentine history to preserve. Florida State University swim teammates who spent their honeymoon tending turpentine holdings at Little St. George Island, they have guarded their legacy ever since. Mr. Allen, at age seventy-two, spry, tan, and white-haired, told his story while selling tickets for Apalachicola's eleventh Annual Historic Homes Tour on May 4, 2002. Later, despite crippling multiple sclerosis, Mrs. Allen hauled out a museum's worth of artifacts, such as aluminum coin tokens, known as scrip, or "jugaloos." Workers were paid 40 percent in cash and 60 percent in tokens that were honored only at the turpentine still commissary.

Allen described working in the commissary from age twelve, and C. C. Land successfully defending himself against a charge of peonage for paying wages in scrips.[5] Allen also explained the turpentine process step-by-step and recalled the rough working and living conditions in the still's twelve shanties. He described a card game called "Skin"; a hog-feed distillation beverage called "buck"; and stove pipe segments used to protect against rattle-snakes, or "Bell Cows." Finally, he extolled fishing in Tate's Hell.

"I went out one time on the dip wagons pulled by a mule, and you rode

Fig. 6.3d. A woodsrider oversees turpentine workers in 1930s Florida. Photo courtesy of Florida State Archives.

for four days. You worked from can to cain't. And they gave you a dip bucket and a little paddle, which you went from tree to tree and dipped the gum out of the cup and scrapped it into this bucket. When that bucket was filled, you took it back to the dip wagon, and it was dumped into a wooden barrel, and around ten o'clock my hands were beginning to really hurt. And the [workers waited] that long to show me to go over to an old rotten tree and rub the rotten wood in your hands, and that insulated it against the gum.

"That's where I learned the common lunch was canned sardines and vanilla wafers. Most of them carried a tin bucket, which their wives packed for 'em in the morning [with] some kind of pork and some kind of bread, either corn bread or biscuits, and always cane syrup.

"The dip wagon was brought back to the still, and one of the biggest men 'headed it over.' He pulled that barrel sideways and rolled it up a ramp to [the loading] platform. Then the raw gum was put into a large kettle, and it was cooked. The spirits of turpentine was distilled off the vapor, and then there was a long trough—6 feet by 10 feet. That had four wooden trays with different size strainers in it, and that hot liquid gum was poured into that, and of course that caught all the impurities so that you had pure gum at the bottom, which was then decanted off and put into a metal barrel.

"The metal barrels came in halves, and we had a cooper bend a flange over it [to make] a complete barrel [and] pounded a lid [on], and then it was ready for shippin'.

"Now the base of that ol' still is still over on the property. It was right on [Route] 98 near 65. It's Gramercy Plantation now. You can't miss it. If you drive on past the entrance real slowly and look over on your left, you'll see a mound and you'll see old brickworks. And there are six or eight barrels of the old rosin, still there.

"The stiller, who is that man that controls the breathing mechanism [for the airtight distillation process] did not have a long lifespan. They kept an electric meter that told 'em exactly what the temperature was, and they kept it that temperature all the time." A temperature of 290 degrees Fahrenheit was required to evaporate turpentine, but if it rose above 290 degrees, the still could explode.[6]

"[In the commissary], we had whole sides of salt pork in a bin, and that was one of the staples. I sold Wolverine brogans, heavy leather work shoes. Tin goods were called 'iron rations.'

Allen added that he found his grandfather's buggy rifle in the commissary and asked to keep it. His grandfather had sawed the muzzle off so that it would fit, propped between knees and floorboards, ready to lift and shoot a panther at a moment's notice. "Panther was really the only problem in those days," he said. "It was the only predatory animal that they were afraid of.

"The wage and hour law is what killed the turpentine business because it was piece work. Whenever that came in, we converted to cattle. An educated guess would be 1948 or '49."[7]

"It was a very rough life," Allen said.

"They carried a cutter, a [foot-long] piece of metal on a wooden handle with a counterweight on the bottom. They had a triangle file, [which] was ground down, and it was razor sharp. They used this [file] to cut up and clean the inside of that cutter head."

"[Land was] a man who had no hobbies—100 percent business. He had an eighth-grade education but could sight-add columns of figures. A very abrupt-appearing man, but he had a heart of gold. On Christmas morning, every [worker] was at the back door yelling, 'Christmas gift, Christmas gift.' After he died, I went through his papers, and he had given money to needy families in Eastpoint.

Fig. 6.3e. Jerry and Anne Allen. Used by permission of the Allens.

"He was a railroad detective [by age eighteen] in Pensacola, and he had a bullet scar that ran across [his cheek] from a .38 caliber bullet. Mr. Land would never sit with his back to a window, and he always carried a pistol."

Allen was along one day when Mr. Land rode his favorite horse into the swamp. Mr. Land used his pocketknife to clean mud from the horse's hoof. The knife slipped, and the horse bled to death. "There was nothing anyone could do," Allen said, "because he had hit a major artery where a tourniquet wouldn't reach.

"Mr. Land was not afraid of anything but a little honeybee. Once a bee flew into the truck cab, and he jumped out and let it go crashing into the woods."

Those summers "showed me that I durn sure better get in school and get an education. I didn't want that life. I graduated from FSU when it was still a branch of the University of Florida. I was lifeguard and waterfront manager at Wakulla Springs," where Anne swam professionally for the motion pictures.

"Anne and I were married and got on [C. C. Land's] tugboat and went to Little St. George Island [for] our honeymoon, checking on the cattle and the [workers] during that two-week period.

"[Mr. Land] had a towboat and a barge, and we built temporary quarters for the [workers] over there. They'd bring the gum down to the dock, and we barged it over. Now, in front of his house there was enough land at that time that he had cattle corrals and enough deep water to bring that barge in there. Now it's so eroded and filled in that you couldn't do anything with it.

"All of the [workers] who had worked turpentine had to find jobs elsewhere. I think he kept four for his cattle operation. Back then he paid $10,000 for his prize bull and even had a insurance policy on the thing."

Jerry Allen retired as vice president of Mortgage Lending after twenty-one years with Apalachicola State Bank. Since 1989, "I fish everywhere. I just got through fishin' off St. Marks light and the Ochlockonee River. But I have a camp up on [State Road] 65, and I bass fish up there two weeks outta the month.

"[Whiskey George] Creek that I'm on goes up and splits into five channels and then comes back together and goes on forever. You've got to know which channel to go on, and then it's just a straight shot up into the National Forest. It's jet-black water.

"Over here [in Apalachicola], you have to wait to launch your boat. I don't like people pressure. 'Course it's fished harder now with the influx of

Fig. 6.4. Tate's Hell road builder Billy Kersey with the "splinter" that was surgically removed from his leg. Photo by Faith Eidse.

people, but you still catch the same species of fish. I caught bass, several varieties of bream, striped bass, which have been introduced to the river, large mouth bass, speckled trout.

"The spoil piles that they're putting on the sides of the river are stopping the bream from going out in the river at high water to bed. I don't fish over there.

"[Oysters are] on the decline. Now what they are catching we threw away when I first moved here. We could go on the inside of [St. George] Island and wade and we'd see just this bill stickin' out of the sand, and when you pulled it out, that oyster would be like this." Allen measured 8 inches.

Allen has hunted for years along Whiskey George Creek for three slaves' graves, reportedly located there. He and Anne recommend novels like Rubylea Hall's 1947 *The Great Tide*, which provide an emotionally rich history of the area.

Billy Kersey: Building Roads through Hell

Billy Kersey was born in Carrabelle in 1937 and raised his family on the road to Tate's Hell. A descendant of the original Creek inhabitants, he worked three decades in the legendary swamp, operating heavy equipment and facilitating pulpwood pine production. He also told about his father, a forest ranger, killing a truckload of bear in Tate's Hell, and narrated many other swamp survival rules.

Kersey was among the work crew that discovered the unique dwarf pond cypress at Dry Bridge and John Allen roads. Trees estimated at 150–300 years old but only 7 to 10 feet tall. They are the same species as pond cypress but were stunted by low nutrients, hard clay soil, and year-round flooding.

Kersey also noticed the hollowed topography and layered sediments that indicate once-submerged land. Millions of years ago, ocean currents eroded a wide trough into the continental carbonate rock, which became known as the Gulf Trough. Subsequent deposits pushed the carbonate crust down and created the Apalachicola Embayment. It was reworked by rising and receding sea levels, wave action, and rainfall drainage.[8]

The blue and white marl Kersey turned over while road-building are Miocene, Pliocene, and Pleistocene sediment deposits,[9] atop limestone that plunges so deep that pioneers had to drill 300-foot artesian wells to access the Floridan Aquifer.

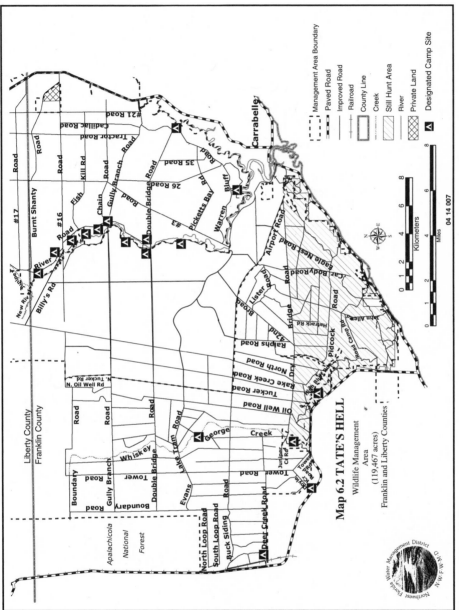

Map 6.2 TATE'S HELL

Wildlife Management
Area
(119,467 acres)
Franklin and Liberty Counties

Management Area Boundary
Paved Road
Improved Road
Railroad
County Line
Creek
Still Hunt Area
River
Private Land
Designated Camp Site

04 14 007

Kilometers

Miles

Map 6.2. Tate's Hell

Kersey's wife, Martha, also joined the oral history on December 3, 2001. She discussed teaching during integration and her rise to assistant principal in Carrabelle.

"We watched the whole neighborhood build," Kersey said. "Goin' on down River Road there was an old Indian house. Indians [had] lived in it years ago. I have no idea what tribe or nation," Kersey added, "but my grandmother's mother was Indian. In my younger life I stayed in the woods, [and] we found all kind of arrowheads.

"I went to work with Buckeye in '59; 1960 they put me on St. Vincent's Island marking the timber. The inside beach was old shell mound near 'bout the whole length of the island. I ran [my machine] through a pot [that] still had charcoal in it. The fire box was square, and then it had a bowl built on top of it.

"Another time I was on the north end of [Tate's Hell] when we was pushing the boundary line road—Road 17 next to New River—and we had crossed a tram [road] and pushed the tram off to leave the tractor there. There laid a [rusted utensil]. It was heavy, and I hit it on the tractor, and it busted all to pieces, and it was clay filled.

Kersey opened a map of Tate's Hell. "[Buckeye] owned Tate's Hell [to the] Apalachicola National Forest. We found flint chips where they had built the arrows; broken arrowheads most any place you'd find a ridge cut pretty close to the river. There's 182,000 acres that the company owned. We built nearly 800 miles of road on it. Northwest Florida Water Management is trying to correct what we did. And you got a road nearly every mile and every half a mile, [and] we planted pine trees on it all the way across that property.

"To start off with, we had four draglines. And then we got excavators, back hoes on tracks, four of those. There was Mr. Davis, and Ralph Kendrick, Harry Simon, A. J. Taylor, Zeke Corley, J. P. Incolade, Herbert Davis, and myself over the period of years. The roads was built actually to get the logs out and to drain the water and to do our choppin', plowin', and plantin'. All of our big dragline roads, water's gonna hit [from the north] and run east. We'd run some of them north too. Up here's the only place it ran north next to New River [into the National Forest].

"Well, some of them go to the west too," Kersey said. "See, it has three breaking points [draining divides]. And I don't remember exactly where they are." Dry Bridge Road was so named after work crews dug a ditch, bridged it, and then received no water in that direction. "In here it would run down [to East Bay]. This was Highway 67, and the water will about stand still on the east side of the highway."

We built nearly 800 miles of road on [the swampland].

"There was Harbeson City [north of Carrabelle on State Road 67]. During the Second World War, [trainees] shot it all to pieces, see?" Kersey said. "And my daddy was the county ranger, Florida Forest Service. But when I was a kid, Harbeson City burnt. And belts of machine gun bullets, hand grenades was goin' off. And then after I went to work with Buckeye, we burned it again and then planted it.

"Camp Gordon Johnston was on St. Joe land [stretching 21 miles east of Carrabelle to Ochlockonee Bay]. Lanark was where the officers lived. And then this [St. George Island to Alligator Point] was an amphibious training camp—one of the largest in the United States.

"I don't know when the last people lived in Harbeson City, probably [at] the mill pond out there. There's some flowin' wells out there, artesian wells. The government made us stop 'em up.

"All of the little creeks and drainage that was naturally there, every time we throwed a bed up on it, that was a dam," Kersey said. "There's thousands of them. I know over time they wash down. We planted it all. The only place we didn't really plant was in Picketts Bay [at the confluence of New and Crooked rivers above Carrabelle].

> Every time we throwed a [road] bed up . . . that was a dam.

"See, at Gully Branch that was a big turpentine still. They got a 6-inch flowing well there. At the Parker Place on New River, there's a big flowing well there. It's below Cat Branch. And over in here [off State Road 65] there was another big one. Now, when the tide rose, the well would flow harder and higher. Them wells is over 300 foot deep. And all of them drilled by hand.

"[Before pine plantations, there were] titi, wiregrass flats," Kersey said. "And then you'd have ponds that would be black gum and cypress. Well, all this in here, what we called flat-top cypress, when it quits growin' [the] top flattens out in it. And it's juniper. Juniper everywhere.

"[The dwarf cypress] are just about 5 miles up behind the house here. I was in the crew when we found them, when we went to build a road through them. That had to be in the sixties. And when they bored 'em for age they was 250 years old.

"[From State Road 65] go down Buck Sidin' Road until you hit Barry Road, turn down it 'til you get [to] Dry Bridge Road, left on it a little ways, and there they are.

"And when we first found them that was a beautiful thing. And after we put the road through it for the first years, it was beautiful. But then the titi and the pine tree began to encroach on them, and so it took some of the beauty away. You could go through there at certain times and catch the mist rising, and it was spooky looking. And then you'd come through there at times with the clouds casting shadows on it in places, and it was real pretty.

"Like I told Dan [Tonsmeire], 'I don't care what you do in none of the rest of the park, just don't kill them trees.' I think at one time Tate's Hell was either a branch of the Apalachicola River come acrosst here or something like East Bay or Big Slough that ran up in there.

"Diggin' roads you get up next to the river; we called it gumbo, marl, or whatever. Some of it would be blue, some of it'd be white. It was like clay [but] when you get a distance away from [the river], then you start hittin' reg'lar dirt. So that tells me at one time this creek or river, was yay wide, and that was [sediment] that had filled in over the eons of years.

"I even flew it in a airplane, just through my work, and you can take these little cypresses all the way to Owl Creek. They're not as small as these are down here, [which are] 7 foot high, if that high.

"[The most unusual animal I collected] was the [exotic] walking catfish; walks with his fins. He can walk across land and go to another pond. In [my] aquarium I never seen them swim. They'd always walk on the bottom.

"The tram roads were dug by Harbeson City, and I guess the [saw]mills that was in Carrabelle. We'd find a piece of rail every now and then, and cross ties. If they were finished logging here, they'd pick 'em up, move 'em. When they hit wiregrass flats, a lot of times the track floated. When the train hit it, it sank, see?

"We prob'ly got the cull of the original growth and second growth. I was told that Harbeson City, the [pine] tree that they cut down had to be at least waist-high, layin' on the ground. There [are] pictures . . . of pine forest, and a man looked like a matchstick standing up 'side trees. And I seen [old-growth] timber between here and the Burnt Bridge; it was a place there called Section 10. And that had been turpentined, and my understanding, there was a lot of bloodshed over that. Those [old-growth] trees was big enough when they was cut I could walk a D-6 Caterpillar up on the stumps. They was prob'ly pretty close to 4 foot in diameter at the ground.

"Oh, Lord, if you send me a gun, I'll send you a soul."

"C. C. Land owned quite a bit over here just east of 65. And I've heard they had a cuttin' over there. One [worker] cut one's throat, said he stuck the turpentine and wiped it all over his throat; sealed the blood off. He walked about 6 miles to a house. And he beat on the door, and they wouldn't give him a gun. So he looked up and said, 'Oh, Lord, if you send me a gun, I'll send you a soul.'

"[Burnt Bridge] got set on fire during a strike. That one burnt bad and several more smaller ones. And roofing tacks was scattered all over the highway. It was townspeople [who] thought they was helping. We went back to work for 25¢ less than what we struck for. See the mill at Perry there was 800-som'm workers down there. Over here there was only forty-two.

"[The army] used to use St. George as a bombing, strafing range. We caught a lot of bombs that went off [in our nets]," Kersey laughed. "Concertina wire, jeeps.

"Saw a lot of bears. My daddy was [the ranger] at St. James Tower, between here an' Sopchoppy. He was goin' up the tower, heard a hog squealin.' And he looked down the road, and that old sow bear had caught a hog and was tryin' to train her cubs how to kill the hog.

"That night Daddy and his first cousin, Mr. Don Hance, they killed a pickup truckload'a bear. The bed of the pickup truck was rounded out with bears.

"Mr. Don owned bees. We would take turns a-settin' up with bees. Mr. Don and his boy Donny would set with them one night, and me and Daddy set with them the next night. He'd move 'em next to the river, where they'd get tupelo. And the rest of the time he moved 'em where they could get titi or wildflower. And there's always a bear there. I mean, he just moved it from one bear to the next.

"Game department came to Daddy and Mr. Don and asked them, said, 'Would you all please quit killing the bear?' So they built a trap out of chain-link fence, but the bear picked the gate up and walked out. So they had to come up with a locking mechanism. And then they would take and punch holes in his ears and put a forest service tag in and haul him all the way over to the Big River. Three days later they'd catch the same bear again."

Kersey chose a red and white marbled arrowhead from his collection, the center shot through with solid garnet. He contrasted it with an asymmetric arrowhead. "Now, see that? They made mistakes. I always say that one's for shootin' around curves." He selected a 3-inch tooth. "That was a gator. [We] found the bones and the scales on [Route] 98 where Tate's Hell Trail begins. You hit the sign goin' one way, it says, 'Enterin' Tate's Hell.' Come from the other way, says, 'Leavin' Tate's Hell. Aren't you glad?'

Kersey pointed out an eight-point trophy on the wall. "That was the largest deer I ever seen right here [in Tate's Hell], not countin' the [Edward] Ball and St. Vincent [parks]. They came from India. They are 600 pounds, 800. Used to there was zebra, eland, black buck," Kersey said. "[Eland]'s the largest antelope in the world. Back when the government bought [the island] they had 'em killed.

"I haven't hunted in twenty years," Kersey continued. "There're just so many people in the woods. I had my machine shot, with me working [in it]. That's the reason why I quit, on 'count of the kids with high-powered rifles. Today they just throw 'em out and give 'em a gun, and that's all the supervision they get.

"There was a woman lost on the property for four days before she was found," Kersey said. "They was camping. And her and her son, four, maybe five, left camp to go to the store. She had a little bitty car. When she ran out of gas, she pushed the car out of the road underneath some trees. The airplane couldn't see it. Anyhow one morning, man goin' to work drove up on her. They was hungry, didn't have no water. She wouldn't drink out of the ditch. Which I did, out of a pond where it wa'n't nothin' but green scum. Pushed the fish out the way, lay down in the ditch, drink all you could hold.

"Carry your lunch bucket 'cause that was weight you had to carry. You took all your pennies out of your pocket. Most of those roads we cut [waist-] high with a machete, some of 'em purdy near 15 miles long."

Martha, Kersey's wife, is concerned for the livelihoods of Carrabelle's students. "They're thinking, 'I'll always have the bay to make a living with.' And you just kept trying to convince them that it might not be there in a few years. When huntin' season started, they evacuated the schools, and we finally got through to the parents, and it got where they would wait until the afternoons and bring 'em back the next day."

"You can't believe this in Carrabelle now," Kersey concluded, "the waterfront [of] five years ago, it's not there no more. [Land dealers] bought and then the condominiums is goin' in. See when I was young, there were fish houses 'n' frame rails and gill net spreads."

7

Logging "Eternal Wood"

This area was cut so clear you could see all the way from Hosford to Wilma with hardly a tree to break the view.
Betty M. Watts

The Apalachicola floodplain is home to a hundred plant species, many of them northern varieties carried downstream from the Appalachian Mountains. Cypress, tupelo, and mixed hardwoods thrive in alluvial wetlands dominated by variable flow, substantial flooding, and heavy sediment loads.[1]

The area was intensively timbered from the mid-1800s through the mid-1900s. Cut-over lands in the Apalachicola National Forest were replanted by New Deal work programs, to feed large regional steam-driven sawmills.[2] Those mills have given way to dozens of privately operated electric sawmills. It is estimated that only 3 percent of the original longleaf pines still stand, less than 3 million of 90 million acres that once covered the land from Texas to Virginia.[3]

About 10 percent of the logs were lost to the river as they were floated to mill in Apalachicola. The value of this heart pine and cypress is about $7.50 a board foot, almost four times that of a fresh-cut, "green" tree, according to Gordon Roberts of the DEP.[4] Growth rings are close, and the wood is impervious to anything but fire.

In the mid-1970s, the Florida Game and Fresh Water Fish Commission (now FWC) determined that pulling up sunken logs removed fish habitat and river structure, and the practice was prohibited for almost twenty-five years. An economic downturn prompted renewal of deadhead leases by 2000, but with regulations. A $5,000 sovereign submerged land permit was required to retrieve such lumber. The DEP uses inspectors, environmental assessments, harvester education, and random inspections to control recovery of sunken lumber. A charge of logging sovereign lands led to sawyer Cairo Ingram's arrest and eventual exoneration. Ingram's story is featured in this chapter.

Fig. 7.1. A logging crew uses caissons (high-wheeled ox carts) and a locomotive to clear woods in 1900s Florida. Photo courtesy of Florida State Archives.

The government is actively restoring longleaf pine forests as Americans consume a pickup truckload of paper per person, per year. Currently logging is managed on District lands, with old-growth pines harvested at about fifty-plus years, and hardwoods, depending on species, at 75 to 150-plus years.[5]

Don Ingram: Milling "Old-as-Christ" Cypress

Cypress sawyer Don "Cairo" Ingram came to Apalachicola from Cairo, Georgia, with the Florida Power Company while still in his early twenties. After work he'd watch Bud Seymour build shrimp boats. One day, Seymour offered to build Ingram a boat if he could find some good hardwood.

"I got a sawmill 'cause I wanted a shrimp boat," is how Ingram told it on February 2, 2001. The last big sawmill in Apalachicola, Tildon, had closed in the 1950s, having milled 50,000 board feet a day.

Even before he secured an old sawmill, though, Ingram found the largest deadhead he would ever scale on Johnson's Slough, while lost on a squirrel hunt. The year was 1968 or '69, and Ingram stayed with the log until a fishing boat found him.

That experience started a business that lasted twenty-five years and shipped cypress around the world. For another four years, Ingram ran BBT (Big Boys' Toys), operating bulldozers and tread cranes for fill and lumber operations. He retired at fifty-five and sold his sawmill site on Bluff Road in Apalachicola for a housing subdivision.

"I heard the largest [deadhead] Sheip's ever got was 88 inches [diameter] up, high," he said. "You scale a log by its small end; the scale figures in the taper of the log. So it's always 'inside bark diameter,' ibd.

"That log [I found] was 52 inches, so you got 26 inches—that's one side of it. And let's just say it's easy fifty to eighty growth rings per inch. So let's say, times 26. [That's 1,300 to 2,080 years old.] And guess what? We didn't have the bark or the sap on this log; it'd rotted off, which was then about 2 or 3 inches thick.

"I found it before I ever had a sawmill. It took me two years to find it again. [The first time I found it] we'd go up on the houseboat and saw us trees the night before hunting season. So everybody went hunting at daylight, generally. But nobody went huntin' with me 'cause I shot a rifle; everybody else shot a shotgun. But in Georgia you done shoot with a rifle [so you can eat it].

"And you generally had to shoot it in the head. So I got off of the boat, and I took off. And everybody else, they went one way, and I went another. And I got lost. And I found these logs—just a lot of logs in these sloughs. And so I went back as far as I could, and it got so much water, I couldn't cross it. And I said: 'Well, I got plenty of squirrels and matches and a gun. I'm'a wait right here 'til somebody comes up here.

"Well, I wa'n't there very long, and I heard a boat. And I hollered, 'Hey.' I heard that boat crank up and come closer, and it was Anthony Taranto and his wife. I had got two creeks over from where I was s'posed to come out.

"I got two brothers I told 'em about it. We was just up there lookin'. And one of my brothers said, 'Hey,' lookin' through the woods. He said, 'Someone used to build a road through here.' Now you talkin' 'bout swamp, you know. He said: 'Look through here. Look both ways, far as you can look. There's no trees any bigger than about that big around.'" Ingram indicated 4 inches. "Sure enough—that was the pole boat road they had cut to go get this timber. And for some reason it must not got enough water that year or somethin', and they never went and got any of these logs.

"Okay, let me tell you. All the years that I logged a sawmill—the boys always called it a 'hit'—they'd make a hit right before Christmas. The water'd come up in December; they would go get a bunch of logs. And then the big [flood] was in April. We could always tell when things started puttin' out [of] the woods, you could bet it was gonna be some water comin' down there. Now we got water—and you generally needed about 20 foot at Blountstown, [which is] about 88 miles by the river.

"[Johnson's Slough was] fifteen minutes from my house in the boat. See what happened, there was about eight sawmills here when I started. And then everybody went out except me. Mr. [George] Walker was one of the old-timers, but he's already gone. He showed me where all the jillion board feet were.

"He worked for Sheip's. And everybody worked for them big sawmills back then, and they knew where they cut down timber and the water didn't come up and never get 'em.

"He came out one day, told me my sawmill wouldn't work. See I hooked mine up electric, and it didn't make no noise, so when you clicked mine on, you heard just a saw blade turning, and he says, 'You got to listen to that engine,' he says. 'Them old gov'nors open up,' and he says, 'that's how you know you're sawing.'

"I said: 'Well, Mr. Walker, mine's not on chain speeds. The electric motors will maintain my 540.'

"'Nope. Never do. It won't work.'

"The day he died he was sittin' at my sawmill, and they took a picture. He wore a black hat, and he stuck his tongue out. He said: 'I b'lieve I'll go home. I ain't feelin' too good.' It was real hot. He went home and had a heart attack.

"The best trees was cut down with an axe and cut off with a cross cut. The best reason I ever heard, a person got paid by the tree when the tree fell in the woods. They might have got a quarter. Every log back then had a mark on it. Whoever cut it down put their mark on it.

"It'd be like a four-leaf clover, it'd be like two *x*'s, it'd say, 'This is Sam that cut down this tree.' And people got paid so much [to] cut it in two. Ninety percent of the logs that I sawed—out of the river—was cut down with an axe. And probably 20 percent of them was cut in two with an axe.

"I saved one log one time. I went up in Jackson River and found a pine log that was 54 foot long and about 18 inches on the small end. And it was cut down with an axe and cut in two with an axe, and it had a diamond shape with an *S* in it, and the best we can tell—that was Sheip's burned into it. And I cut that off and gave it to George Wefing. Now, one of the boys that worked for me, I cut him a keel out of that log—Ronnie Martina. His daddy built him the most beautiful boat. Go down there to the millpond—you'll see it sittin' there–the *Night Stranger*. And it's about 60–65-foot shrimp boat.

"Never did [get a shrimp boat]. What got me in the sawmill business was watching Bud Seymour build *Buddy's Boys*. When I moved here that was the biggest boat I ever seen sittin' in a man's yard. And onliest thing layin' there was the keel, the bow stem, and one stern board, and there's this real peculiar Buddy. And he made everything with a hatchet. He'd cut all the knuckles and everything. He had a hatchet that was filed two different ways. One second he was cuttin' this way, and 'fore I knew it he was cuttin' this way.

"Joe Lindsay in Sumatra was the only miller around when I wanted logs sawed. And Joe was ancient. He had bought a lot of land around Sumatra, Apalach, Eastpoint.

"We got [the log in Johnson's Slough] with a set of blocks. Boat blocks. You could run up there, hook 'em to a tree, and take a boat and pull it out. The ancient way.

"And when we got it in the river, of course, it sunk. So we drug it. And we brought it down—and it stayed down at my landing for like, two years. My dozer wouldn't pull it out—just got one end way up—and that's where it stayed. We didn't have nuthin' big enough.

"My brother came down one time. I says, 'Hey, let's go down and get that log.' We went down there on a real cold, cold day. It looked like the river was on fire, so much steam. And we took two axles like out from underneath a truck. And we took a skidder and my D-4 [Caterpillar], and we picked that log up with a winch, and we put logs under it—little short logs? And we rolled it out on the bank, and then we dug a hole here and hole here, put the axles in there and then spun the log back, and we made the log—the trailer. And then we slanted these holes, and then we took the dozer and the skidder and pushed 'em out, and that's how we brought it home.

"At the old sawmill, the front axle or something broke on it, and it rolled off, and it stayed there for two years. Right there 'side the road—everybody remembers my sawmill, remembers that log. This is what was so crazy—it was like a princess, it was so pretty. I mean no doohicks—nothin'.

And Busch Gardens—I drove to St. Louis—sent 'em pictures of the log, and they said, 'We would'a bought it—and we will buy it in two years from now—but we've already started the Dark Kingdom,' or something down there. They had no place to put it. The state, of course, wanted me to give it to 'em. I said: 'Uh-uh, no. I'm not givin' it to ya.'

"So I was shippin' lumber to Caldwell Tank, back then—in Louisville, Kentucky—by rail. And one day I [said], 'I'm gonna cut that log.' So I went up there and cut it in three sections. And I got me a new chain saw and split the first two sections. Cut it down one side with a chain saw, rolled it over, and cut it on the other side. Took wedges and busted it open like an apple.

"The butt cut—I had to quarter it and cut it up. And I sawed it and I sawed it. Five thousand foot of tank cypress out of it. Took me one day to split it and one day to saw it. It was used for food processing tanks. All your food, this day and time, all your chopping blocks, gotta be made out of cypress. They done away with oak, 'cause oak is porous. The last big project,

> It looked like the river was on fire, so much steam.

> [The log] was like a princess, it was so pretty. I mean no doohicks— nothin'.

they built three tanks for Tabasco, and the tanks was 150 feet in diameter and 17 feet in height, and they age Tabasco Sauce in them.

"Yeah, Caldwell Tank told me that cypress wouldn't let anything penetrate it, and then, in the same [way], nothing would come out of it. Water gets in it, [and] it preserves it actually. They say these tanks will last forever as long as you keep liquid in them. Cypress will dry out. If you let it get just dry, that's about the worst thing you can do to cypress.

"My house is built outta cypress. Now, it will not rot. But in log form it will rot if it dries out. But if you saw it and put it in a house or a boat or whatever—it's there for life. Forever. They call it 'eternal wood.'

"The house I built at the sawmill, I used juniper, which is white cedar—and I used yellow pine, which is a fat pine, what we call lightered pine. And then I used deadhead cypress. I've used all [pine] beams underneath the open deck, and I nailed cypress on top of it. Three or four years later [we] tear up that deck. The pine had no visible decay between the boards; it was something that stayed wet continuously. The juniper was next, and the cypress was next. The pine was the least decaying.

"I sawed a jillion feet of pine. But it was green. Now we logged it, you know, standing. Cypress was the thing that put me on the [map]. I got known by it, put it that way.

"I sawed only selected grade. In other words, it's got to be purty. It's got to be clear. Can't have pecky in it. It's got to be all heart. It's got to be something that a rich person'll buy. It can't have a knot in it, can't be a split.

"Now tank cypress was two below boat stock, [which] is the top. And then you got tank and number one tank and number two tank, and it goes down to where it says, 'On a 10-inch board you could have one unsound knot, or you can have three little knots.'

"What's a little knot? Is it that big? The grade book was wrote by a sawyer, Lee Tidewater, who graded his own cypress. He had one grade of cypress called tidewater red. You know how they got that hardwood to float in the old day?

"[They girdled it], depending on how long it had grown. If the leaves were still on it—because cypress will grow so old it might only have one branch with leaves on it.

"Apparently [it doesn't need leaves to live]. There's a cypress [17 feet in diameter] at a state park [near Sanford and Maitland]. It has only one branch with a few leaves high in the tree.

"Anyway, after they girdle it, the leaves will fall off and ten days later—all the sap has run out—it will float. I had an FMC—it's like a World War II tank on tracks—but instead of a gun it had a big winch. It could climb over logs.

"If [a deadhead] cypress got waterlogged, it wouldn't float—but, also, deadhead had colors in it. Black cypress was colored by tannic acid—decayed leaves in the water. Light orange, brown, etcetera. If it's quarter-sawed, you can cut it so you can see the face grain. It don't wear as bad. It looks like paneling, though, with all the grains in it.

"I went to Georgia [to get my sawmill]. I'm the youngest of eight children. I went home, and I asked my family, 'Where's that old sawmill?' It was run by a big man, called it the Pritchard Brothers. It had been shut down for years.

"It had been sittin' [so] long, trees that big around [4 inches] had grew up though the sawmill. The old man says, 'What part of it you want?' I said, 'I need what it takes to saw.' And he says, 'Well you need the husk frame; you need so many feet of this; you need the edger, carriage, and the trap.'

"I said, 'How much it gonna cost me?' And I'm thinkin' big bucks. He says, 'I'll let you have all of that for $300.' And I'm thinkin', 'Hm, I don't have $300.'

"We were back on the road about 4 or 5 miles goin' back home, and I said, 'What's ya think he wanted?' And one of them said $3,000, and one said $2,000. And I said, 'Nope, he said $300.'

"And Uncle Grady looked at me. He said, 'Son, you don't want no sawmill unless you buy that sawmill.'

"That sawmill ran five years—I ran it on the weekends and afternoons—before I quit Florida Power. So the sawmill was makin' more money than I was makin' with Florida Power before I ever quit.

"I tried to get a leave of absence from Florida Power. They wouldn't give it to me. The vice president did come all the way up here and explain it to me: I would set a precedent. So, I looked at my boss man and said, 'I quit.'

"I had three-weeks' vacation. They said, 'You can come back any time to this date and keep your same job.' And when that Friday went by at 4:30, I realized I didn't have a job. You are on your own then; you ain't gettin' that sweet paycheck every other Thursday from now on.

"[But I was already making] five times what I was making at Florida Power. In one month I had over $20,000 in my pocket. Cash dollars. Everybody bought lumber in cash then. I sold everything I got—as long as it was good, mind you. I've never advertised anywhere except for business cards.

"I shipped it also all the way to Osaka, Japan. I was the only one really sawing deadhead. And I sawed deadhead like for twenty-five years. I thought that there'd be no more logs. After twenty-five years I did run out of logs—I did and I didn't.

"I ran outta logs because [of] modern equipment called wood monitors—these little sawmills? See, I hauled logs everywhere within a radius. If someone had logs, I sent a truck after 'em, if they were cypress. [After] wood monitors come out, and where, say, I would get five thousand logs a year—now there's fifty little wood monitors set up, and everyone divides those five thousand logs between fifty sawmills. So everybody gets one hundred logs. One man can operate it; it took seven to run my mill.

"So all of a sudden everyone's standin' around lookin' at me. 'What we gonna do today?' That's when I started a construction business—to keep everybody busy. I went to the state, got my septic tank license, put in septic tanks—and that's good money too.

"There for like two or three years after I slowed down, I would buy all the [wood monitor] lumber and ship it. 'Cause see, you have to have approximately 7,500 board feet to put on a semi, depending on the thickness. But these little wood monitors, they'd be lucky to saw 200 foot a day that I would buy. They're very accurate, but they're slow.

"R. J. Brown? The guy that died, I bought his wood. I bought the McLemore's wood, I bought logs—I bought everyone's wood. I would buy it for like $1.10—let's just say $1 a board foot. I'd ship at $2 a board foot. So I'd buy 1,000 feet, put it on a truck, make $1,000.

"They think they're makin' a lot of money if they sell one [log] for $20–$30. And I told 'em: 'You make a hit if you put it on a truck. You gettin' thousands of dollars. That's something you can go to the bank and save a little bit at.' When you get $20–$30, you stick it in your pocket and go buy a beer with it. You never get ahead. I told one boy: 'Saw you lumber, keep your best, ship it. Get you a little [blue]print sittin' right there 'side'a your sawmill and saw out a house. When you hit number two lumber, start sawin' out your studs and your beams.' If you see all the cypress houses goin' down Bluff Road—I built all those houses from my sawmill.

They done everything and did lock me up.

"The last house I built is on Bay City Road. I built the replica of a log cabin [I noticed] in Georgia—just didn't use logs. I just drew it up and knew how many beams I had to have and put it together. And it turned out real good, sold—like—a week before I got through with it. And everybody said I sold it too cheap. They didn't realize I sold it for [about] $120,000. It's 1,700 square feet with two-story decks all the way around it. I had figured all my lumber at $1 a board foot. This was number two lumber. I had 70,000 board foot in the house. So in reality I sold $70,000 worth of lumber one time.

"They done everything and did lock me up. Oh yeah. I wanna tell you a good story. I've spent time with the federal boys. But every time they would come up—the game warden, the Florida forestry investigators, the state park people, everybody was on my case—they, for some reason, thought I was stealing these logs. And everybody was gettin' 'em, but no one was gettin' as much as I was getting.' So it was a big jealousy [thing]. I got rid of most of it when I moved my landing right above my house. No one knew what I was doing then. 'Cause what got these boys in trouble a few years ago, they blocked all the public landings. Someone on TV said that's when the state come down and start makin' them get permits.

"Now [a permit's] about $5,000. Per year now, we're talking. They're taking $10,000 off the top. So you set out $5,000 for the permit. You've got to be insured. You've got to be—it's a lot of things. When it's all said and done, it's a lot of things. And they monitor you—where you can be, what you get.

"The state claimed they own the logs, and the federal government claimed they owned the logs. And I'm claiming they're free for taking. In other words, I would just ask you, if your boat sunk in the Apalachicola River—your boat—how many years would it be before it belonged to the state?

"In '87, I was called to the federal grand jury—in Tallahassee—clear all my paperwork. And I'm thinkin': 'Hm, what am I doing? I'll call my accountant. You know anything about that?' 'No. No.' Somebody of them kind'a found out they's investigatin' me–me and me alone.

"And on December the seventeenth at six o'clock one morning they walked out there—the federals–and handcuffed [me] and charged me with three counts of grand theft, conspiracy, and everything, for stealing logs off of the National Forest. And they would not let me call my attorney. They would not let me call my wife. They would not—and I said, 'Well, can I at least tell some of my workers that I'm fixin' to leave here?' And I called one of the boys and I said, 'Hey, they're fixin' to take me to Tallahassee; call my attorney.'

"The federal marshal says, 'Hey, you ain't cuffin' Cairo behind him.' Says, 'You can cuff 'im in front.'

"So we was goin' down the road, you know, to Tallahassee—and I was smart enough I just sunk up like a turtle in his shell. And all of a sudden it hit me—the guy that just arrested me was one of the loggers. "And I turned around, and I says, 'The day I shook your hand I knew you wa'n't a logger.' He said, 'How's that?' And I said, 'You don't have calluses.'

"They wrote all this up. I spent twenty-nine days in the federal court-

Fig. 7.2. Sawyer Don "Cairo" Ingram built his house on the Apalachicola River from pine, juniper, and sunken cypress logs, or deadheads, he retrieved from the river. Photo courtesy of Don Ingram.

room. Four mistrials. And it about broke me. I was paying two attorneys $2,000 a day each. So just tote that up for twenty-nine days. That's four [thousand] times thirty—$120,000, right there. And outside of days and days, we went over [testimony]—and this was over $128 worth of logs.

"I prob'ly had twenty sawmill owners comin' to my defense. And—I should'a got [the feds] for entrapment. [The investigator] was dealing with two boys I've known ever since I was in the loggin' business. He bought 'em gas; he even brought the chain saw down. He took and had the trailer and even showed 'em where to cut down the trees they brought to me.

"It was comin' off of the National Forest. These old boys, you'd pay 'em $34. You'd see 'em next, four or five days.

"On the tape, I said, 'I really don't [care] where the [logs] came from as long as you paid stumpage.' Stumpage is what you pay the landowner for the log. So I said that three times in about three hours. And one saw-miller got up and says, 'We bought 'em on sleds,' he said, 'on wagon, we bought 'em comin' into the sawmill pulled by a mule.' He said, 'We ain't never asked where they come from.' He said, 'If we asked 'em, they might not bring us no more.'

"We used the defense: when you stop on the road to buy a watermelon, do you ask the person, 'Is it stolen?' I mean, you gotta have a good faith. My accountant got on the stand and testified I'd bought over $700,000 worth'a logs that year. They started [prosecuting] in March and ended in September.

"I was shippin' logs to Osaka, Japan, and making more money. So I didn't have to be in there sawin'. They was rebuildin' their [shrines]. They was always lookin' for big logs. They wouldn't buy nuttin' but the best cypress. They would not buy deadhead cypress either. They wanted the constant color.

"It came out in the newspaper that they had spent over $8 million to try and convict me of a $128 crime. I have very little beliefs in court systems anymore. And let me tell you something—defend yourself. Don't get no public defender.

In discovery, Ingram said, his signed statement that was originally one paragraph long grew to a whole page. Both were signed, though only the short one was found to be genuine. Judge Stafford "got so mad, red as ketchup.

"[My attorney] stood up and he says, 'We'd like to have a mistrial.'

"And [the judge] just took that [gavel]—bam! 'Mistrial.'

"I said, 'Oh yeah, I wanna go tell my witnesses.' I opened the door—and you ever in the witness room, don't tell nobody about what you're doin' 'cause they put snitches in there. 'Cause they found out I'd flew the sheriff around, that I had a airplane. One of my witnesses was tellin' a federal person that.

"That was it. They never sent me back. That was the end of the fourth [mistrial]. It went to the [grand] jury, I think, once, and it was a hung jury. Another amazin' thing, you know who the jurors is going to be too. You got their name and address. I even had Florida Power brothers—on the crew that'd worked with me. I knew that one or two on the jury was with me. Always.

"Oh, and hadn't you always heard, you're innocent until proven guilty? Do you realize once the federal government charges you, you on probation?

"I could not go no fu'ther than Jacksonville, which you can't go next to water, can't go no further than Pensacola. I could not go near Georgia and no further 'n Gainesville. I had to report to a parole officer every month. They carried me up [to Tallahassee], put me out, put me on a $200,000 bond, turned me loose on my own reconnaissance, and I says, 'How do I get to Apalachicola?' And they says, 'The best way you can.' [I] called my wife, 'Come get me.'

"You want to talk about high-water logging. On pine, these McLemore boys hauled for me for years. They get in a little ol' wooden boat about this wide and go throw these trees down with a chainsaw—out of that boat. Done cut the tree in two—and a yellow pine [longleaf pine] will float—it don't have to be dead, pop like a cork. And go saw the top of it. That's the way they did on high water.

"But see, you didn't do pine earlier, 'cause if you kill the pine, it hits the ground—it will soak up water, and it won't float. You dry out the sap in the cypress, and that's what floats it. And the heart—the inner part of the pine— that's what floats the tree. They don't have any water in it.

"I had three foresters out in the woods at one time, and all of them's arguin' what kind of pine this was. It's very dense, had very large hearts in it—that's what you sell in a pine—heart wood. That's the kick now—pine flooring. And they come to the conclusion that it was slash, grew in adverse conditions. It grew right by the cypress. Slash pine is what most people plant now for pulpwood. But this came up for some reason up here in Lake Wimico before we logged it. All the years we was up there, we was in water.

"I can never figure out when it got dry enough for a tree to come up. Now each one of these trees was somewhere around a hundred years old. So sometime a hundred years 'go there was a drought. I was in there for the old girdled cypress they missed when they put the tram tracks in it, but I realized that the pine had some value. So we logged a lot of pine. Just square the log, ship a big old chunk of wood.

"Dora, [wife of] my boss when I worked for Florida Power, she filmed it from the plane and called it 'The Unreachable.' Back then it was unreachable to them.

"And they had logged right on by this tree. And everyone was in water about up to the knees—that's about how deep the water was. And [the video] shows [a logger] cuttin' on this tree, and it's a big chain saw, and the thing is just too big for the chain saw to reach through, so he has to block the tree.

"So he hollers, 'Timber.' And I'm holding my two dogs [a cocker spaniel and a rottweiler. "Rott" weighed about 160 pounds]. Here goes the tree— crchwa-crchwa. Hits the bank. Somebody yells, 'Bear! Bear!' A bear, must'a weighed 200 or 300 pounds, was on top of that tree.

"And them two dogs run out there and smell that bear and come back to me. They wouldn't even chase that bear. The only reason it didn't kill that bear is because they had notched all the trees in front of it. And the tree, when it started over, weighed too much. It just went—chock, chock, chock—and crushed every tree 'til it hit the ground. So it didn't go real hard," Ingram clapped. "But it stunned the bear, and the bear rolled out and got up on his all fours and just—

"And these crazy boys from Wewa started chasing the bear. The biggest one of them is only that tall [5 feet]. And they run him until the old bear got up momentum too. One chunk of that tree I got over $1,000 for it—went to Japan.

"At the bottom [it was] way more'n 6 foot [across]. The boy was cuttin' it above his head 'cause it was so huge. By the way, most cypress's got a flare butt to it?

"I can tell you where—down there on [Route] 17/92 down at Sanford there's one there that scales 50,000 board foot—standing. They call it the Senator. Seventeen feet through it—that the way you'd saw it down. And it goes all the way up, and it got a little limb stickin' out about 100 feet up.

"I like to saw it down, though, wouldn't you? I'd love to hear that rascal hit the ground. I could just imagine what I could do with that one. That is the largest I've heard about. In the newspaper I've been readin' about in the Carolinas, big cypress. Naw. No, they ain't never talked about one as big as I logged. Good golly.

"[With the Senator], now, they got a chain-link fence around, and they got lightnin' rods on it. Do you know why most older cypress trees don't have tops on 'em? It's just a characteristic of cypress. And as the cypress tree gets old, they startin' to havin' pecky. And it weakens the tree and anything that comes by breaks the limbs.

"But see what a cypress tree will do, if all the limbs broke out of it, it'll put out more limbs. But from the trunk. Not like a pine tree. If you break off all the limbs off a pine tree, it's gone. But a cypress tree will put out.

"Matter of fact, you can take one and throw it in the river, and if any of that bark stickin' out, it'll sprout out. The stump will sprout out. And pecky at one time was a fad. The recording studios [in Tennessee]—it's in there. You know why? All the little holes absorb the sound."

Lewis Jamerson: River Swamp Forester

Lewis Jamerson is a tall, silver-haired forester in plaid, denim, and suspenders. He evolved from thirty-four years of selling clear-cut timber to five years of forest restoration with the Northwest Florida Water Management District. In 1985, the District purchased 35,500 acres from Jamerson's former employer, Southwest Forest Industries, which had bought it from International Paper Company (IP) in the late 1970s. Jamerson was familiar with the land, so the District hired him to help manage it. He helped locate and close

Fig. 7.3. Forester Lewis Jamerson helped end pollution of public lands. Photo by Faith Eidse.

down at least thirty river camps on land leased from the forest industry. The District wanted to end pollution of the watershed and eliminate exclusive private use of public lands.

Years earlier, Jamerson wrote in a 1973 IP management report that operations included 49,000 acres of hardwood river swamp and 7,000 acres of "the best pine growing lands in the Panama City Region." The Wewa Barge Landing, operated by an IP wood yard foreman, crane operator, and log machine operator, trucked lumber to four sawmills, and hard pulpwood on trundle trailer to the IP mill in Panama City. In 1973, IP cut 21,400 cords of pulpwood and 7.5 million board feet of saw timber.

Jamerson, who has served twenty-five years on the board of the Tupelo Soil Conservation District, also noted in his report that some of the largest tupelo blocks in the state were located on IP land. Apiaries accounted for twenty to forty leases on that land, each supporting 150 to 200 hives.

Jamerson's report continued: "During hunting season we have 1,500 to 2,000 hunters in the woods camping out on the riverbank for three days to two weeks at a time. The fishing is excellent most of the year except during periods of high river. There is an annual rivercade from Columbus, Georgia, to Apalachicola, Florida," headed for "the most delicious oysters and shrimp this side of heaven."

Jamerson was raised in Alabama and moved to Wewahitchka permanently in the mid-1950s. He told of working first in forestry, then in restoration, at his tree-shaded bungalow on Church Street, on January 24, 2002. He was joined by his wife, Vivian, and daughter, Mary Ann. The Jamersons also have a son, Ralph.

"I worked for the Water Management District for about 4½ years, 1988 to 1992. I worked for International Paper Company for twenty-seven years, and I worked for Southwest Forest Industries for seven years. And whenever the Stone Container Corporation, which is out of Cairo, bought the property, they dismissed most of the personnel in the forestry end and in the wood yards end.

"I stayed out of work for about a year, and then somebody said, 'Well, you need to talk to Water Management District.' Sure enough, they hired me right off of the bat.

"At that particular time, the Water Management District was having a time because of these camps. They had a bunch of people that had built camps over there, and they figured I'd be a good one because I knew the people and I knew where the [shacks] were.

"What we did, we put up [notices], and then later on we posted, with the help of the sheriff's department, that these buildings had to be vacated or else we were going to do away with them. They were gonna be eliminated," Jamerson chuckled.

"[IP] had camp leases," Jamerson said, "$10, $15, $20 a [month] for just puttin' up a camp out there. And some of 'em were permanent-type-lookin' things, and some of 'em you wouldn't even sleep in if the storm come along. They were huntin' lodges is what they were, your fishin' places.

"I started in business with IP. IP originally bought 50,000 acres," Jamerson said, "and then they sold part [of it] to Water Management District, from Brickyard Cutoff, back [north]. And then the State of Florida bought [part of it], which is still under the [Florida Conservation and Recreation Lands].

"I knew the thing from one end to the other. See, I was in the midst of the cuttin' of timber. When International Paper Company bought it, we bought it with the idea of hardwood log, pulpwood, for the mill in Panama City. At that time they had some orders [to fill], you know, what they call bleaches—pulp.

"[Pulp] is a mixture of 40 percent pine and about 60 percent hardwood. And they shipped some of it to Israel, and [they] would drill holes in [the 4-by-2-foot pulpwood sheets], and then they'd make all kind of fine stationary.

"It was my responsibility to draw up timber sales. You would draw up a block, correctly estimated [for] volume of each species. See, what we had to do whenever we were sellin' timber, we had to divide it up, say all gum was in one amount of money. And then mixed hardwoods would be another, which would be sycamore and willow.

"It mighta been that it was virgin," Jamerson said. "Whenever they were first cutting timber in the river swamp, they did not cut anything but just gum and cypress, you know. And the rest of the species was still standing there. That was really what's called virgin timber. But it wasn't really because they had already been through and cut ash, they cut gum, they cut cypress, you know, high-quality species. But they had never ever cut anything like, you know, the lower-grade species. Oak especially. But [there's] no market for that stuff in the river swamp because it costs so much money to harvest. But whenever we went through, we cut everything from 7 inches to the top, 7 inches diameter breast high [dbh].

"All foresters know where the dbh is," Jamerson said. "That's 4½ feet from the ground. Take a stick if you're cruisin' timber and be sure that you measure that diameter properly, 4½ feet from the ground. That's just a standard term in forestry.

"I mean, when you cuttin' other timber, why you can cut it slam that big [5 inches]. You see this timber goin' to the mill over there now? Some of it ain't 5 inches hardly, dbh in pine, you know.

"But anyway, we cut everything from 7 inches to around 11 inches, and everything from 11 inches up was saw timber, and everything 11 inches down was pulpwood. It looked like a ruptured duck when we got through with it. It sure did. What it is, see, them using tractors and heavy equipment, you goin' back and forth and knockin' that stuff down and actually, when we were cuttin', we left more timber if we were cuttin' the saw logs in the tops than we harvested. You still have a lot of woods that you could convert to pulpwood even though you cut the saw logs.

"That's a load of pulpwood," Jamerson said, selecting a photo of thin logs on a river barge. "[There's] nothin' fit for sawin'. There's a big barge right there, with a crane loading.

"The saw logs all went to four different buyers—Direct Lumber Companies, which is the old mill in Graceville. If you've ever been to Graceville,

It looked like a ruptured duck when we got through with it.

there's a mill there that they shut down, and they're in the process of trying to crank the thing back up now.

"We sold some timber to New Lumber Company, which is in Blountstown. We sold some timber to Oldham Hardwood in Hosford. That was a big veneer mill. That's a log that you put on a turntable, and they peel the thing. It's thicker than that right there." Jamerson indicated a thin-veneered coffee table.

"But they make furniture out of it. They peel it to make the plate that goes on there." He slapped the table again. "The inside would be made [of] some other species.

"In the beginning, we'd load it on a barge and carried it to what they call Stiff-n-ugly [Estiffanulga], which is just below Bristol there. And they off-loaded it there and hauled it on trucks to different sawmills. And later on they kept tryin' to find a place to unload logs.

"See, in that paper company we tried to get a sawmill down here, build a sawmill down here. We had people up in Georgia and everywhere else tryin' to make a deal. But they never did, so they found this place on what they call a cutoff. Not, you know, Chipola River Cutoff. And they leased it from Neal [Land and Timber] Company, and that's where we began bringing the logs and pulpwood. And then, from there, it was trucked to those different sawmills.

"That's the boat I used on the river," Jamerson continued, selecting a photo of a sleek white boat. "That's a Polar Craft boat with an 80 Evinrude. They were primarily personnel [carriers]."

"In the beginning, we [were] tryin' to get people to come over here and build a sawmill. We went back and forth, up and down the river carryin' different people. We even carried a guy from Caterpillar tractor company. Caterpillar was gonna buy the land and nah—no way in the world. They didn't want to put the money out on it, apparently," Jamerson said. "I mean, at that time we were enjoyin' a whole lot of rain. And these people would come over here and see the river when the river was up, 12, 14, 15 feet. See most of this river swamp is wet anyway, you know, whenever it's raining. And the river up too, that multiplied it because you can't go loggin' the real rivers.

"The river was up, and I mean it stayed up," Jamerson said. His records showed a 23.41 foot crest at the Blountstown gage in the flood of March 8, 1971. "At some time we'd have six months of high river, you know. I mean that'd be alternatin' all durin' the wintertime.

Jamerson selected a picture of the 1971 flood, when he boated to his of-

That was a big veneer mill. That's a log that you put on a turntable, and they peel the thing.

fice. "The water was in the floor of [the trailer office] because this whole place was under water. And I had my IP flak jacket on and had my IP symbol on the side of the boat and IP on everything, and this plane started flying around. He says, 'Where're you goin'?' 'I'm goin' to my office.' And this guy, he sent for the Marine Patrol, and the Marine Patrol came up there and said, 'What are you doin' in here?' And I said, 'Come to see if the water was in my office floor.'

"What it is, see, when the river was up, why, people would go and steal out of these camps. Characters from Alabama and Georgia would come down there and steal motors and steal stuff out of people's houses.

"[The river level dropped five or six] years ago like it is right now. Somebody went out and set [Cutoff Island] on fire, and I walked through from about the middle all the way through that swamp, and it was dry completely, and the fire was about 7 or 8 inches high.

"[The river] is 2 feet at Blountstown," Jamerson said. "You got a Corps of Engineers gauge up there. So that's way down for the river, and it surely affects everything. [It's] two years since it's been up of any consequence. There may have been [a] 7- or 8-foot river, some'm like that.

"Sometimes you pull [those barges] up to the bank of the river, and the Corps of Engineers would dump water out of Lake Seminole. We would come out on Monday morning, and the barges'd be out on the hill with the logs on it," Jamerson said, laughing.

Jamerson selected a photo of a barge tug. "See, that's the *Bonnie B.* This is Glen Tarrow Warren with the hat on. Sometimes he'd run four and five cruises over there, be loggin' in different areas. That's his tugboat captain, Griffin. I think that's his name, Griffin from Blountstown. I would say 1980, '81.

"This is logs that later Water Management District sold," Jamerson said. "Logs that [foresters] had girdled back many, many years ago. Otherwise it'd go slam to the bottom of the river. They're still doin' deadheadin' out there.

"[I] was [with] Southwest Forest Industries [when it] bought out International Paper Company," Jamerson said. "That's out of Phoenix, Arizona. Now they are no longer; no such thing because [Smurfit-]Stone [Container Corporation] bought 'em out. I didn't work for Stone. Whenever Stone bought it [1987], my headquarters up between Franklin County and Gulf County, Clarksville, told me, 'Get the men with you and come in Monday morning.'

"They didn't say what was gonna happen, but that was the day that Stone handed out the little brown envelopes," Jamerson laughed, "and terminated, see, a bunch of us. I'd say twenty men, more or less, men that worked in the wood yard, foresters." Jamerson was sixty-four or sixty-five years old at the time, but, "I wanted to work. I needed to work.

"[When I joined the District] we planted some [trees]. But in order to plant hardwood, you've got to plant it just like you gonna plant peanuts and corn and cotton. You gotta completely annihilate everything out there. Whenever you plant your trees, you got to go back and disk it this way and then disk it that way. Keep down the grape vines and the bushes and all kinda stuff. It's not a practical thing to be plantin' hardwood because it costs too much money to do it. They did a world of it, Lou'siana. Planted cottonwood and gum and cypress and ash. The experience I had within that fir company was we planted it and then the river came up. Whenever the river comes up and it gets over the top of the trees, it kills the trees. Cypress can withstand that.

"Bill [Cleckley] and I went over there and planted cypress, and planted gum and—well, he got some Shumard oak. And the river came up and left some of it standing. And we went back in there and planted. You know, put acorns in the ground about every 5 or 6 feet, and the 'coons had gone down the rows and eaten every one of the acorns.

"I would say we increased wildlife 'cause in pine trees, whenever you let a forest just [thicket], the wildlife decreases, but if you cut timber—the sprout? That will attract deer. In fact, when we cut hardwood up above the upper end, you come out there and see where the deer had been, and looked like they had grazed everything that sprouted about head-high.

"All we ever had over there was deer and turkey. Of course, we had a lot of otters and a lot of beavers and—" He selected a photo of a felled tree, shoulder-high to a man standing next to it, about [60 inches] in diameter. "That's a deadhead cypress. That's a cypress that we hauled to Oldham Hardwood. That's one of the Mr. Oldhams that's standing next to the log. He scaled the logs. [That tree is] at least 1,000 [years old]," Jamerson said. "Very seldom did you find those except in a deep swamp, you know, where they were unable to get the thing out. That [was] found on Florida River.

Vivian, Jamerson's wife, appeared from the kitchen and said: "Lewis got lost one time. I was worried about him, and usually he comes in before it gets dark."

"Water pump froze up," Jamerson said.

"So he went on down to this man, Old Zee Thomas," Vivian said. "And he has a turnip green and a vegetable lot on the river—or he did—he's not living now. And here I was worried to death, you know, fixing to call and get together a search and rescue. And he was over there eating turnip greens and corn bread."

"See, when it happened," Jamerson said, "see, I lost my oar. I was tryin' to get to Ocheese Landing, and I mean it was about three-fourths of a mile or so, and I got down there and hollered, 'Old Zee, you home?' He took out a gun and started to shoot, bang, bang, bang. And I said, 'Old Zee, don't shoot me,'" Jamerson laughed. "So that's when we had the coffee and turnip greens," Jamerson laughed. "No such thing as a telephone. I mean he was in the middle of that swamp. He had 'im a floatin' hut," Jamerson said.

"He'd go barefooted a lot," his wife added.

"All the time—no shirt. The Corps of Engineers had what they called a snagboat," Jamerson said, "which was a [gantry] that reached out there and got the logs. And then they had a dredging boat, had the big hole in front of the [gantry], cleaned out the channel. Some of the best cooks in the world. If you didn't have a good cook on there, he was dumped, and go'ed you get a good one. Most of those men are the nicest men you ever skippered. They'd see me go by on that boat and wave at me, 'Come on and eat.'

Jamerson selected a photo of beehives high on stilt platforms in the swamp. "[L. L. Lanier] protested. He said, 'Lewis, you gotta stop cuttin' my tupelo 'cause that's how I make my living, on tupelo.' He wrote a letter to International Paper Company in New York, protesting IP's crews cuttin' tupelo gum in the river swamp.

"The vice president wrote a letter back to the people in Mobile and specified that we were not [to cut] the trees that would ordinarily be used for the production of gum. This man had a wife, and they run these two-wheel horse trotters. Come to find out he was buyin' the honey from L. L., and he fed it to them horses," Jamerson laughed. "At one time, [Lanier] and the Whitfields were two of the biggest honey producers in the world." Jamerson added that the Whitfields placed their hives on Battle Bend, and when the Corps cut off that bend, it left their hives on dry land.

Concerning the Dead Lakes dam removal, he said: "They put a lot of people out of business when they decided to tear the dam down. A bunch of fish camps up there right now is just high and dry because they do not have access to the Dead Lakes. While the dam was there, the [water] stayed up where they could fish. Out West they built ramps for the fish to get up into the river. But here I don't know if they could ever get them trained to jump over a dam.

Jamerson selected a photo of himself standing against a large loblolly pine growing on Coon Island. He opened a U.S. Geological Survey topographic map of Orange, Florida. "This is Florida River; [and Coon Island's] not too far from the Apalachicola River.

"When I first came over here, I went with the Larkins by boat into these

[The timber] came back thick as hair on a dog's back.

islands. Most peculiar thing. Looks like it's got banks on it, 12, 14 feet high out of the water at that time. And what they think, at one time the Apalachicola River moved over here, and that's how [it cut those banks]. There're two of 'em, Pig, Coon Island, right there. And we cut all the timber off of those things, and it came back thick as hair on a dog's back. With pine trees.

"The Water Management District owns all this except this old part of it up in here to Mitchell Larkin's. [The] District contracted with the state, and they built a road all the way to those islands. You just rogue it up, take a tractor, and push it up, you know," Jamerson said. "Yeah, I'm sure Water Management could not dig. But we had already built a road in there when we were loggin'. The river landing is right there where you come off the highway."

The District was restoring wetlands impacted by a new U.S. Highway 20 bridge "and trying to pacify the hunters and the fishermen to get back in there. Where we [foresters] had built wooden bridges, the [District] went in and tore them out and put in lower water crossings. But when Bill and I were planting in here, those old wooden bridges were falling apart, and we'd take a chance on the Jeep to get back in there.

"You see, the beekeepers have just about gone out of [the Florida River area]. They no longer do this. L. L. bought land where he can get his bees up without having to haul them. That's an expensive operation goin' to that [area] over there. You had to haul your bees in there, and then you had to feed 'em prior to the time the tupelo blooms just maybe two to three weeks during the year. And it gets rain and ruin. The wind can blow and blow the blooms off the tree, and poor L. L. just, he switchin' out every time a tupelo bloomed."

Jamerson pulled out a yellowed 1971 *Tallahassee Democrat* article and photo of forester Owen House dwarfed by the largest *Carya aquatic* in the United States. "Now, this is a water hickory," Jamerson said. "That thing was 22 feet, 2 inches [in circumference]. That's the world's record for that species. It's in Calhoun County right around Blountstown."

The tree—which could once be seen from a point just north of Ocheese Landing–was certified by the American Forestry Association in its National Register of Big Trees. It was 150 feet tall and had a crown spread of 87 feet. At the time, Florida led the nation in champion trees. Now it has only three: a Black titi in Wakulla County, a *Hawthorn consanguinea* in Tallahassee, and a Florida yew in Torreya State Park.

"I don't think [there's any virgin forest left] in the river swamp," Jamerson said. "I think it's all been cut over. Many, many years ago they were cuttin' gum and the more valuable species, and then they started cuttin' everything else. I don't believe there's any areas left on Florida River where it hasn't been cut, they've cut through it so many times.

"They used to use the cable skidder. And they'd get out there, and they'd run the cable out on the swamp, way out yonder, and then they'd cut trees. And cut 'em toward this big cable, and they'd tie smaller cables to those trees. I tell you what, we had a place down there right below Kennedy Creek where it was done like that. It looked like somebody'd dug a gulley. In other words, the big cable went out, and the lesser cables comin' this way, and they had what they called a steamin' skidder, and he'd pull a pile of those things, and it would just literally clear everything in its path.

"International Paper Company was gonna do a study at Auburn and U.S. Forest Service, and they hired this man [who] got up there in the middle of that swamp, and he fell in[to] one of them gullies, and he couldn't get out. And it just so happened that the Corps of Engineers was not a quarter of a mile [away]. And he kept hollerin' until finally Johnny Hutto on the dragboat heard him. So it was gettin' late, and all the crews lined up, and they went out to the swamp like this," arms linked, "to find the man. [He] had a bad back, and that was the reason he couldn't climb up the bank of that thing.

"I went down there, and I pumped it dry. And then we were able to clear that with the logger. They were gonna do a tractor-type loggin' in that thing. I said, 'You all are crazy.' It was a low swamp. You have to have a table to go out [on] that, pull the logs out, 'cause it's land won't hold up a piece of equipment. It'd go head first into that thing. And then they were loggin' ditchy-do.

"I mean, the ditch wasn't there. They just, whenever they pulled 'em out, all the logs made the ditch. Whenever they put the main line out there they had to be sure and keep it in a good straight line. It was a dangerous business. Many, many men got caught in the middle and that log run over him.

"Hardwood is difficult to cut anyway because a lot of it [grows] one-sided. You have to look at the top. Be sure you know which way it's gonna go. You just don't run up and run a saw in it.

"There's a guy here in Wewa that could take a saw and keep two rubber-tired skidders goin' in that river swamp, he was that good. He could cut 'em, and next time you'd see him he'd be leanin' against the tree, and it'd be trees all over the woods where he'd cut 'em."

They were loggin' ditchy-do.

8

A System Rich in Scientific Treasures

We couldn't understand that anything bad was gonna happen to the river.
We just took all that for granted.
Angus Gholson

The Apalachicola basin's wide species diversity and range of habitats inspired pioneering naturalists of the Southeast. Here botanist Hardy Bryan Croom discovered the Florida torreya (*Torreya taxifolia*), samples of which he sent to Dr. John Torrey in New York to verify as a distinct species. He also discovered the now-endangered flowering croomia (*Croomia pauciflora*) and *Baptisia simplicifolia*.[1] Moreover, he met a beginner, Dr. Alvan W. Chapman, and they determined to botanize throughout Florida in search of new plants. Croom got a good start in the steephead ravines of Liberty County when he leased a plantation near Aspalaga Landing in 1832.

However, Croom's short, productive career ended in 1837, when he perished in a shipwreck. Chapman continued Croom's work, traveling from Marianna to the Apalachicola River on a white horse, botanical samples pressed in his saddlebags and hat and strapped to his back. He spent so much time on his horse that he claimed it was "nearly as good a botanist as I am."[2] Dr. Chapman gained a solid scientific reputation with his 1860 classic, *Flora of the Southern United States.*

The Civil War disrupted Dr. Chapman's work. He was a Union man, born in New England, and so devoted to the cause that he and his wife, a secessionist, separated for four years, according to family friend Virginia Kimball.[3] Mrs. Chapman went home to live in Marianna, and he stayed on in Apalachicola, where his pharmacy was often targeted by fighting men.

He owed his life to his profession, Kimball wrote, since he was the only surgeon in town, skilled and protected by his friends who warned him of approaching enemies. Sometimes he only had time to hide in the Trinity Church, where he'd spend the night in his pew.

Kimball added that he had once shown her the spores of a fern coordinated in multiples of four and told her, "If the All Seeing has carried his law of order to even these minute spores, has he not so governed the whole world that no man need fear?"

The Confederate's Andersonville Prison was located near the Flint River, and Union escapees who made it to Apalachicola would hide in the swamp until word reached Dr. Chapman. Then he or a young devotee, the son of a patient, rescued them and rowed them out to blockade ships in the Gulf.[4]

The scientific legacy of Croom and Chapman infected Angus Gholson Jr., a field botanist from Chattahoochee whose interview follows. Gholson grew up among healthy torreyas, and over a lifetime he has collected about 16,000 specimens of Apalachicola flora. Recently Loran Anderson documented a new blazing star species on the Apalachicola Bluffs and Ravines Preserve and named it *Liatris gholsonii* to honor Gholson's tireless field botany. Chattahoochee also named a 100-acre riverside park for Gholson, boasting that it ranks sixth in the world for varieties of rare species.[5]

The eastern watershed from Bristol to Chattahoochee is a primary preserve of rare and endangered plants, its steepheads a refugium that have protected the Florida torreya, croomia, and Florida yew from extreme climatic event for millennia. E. E. Calloway, a Bristol resident in 1950, regarded the Apalachicola Bluffs as the biblical Garden of Eden since it was near a four-headed river. He counted among them Spring Creek, which rises to join the Flint and Chattahoochee at the Apalachicola. Moreover, the torreya is also known as gopher wood, the lumber Noah was instructed to cut from the Garden to build the ark.[6]

Of the forty-seven species of trees in the Apalachicola floodplain, the most common grow in permanently saturated soils—Ogeechee tupelo, bald cypress, Carolina ash, and swamp tupelo. The Apalachicola River basin contains one of the largest remaining stands of tupelo in the world.

In this basin reside sixty-four identified reptiles and forty-four amphibians, among the highest such densities in North America, north of Mexico.[7] The Barbour's Map turtle is a species of special concern, having suffered from river damming and local harvesting.

The blotched kingsnake is believed to have evolved in the Marianna Lowlands; the alligator snapping turtle is threatened by habitat impacts. At over 155 pounds, it is the world's largest freshwater turtle. The gopher tortoise is a keystone species whose burrow loss to agriculture, timbering, and development impacts the Eastern diamondback rattlesnake, the Florida pine snake, the indigo snake (threatened), the Florida gopher frog (a special concern), and many others.

Windrows on Steephead Streams at Rock Bluff, 1986

In this chapter, Angus Gholson and Marilyn Blackwell speak about these treasures from experience, Gholson as a field botanist and Blackwell as a river camp dweller, naturalist, and activist.

As he spoke, Gholson focused on logging impacts on the rare and endangered Florida torreya tree, which grows naturally only in the steephead ravines of the Apalachicola basin. Springs vent from the bases of these porous seepage slopes, which were once ancient shorelines. The sandy edges slump and are carried away as the streams carve steep-walled valleys that migrate headward. Unlike the rain-cut, gully-eroded ravines of the adjacent red clay hills, steephead valleys—such as those between Sweetwater Creek and Bristol in northern Liberty County—are ever-flowing and maintain a constant temperature. Darters, snails, lungless salamanders, and crayfish depend on this constancy, summer and winter.[8]

Steepheads are critical conservation areas because each contains four major ecosystems: aquatic streams, seepage-slope wetlands, lower-slope hardwood forests, and dry, upper-slope forests. After these ecosystems were touched by perimeter logging and road building, Gholson said, the torreya was threatened by a fungal disease of the stems.

Angus Gholson Speaks for the Torreya Trees

Angus Gholson Jr. is tall and trim, his hair iron-gray, his demeanor warm. On a hot day, July 23, 2001, he told his story at his birthplace in the center of Chattahoochee, a grand three-story house fronted by Doric columns. As he began, he was riveted on a live oak in the yard, its long arms covered in brown ferns. "They need rain," he said, his voice gravelly.

Gholson is a Beadel Fellow with Tall Timbers Research Station, north of Tallahassee, and mentors graduate students from the University of Florida, his alma mater. Tall Timbers called him an "Ambassador for Botany" and promoted Gholson's study of flowering and growth patterns in vascular plants as "one of the most comprehensive studies of its kind." The Beadel Fellow program, named for founder Henry Beadel, supports senior naturalists.

Gholson's office is an enclosed carriage house, its air conditioner wafting a cool blast tinged with mothballs. Over fifty years he's collected and catalogued 16,000 plant specimens of the Apalachicola River basin. They are pressed and stacked in sample cases around the room. He has files on taxonomy—the rules for naming genus and species—and bookshelves of botany texts, several dedicated to him.

"I was born right here eighty years ago on September the twenty-fourth,

Fig. 8.1a. Field botanist Angus Gholson grew up among thriving torreya trees at his home in Chattahoochee. Photo by Faith Eidse.

1921," Gholson said. "Lots of our time was centered around the river and fishing and playing and swimming on the Apalachicola River and the Flint and on the Chattahoochee. We couldn't understand that anything bad was gonna happen to the river. We just took all that for granted.

"Now, of course, the Apalachicola National Forest was there and—let's see—Torreya [State Park] came in the thirties, and I think so did the [Marianna] Caverns. But just about everything was pristine in those days. In my early boyhood, U.S. 90 wasn't paved, and the first bridge over the river was completed [the] year I was born.

"We used to walk up the east side, and then we'd find a partly rotten log, and we'd ride it back to the bridge down here. And in between the rivers, there were some beautiful springs. Over on the west of that Flint River, just within 3 or 4 miles up there, the water was freezin' cold, but we didn't have to worry too much about that; the sun was real hot too.

"My father and mother both were real close to plants, so it wasn't too hard for me to wanna be outside. My mother married a Mr. Scarborough first, and he died during World War I. And she married my father, who worked for him. Down here on the corner [at Route 90], on the northwest quadrant, is where that store was. It was a big two-story [general store].

"They had about everything people needed in it. They even sold caskets there. They could've used [a motto] like 'From the cradle to the grave.' I understood during World War I they ran out of caskets in this part of the country because of the flu. They couldn't get 'em buried as fast as they were dyin'.

"In the Great Depression, certain outfits bought up all this land. People were hungry, and land sold for as cheap as 25¢, 50¢ an acre. The way they've managed it and taken care of it, there's a terrific impact on the use of the land. Maybe we brought that on ourselves by not being respectful to the land, too, you see?

"Now, from that point on, it's a biological question. When you go clear a place, and you bring things in that weren't there originally, you've upset something that's been working to come to a climax from the beginning of time. But when you change a place like between here and Bristol on those sand ridges, first off, when they clear-cut it, that was pretty rough. There were [plants] on there that were adapted to that. There was longleaf pine, wiregrass, turkey oaks. There wasn't the biggest and the prettiest trees, but at least they were adapted to it.

"I guess in the 1950s, the first time they cleared that, they pushed it up in windrows. Aerial photographs show they were about 100 feet apart. They pushed the topsoil up too. Then, in between those windrows, they planted slash pine. They had nothing but sterile soil to grow in, so they didn't grow. In about thirty years, the slash pine were about 4 to 5 inches in diameter. So even St. Joe [Company] had some failures.

"There used to be a beautiful forest all the way from here to the bay at Port St. Joe and around Apalachicola. And that helped to moderate these bad storms that come. But that's all been cleared now, and weaker trees are down there. I'm sure for the ambient temperature it's prob'ly made a difference.

"When we went to World War II, there wasn't anything wrong with the torreya. It seemed to be in pretty good shape. But after we were back and all that land was cleared, when you cut all of the trees off a place, and you push up all of the grasses and even the topsoil into windrows in those sandy areas, you increase the evaporation tremendously, and you raise the ambient temperature considerably. And the moisture regime is certainly altered. Now, torreya grew in all of the [steepheads]."

Gholson unrolled a topographic map of Rock Bluff. "Now, see, this is the

> When you cut all of the trees off a place, and you push up all of the grasses and even the topsoil . . . you increase the evaporation tremendously.

Fig. 8.1b. Torreya flowers no longer appear in steephead ravines, where the trees succumb to blight before reaching maturity. Photo courtesy of Florida State Archives.

junction of [State Route] 12, comes out of Greensboro to Bristol, and this is [County Route] 1641. This is the head of Sweetwater Creek. And here's the head of [Upper] Sweetwater Creek. And you notice those contours now are very, very close together. They're steep. Every one of these branches off of it is a steephead. They look like an amphitheater. And they erode from beneath.

"So right here [above the amphitheater] the water drains down through [sandy] soil and runs under, and the trees fall over and these grow back this way. All have been altered by these roads. See, the people building those roads, they didn't understand it. You look at these systems—and the one nice thing about this right now, the Nature Conservancy, they own this system, but St. Joe still owns the rest of them. They are significant biologically.

"They cleaned all in [above the amphitheater]. And then, in a lot of cases, they pushed [berms] over in here [against the steepheads]. And, when [clear-cutting] interrupted that moisture regime, that weakened those trees, and whatever the pathogen that was traveling, it exploded, and it contributed to the demise of torreya in the wild.

"There's a berm just about all around [the steephead]. Rain would evaporate immediately, and before you had wiregrass, you had dog fennel, all the andropogons and a lot of other things, plus turkey oaks, runner-type oaks,

The most conspicuous element [from here to Bristol] in those ravines were torreyas.

and then longleaf pine and duff, leaves and things on the ground, that would prevent evaporation.

"The torreya grew on a contour in each one of these places. That was home to them. And [clear-cutting] weakened those trees. And that's in our lifetime, that's just [since] the 1950s. You think about it now, that's not gonna be here anymore. That's gone. Now, I like to admit [that] in our lifetimes, maybe for a long time before then, maybe torreya was just hanging on. Because the timber was cut from time to time—but it wasn't clear-cut. They were selective, and you left something in the woods.

"When I went to school in 1942 and '3 and then the war came along, the most conspicuous element in these ravines were torreyas. In those days, the Florida yew was a lot rarer than torreya. Now that's reversed. Lord only knows all the other elements that went with the torreya.

"Well, I don't see it slowing up. You see, you're right in the middle of Georgia, Florida, and Alabama arguing about the water. It's selfishness. Why not leave the streams like they were? Atlanta wants the water, and you can well understand why they want it. But then, see, when they build these projects, they have to have some purposes for doing it. You have some of the other [reservoirs] further up the river where recreation was one of the authorizations. They got lots of money for those things.

"This was one of the best turkey countries in the world. Most of the time in the fall those river swamps were full of water. Well, those turkeys could fly off of these hills, and they'd roost over that water. They're a pretty good match against a good hunter because they had the water on their side.

"And then the food that the swamp [provided], and of course we cleared most of that when we cleared for the [reservoir] project. I can remember some of those biologists for the state coming to this area and trapping turkeys and taking them to other places down the state, see?

"Growing up here, it was just about like being in heaven. Mr. Calloway, he started this Garden of Eden down here at Bristol. I kinda agree with him. We're fast losin' it, but we had it at one time. The torreya's a good example of that.

"Unfortunately, we especially don't know about the things we couldn't see. And maybe the reason why we didn't have some of these viruses is because maybe we had things to take care of them; maybe we've eradicated those things. Either with herbicides, fungicides, insecticides, or whatever we use.

"I worked [at Lake Seminole] during the clearing of the reservoir. The first reservoir manager was R. H. Alcorn, and I was his assistant for twenty years or so. When he retired, they made me the manager.

Growing up here, it was just about like being in heaven.

"Don Vickers was our entomologist, and in those days, Georgia had a law that if an adult anopheles mosquito occurred within a mile of a residence, you had to do some sprayin' for it. DDT was authorized, and Don Vickers did a thorough job of it. He was a quiet, easygoing guy, [but he died suddenly].

"We did a lot together, and on the weekends we botanized. His name is in here." Gholson opened a shelf door and revealed stacks of manila file folders.

"I hope this is a record of my time being here on the Apalachicola River." Each file folder contains leaf, stem, and bark or flower. "That's things that would be necessary for identification. I'm interested in all types of flowers and trees, and—I've given it to the University of Florida whenever that indefinite period runs out. They'll move it down to Gainesville, either incorporate with their herbarium or maybe they'll keep it separated along with the library and the file on the Apalachicola region.

"When I gave this herbarium to [UF], they requested that I have it appraised. I was able to get a little bit of relief on my income tax for five years. But it seems like the IRS doesn't think nearly as much of these specimens as I do.

"Taxonomy is a very important science, and unfortunately a lot of names get changed, and I have a lot of work to do. Everything's got to have a name. You can't say, 'that plant we picked up over yonder on the other side of Tallahassee.'

"And I have a fair number of graduate students that come by, and if I can help them, they can do in a few days what it would take months to do. I have a good workin' arrangement with the University of Florida, Florida State, Mississippi State. If they can use [this collection] and reduce time, it means something to them.

"I had a [group] out on Lake Seminole that did a lot of work on aquatic plants. And it was a big problem because this is a shallow reservoir, [nutrient rich], and there was just a beautiful place for aquatics to thrive. And I don't know a better place in this latitude, to study aquatic botany than right here."

Gholson selected a book by Bob Godfrey, *Trees, Shrubs, and Weed Vines of Northern Florida and Adjacent Georgia and Alabama*. It was dedicated to Gholson, 'not to pay a debt but to acknowledge it.' Godfrey and Herman Kurz, both FSU botanists, were the first to notice the torreya's decline in 1962.

Walter Kingsley Taylor, a professor at the University of South Florida, dedicated to Gholson his 1998 pictorial book *The Florida Wildflowers in their Natural Environment*. 'A dedicated friend of our wildflowers, a southern gentleman who has given his time freely and shared his exceptional knowledge of these plants with thousands of folk scattered through the United States.'

"People are kind enough to recognize your help," Gholson said. "Gail Fishman has a recent book out about the early botanists. She recognized I encouraged her a lot to do it." *Journeys through Paradise: Pioneering Naturalists in the Southeast* was published by the University Press of Florida in 2000.

"What botanists generally do, they enter into an agreement that they'll collect in duplicate or triplicate and then they'll swap. I've given a good many specimens away, but I'm out of room. Georgia, Florida, and Alabama is what I like. That book [by Godfrey], I collected with him and worked along with him—and so that's about what's in here. I think it's a pretty good collection of aquatic vegetation.

"Dr. Chapman was an outstanding person," Gholson said, revealing a kindred spirit. "[Chapman's] first love was botany; there is a very rare plant that grows around here, and it's called *Spigelia gentianoides*, and it's in the *loganiaceae* family, one of the [most] poisonous plant families we have.

"So he was on his way from Quincy to Kentucky Landing on the Apalachicola River [across from Florida River, north of the Chipola Cutoff] to perform an amputation. He happened to see that plant, and he knew that was new to science. So I'm just wondering—that fellow that was suffering with the leg—if he noticed he had to wait a little longer on it.

"If later botanists find that you have screwed up in identifying or either classifying the plant, then you're supposed to change that name and annotate that plant, see? What was so unusual about Dr. Chapman, very few of his plants ever had name changes. And he had to learn Latin before he could read the books.

"My degree is a bachelor of science in forestry, with honors. I went to the war and came back and [graduated in early] 1948. At the time I wanted to get going.

"You see, when they backed up Lake Seminole in 1948—two years later we had a serious hyacinth problem. And so, from that time on, I had my hands full with aquatic plant control. That was the Corps' responsibility to keep the channels open and the launching ramps free.

"If you didn't have plants, you wouldn't have anything. You eat hogs, chickens, cows—well, what do they eat?

"The Water Management Districts have a tremendous responsibility. And I was hopeful that [they] would be able to control all the bottomlands between here and the coast and manage them for the betterment of mankind. People are constantly clearing land, and they have creeks. I think it's utterly ridiculous if they say, 'You've got to stay 10 feet from the creek.' You got to stay a lot further from the creek.

"Go out [State Route] 69 and just see what [landowners] have done already now. They've clear-cut the timber, and then they have herbicided it, just killed everything. So they're gonna plant it back in pines. And what're the squirrels going to do? [They] have to have acorns from oak trees. But you can see what little bit they have left, by a little drainage and how terrible it looks.

"In this country, if you have a deed to a piece of land, you do to it what you want to. That's not true in other countries. We don't have any land ethics here. And you get in trouble if you say anything about it. Well, I don't pass up an opportunity. It's going to have to happen to us where food is gonna have to get short and then, maybe.

"And so the Water Management District, they can do the best they can, but they got to [have the] help of the people who own the land too. And once they own [it], then they have a responsibility to manage [it], and for the best of the most.

"Look at wetlands. [We]'ve modified that [definition] 'til there's no such a thing as a wetland. [We] had all kinds of criteria where you could base it on soil moisture, you can base it on plants, you can base it on just lookin'.

"And, of course, we have more and more people. We know an acre will take care of so many this, so many that. You can't overdo it. And water now, you can't do without.

"So your project is the Apalachicola River basin, and it's not natural anymore, but some of its drainages [are]. It's a beautiful system. 'Out of the Hills of Habersham and down the valleys of Hall . . . ' You know, that's the 'Song of the Chattahoochee' by Sidney Lanier. [The Chattahoochee starts in Habersham County and winds through Hall County, Georgia; the poem is a melodic defense of duty over pleasure.] I've been up there where it is just a little trickle. It picks up things as it comes down. We're either gonna have to drink less or take care of what we have.

"The Flint headwaters are under the airport; Atlanta covers all of that now. And of course they're gonna have to have more water.

"Whenever we compromise with the things that we know are wrong, there can't be a thing in the world but trouble to come. And it's not just the Water Management District's, it's not just the politicians' but it's everybody's problems.

"[With the torreya], whatever this pathogen is, it kills it back to the ground. And sometimes it'll sprout out from an old stump [if] there's

In this country, if you have a deed to a piece of land, you do to it what you want to. . . . We don't have any land ethics here.

Whenever we compromise with the things that we know are wrong, there can't be a thing in the world but trouble to come.

enough energy in that stump. That'll grow up and look pretty good for awhile, and then this pathogen consumes that too.

"Someone [at] the Atlanta botanical gardens propagated some of the torreyas, and then they put 'em out—because there's none of the pathogen up there. But you can't move those things back down here until such time as the pathogen is gone. Otherwise you prolong it.

"Torreya grew in a couple of ravines above the road down to the Jim Woodruff Dam. And so far as I know, except for some south of the Resource Manager's Office up there, all of it above that is gone completely.

"Back in the thirties, people selected Torreya State Park [at] the place that had the greatest concentration of torreya in it. Now most of that is dead, and they planted some back in there, and that's dead. So they don't need to move it back. And over at Tallahassee, if you go out there to Maclay Gardens, they have some torreya out there, and it looks terrible.

"That plant is dioecious. You have the male on one plant and the female on the other, and it has to cross. So last time I saw it, there was some trees that were producing fruit." Lavere and Thelma Walker, Gholson said, planted a male and female torreya thirty years ago—and one still looks healthy. "I think that the male tree has already fallen. That's the female that's there, and it produces fruit, and I've passed it on to people who are doing research on that.

"There is a tree up in North Carolina that produced. As far as I know, it was a female tree. So in the plant world, under some conditions [a tree] can fertilize its own eggs."

Gholson found, in an old book, a glossy photo of the North Carolina torreya, a healthy 45 feet high and 40 feet in branch girth. "[It] is in real bad shape now." He opened a portrait frame, revealing the same tree, ragged and thinning. It was surrounded by rusted cans and barrels. Gholson read from a 1995 letter, "'The big torreya in North Carolina, photographed last year when I was down there collecting cuttings.' It could be [the pathogen], or it could be, they all were just hanging on.

"Now we might speculate just how that got up there. You see, Hardy Croom was down here from North Carolina, so he might have carried it up there a hundred years or so ago. He was a lawyer, but his great interest was botany. The Croom family owned Goodwood Plantation over in Tallahassee.

"North Carolina arboretums were growing some torreyas [in 1991]. They got people that was outside of the area of the pathogen to grow 'em.

"Right now I'm doing a plant list for Pebble Hill Plantation [north of Tallahassee]. I record when they're in flower. Chuck Martin is putting [my work] on [the computer]. You know a lot of these things turned out to be in spite of you, rather than on account of you. You start off doing something, and it just happens, but it's been a lot of fun happening."

Gholson's botanical knowledge sets him apart, but the river has attracted many other naturalists as well.

Marilyn Blackwell: River Warrior

Marilyn Blackwell, of Dalkeith, founder of Help Save the Apalachicola River Group, looks spare and focused in her trademark plaid shirt, jeans, dark glasses, and blue bandanna. A quarter Cherokee, she camps in the creeks her ancestors were named for, more river-centered than self-centered. In recent years, she has rallied newspaper editors, businessmen, and the Apalachicola Bay and River Keeper group with her eyewitness accounts.

At the Big B Restaurant in downtown Wewahitchka on March 22, 2001, Blackwell told her story of life on the river, its natural mysteries, and her survival practices. These include deadheading, worm grubbing, turtle and snake collecting, chemotherapy, and home remedies. She came to Florida from Tennessee twenty-five years ago. When a friend took her to Wewahitchka and they spent a day on the Apalachicola River, Blackwell knew where she belonged. "Then, you could get back in the swamp," she said. Now many sloughs and tributaries are blocked by sand.

"People think you can separate the river from the tributary," she added. "But you can't separate your heart from your body. A river is more complicated and unique than that. It takes a lot of different things to make it work right. The swamp is full of trees, and no two trees are alike. They're like a bunch of people out there.

"The turtles and the frogs are part of it too. At certain times in the summer, one frog will start up, and the others will join in. Then they'll all stop on a dime. We think we know so much; that we're so civilized. We don't know a thing. The swamp seems like man came out of it because it's got so much life in it, and all of it works together.

"When I first came here there was a lot more high water than there is now. You could go out in the swamp; you didn't have to stay in the sloughs. Now you can only get into the sloughs in high water. You can go out on the mud flats, and you only find turtles in small pockets. They feed on bugs and minnows so they need the water. [At low river] the turtles will come out and go into the river.

"I was at Virginia Cut, campin' in a tent. It was the first [river] rise in fall,

Fig. 8.2. Marilyn
Blackwell is an out-
spoken "earth
guardian," asking
for accountability
and justice for the
Apalachicola River.
Photo by Faith Eidse.

and the dog would go out there barkin' when he found a turtle. Some of
them were alligator snapping turtles (*Macroclemys temminckii*). The turtles
were layin' [eggs] there. Well, during these navigation windows the river
would rise suddenly [and] drop down fast, and the turtles and eggs would be
stranded. The softshell turtle is almost gone. It lays its eggs 3 feet above the
water level, and when the water is raised, the eggs drown. The way they bring
the water up fast and let it down fast—it leaves the fish dry in isolated pockets where they are prey to birds, raccoons, and other animals. It sets the fish,
turtle, and crawfish off balance.

"Did you know that the black fish is the only fish that protects its babies?
I found one once in a mud flat puddle, and she come and hit me on the leg
every time I tried to get close to her wad of babies.

"[Twenty-four years ago], my daughter and I said we were going to come,
and we had a little boat. We went to Lester's Landing, and we floated down
river to the Mushroom Camp, which was abandoned. [It] was like 8 foot by 8
foot, and it was on stilts, and it had a mushroom spray-painted on the out-

side. It had been there for a while, but nobody lived in it. You know the guy that had built it several years before went to prison right after that for four years, I think it was, so he wadn't using it then either. Off and on I was there maybe two years."

After the first six months, however, Blackwell developed sores that wouldn't heal. Buddy McLemore (the late Gulf County commissioner), who often checked on them, told Marilyn, "You gotta come off the river or you won't get well." Blackwell moved off the river into a little house near Wewa, and the sores healed up.

"I came off the river, and I'd wash [my sores] like three times a day, and they healed right up. But, you know, in the summertime in that swamp, I guess it's the bacteria.

"Oh [mosquitoes are] horrible sometimes. Horrible, horrible." She pointed out a white welted scar where a bite had become infected.

"Yeah. My kids got [impetigo] one time. And a grown-up person can catch it from a child. Mostly it's bathin' them three or four times a day, keepin' them real clean."

When summer came, Blackwell moved back to the river. She became adept at surviving in the swamp without electricity or air-conditioning. During sweltering summer nights, "we wet the sheets [and slept under them] until they dried out. Then we'd wake up and wet the sheets again. It's not so much the temperature; it's just that close air. It feels like you're going to smother."

If the mosquitoes were bad, Marilyn would set their hammocks swinging. When they slowed down, "the mosquitoes would cover us again. They're so tiny and light that if a wind is blowing it will blow them away. But you have to wake up as soon as the hammock stops or they will cover you again. The Indians used bear grease.

People that do not deal with nature in any way —and we came from nature, we are nature— they're handicapped.

"We lived on boiled eggs, fried corn bread, fish, and potatoes," said Blackwell. "We wanted solitude.

"Once when Monica and I were fishing, we went down a little slough and the motor quit. We paddled out, hanging on to tree branches. Then we floated downriver trying to get the motor goin' again. It was wintertime, and nobody was on the river. A boat went by, and the man aboard throwed up his hand. I throwed up my hand. It was Carmen McLemore. He was a godsend."

McLemore took them to their camp, and from then on "he checked on us. We'd have a fire going—he'd stop by. My daughter fell in love with his son, Grant. He'd bring us a cold drink and a candy bar. Each. Grant is a real part of this place—real easygoin' and down to earth.

"I ran out of money, and I asked him, 'What do people do around here for money?' He told me about worm grubbin' and deadheadin'. He said, 'There's a log on so-and-so creek if you all can get it out.'

"By then I had got another little tore-up motor. But I believe he went in there and cut it down. It took us forever to get it out. But the money from that one log lasted us several weeks. All we needed [for food] was grease, eggs, and cornmeal.

"And, too, we catfished. We didn't have dip nets. We used jump lines. Moni had one on a line. I could tell it was a big fish, and I told her to let it fight and then to pick it up like this"—Blackwell demonstrated, two hands hooked over its body—"and dump it in the boat. It was an 11-pound catfish. We went all the way to Douglas Landing, and someone there said, 'Jean Pippin will want to put it in her pond.' So we went on to Bryant's Landing and carried it in a bucket about half a mile to Pippin's.

"She said, 'I'll buy it if it'll live.' So we went out there to her pond and put it in the water, and you know, its whiskers barely moved. And we rubbed it and rubbed it and rubbed it, and it took a long time. But finally it swam off. And we was squatted down right there by the water, and the dang thing turned around, came right back toward us, stuck its nose out of the water right at us, and flopped back and went on and went in the pond.

"Maybe we just don't have enough knowledge to know that [fish have] knowledge. It was just one of many things that happened on that river, that'll sure let you know you don't know it all. But people don't get that balance. When they don't get that balance of reality, it sets them back, it retards them. People that do not deal with nature in any way—and we came from nature, we are nature—they're handicapped.

"When we first went down there, [Moni] was sixteen. She was always like a old woman. I don't care what happens, she's got something in that pocketbook that'll take care of it—screwdrivers and first aid. Of course, it weighs a ton. It ought to. But she's a real sweet person.

"[We lived on] practically nothing. One time—now, my son, he was in Texas working—so he came down here. He was going to live on the river with us. He put him up a tent—

"And another thing you could do—you could catch snakes and sell them. There was a snake man that came around from Tallahassee buyin' all the snakes. They were like water bandits. Not poisonous snakes. They look big and ugly, but they're not.

"More than likely a lot of them is fed to other snakes, you know, people that collect snakes, like zoos and all. There's some snakes like a kingsnake, he eats other snakes—

"So we was catching snakes, and we had 'em in a big old 55-gallon drum, and the top had been cut out. You can take a hatchet, but it leaves it real ragged around the top? So somebody came by, and they was lookin' at the snakes. And there was one that Buster was tryin' to show 'im, and he put his hand down in there, and one struck at him, and he jerked back and cut his arm on one of them jagged edges. And it was deep, but I had some Betadine, and I had some of that tape that you can't hardly get off when you get it on. And I washed it out and pulled it together and taped it up and told him: 'Forget you even done it. Just go on like you didn't even hurt yourself.' He hadn't even got a scar now."

"Sold some turtles, the little ones like at the Snake-a-torium in Panama [City] at that time. They gave them to the little alligators and things like that. Just little Stinky Jims, they call 'em [*Sternotherus odoratus*, which can emit musk when handled]. In spring, there's a thousands of them things. But then when we got acquainted with the McLemores, they'd do the fish-baitin' [or worm grubbing], and we'd go fish-baitin' with them.

"A lot of people in this area, for many, many years, used to do that. Now a can that's got five hundred worms in it, they're like $25 a can. But that's an art. And when we first started doing it, the McLemores, they was experts at it, and Buddy Jr. and his wife, Faye, they was the best ones. They could get more worms than anybody.

"You look out over the land, they'd say, 'Can you see that ridge over there?' I couldn't see a ridge. It was flat; the whole dang thing was flat. But I finally learned how to tell where the ridge was. 'Cause it'll just be [she spread her fingers a few inches] higher than the rest of it. And you drive the stake down, and you grunt [rub a board across it, which makes a grunting sound] like for ten minutes. In ten minutes, if any's around, they'll be up. And whoever's pickin' up, they'll be real still while the other one's gruntin' the worms. It vibrates the worms, and they can't stand it; they'll come up. Awright. If you hit 'em real good, there's these worms everywhere, and you walk around, and you pick them up. You can put 'em in old cypress sawdust, and they'll live.

"You can take a bulldozer in the woods and let it stand and run, and if there's earthworms around, they'll come up. But if they come up from that kind [of rumbling], they don't live good for some reason.

"But then if there's just two or three worms come up, you watch, and wherever they come up at then, you [grunt] over that way just a little way because you might go from here to there," she motioned a few feet, "and you can't hit 'em, and then you do that [again], and you see where they come up the quickest, and you go that way. Usually it's on a field that's been [timbered], and it's been burned. When you come out of the woods, 'cause the damp's still on there and it has all this charcoal, you're black all over.

These worms are used to bait "bream, shellcracker, warmouth," she added. "At that time there was this guy, Whitfield. He come around and bought anybody's that were sellin' them, and then he resold them in White City, this side of White City where they call it Whitfield View—where the Whitfields used to live?

"A good fish baiter [will] count 'em as they're puttin' them in a can? I could never count to a hundred 'cause my mind be out there lookin' at this 'n' that, and I'd always have to recount mine.

"My father was a woodsman. He loved the woods. He hunted a lot, fished. See, he had five girls and no boys. We'd go squirrel hunting, and he'd hunt with the rifle, but he'd take the shotgun in case a squirrel got hung up on the limb, you know, blow 'em out with the shotgun. Well, I'd come tote the gun when I was a little bitty thing—oh, eight years old.

"I was born in Birmingham—but when I was two years old we moved to Coosa County, and up in that area there's hollows. And I'd walk one side of the hollo', and he'd walk the other side, and he'd slip along, and I'd just be blunderin' along so all the squirrels would go to his side of the trees and he could kill 'em. And twice I didn't keep up, and he pretended that he left me.

"And always those times he'd come back, and he said, 'Now if you ever get behind again, I'm not gonna come back and get you.'

"But he'd have Momma take us in the car way out and put us out and we'd walk miles, I mean miles, and he had a lot of people that you know would wanta go huntin' with him 'cause he was good. And they'd go huntin' in the morning and come in and go down again, and I'd have to clean it by the time he got in that afternoon with another load. And then when I got toward gettin' grown, every time he'd say, 'I've got this little place in my finger, and I'm afraid it'll get infected if I clean that stuff.' He made excuses, but I never did learn. I always worshipped him.

"He was in World War II, and he got separated from his company when the company retreated. Somehow or another he and another guy had to hide out in a foxhole for two weeks, and it got real cold, and he got double pneumonia. It just messed him up.

"I'm sure he would have loved to have had a son, but when I was little I'd get a sugar biscuit—butter biscuit and put sugar in it—and put it in my pocket, or two or three of them, and stay off in the woods all day. And I know Momma'd come and see about me. I'd go out [on] the branch and stay there all day.

"[I finished] twelfth grade. And sometimes the way I spell, you wouldn't think I'd passed the third. I've got a little block when it comes to computers. A friend got me a new computer and a printer, and it just sits over there like a—[she wiggled her fingers as though at a cursed object]. I've got it covered up. And I told her I had divorced it.

"I've fooled with it a little, but it's not my thing, and I can't make myself. You know it would help a lot in [our] efforts [with] the river and the dang pollution and everything.

"When I was little and we had doctors, they was doctors 'cause they wanted to be doctors. And now a kid thinks, 'Well, what can I do to make the most money?' You know, doctor, lawyer, Indian chief. And I don't care if you're perfectly healthy, if you go to the doctor they're going to find something—a test you need—something that you need.

"I've seen cancer patients that they've treated—up 'til a few days before they died—with dang chemotherapy. And you know, even a buzzard waits 'til something dies, stops breathing, to start feeding on them.

"I'm sure there's things you have to get treatment for. Like my arthritis. If arthritis hits you, it's just as likely to leave you. A friend's shoulder swelled up, was infected, real red, and the doctor told him that he would more than likely, within a couple of years, be in a wheelchair. I'd rub him [with] this old horse liniment, that's real strong-smelling, and right now he ain't got no arthritis, and that's been years ago.

"My thyroid got messed up. But I had polio when I was thirteen, and it messed up the bones in my neck. Well, it got to hurtin' really painful. So this man, he come up with this medicine that he made out of tupelo berries. I'd have to go there, drink it, and stay for like thirty minutes after I drank it, and it cured it; it quit hurtin'. It was a miracle."

Blackwell said she's on thyroid medicine and has to go to the doctor and pay for it. So she tries to cut down, but "when I try to get off of it, I can feel it. It's like withdrawal. I get jittery, my heart feels like it's speeding up."

"It's sinful to take a system that took years to develop and deliberately destroy it so they can play money games. You've got a lot of vegetation that was still along the river, ponds, and lakes when we came here. But sand has filled them up. A lot of mud flats are filled with the sand they dredged here. Common sense is a thing of the past like a horse and buggy. It's gone. There's already a kind of insanity that's got hold of people. Most of that cargo that goes up the river goes to a big corporation that is not human. It can't think. It strives to make more money. It's like a monster.

"I'm one-quarter Indian. Cherokee. They didn't pile a bunch of [stuff] in their teepee and say, 'Look, see, I got all this [stuff].'

"All the agencies that are supposed to be protecting us are not doing it. It

It's sinful to take a system that took years to develop and deliberately destroy it so they can play money games.

frustrates the people living here. I was never outspoken before. But, like the McLemores, most of what they ate came off that swamp. And then watchin' [the river] myself. It's just senselessness. The leaders are destroying something.

"There was not even a quarter mile [of spoil banks] when I first came here. Several people made their living off catfishing. I went out to catfish a few years ago, and the dang fish was dead in the basket. Sand would get in their gills and kill them. In your mind you can see fish hauling, trying to get away from it.

"I commercial catfished in the spring for three or four years in the late seventies. I crawfished for about four years, six years ago. When they cut off the water, the crawfish go into the ground. They stayed down there for months, through April, May, June; one year it went into July before it flooded. They've been in the ground now for two years.

"I've been steady working on something. There's pollution at the mill site. They're puttin' sludge on the ground. I've been working on the commissioners [to request health studies by the Centers for Disease Control. In October 2001, the DEP and the landowners, Port St. Joe and Smurfit-Stone Container Corp., agreed to appease concerned Gulf County residents by having a third party test the site].[9]

"The Chipola River and the Intracoastal Waterway have health advisories. There have been fish kills in the freshwater canal to Port St. Joe. The wastewater treatment plant in Port St. Joe makes foam in the Intracoastal Waterway," Blackwell said. She publicly opposed St. Joe Timberland Company's game resort on the Brothers River. "The idea that someone is trained in wildlife, and attracts ducks to an enclosed pond just to shoot at them."

A sign she posted in Gaskin Park warned that the Apalachicola River was ruined by dredging. Blackwell wrote to the Corps pleading that they end the destruction. "The Corps has no heart. Then [it] proposes [on August 15, 2001] cutting back water to the Apalachicola 20 to 40 percent when the river is at an all-time low. Who's representing the environment and the needs and wishes of the people on the river?"

Blackwell adjusted the blue bandana on her lined forehead and lit a cigarette. Her brown eyes glinted. She looked like a backwoods warrior.

9

King Cotton, Tupelo Gold, and Cracker Cattle

He planted where the deluge ploughed,
his hired hands were wind and cloud . . .
Ralph Waldo Emerson

Joseph Harris was just eight years old when he was sent from home to earn a living. It was during the Depression, and his mother, half Indian of the Cloud Clan, worked as the family field hand. His aging father was supporting a second family, and childhood was over for Harris as soon as he could follow the plow. One of the last sharecroppers in Jackson County, Harris finally got out when the federal government began controlling market crops.

At the time he was providing all the labor for the landowner and receiving half the profit, from which he paid half the costs of seed, feed, and laborers. His wife, Jewel Dean, also reared on farm labor, worked alongside him. But after their first child arrived in 1951, Harris switched to forestry work, the dominant industry in the basin.

The northern third of the Apalachicola basin is made up of cropland and pasture, most of it concentrated in Jackson and Calhoun counties, according to the U.S. Department of Commerce. Land use affects river health, and farming along the Flint River contributes fecal coliform contaminants, somewhat mitigated in the Apalachicola by the Woodruff Dam. The southern two-thirds of the basin is forested floodplain.

Tupelo swamps flourish as the river descends into coastal flats, and that's where beekeeper L. L. Lanier lives, on an island surrounded by wet feet trees. Lanier, of Wewahitchka, was so dismayed when sand began filling in the tupelo swamp after the Woodruff Dam was completed and the Corps began dredging and cutting off bends in the river that he bought 400 acres of tupelo swamp to conserve. He wanted to guarantee the highest-grade honey for market. His story of collecting noncrystallizing, hint-of-lime tupelo honey follows that of the Harrises.

On the barrier islands of the Apalachicola Bay, the late Pearl Porter Marshall, St. George light keeper's daughter, inherited her father's cattle, and, with her husband, bought the French-imported Charolais stock belonging to turpentine legend C. C. Land. An excerpt of her written memoirs is included in this chapter as well.

The Harrises: Jackson County Sharecroppers

For years, Joseph and Jewel Dean Harris lived, breathed, and dreamed holding the plow. When their children came along, however, they sold their mule team, corn, and the crib and escaped sharecropping with a few hundred dollars to their names. Harris then helped the Apalachicola National Forest plant and harvest enough board feet in a year to build 2,500 homes.

Joseph's nose is scarred from a field hoe accident, and he faces other health problems. Still, he bears up after seventy years of physical labor.

Jewel Dean's hair has silvered, and her feet are bruised, but she smiles frequently through bare gums. The couple's survivalist values are evident from the animal pens in the side yard where chickens squawk, pigs root, and a field horse gallops.

Harris was born in Jackson County on September 27, 1924. Descended from Native Americans in Sneads (near the original Apalachicola), he recalls people waiting for the steamboat to load cotton, watermelon, and passen-

Fig. 9.1. A laborer with hand-held ox plow in West Leon County, 1958. Photo courtesy of Florida State Archives.

Fig. 9.2a. Jewel Dean and Joseph Harris with his mother, Georgia Ann Simpson Cloud. By permission of the Harrises.

gers, and unload food and supplies. The Harrises told their story at their brick-front home south of Bristol on August 21, 2001.

"I know what [the Depression] was like. It was a bad time. You worked for 50¢ a day, sun-up to sundown," said Joseph Harris. "[My dad] did farmwork, whatever he could get to do. He logged lots of times. They pulled those logs out with oxen, and then they'd load them on flat cars and pulled [them with] an old steam engine. They had a regular railroad, and then they had spurs.

"[He worked for the] Graves Brothers when they logged absolutely all through here. The Park Service owns it now. I can remember the old log trains. [My father] came from Mississippi, and my mother was raised here in Florida.

"Oh, Lord, I expect I started [farmwork] about eight or nine years old, with a hoe, plow, and mule.

"I had a pair of mules of my own, back in the fifties. And I named one of them Blue and one of them Ada. They were big mules too. You had one that was called an iron-gray. She was a very big mule.

"I planted corn, cotton, peanuts and watermelon, cucumbers—all kind of stuff for the market. I raised hogs.

"[In sharecropping] the man that purchased the land furnishes the land, half the seed, half of the fertilizer. And you furnish half the fertilizer, half the seed, and [all] the labor. And you get half of the cotton or whatever. There's no sharecropping today like there used to be.

"Yeah, I made a living. What one had, you know. If you had your own [corn], see, you took [it] to the grist mill also and had cornmeal made. Which you don't see them running today. And you had your own meat, your own chicken, that you didn't have to buy, like you do today. You could live. I mean, heck, you didn't have a whole lot of money, but it didn't take that much money back then because things're cheaper than they is today. I could live on $600 a year, gross."

"I made 5¢ a day," Jewel Dean said. "That was in '45. I picked [cotton] by hand."

"If you had cotton, you picked it by hand," Harris said. "You hired whoever you could get, and you paid so much a hundred. You picked 100 pounds of cotton, you made 50¢.

"I got to where I could pick 100 pounds a day," Harris said. "I hired some people one time out of Greensboro up here, and I lived over in Jackson County. [One] guy, could pick 400 pounds a day. But he had a lo-o-ong sack. And he'd get down on his knees, and he'd pick two rows at a time. Crawl and pick it, or you can bend over and pick it because there wasn't no machines.

"And you shook peanuts out by hand. You plowed 'em up by mule, and you shook 'em by hand. At the end of the day, they'd go back and put 'em on stack poles. Today, you plow 'em up and pack 'em and carry them out to the dock.

"The piles were big," Jewel Dean said. "A pretty big size slat across the pole."

"You take 'em up in about September or first of October, and then you pick [the poles up] in November and December. Take your mules, pull up beside your peanut pole. And you pull 'em up and take it right on to the peanut picker.

"You had 'em dried, you know. But what I'm saying, you'd take that cup-n-tongue loose and use the chain on your wagon with the body off of it. And you just back up to your peanut pole, hook your chain here, jump on your wagon, and tell your mule to 'get up.' He'd pull it up 'cause it wasn't buried that deep.

"And then you would have a guy pullin' the poles. And you had a guy feedin' the peanut picker. The old Livingston picker? Was the first peanut pickers to ever come out.

"And they'd pull that pole and pitchfork those peanuts in the picker, see? And you had one guy catchin' the peanuts down here, and you had one guy maybe behind it, balin' the hay. And they had an old mule hay baler. You had

Fig. 9.2b. For 100 pounds of cotton, pickers earned 50¢ in 1945, according to Joseph Harris. Photo courtesy of Florida State Archives.

to feed [the baler], and you had to tie the wire. But the mule, he'd go around and around for ya. And then they come out with a power baler about the last part of the forties, maybe the first part of the fifties.

"I was using mules up until '55. That's when the tractors began to really take over. And 'til the government got to cuttin' the acreage on your money crops, I just sold out and I got out. I quit.

"You'd plant in the spring of the year; you planted your watermelon about the last of February. And you plant your corn around March, and your peanuts around March and April, and your cotton. You planted them by hand with a hoe, but you made your rows with a mule, see? You had to plant them in hills so far apart. And your cucumbers, you had to plant them by hand. And you gathered them by hand; you gathered the watermelon by hand.

"We had about 25, 30 acres of watermelons. Reckon what happened, we got so much of it on the market 'til the market went. You didn't get a good price for it.

"Peanuts, you sold them by tons. And then your cotton you sold by the bale, whatever size bale it was.

"The cotton was all right, but you could grow more peanuts per acre than you could cotton. Sometimes I had 15 or 20 acres. It was accordin' to what the government allotted you. The government got to allottin' this stuff back in the fifties. And they had the little man, you see, like I was. In 1955, I had to go 'cause I couldn't make a living.

"You know, a lot of times I got all the crop laid by, I'd get out and public work for a time for the government. I'd get out and maybe log or work at the sawmill.

"Where I sharecropped was on the other side of Altha. About 3 miles from Cypress, really. Out at Little Rocky Creek, Rocky Creek Settlement. That's where I was.

"The man that I worked with, he had 700-and-something acres. A lot of it wasn't farmed. My daddy could have bought it and he didn't. A Drew Peacock [did]. He's dead and gone. That was a good deal for him. Actually, see, you'd get money from him to pay your hands. You hired who you needed to work. Toward the end of the year, you owed him most of the sell-off from the land. I mean, he got to keep his end up. You wound up at the little end. That's the way it's always been with a lot of things. And still is today. The little guy's still down here, and he can't get up because all the other big guys are holding him down here, see?

You owed [the landlord] most of the sell-off from the land.

"When I sold my mules, I sold my wagon, and I sold all the corn I had in the crib, and I sold my hogs, I must have got out a coupl'a hundred dollars. And I moved down south to work in the orange grove. And I think I stayed down there about two, three months, but I didn't like that. I had pretty young'uns at that time. I come back home and went to work for the U.S. Forest Service, and I worked for them about twenty years.

"I done everything," Jewel Dean said. "I did plantin', shucking peanuts, totin' peanuts. I hoed peanuts, hoed corn, walked behind the oxen. I planted with the oxen," she said proudly, "peanuts and corn. I worked with my daddy. I started working when I was a girl, from about the time I was eight. My birthday is April 16, [1928]. I was the second of twelve children, nine of us living now.

"There, see, her sister was older than her," Harris said, grinning about the sister Jewel Dean didn't want him to date. "I didn't have but one big brother and one little sister. And they died when they was just babies. There was nothing like today's [antibiotics]. And they didn't have doctors like they have today. They just had an old country doctor, and he didn't have that much medicine.

"We built bridges, we built roads, and we planted pine seed. Done a little construction workin' on all the houses. They used to have a lot of houses down there. We had to keep up the houses, too. The roof and the plumbing and all that. I done a little of a whole lot."

The Harrises have bricked up the front of their own shotgun-style clapboard house, added a porch with pillars, added kitchen, bathroom, and parlor. "You oughta seen it when I first bought it. Little old four-room plan with eight children. [We] married in 1950 in Bainbridge, Georgia. I reckon in a way we did [elope]; in a way we didn't."

"We didn't have a lot," Jewel Dean put in.

"I just didn't ask her, and we didn't tell anybody," Harris said. "We've been married fifty-one years this July." The family celebrated at Torreya State Park.

"I got eighteen grandchildren, twelve [greats]," Jewel Dean said.

"Before they put this dam in up yonder," Harris said, "you used to go back in that swamp and creek. Blue Springs up there—which that water's all back in there now [Blue Spring's run dried up during the millennial drought]—I done a lot of fishing there. And I worked with a fellow—this was in the forties—he had hogs in that swamp. And we'd collect what they called wild mulberry for fence posts. We'd go in there and cut 'em. Bring in a saw and haul 'em out with a wagon. He'd turn around and sell 'em. They would last.

"And we cut some of what they called a pig nut hickory. It's not like this hickory out along the sandy land. It makes a lot more hickory nuts. And we cut a lot of that for posts. That's hardwood. [My brother Alvin] uses pine," Harris added, referring to an adjacent post factory. "Small pine, up to a certain size.

> We sat on the bridge, and we caught close to 200 fish.

"I remember once we went to the creek," Jewel Dean said. "And we sat on the bridge, and we caught close to 200 fish, about that big. [She held up her hand.] That was back, right when me and him married. It didn't seem long [between the time] we sat down and we fished and time we got home. But you can't do it now."

"Back to when they dammed up that river back up home," Harris said, "you could go in 'most anywhere and catch fish, I mean good-sized fish. For one thing, see, back then there wasn't as many people fishing like they do today. I mean now there's somebody fishing every day.

"Maybe on Saturday [I'd take a day off]," Harris said. "See, I was the second family of my dad, and he was old. And I had to work to help make a living for my brother and my sister after he finally had to quit work. And he only got $15 a month. And I worked all my life since a chap. When I retired, I went back out and I worked for five more years.

"I worked for Georgia Timber Company, out over in Blountstown. I was running knives through a chipper, sharpenin' [them]. And then I worked out in pulpwood too. And I also worked down here at Florida Veneer Mill. It's not in business anymore.

"I logged, I pulped wood in a sawmill. You had to push the wood through the blades. You had to push hard. They had big old engines, and they were pulling old circular saws. It was very dangerous. One man fell into the saw blades" and died. "You could very easily get killed.

"I never did work at none of the big mills. In fact, I quit at the sawmill and found me something else. It was hard work. I mean, you take these slabs and you stuck you some of them up on skid poles, and you kept your poles kinda greased where it'd slide? And you stacked you up a pile of that, and you'd get your ring startin' right down there into the fire pit. You'd get all hot in June, July, and August. I've done a lot of hard work.

"You take, here I am, I should be seventy-seven years old [next month]. Everything I get I have to work for. I don't get no handouts whatsoever. I don't get Medicaid; I don't get my medicine paid for.

"But you take a lot of these people that's out here, that's got children? They can get Medicaid, they can get to the doctor, they can get medicine, doesn't cost 'em nothin'. Some will not work, and that's not right. Every one of my children is hard at work, every last one of them. I raised them that way. They're out making their own living. They're helping pay another kid out of their own money. So you see, there are people who are getting benefit of it that should not be gettin' it, because a lot of the older people did not get it.

"I'm proud as I don't have to sit there beggin' for nothin', and I'm proud if my children don't," Harris said. "I keep losing weight. Found out my lung's about to collapse. I had a bronchial infection, and I had bad lungs too. I had pneumonia way back years ago. In fact, I had it three times. And the first time I had the flu and pneumonia, the doctor give me up. No chance for me.

"That was back in the thirties. They had a nurse, Miss Kittrell. I will never forget her name. She came to our home and stayed there day and night. My mother was sick. My father, he come down [with it]. And back then you didn't have a bad cold and call it the flu. You had the flu, and there wasn't any people come to see you because they were scared.

"I didn't even know when I came down and when I come up. That's how low I got. The nurse said she had her doubts and was about to told one of my aunts that there was no chance for me. She had done everything she knowed to do.

"But anyway, I got mad when I was in the height of [illness]. They say part of it was, I worked through my lifetime [with] chemicals that you don't even have today. The government has banned them, you see? The doctor told me when they operated on me that I was exposed to some kind of chemical. It weakened my system.

"Well, DDT, you put it on trees or inject it in that tree. That busts the bark on that tree. What in the world is it going to do to you? We used to use it here in the Ochlockonee River swamp, and you had what you called injectors. And you hit that tree, and it would squirt so much of it in that tree. In about a week, the bark was stripping off the tree. It killed the 'undesirable trees' such as ironwood. They just wanted something else to grow there. I mean something like over cut oak, pines.

"I worked with zinc and lead, and I worked with some kinda stuff you spray the crops with. You put it on the pine seed, and then we planted them pine seed with what we call cyclone seeders. And that dust just get all over you. That would kill the birds and stuff that picked up those seeds. I'm curious now, though, on that science that's come out. Really, you weren't supposed to work with this stuff at one time [for more than] one year. I worked in it two or three years. And we set out a lot of pines too, with machine and by hand. I've planted several thousand. We planted anywhere from three to four thousand a day, sometimes six or eight thousand.

"But the forest is not like it used to be when I worked down there. 'Cause they've let a lot of the roads go bad, a lot of the bridges. We have repaired and built bridges that are all gone now in Liberty County.

"We picked up garbage, we cleaned bathrooms, we mowed, just everything in general all through the [Apalachicola National] Forest. We had [facilities at] Camel Lake, we had Wright Lake, we had Hickory Landing, we had Cotton Landing, we had Porter Lake, and we had Hitchcock Lake. And then we pumped out the bathrooms across the river. Actually you really don't know nothin'·'til you get out there dealing with the public. They want this done, and they make a mess and make you clean it up.

"[While sharecropping] I always had something to eat. And I didn't have no bills," Harris laughed. "Back then you didn't go into debt too much. We drove mules when other people were driving cars. Oh, I can remember back in the Model T and Model A days. I didn't own one 'til after I was married. My momma and daddy were always: 'Well, you don't need this, and you don't need that. You don't need to throw your money away to certain people.

"I've lived a hard life. I can tell you when wages went to $1 a day—1940."

"I bought flour," Jewel Dean said. "Flour, sugar, coffee, milk. I canned a lot, peas, beans, okra. They don't can nowadays."

"I would be able to live on around $300 or $400 a month," Harris said. "I mean back when you're raising my kids, you know. We rented until sometime in '63. I bought [this house] with money I didn't have. I borrowed the money and paid it back by the month. I got a deal on a little place right there. The old lady and the old man that lived here, they wasn't going to finish paying for it. I got the place for $700. That's what she owed on the place."

"He paid her a lump sum," Jewel Dean said. "The first time he ever got any income back" on taxes. "And he got that money he spent on this house from my daddy. It didn't have a bathroom, but we did have a kitchen."

"This wall I built out 6 feet all the way down," Harris said, indicating the east wall. "And I come back later and built this here," he indicated the front, north wall. "Built the porch out front, built two rooms back yonder, and added a bathroom and built the kitchen. I built the kitchen in the last part of '77."

"He worked all day, and then he worked all night," Jewel Dean said.

"It's eight rooms," Harris said. "I tell 'em I put my life earnings in. I did a lot of the carpentry by myself, before my children got big enough to help me. I taught myself," Harris added. "One old fellow that worked on our forest service, he was a good carpenter, and I worked with him a whole lot. And I worked to see what he was doing, and what he told me to do, I'd do. I'd do my own plumbing. I done all my own work back when I could see good.

"I set my children down, and I tell them, 'Living is hard, but you make more money in one day alone now than I made in two or three weeks.'" Harris laughed.

He often walked 6 miles to go visiting, Harris said. "I walked from Little Rocky Creek several miles to Sneads time and time again. It'd take me about an hour a day, but I was just going to see some of my people. Young boy, young man, like. I walked out in the country where I had a [great-]aunt and an uncle right there."

"We walked to church," Jewel Dean said. "It was about 2 miles, sometimes farther than that. We went to Antioch Church, went to Saint Creek Church of God. We went to the Church of God and the Church of Baptist at Antioch, Free Will. We went to different churches on Sunday night and Saturday."

"Yeah, that's when we were at Sanger," Harris said. "I walked to church many a day too. I been just about all kinds. I've been Holiness, I've been to Baptist, I've been to Methodist, and I went there more than one time. I been to about everything but Catholic," Harris said. "But actually, I'm more Holiness than I am Baptist.

"My mother, she finally in her later years, she went to Baptist," Harris said.

"And I never did know my father going to church. I was brought up, mostly I wasn't at home. I was with other people.

"And I mostly [was] brought up around other people," Harris said. "You know I stayed with them and worked with them and all that. To really know what a real home was, it's still other people. This is another reason, a lot of people said, 'You're crazier over your children than any man I ever seen.'

"But I think one of the reasons I love my children and I stayed at home and I kept them together, I actually do think people should do that. I raised my children and schooled them and done it on my own by knowing where every last penny went. If I done on what little I made, I made less than what I'm drawing today."

"I didn't throw away anything," Jewel Dean said. "I turned old dresses into work shirts. Just cut up old dresses—what part was wore out, I didn't use. What was good, I made dresses and shirts out of 'em. I'd take pants legs, if he wore the seat out, and make pants [for the boys]. I might have to mix colors; it might not be the best-looking dress in the world, but it was worthwhile to make it. And it ain't what you wear, it's if it's clean. Nowadays you don't have to do that. My children don't. And I don't, but I still wear my old clothes."

The Harrises keep pictures of their parents in their living room. Jewel Dean's parents were Joseph and Roxanne Daniel Williams. Joseph's mother was Georgia Ann Simpson Cloud. "The 'Cloud' was Indian," he said.

In the yard, the Harrises have collected a museum of relics. There's an old hog-rendering kettle and an old cane kettle from days when sugarcane was grown and processed in Gadsden County. Mr. Harris also displayed turpentine hoes, cross saws, plows and seeders used for corn, peanuts, and, later, cotton.

L. L. Lanier: Honey Philosopher

For more than a century, the Lanier family has been harvesting honey from the Apalachicola River swamps. Their tupelo honey was selected from a world sampling by Chivas Regal to make Lochan Ora liqueur in the 1970s, and the family has been celebrated in print and film for half a century.

In the 1978 WFSU-TV documentary *Watermarks*, L. L. (Lavernor Laveon) Lanier Jr. speaks for keeping the Apalachicola natural and free-flowing. A plan to dam the river at the Chipola Cutoff and permanently flood the tupelo swamps for 45 miles was later withdrawn.

Lanier's bees were featured again in the 1997 Golden Globe–winning Sundance Film *Ulee's Gold*. Lanier, who learned beekeeping from his father

Fig. 9.3a. Beekeeper L. L. Lanier Jr. with his spitz, Dolly, at home in the tupelo swamp. Photo by Faith Eidse.

and grandfather and passed the business down to his son, Ben, says the bee-keeping was true, the story was fiction. But at his home on Lanier Island in the Chipola River swamp on March 22, 2001, he revealed many parallels with Ulee, the character played by Peter Fonda in the Victor Nunez film.

The story turns on the critical timing of taking pure tupelo honey to prevent bees mixing it with darker, lower-grade sources. Certified tupelo will not granulate, due to its high levulose to dextrose ratio (43 to 26 percent).

"I'd say that, to any degree, this is the only place tupelo is commercially grown. A lot of 'em put other honeys in it and call it tupelo," said Lanier. Only a quarter of the 20 million pounds of honey produced in Florida in a typical year is certified tupelo.

The swamp around Lanier's home was alight with egrets, ducks, and "Lord Gods" (the exclamation evoked by ivory-billed woodpeckers and then, as they vanished, by pileated woodpeckers), and the yard was filled with wet feet trees—white tupelo, water-elm, and black gum. As the wiry, white-haired raconteur wove stories and philosophies, the water rose, but Lanier assured us his house sat well above the flood crest of 1929—on 4 feet of fill and 4 feet of foundation. It was a crest his father had accurately predicted and marked on their walls when Lanier was six. "We had 18 inches to spare in [the flood of] 1994," Lanier said. "We were close. [Dad's] contention and mine is, too, you cannot raise that Gulf.

"In 1933, now—that would make me ten years old—the river did something it had never done before. There wasn't any dams. She dropped, just like you shut it off at Chattahoochee. Fish died by the ton. It formed a barrier at the mouth of every slough.

Then they cut it off with the dam. That dam is killing the tupelo trees. Mud used to come from Alabama and Georgia and enrich the swamps.

"I was born in the bee business," Lanier said. "I was two months old when my parents carried me down that river in a super." A super is a box on top of a brood-box that houses a queen bee. "They had me nestled up there in one of those supers. And the *Callahan Sr.* (a paddle-wheel steamboat) had just sunk [March 25, 1923]. Daddy had always paddled up that river. But about that time he bought a 2½-horse Johnson for $50. It was a small motor. He would sight on a tree and say, 'Yes, I'm moving.'"

"There's a lot of history in this swamp," said Lanier, who lost his brother Ed to the Big River. Ed read to him by lantern light at their bee camps, so that Lanier could read when he entered first grade in Wewahitchka.

"My brother was down at Richard Lake. He had no gun. I was six years old. I wadn't scared if Ed was there. While we were sleeping, something scratched on the door.

"Ed said, 'Are you scared?'

"I said, 'No, I ain't scared.'

"We had a bright ole kerosene lamp. I said, 'What do you think it is?'

"He said: 'It's a bear. I'll open this door, you get behind it, pull it open, and I'll hit him with this hammer.' He pulled that door open. I got up behind the door. He was protecting me, but he was facing the bear.

"That bear looked and ran, and that's all we could see was just a black spot. He dumped over a hive of bees and stole a ham of meat that we had hanging up. It was under that big oak tree there at Richard's Lake, behind where our bees are now."

Lanier complained to Bob Sikes, the original "He-Coon," about the Corps cutting off a double elbow near his apiary, straightening the river, increasing the current, and making it harder to navigate upstream. "And once you cut that point off, it will fill up so quick. Willow trees and sweet gum marched

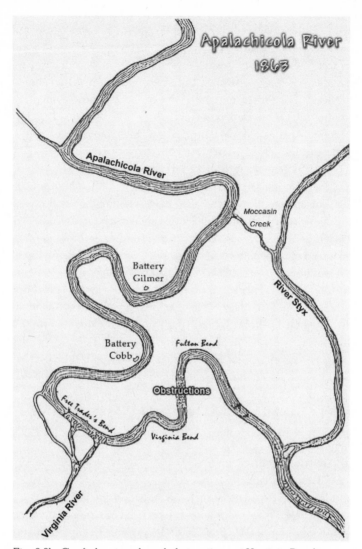

Fig. 9.3b. Confederates placed obstructions at Virginia Bend, forcing boats through Moccasin Creek and the River Styx. Later that route was dredged open, increasing the current and making it harder to navigate upstream, Lanier said. It also cut off Virginia Bend to tupelo honey producers. Map adapted by John Crowe from an 1863 U.S. War Document map.[1]

across it like soldiers. You straighten the river, you drain it." The year was 1955, and Sikes wrote him back, "Dear Junior, there will be no more straightening of the river."

"One day," Lanier said, "I was carrying bees on the River Styx [a crooked river that circumvents 'the Narrows,' where Confederates dammed the Apalachicola against the Union], and there was a tugboat grinding against the current. The river was up 24 feet at Blountstown, and they had just cut that river straight in the previous year. I was carrying thirty to forty supers. I slowed down and waved at him. He invited me on board and poured me coffee.

"'You one of those Cajuns?' he asked. I said, 'We came down on an alligator and got lost in the swamp.'" Lanier's ancestors are French Huguenot, though not via Acadia.

"But I asked him, 'Wasn't it easier to go upstream when this was crooked?' And he agreed it was. See, you can make it up around those bends when the current is slow.

"I worked for the U.S. Engineers a year on that river on a snagboat—*Albany*. Used a bucket snag to pick up trees and lay [them] on the bank.

"I worked from Apalachicola to Bainbridge. Must have been '41, just about the time the war started. Hezekiah Tant, 'Captain Hezee,' was the captain of the boat. And Ira Campbell was the district engineer for the Corps.

"Well, we dynamited King's Rock, which is above the dam at Chattahoochee, comin' out of the Flint River. It was a detriment to the steamboats. If you're comin' down, it'd carry you right into it, rip the bottom up. We put a case of dynamite on it, dropped into the river, and it'd go 'bloop,' 'bout like that. It never shattered that rock one bit. That rock is covered up now with all the dam.

"This dam ruined the river. It began to fill up immediately after that dam. Sand goes all down the river; the tupelo can't get the nutrients. Not only that, the sand covers up the new trees so they can't sprout. One day the swamp [will] be like the Dismal Swamp of Virginia, just eliminated. But the most dastardly thing they did was pile all the spoil out on the banks and then dig a ditch behind it. In high water, the water'd come back around and wash it in the river.

"My daddy said [sturgeon] used to stand up and shake and fall like a tree. He said you could hear 'em. He said if you seen 'em you could kill 'em with a shotgun. And said they'd be up to 16 feet long. And then fall, 'KAWOOP,' in the water.

"After [snagging], I worked grading citrus—oranges, tomatoes, peanuts. I was workin' peanuts in Americus, Georgia. We got to know all these farmers.

This dam ruined the river. It began to fill immediately after that dam.

One of them was named Carter, James Earl Carter Sr. I'd take a li'l ole electric heater [with a] brass lap. I'd take some shelled peanuts and put 'em around that and let 'em parch. And these farmers—and Jimmy—he'd come in with his daddy. He'd say, 'L. L. you got some hot, parched peanuts tonight?'

"In 1978, we just normalized relationships with China. Jimmy was still president, and I wrote him a note when he came back. I said: 'Jimmy, I appreciate you normalizin' relations with Chinese. There's ten of them to us one, and it's better we have them as friends than a enemy.' He wrote back and said, 'Thanks, L. L., for agreeing with one thing I did.'

"I was in the group," Lanier said, "one of the first" to enter China in 1979 after a ban on visitors was lifted. "They found out I was a beekeeper, and they kept my interpreter busy. See, over there a beekeeper is number one. Those Chinese just flocked around me. I'd heard the tupelo was over there, too. Well, I didn't find any trees 'cause they've cut most of their trees around Shanghai. But there where the Yangtze River [flows] looks just like our river—muddy.

"Did you know that during Caesar's era [honey] was worth more than gold? There was no other sweet. There wadn't any beets, any corn in Europe to make sugar out of, even if they'd 'ave known how. Sugar and salt were the two main things to fight about—and women—three things.

"You know, I've worked with REA [Rural Electrification Administration] and Farm Bureau statewide," Lanier said. "That's what lighted up the river valley [after 1935]." Each family invested $5 against costs, measured in customers per mile. Lanier is past board chair of Gulf Coast Electric Cooperative, Inc., Wewahitchka, which pays dividends on electric bills, pays $500 to each fire department, and sponsors community events and scholarships.

Lanier left the river and the bees for thirteen years to grade produce, but like Ulee, Lanier's life turned black when he left the blooming, trilling swamps.

"This was fifty-odd years ago," Lanier said. "I was all by myself. This fellow just came up out of the blue. He says: 'We want to hire you. We know you're trustworthy; you don't drink. We want you to take this little black bag; you go in a bar and set it down. You don't know what's in that bag. You haven't gotta know. Another fellow comes in, unknown to you, got a bag just like it, sits just as close to you as he can. When he gets up he gets your bag by mistake, goes out and leaves you his. You still haven't gotta know what's in it.'

"That scared me. Three days after I refused it, the guy I'd 'ave replaced wound up with six bullet holes in him, right there on that dreaded Highway 4. I didn't wanna go to work for 'em 'cause you can't get out from under it. They bought you. That's why I came back. I looked up that night and said,

Fig. 9.3c. Beekeepers examine honeycombs at Whitfield apiaries near Wewahitchka in May 1960. Photo courtesy of Florida State Archives, Charles Baron photographer.

'Lord, if you'll let me go home, I'll work twice as hard for half as much to make those bees go.' I came home and buried myself in those bees," he said.

There's "nothing I can do" to encourage the tupelo, Lanier added. "I guess I own as much swampland as any small landowner. I'd say maybe a total of 400 acres. I bought that so I could put bees down here and they couldn't run me off.

"I'm an environmentalist, but I believe in using your renewable resources. It's like a can of preserves. You [don't] set 'em on the counter and let 'em ruin. You got to use your environment as you go through, with care. You've got to have a match between the environment and the use of all this stuff.

"I put [honey] in my eyes almost every night. And I told the eye doctor that. He had to take cancer off the inside of my eye. See that little scar?" Lanier pointed to a nick on the bottom lid.

"[The doctor] said, 'What kinda salve do you use—eye drops?'

"I says, 'tupelo honey.'" Lanier laughed gleefully. "He didn't correct it. Yeah, it's one of the best things in the world for burns. See, it re-moistens. You're drawing the heat out. I read this article, confirmed my thinking, 'cause you've been burned over half of your body and you got to peel [the bandages] off of you every mornin' and every night. They put you in honey and just let you slosh in that honey, and turn you over and over. You'll heal up without a scar.

"You know, there's a disease that's cured in honey. It's harmless to people. There's a spore. It's called foulbrood, 'cause it has a foul odor. See there's an egg, the larvae, and the pupa in an insect, you know that. Well, it rots in the larvae [or brood] stage. It smells like rotten fish.

"We was way down the river there one day; we'd burned 300 colonies. Pete [the inspector] says: 'Lavernor, I'm gonna get it in that hard head'a' yours about the foulbrood—how dangerous it is. You throw it in the barrel and throw gas on it, and it goes 'foomp.' That spore can go up there on the leaf of a tree or on a cypress log. Twenty years from now if, accidentally, honey just dropped on that same spot, that spore comes out of the wood, into the honey. Your bees go pick it up, take it home, and they've infected their young.'

"All the beekeepers forgot this," Lanier said. "They call me an old crank because they can give 'em an antibiotic. But it only covered it up. It didn't shoot it. But you see my point? Foulbrood. Without the bees, we can't live.

"I'm not scared of the atom bomb. I'm not scared of Jerusalem causing the world war. I'm scared of the bees bein' wiped out by diseases, and then we will be hungry, in three short years. We won't actually starve to death in three years, but your cucumbers would go, your tomatoes, your watermelons. [Bees] pollinate your vegetables. And they pollinate [fruits and other edible plants].'

"Now, I don't know but there's 300 plants that your pants leg, walkin' through the dew, will not pollinate. Or the wind or a bird—nothing but a honeybee.

"The steamboat going down the river—that's the prettiest thing I ever saw. I seen the steamboat tied up to the old cypress trees. Go in that saloon and there was cigars and candy and cigarettes, and I was raised up as a kid who'd notice.

"Well, the steamboat hauled the bees. They'd tape 'em together with sticks, cleats, and nail 'em up the side (8 feet high) and hold 'em together, in case it shifted? Well, the steamboat hit the mouth of the [Chipola] river down there, and they'd get out on the river and holler—and say, 'Captain of the boat be in about 15, 20 minutes.' So help me. Daddy'd get out there and holler and answer him. See, they had a code worked out.

"He says, 'Son, put your ear against that post and you can hear that steamboat.' Sure enough, I could: shoo, shoo, shoo, shoo [imitating the rhythmic

Fig. 9.3d. Lanier's mother slept one night at the Gregory House to confront the ghost that walked these stairs. Photo courtesy of Florida State Archives.

churn of a paddle wheel]. Well, you can go free, with your bees. Overnight you had to pay a 25¢ fee to go to a steam mill, Donalsonville, where the train bridge used to be. That's where they put 'em off, and Daddy'd rent a wagon and march with a horse and carry them out to various farms.

"Well, Uncle Alfred got caught up there one day, and he didn't have a quarter. And the captain and purser just hollered, more or less as a joke, 'Tag him out in steerage.'

Captain of the *J. W. Callahan Jr.*, Mason "Mace" Nisbet, "was a good friend of Daddy and Mother. So finally they say, 'All right, you take Junior up there.' So I get on the steamboat with 'im—. We come on up the river, and they had just told Daddy: 'Mr. Lanier, We want to quit. The steamboat's gonna shut down. The trucks are puttin' us out of business.'

"Well, I was on there with a kid, and I was having a ball. Lookin', I'd come up that river. And the dad-blame thing broke. One of the arms had twisted, like an oil rod, or drivers broke a piece of steel. And there we were; we tied it up. There was nothing we could do. Jim Harris comes by—a local from Wewahitchka—and he's a metalsmith. I remember walking out from Cochran Landing. Doggone if he don't pick us up and bring us to Wewa. But anyway, that was the last trip of the *John Callahan Jr.*

"See, that river was the road into Wewa. Our Daddy came down that river with his family, his Daddy's family and brothers and sisters; traded his farm for a floatin' house. They went from Birmingham to Anniston, Alabama, to Apalachicola.

"Another story I'd like to tell you. You know where Torreya Park is? That old [Gregory] house was on the Ocheesee side, way down the river from where it is now. When I was about ten years old, the [Civilian Conservation Corps] took that apart and carried it up the river.

"Aunt Essie, the oldest of Daddy's family, married a Gregory, the son of the man that owned that house. But he was a riverboat gambler. Daddy said he wore a fancy hat and a chain across his chest, you know, and he'd go down the Apalachicola River and across the bay where maybe he would catch a schooner, and go to New Orleans, and go to Mississippi—gambling. And one time he didn't show up, and they don't know any more than that. That ended him.

"And that's corrupted my mother. She came from Carolina here. But that house was haunted and still on this side of the river—at Ocheesee. She was a schoolteacher, and she got a college degree at Blountstown. Can you believe that? But she and [two friends], none of them were scared of him. She come to settle this haunted house. She said it sounded like the headless horseman, you know, that was holding his head and his chain?

"So middle of the night she hears him. And all three of them go and lean over that banister. And they seen that flying squirrels carrying crab apples down the stairs, and one of [the apples] gets away from them once in a while and goes down the steps—bloop-bloop-bloop-bloop-bloop."

Pearl Porter Marshall: Lighthouse Keeper's Daughter

Pearl Porter Marshall, daughter of lighthouse keeper Edward G. Porter, was born in 1900 and raised in the paradise of Little St. George Island. Before Bob Sikes Channel was cut in 1957, the barrier island sometimes connected

Fig. 9.4a. Cape St. George lighthouse and keeper's house in 1950. Photo courtesy of Florida State Archives.

with big St. George Island by a narrow, sand isthmus. To the west, separated by West Pass, was St. Vincent Island. It was this western approach to the bay that the Cape St. George (Little St. George Island) lighthouse first marked. The 1833 lighthouse stood about 2 miles from the second (current) light, built in 1847. The keeper's house, damaged in the Civil War, was rebuilt in 1879 to withstand hurricanes. It featured a hip roof and a strong central chimney, which supported ceiling joist and rafters.

Before her death on February 4, 1992, Pearl Porter Marshall wrote an account of her life. These are her words, as nearly as possible, used by permission of her heirs:

I am the daughter of a lighthouse keeper. My father was a lighthouse keeper on Little St. George Island, where I was raised until 1913, when my father died. He was assistant keeper at Cape San Blas when he was sent to St. George Light. While at St. George, he and Mother had six children. I was the fifth and always his right-hand man with all the stock, gardening, and outside chores. There was two boys, one older and one younger than I.

There was only two families on the island, the keeper and the assistant keeper. We only had a woodstove to cook on, outdoor toilets, and a big washroom where we did our washing and took a bath in a big zinc wash tub. Our house had two big cisterns.

We went to school two years on the island. [Our] schoolteacher, Miss Ola Rhodes, boarded with the assistant keeper's family. We had to walk about 2 miles to the school, which Dad had built for a storm house.

When Dad knew there was a storm on the way, Mother would cook and bake all day as we only had a tiny oil burner in the storm house. Dad would have me hitch up a mule and a horse to the double team wagon, and we would all pile in, except Dad, [who] had to stay at the light.

I remember one time we stayed at the storm house about three days, and one time when Mother thought the hurricane was over, she had me hitch up the team and we started home. We met Dad about halfway. The wagon was practically floating, and Dad was wading waist-high.

Dad said: "Where are you going? This is only the eye of the storm. Go back to the storm house." In a day or so, the storm blew over, and you could just see the top of the garden posts, the water was so high. Dad said the tower would just rock during a bad storm.

One time we had a real bad northwester, and there were hundreds of little birds, all colors, all over the island, some dead. We kids caught the live ones and put them in the wash house until they could fly again.

Dad had lots of cattle, hogs, and goats, and he would butcher a beef once a week and send it to market by the assistant keeper. The only part we had was the head meat, brains, and tripe.

The boat only came once a week for supplies, so Dad always bought can goods, flour, sugar, and meal by the case or sack.

Dad had built a [retirement] house up close to the bay side and hadn't quite finished it when he died. He was teaching us how to light the lantern, as it was hard for him to climb the stairs. The lighthouse tender would anchor in the Gulf, and men with yokes and a can on each side carr[ied kerosene] to the oil house where it was stored.

The Hammock House [was built] on a big hill we named Pike's Peak. At night the cattle would go to the beach to get out of the insects, and the next day Dad would send [little brother] Bunks and I down with the mule and cart to pick up chips. The horse was Sampson, and the mule was Mack. He was the sweetest and prettiest little mule I have ever seen. When Dad [plowed] his garden, I would ride Mack.

The lighthouse inspector came about two or three times a year to inspect the light, and everything had to be spotless. Dad would have to meet him in the horse and buggy and bring him over to the light, for the lighthouse tender always anchored on the bay side. [The inspector] would bring us a [new] library about once or twice a year and pick up ours to take to another station.

Fig. 9.4b. Josephine Porter, Hazel Nickmire, Pearl Porter, Eleanor Porter, and Rosa V. Montgomery in a rowboat at St. George Island, about 1916. Photo courtesy of Florida State Archives.

The light was under the U.S. Lighthouse Establishment, but the Coast Guard took it over. Dad had bought the island from a Mr. Williams, except 6 acres where the light and two houses were.

When we lived on the island, crowds would come over and fish off the Government Dock, which is on the bay side of the island. They [had] the fish strung on a pole, and two men carrying it with trout, red fish, sheep head, sun fish, mullet, spade fish. The water was deep there then, but there has been so much erosion to the island, it is real shallow around the dock now. There are still some good fish in there at times and oysters on the pilings, which I have gone down and shucked many times.

Sometimes some of our cattle would get stuck in a bog, and if we found them in time, we would pull them out with the mule or horse. One of the mud ponds was right back of the house, and we usually found them in time and could save them.

[In] a saw grass pond right back of the house we kept our small playboats and one skiff. One day Josephine, Eleanor (my two older sisters), Hazel Knickmeyer, the assistant keeper's daughter, Rosa Vee Montgomery (Hazel's cousin), and I were playing in the skiff, and we had our dresses tucked in our panties to keep them from getting wet. One of us said, 'There comes a man down the beach.' Well, we started pulling our dresses down. Josephine just sat down on the bow of the boat. It was Mr. Vessels, a photographer from

Apalachicola, and he said: 'No, don't do that; I want the picture just as you were.' I really do cherish that picture.

This pond would get filled with water during a rainy season, and we would open it up to the Gulf to keep from breeding mosquitoes.

One day Hazel and I were playing horse and driver. The beach looked so smooth and pretty, we started across it and we both bogged down waist-deep in quicksand. We had a time crawling out [and] were always cautious after that.

Dad taught me how to milk, and I milked four or five [range] cows every morning and night. I had many a sore hand where the calves would bite me, [but] we had all the milk we wanted, and mother made butter and cottage cheese.

We always had a lot of chickens, and Dad had a dozen white leghorns at the Hammock House. We always had plenty of eggs.

We would get up early and go out in the woods and look for terrapins, or cooters, and when we found five or six, Mother would make turtle soup or stew. It was really good.

Dad had built a dock about 3 miles up from the lighthouse. He also built a cottage for people who wanted to come down for a week or two. There is where I met Herbert Marshall. I would hitch up the double team and haul their things to the cottage. If they had any ice [or] watermelons [left], they would always give them to me. Dad had built an icebox of wood and filled it with sawdust, and that's the only way we could keep ice, which we seldom had.

Dad was taken sick in 1913, and Mother was in Apalach canning figs. Rudolph, Herbert's brother, had a speedboat, so Eleanor and I put Dad in the wagon and took him to the cottage, and Rudolph brought him to the doctor.

He lived four or five days when he died with uremic poison or Bright's disease. On his deathbed, he told Mother to take us to the island in the summer and live at the house he was building, which she did, until her death in 1924.

When he called me to his bedside, he said, "Pearl, take care of all the stock," which I tried to do, as I always loved cattle, horses, goats, and pigs. They just seemed part of my life.

I went to the island with mother every summer as the other children were either married or worked in Apalach. Mother had given me six cows as the others didn't seem to care about them.

Mr. Walter Roberts would butcher a beef for mother once a week. One time Mr. Walter said, "Pearl, here's the rifle, come on and kill the beef[;] you have done everything else."

Fig. 9.4c. Pearl Porter Marshall, niece Mary Virginia and Bess Marshall Porter take aim on St. George Island in 1924. Photo courtesy of Florida State Archives.

I said, "No, Mr. Walter, I draw the line there."

When I was in the twelfth grade, Herbert decided to join the navy and was gone two years. When he got out, he came by Jacksonville, where I was taking a course in telegraphy. Mother got sick, and I had to come home and take care of her. October 24, 1923, Herbert and I were married.

Herbert got a job dipping cattle to eradicate ticks, so we moved to the island. He built three vats—one on our island, and one on the big island, and one on St. Vincent Island. We would pack a lunch and go to East Pass, opposite Carrabelle, and drive the cattle from there to our dipping vat, dip all of them, including our horses, and next day go to St. Vincent and dip their cattle.

Herbert gave me a Remington 16-gauge shotgun on my birthday and taught me to shoot it. I got where I was nearly as good a shot as he was. I went hunting quite a bit while Herbert and I lived on the island, and I surely do miss it now.

When the taxes came due on the island, we borrowed the money [and bought] three of the Porter heirs' shares of the island (Josephine wouldn't sell her share). We [then] leased the turpentine to Mr. Clifford Land. Herbert and Clifford went in the cattle business together, and finally Herbert bought him out.

We dipped cattle down there for about a year and moved back to town. Herbert went to work for the State Road Department. He also did some carpentry and later was sheriff of Franklin County for sixteen years.

When the air base was closed in Apalach, Herbert bought two of the army barracks, hauled them to the island and made us a home on the bay. We would go down whenever we could.

The Coast Guard [was] going to burn down our house at the light. Herbert said he would like to have the lumber and floored our house. We both loved that island. In fact, the happiest days of my life were over there from the time I can remember until Herbert was killed in a boat accident over there, September 12, 1976.

Before Herbert left, we sold all but 160 acres on the Gulf side and 80 acres on the bay side, where our house was built. We were to have a lifetime estate on it, but it wasn't written in the final sale, so they told me to move.

Little St. George is a beautiful island, far more beautiful than Big St. George, and I had a wonderful life on that island and had a wonderful father; a well-built and good-looking man, and a wonderful husband and father.

10

River as Trade
and Commerce Opportunity

The river is more valuable as river than as water.
Pedro Arrojo Aguda

A river is much more than a canal. It is the life, sustenance, and opportunity of a community. It creates local meaning, cultural values, and social identity.[1] It offers connection to a vast world and expansion into it. It is a source of learning, a key to natural and local knowledge, as well as a starting point of contact, comparison, and contrast with other cultures. The river embodies identity and changes it, even as river uses change.

Apalachicola was once a center of river commerce, and shoppers spent their money locally well into the 1900s. Its large houses teemed with tentable bridge parties and society balls. When the St. Joe railroad arrived, the town turned out to see the engine back into town, pick up picnickers for the beach, and pull forward back to St. Joe. Trains, bridges, and pavement eventually lured shoppers to Panama City and Tallahassee. Boats stopped supplying the city's riverfront stores. Buses departed the ever-more-remote port city for the increasingly central state capital.

When the 1994 net ban left commercial fishermen reeling, guided fishing parties proliferated, making Apalachicola a recreational fishing destination. The popular annual seafood festival the first Saturday of November draws Floridians, Georgians, and Alabamians. They move in and sometimes take up preservation causes to protect beaches against a development boom. Do neighbors still know each other as they did in Clifton Lewis's memoirs of historic Teresa Beach? Has Apalachicola retained the hard-working, hard-playing edge recalled by Kathleen Hayes, Jimmie Nichols, and Robert Howell?

Edward Tolliver, Apalachicola's first black mayor pro tem (appointed temporarily), who died in December 2001, recalled swimming through Apalachicola along creeks, marshes, and embayments that are now filled in.

Numerous commerce communities, service bases, religious denominations, schools, and fishing communities have imprinted the region. The relationship between a river and its people is historic and changeable, constantly in flux as shrimpers replaced spongers, who replaced steamboat rousters, who replaced slaves.

Jimmie Nichols: Four-time Apalachicola Mayor

Jimmie Nichols, a native of Apalachicola and descendant of Greek immigrants, was interviewed on videotape in 1989 by Frances Ingram, then employed by the Apalachicola National Estuarine Research Reserve (ANERR). Following is an excerpt of that interview.

You couldn't hear any English spoken. It was either Greek or Italian.

"My full name is Jimmie J. Nichols; been in Apalachicola all my life. My father worked in seafood, helped open the Owl Café (1907), married in Greece, raised three boys and operated the Economy Cash store. When I was a teenager, downtown Water Street and downtown Commerce Street were

Fig. 10.0. Oyster shells on Water Street, Apalachicola, about 1906. Photo courtesy of Florida State Archives.

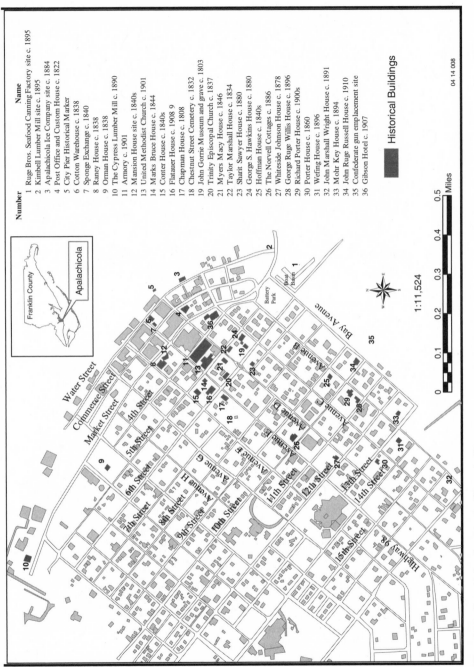

Number	Name
1	Ruge Bros. Seafood Canning Factory site c. 1895
2	Kimbell Lumber Mill site c. 1895
3	Apalachicola Ice Company site c. 1884
4	Post Office and Custom House c. 1822
5	City Pier Historical Marker
6	Cotton Warehouse c. 1838
7	Sponge Exchange c. 1840
8	Raney House c. 1838
9	Orman House c. 1838
10	The Cypress Lumber Mill c. 1890
11	Armory c. 1901
12	Mansion House site c. 1840s
13	United Methodist Church c. 1901
14	Marks Bruce House c. 1844
15	Conter House c. 1840s
16	Flatauer House c. 1908 9
17	Chapman House c. 1808
18	Chestnut Street Cemetery c. 1832
19	John Gorrie Museum and grave c. 1803
20	Trinity Episcopal Church c. 1837
21	Myers Macy House c. 1846
22	Taylor Marshall House c. 1834
23	Sharit Sawyer House c. 1880
24	George S. Hawkins House c. 1880
25	Hoffman House c. 1840s
26	The Norvell Cottages c. 1886
27	Whiteside Johnson House c. 1878
28	George Ruge Willis House c. 1896
29	Richard Porter House c. 1900s
30	Porter House c. 1860
31	Wefing House c. 1896
32	John Marshall Wright House c. 1891
33	Mohr Key House c. 1894
34	John Ruge Russell House c. 1910
35	Confederate gun emplacement site
36	Gibson Hotel c. 1907

Historical Buildings

1:11,524

0   0.1   0.2   0.3   0.4   0.5
Miles

04 14 008

Franklin County

Apalachicola

Map 10.1. City of Apalachicola Historic Sites

Fig. 10.1a. Mayor Jimmie Nichols, Jim Woodruff Sr., and Congressman Bob Sikes at Harbor Day celebration, Apalachicola, 1958. Photo courtesy of Florida State Archives, photographer Karl E. Holland.

full of Italians and Greeks. They were doing their fishing and oystering; they even had some sponging going on. And that was a time [about 1900–30] that you walked down those streets, you couldn't hear any English spoken. It was either Greek or Italian.

"Down here, around where the courthouse is located now, there were three Italian bakers makin' these round rolls of bread. When it first came out of the oven, those Italians would open it up and put olive oil and black pepper on it. But after two days it got so hard they used to call it bricks, and there was a Greek bakery in the area too. There were a lot of coffeeshops around. There were a lot of restaurants downtown that were Greek-owned.

"I remember the first time they had a fire in Apalachicola—when the new fire truck came to town on a flatbed truck—and they had three fires that day. So that started some questions, now.

"Back in those days the kids in the neighborhood would get together and have their own games. There used to be a Irish town baseball club. There was one up on the north of town called the Gallopin' Goats.

"We used to have two trains come to Apalachicola every day. The name of our railroad company was called the Apalachicola Northern Railroad, and they also said it stood for Absolutely Nothin'. There used to be a train come in every morning, around ten, from River Junction, which is now called Chattahoochee. At River Junction, the Apalachicola Northern connected with Seaboard Rail Line.

"Every morning we got fresh Merita bread from Jacksonville, sold at Russell's Meat Market. Every night the American Railway Express train was goin' out of here. That's how all the seafood was shipped at that time. There used to be a lot of wooden barrels that shipped out, with ice on the top, covered with a croker sack. To go as far as New York, they had to take the croker sacks off and re-ice it half way up the road.

"There were twenty-one seafood houses in Apalachicola, including several canneries. A lot of seafood houses had special carriers with their name stamped on 'em, like Standard Fish and Oyster Company or United Seafood Company. They would ship oysters in gallons packed in ice and would go up to 500 miles from Apalachicola. Those restaurants were supposed to ship the carriers back, but I imagine a lot of 'em kept 'em.

"I can remember in 1942 when this *Empire Mica*, British ship sank off Cape San Blas, and they brought all those people in here. Captain Randolph and the *Sea Dream* was comin' in with a party, and he was alerted so everybody got on his boat, and they went back out to the *Mica*. According to [his] story, they circled around and saved fourteen people, and after these people recovered, they even had a [memorial] service in the Episcopal Church.

"One or two of those fellas came back here and settled in this country. One of 'em came down here about two years ago. I believe they had an article in the paper. I know the City of Apalachicola got a letter from one of 'em. He's now livin' in New South Wales in Australia.

"And they tell me that during the war when the Apalachicola Gunnery School was stationed out at the air force base, that Clark Gable was supposed to have flown over Apalachicola and said, "Gosh, that certainly is a beautiful little city down there." Because Clark Gable said it, we still remember it.

"Italian and Greek families were real close-knit; they observed their special holidays. There wadn't no television, and everybody came downtown every night. There was several butcher shops, and there was a lot of people didn't have refrigeration. They would come down on Saturday night and make their selections, then go back the next morning, pick up their meats, and go home and cook 'em.

"The drugstores used to stay open 'til twelve o'clock at night. You could come downtown and park your car in front of John Joe Buzzett's drugstore, and he'd come right out and say, 'What do you want?' He'd deliver [ice cream cones] right to your car.

"In the summertime a lot of the churches went on excursions to Port St. Joe on the train. The whole church would go and have their picnic and come back that night. You could smell meatballs all over the place down there.

"Well, the first talking movies in the Dixie Theatre were around 1928 or 1929. Al Jolson had one of the first ones. It cost you a dime to go to the show if you were under twelve. An adult pass was 35¢. The theater was segregated, and the upstairs balcony was split in two. On the east side only black citizens were allowed to sit and went through an outside entrance. On the west side were people who loved to smoke.

"Every week they'd play fifteen minutes of some serial [like] *Hopalong Cassidy*, Ken Maynard, or Bob Steele. They also had *Happening News*, what was happening in the world. Then they had the main movie. It all lasted about two hours. Mr. [Alex] Fortunas was the main operator. He also had a seafood house. He had two sons, George and Nick, and he also had a daughter, Emma Fia. I think people in St. Joe, if they wanted to go to the theater, came to Apalachicola. They had plays [and] a beauty pageant in the theater, and it seemed like Fred's Sawyer's wife, Dottie, was selected [as Miss Franklin County]. Her name was Buck.

There wadn't no bridge between Apalachicola and Eastpoint. . . . It took exactly one hour to go across the bay [by ferry].

"I can remember when there wadn't no bridge between Apalachicola and Eastpoint. We had Captain Andy Wing's ferries. Each ferry carried about twenty, twenty-five cars. It took exactly one hour to go across the bay from Apalachicola to Eastpoint. Then there was a paved road trunk from there to Tallahassee via Carrabelle. There was also a railroad that went from Carrabelle to Tallahassee, and Captain Andy Wing also operated the passenger boat called the *Jesse May* that went from Apalachicola to Carrabelle, and then you could take the train on to Tallahassee and points all over the country.

"Back in those days we didn't believe in going out of town for shopping. Everybody shopped in Apalachicola. I remember putting out [dry goods] circulars for my daddy in Port St. Joe and Wewahitchka. Now it's the other way around. Everybody I know now goes out of town and shops.

"The most outstanding teacher in Chapman High School was Miss Stephie Rice Porter. She always used to say, 'You've got plenty of time but none to waste.' Then we had Miss Emily Porter (her daughter), Willis Anthony, [and] Grace Alexander Norton. She really worked with every student.

"They had a lot of snapper boats fishin' out of Apalachicola. Captain Mosconis and his son Nick, they would catch snapper and grouper and be out ten days. When those fellas went out on those boats, the cooks always ordered the best of steaks and things. I think they ate better on the boats than they did at home.

"Whenever they'd come in, they must'a had lots of dough 'cause I betcha they gave away fifty snappers to different people. They used to cut the heads off for processing. A lot of the local people would cut off the [neck]. It was about 2 inches square. All the debris, shrimp heads, and things were thrown overboard, which you cannot do anymore.

"Everybody had an icebox. We used to have a [paper sign for the window marked] 10 lbs., 15 lbs., 25 lbs., and 50 lbs. [That] way the ice man would know how much ice you wanted, and he'd bring a piece off his truck. You used to see [the] 300-pound size; it cost 75¢. It's $10 today.

"[In] the Depression, all the grocery stores competed, and they would deliver $1.50 of groceries to your house free. Bring it to your kitchen, take your groceries out, and bring the box back.

"Willis Glass and his brother Chancey had the Glass Dairy right beyond where C. T. Ponder lives. In fact, the house is still there, and so is the place where they bottled the milk. Every morning around six o'clock, Willis and his brother would deliver milk. They also delivered milk in the afternoon.

"When Sheip's Mill was in full force, they used to make this lumber for cigar boxes. Fifth Street was one of the very few streets north of Bay Avenue that was paved. It was paved all the way to the mill. When [the] twelve o'clock whistle blew, everybody went home to eat. That was the busiest street in town for like one hour, comin' and goin'.

"Sheip's also had a commissary. In the beginning, Mr. Sheip [gave] a percentage of [pay] in scrip. You had to spend that scrip in their own store. It controlled the prices, of course. There was nothin' cheap in there, but you had no choice because there was still a depression going on.

"There's a real loss of the buildings. I don't believe they had any business tearing down the old school building. And that was where the courthouse was. Behind the courthouse, where the mental health building is, was the county jail. The old city jail was down here behind to where the county courthouse is. And where the Rainbow Marina is, Marks Brokerage Company was, and they were a wholesale grocery house, and there used to be two boats comin' in. One was called the *Callahan*, which was a steamship comin' out of Columbus, Georgia, bringing groceries down here and carryin' something back, turpentine I believe. Then we had the *Tarpon* that came out of Mobile. It stopped in Pensacola, Panama City, even went to Carrabelle, and came back to Apalachicola and unloaded groceries. It also carried passengers. If you compared the hustle and bustle of fifty years ago to today, it's a big difference.

"There used to be a lot of grocery stores around town; now there's only two. If [people] had a car, they would average one per family, not soon as you

[turn] sixteen you have your own automobile. There was always two drug-stores downtown. Mr. Buzzett had his drugstore in the original site. I think his license dated from 1905, one of the oldest pharmaceutical licenses in Florida. When Willis Kennedy bought that out and moved, I think he still got the same number, three or five. And down at the corner there was always a drugstore until Lanier moved out. The Robbins brothers operated it and then T. J. Hicks.

"Way out across the street, the faceless building, that was the first A&P in Apalachicola. In between the Gorrie Furniture Company and the A&P building, Kirk had a drugstore. Around 1950, A&P moved across the street and was on the corner where the Apalachee five-and-ten was. And in that former building is where Dr. Photis Nichols opened up his office right after the war. Later on they had the county hospital out at the [former] air base. And I think the first baby that was born out there was Reba Randolph. She's a Braswell now.

"At one time they had four doctors in Apalachicola. There was Dr. J. S. Munroe. He lived in the Rainey house. All he gave you was a pink pill, and it was the bitterest pill I ever took in my life. He must'a brought 2 million pink pills with him 'cause he never ran out. Then we had Dr. Conter, we had Dr. Weems, and we had a [doctor] who had an office above the Dixie Theatre. He had a lot of dogs; he loved dogs. His name was Dr. Steely.

"Sometime in the mid-thirties *Old Ironsides* was brought to Port St. Joe [on tour]. They had people there from all over the southeastern United States come down to see *Old Ironsides*. It was originally named *The Constitution*. They had a menhaden plant at Port St. Joe; we called it pogies. And it was a long dock, way out in the water. But I wanted to go on that boat. Seems like at one time they had a zeppelin called U.S. *Los Angeles* come over to Port St. Joe. There were several zeppelins in America then.

"The National Guard used to go off to camp by railroad. They'd go for two weeks, but our National Guard has been all over.

"We had buses out of here; we had Lee's Coach Line operated out of Apa-lachicola twice a day. They connected between Tallahassee on down and over to Panama City. Back in those days in the thirties they also had a six-team intercity baseball club. I think they had Tallahassee, Apalachicola, Carrabelle, Port St. Joe, Wewahitchka, Blountstown, and Marianna. And of course, the two teams that had it the toughest— It was dangerous to go to a ball game where Carrabelle and Apalachicola played each other, whether it was in Apa-lachicola or Carrabelle.

"On that area bordering Twelfth Street, that's where we played football. John Lovett lives on that property now, and so does McCormick and

> It was dan-gerous to go to a ball game where Carrabelle and Apa-lachicola played each other, whether it was in Apa-lachicola or Carrabelle.

Fig. 10.1b. Apalachicola sponge exchange, about 1895. Photo courtesy of Florida State Archives.

Watkins. That was Porter's Baseball Park. Home plate was down at the corner where McCormick's house is.

"Frances Bloodworth could hit home runs all over everyway. We had some good ballplayers in Apalachicola. [Police chief] G. W. Hendels went down to [try] out in Tampa, but he got homesick and came on back. There was a lot of kids who never left Franklin County.

"[This is my] fourth term [as mayor]. [In] '55 I became a city commissioner, and the mayor at that time was Cory M. Henderson. He resigned to go back to lab work for the U.S. Quartermaster. During the war, he was operating a tent plant in Apalachicola. So I took his place. That was for two years. In 1959, my wife and I had the chance to go to Greece and adopt two little babies, John and Kathy. While I was there, Dwight Marshall was acting mayor, mayor pro tem. Then I sat out until 1971, then I ran [and] was mayor for four years. In 1975, I ran again, then I sat out again [until] May 1987.

"By coincidence the other night we adopted a Florida Power franchise for thirty years, and I sat on the one we adopted thirty years ago. The city attorney was Bourke Floyd, and thirty years later his son is city attorney.

"When we were working on that other franchise it was real controversial, and I was tryin' to get a better deal. They were puttin' out stories that I was

They had a
bank in
Carrabelle
just to take
care of the
Greek
sponges, the
Grecian
Bank.

gonna put Florida Power out of business and go back in the electrical business with my brother, a chief electrician.

"I think by the time I was growin' up, [the sponge industry] had died out.
Around 1895, it was in its heyday up here. Most of the sponges are caught
between Carrabelle and Tarpon Springs and Key West. They used to bring
sponges up here. They had a bank in Carrabelle just to take care of the Greek
sponges, the Grecian Bank. A lot of the sponge folks in Tarpon Springs were
familiar with Apalachicola. The Tarpon Springs sponge exchange, a boat in
there, [the *Aegean Isles*], used to be called the *Apalachicola*. A plaque identifies it was made in Apalachicola in 1935 and who made it, so forth.

"Back in those days there were so many Greeks in Tarpon Springs, so
many in Apalachicola, that if there was a depression in Apalachicola, the
Greeks would just go to Tarpon Springs and visa-versa. Most of these people
that came over from Europe were following a relative or somebody. I had an
uncle that wound up in Seattle, Washington. He said, 'When I came to Apalachicola [between 1901–8], things were not doing so good, and there was an
earthquake in San Francisco.' They were advertising for laborers so he went,
wound up in the salmon business.

"I'll tell you something about Irish Town, [the] section around the courthouse. A couple of years ago the Episcopal Church had their 150th birthday.
I went around there and suggested [writing] a history of the area. They're
printing it now. It seems that whenever the Apalachicola Land Company
needed laborers, the Irish people must'a been a special labor gang. They
went from town to town wherever they were needed. They built forty cotton
warehouses in Apalachicola between 1830 and 1840, three stories high.

"City Hall's one of 'em; the other one is across the street. From the Water
Street entrance you can see an outline of the stairway up to the third floor.
They must'a had a lot of trouble with [the third floor]. That's the reason we
stayed down to two floors. Most of 'em didn't last over ten or fifteen years.

"I can't understand the shape of that building [on the corner down from
City Hall], don't know what it was intended for. And Willoughby Marshall
made a plan for the city when I was mayor the second time. He said that
Apalachicola was laid out on the Philadelphia plan. He said the intent was
for the people to build their houses around the squares. But Apalachicola
was a river town and a cotton town and seems like all the merchants went up
and down Fifth Street and built their houses. In fact, you might have heard
Mr. Marshall talk about taking a strip and rearranging the houses right here.
I told him that you'd have to find a Rockefeller to come in and buy these
houses and shuffle them around like they did in Williamsburg. They tell me

Fig. 10.2b. Edward E. Tolliver with his son, Edward G. Tolliver.
Photo courtesy of Edward G. Tolliver.

that from Riverside Café building, going north, was a marsh and they had a
wooden walkway they carried stuff on to where the lumber mill is.

"Then right across from where James Connors lives, there used to be a
shingle mill. And next to that, Mr. Harrison had an oyster shell crusher. They
shipped the crushed oyster shell out. I think it was part of chicken diet to
[strengthen] their egg[shells]. But there was a lot of [crushed oyster shell]
that helped build Apalachicola's original streets. It worked, or we'd have a
bunch of sad roads like they had in Carrabelle at the turn of the century.

Edward Tolliver: From Poverty to First Black Mayor

Edward E. Tolliver sat in front of his bright orange and blue nightclub, Ed's
Place, on Martin Luther King Street in Apalachicola, tears flowing down his
cheeks. He was recalling the poll taxes (established in Florida in 1888) that
disenfranchised blacks in local elections until 1954, and the laws (enacted by
southern states after the U.S. Supreme Court struck down the Civil Rights
Act of 1875) that segregated them in schooling, worship, public places, and
conveyances, and disadvantaged them in employment and careers.[2] Tolliver
also recalled cross burning and verbal threats on his life.

Fig. 10.2a. Edward E. Tolliver served temporarily as Apalachicola's first African American mayor. Shortly before he died in November 2002, he was at his bar, Ed's Place, on Martin Luther King Jr. Street, Apalachicola, with Thornton Humphries. Photo by Faith Eidse.

He leaned against a four-foot walker, his legs weak, his fingers numb from steroid treatment following a diagnosis of lung cancer and seven courses of radiation. He wore a royal blue shirt and gold cross as he told his river story on November 5, 2001, a month before he died.

He fought back and became the first black to hold public office in Franklin County when he won an at-large seat on the Apalachicola City

Commission in 1975. He was appointed mayor pro tem in 1976 and was reelected to the city commission in 1979. The only one of five commissioners not recalled that year, he served briefly as mayor and was invited to the White House by President Jimmy Carter. Tolliver went on to serve as a Franklin County commissioner from 1986 to 1996. He's remembered for his ability to negotiate and to focus on the welfare of the community.

Ed's Place is a historic movie house and jitterbug joint where blacks could occupy the best seats and were not relegated to the balcony. Ed's son, Edward G. Tolliver, who is pursuing a doctorate in education at Florida Agricultural and Mechanical University (FAMU), leads tours through its rooms. On one side is a century-old pool room with stage and dance floor; on the other is a package store, older than Prohibition.

The senior Tolliver was born and raised in the black community across the tracks from Apalachicola. He attended the segregated Holy Family School for 25¢ a month, more than some children could afford. He spoke in musical tones, as one might if taught by songs and recitations. His friend Thornton Humphries sat nearby.

The second of nine children, Tolliver rose to lumberyard supervisor at St. Joe Paper Company before entering public life.

"My name is Edward T. Tolliver. I was born here, Apalachicola, at a place called Tildon, Florida, October 29, 1927. Memories were running through the woods playing with traps and slingshots. Trapped me birds. Big birds. Quail. Bobwhite quail," which increased rapidly as forests were cleared. "Bring 'em home, [Mom] would cook." Also, "Rabbit [shot] with the slingshot."

"I had three brothers; one is dead. And I had five sisters; two of those are dead. [Charles Watson is] my brother-in-law. He married my sister." Watson, who died in 2002, was celebrated for teaching advanced math and science to black students after they were barred from taking such courses. He created two curricula, one for administrators to see, the other for his top students.

"My dad was too poor," Tolliver said. "He worked at the sawmill. But he did feed us. He fed us good. We never went hungry.

"Never had a nickel or dime in my pocket 'til I was fourteen years old. I wore my old school clothing. When I was fourteen years old I got a job tending wood for Jerome E. Sheip at his house, and they gave me 50¢ a week. And I don't never know a day I didn't have a penny in my pocket. I'd bring the wood down from the swamp. I worked there a year. Then I lived six months without doing anything. I had some money in my pocket. It wasn't that much, but I did have some money. It cost a little bit to get school clothes, and you saved some."

> Never had a nickel or dime in my pocket 'til I was fourteen years old.

Asked whether he was ever lost in the river swamp, Tolliver said: "You'd be up there all night. Then you're a real prisoner. It's real scary. You be goin' round and round in circles and don't know where you're goin' out. Everything looks the same.

"My daddy was a slab trimmer [for Sheip]. It was very dangerous. Saw would come by fast, saw a piece of log, and he would trim that slab and get it off the table in a hurry because the saw would come back for another one. He always kept his mind on his business.

"Mother was a housewife. She had a garden, and we all had chores to do after school. And we had better do it, or we'd get spanked.

"My daddy'd cut the wood, I'd bring it in. And I better take it in right behind the woodstove. And if I didn't, nooo, I'd hear about it the next day. Oh yeah. If you wouldn't have wood to start a fire, oh my.

"We had lamps. Kerosene lamps, woodstove. Then we make some flambouies. You know a flambouie? That's kerosene in a jar, and you get them pine needles."

"Light it," his son said. "And you put it around the house. And you sit outside at night and you'd have a light."

"Our school was up there, end of Ninth Street. The Dunbar High School. And an elementary school there, too, and I went there. It was segregated— oh, it was segregated. In the second grade my sister would teach us; she was a little older. She would teach me to [recite], and I would learn it and stand and recite it. My teacher would say: 'Uh-uh, you don't know that word. You gonna stay in the same place all week.'

"One of my teachers taught me how to spell 'geography,' and I couldn't say it. She said, 'George-eat-ol'-gray-robin-at-papa's-house-yesterday.' And that was 'geography.' So I remembered that for years.

"I 'member a lot about the river. I 'member one Easter Sunday when I was a boy we went to the river. I had white pants on, and the mud was slick. I slipped down in the water, and I took my pants off, and it was embarrassing; washed my pants in the river water. And they turned all cream. I went back home, and my mom said, 'Huh-uh, where have you been?' Oh, boy.

"[On the city and county commission] we tried to bring change [between] Georgia and Florida. We tried to get [the] dredge out so we could change use of the river. But they won't do it. They won't ever dare do it. What happens, see, Georgia is destroying our oyster beds down here, lower part of the river."

"I had three oyster boats. I rent 'em out years ago. I ran a little oyster house for awhile, mid- to late sixties. It didn't make enough money for you.

Georgia is destroying our oyster beds down here.

Money [came] in, but we don't have oysters any more. Personally, I ran a funeral business. Personally, I ran a dry cleaning plant."

"[The funeral business] would've been before I was born," said his son. "That would've [been] in the forties and then into the early fifties because you still used to help Chester Rhodes [with his funeral business] for a little while."

"[I fished] a little bit for fun," Tolliver said. "I went commercial fishing one summer—porgy fishing, menhaden. That was in 1948 to '49. Oh my goodness, we couldn't load 'em all up. That's one you dried up for fertilizer and perfume. It's a strange odor to use in perfume.

"We had a train down here, would come right down to Water Street. Would drive all the way to the bridge. Popham had several oyster houses around there. Popham had big oysters on his bar, big oysters. He sold [oyster beds that weren't his], through the mail. And he got arrested for it. He sold a lot of 'em. He had people down there who invested with him. I know them real good.

"I worked at the paper mill, 1954 to 1989, thirty-four years down there, St. Joe Paper Mill. I went in as a laborer and came out superintendent of the wood yard. I oversaw all the wood that came in.

"I have three [children]. Edward and Veronique, and Joan is the baby. I got one, two, three, four [grandchildren]. They were all here for the [seafood festival] weekend. I had 'em all working. One of my bitty grandchildren, she just runs around and [entertains].

"I have cancer, and I'm dying. But I'm gonna beat it. I'm doing radiation. I have already had seven treatments of radiation. They stopped for about a week or two. Now I gotta go back on it for seventy days. I've got to go in five days a week, Monday through Friday. Back and forth each day."

"And he wouldn't stay with me in Tallahassee," his son said. "He wanted to come back and sleep in his own bed."

"I grew up here," the older Tolliver said. "It was my house for [fifty] years. That house's over a hundred years old." The nightclub dates to 1908. "Some of this is new. That place on the end over there is the first bar room right there. I used to run a projector machine there [featuring] Cab Calloway and Lena Horne [films], some of those. That's the only pictures you'd get. Being a black-owned, black house in the black town." Calloway performed in Betty Boop films; Horne performed in discrete numbers in Hollywood movies that could be cut out for white southern audiences.

Martin Luther King Street runs past the bar, "and that's a shame to name this after Martin Luther King," Tolliver said. "He was a peaceful man, didn't believe in no problems, and you got dope sellers all down the street. And he wanted us to be caught in what was right.

"He lives on in our memory every day. We used to have a poll tax here. [If] you had a job, no problem. [But if] you got put in jail for nuttin', you couldn't vote." Tears streamed down his face, and he paused to wipe his cheeks. "You had to be a property owner to go to the poll. You had to pay to vote, and you had to own property. One person owned all the property down here, and you rent[ed] from them. And you could vote only in the general election, but couldn't for nobody control your life. Couldn't vote for the sheriff, the county commissioner, city commissioner.

"Okay, in 1954, Martin Luther King said for every child to walk hand-in-hand, not because of their color, but because of their belief. [My children] went to segregated schools. The Holy Family School right over there [around the block]. When we grew up, we went over there to a public school. I was schooled over there [through] eighth grade. Went to public school, and you could tell every one of those kids that left Holy Family, the way they dressed.

"We had a convent right over there. And my wife's aunt, she owned a house and sold it to a Catholic organization [for a convent]. Oh, it was a big house. Oh man, big beautiful work in there."

"Nice big stairway goin' up," his son said. "It was just pretty. I don't know what she sold it for. But she's a very stately looking lady."

"She died young," Tolliver added. "Minnie Barfield was her name. [After segregation] things were very, very low. Lower, lower for the black children. And [Charles Watson] was very calm. He had a altercation with one of these parents who came right in and said he failed his daughter at math. [The father] jumped across the counter, and I said, 'It's a good thing he hit Charlie, not me, because I would just hit back.'"

"Took it to court," his son added.

"Oh, Charlie would have classes [after school] even during desegregation," Tolliver's son said. "The whites would come to him and get him tutoring their children. He taught at Carrabelle High School for a lot of years. They loved him over there. He was a commissioner over there. And he taught at Apalachicola High School for years. And Fred [Humphries, past FAMU president] was one of Charlie's prize students. He gave an honorary doctoral degree to Charlie for that.

"I was the mayor pro tem," Tolliver said. "[I represented the] black community and white. I was on the city and county commission. We're trying to get [FAMU a] marine school; a whole city block [in Apalachicola], and we'll try to sell that to [FAMU] for a marine lab."

You had to pay to vote, and you had to own property. . . . And you could vote only in the general election, but couldn't for nobody control your life. Couldn't vote for the sheriff, the county commissioner, city commissioner.

"My great-grandfather owned that—William Ziegler," Tolliver's son added. "He was an enterprising gentleman. He used to go up and recruit men up in Georgia. I think that's when he brought Grandpop Joe down."

"Brought my daddy down from [Lakeland,] Georgia," Tolliver said. "He was fourteen years old when he came down here, and that was seventy-four years ago."

"And Grandpapa Ziegler used to tell me, 'Top dollar was 35¢ a day.' But I made 50¢ a day 'cause I had a truck, and I used to haul the men into [the sawmill],'" said Tolliver's son. "So I guess around that time when things got really depressed, Grandpapa had that store up there, and they came and sold him land for 25¢, 50¢ on an acre."

"[In Eastpoint] they had turpentine," said Tolliver. "They'd go and get turpentine from the pine trees, and you get a 10-pound bucket or a 2-pound bucket, and you'd go and load the syrup and take it down the mill. And a fellow went on at the time, I remember. [The owner had a] compound for black workers. He rode a horse, [and] if you weren't supposed to be there, he'd get you out of there.

"There were crosses burned out there [in Eastpoint]. It happened ten or twelve years ago," Tolliver said. "What happened, they had white and black living in the same project. And they burned the cross on the black people's lawn. They wanted to make them move away from there. But they didn't hurt anybody.

"Carrabelle, Eastpoint? It was much better to live this side of the river," Tolliver said. "And I fish over at Carrabelle mullet dock. Black people couldn't fish [there]. You can eat all the fish you want, but they wouldn't let you fish [at] Carrabelle. My dad went over there. He used to work for a sea-man, fisher. And sometime the weather would be cold, some real pill season, he'd go mullet fishing. Daddy went away one morning early, for a day. And way out on the beach he saw a fire. And he rode out there. [They said,] 'Hey, no, man. You know we don't allow no blacks to be seen down here.' [My father] said: 'Boy, don't you let 'em fool you. They'll throw you down and use you for their bait.'

"They would do it. That was pretty scary. Scary talk," Tolliver said. "That was the feeling they had. They didn't want no blacks fishing on the dock. You can eat all the fish you want comin' from the dock weigh-in, but still they got a problem about blacks fishing over there. Over here, man, if a black likes to go down to the dock, early mornin' stay at it all day, [he can] fish all he wants.

"We have the railroad crossing with the blacks on one side and white on the other," said Tolliver. "It divides the town. Railroad and Highway 98. We

We had our own black beach.

have blacks living down there on the beach side. [But] we had businesses downtown. We had a barber shop down there and dry cleaning. What else did we have?" Tolliver asked.

"In Gulf County the blacks could live across 98, but we had our own black beach," Tolliver's son said. "We couldn't go to the other one, [only to] Money Bayou in Gulf County."

"Oh, we could get on the bridge and go to St. George," Tolliver said. "We could go over there. You could get a boat and go."

"Money Bayou was right in between Indian Pass Beach down there and Cape San Blas," Tolliver's son said. "You could drive up the beach, around until we reached it. Do a little fishing on the point down there, but—"

"Uh-uh, no luau, nothing. Couldn't build no building," Tolliver said.

"I don't know what year they changed that where they integrated the beaches?" Tolliver's son said. "That's been later [than the fifties]. We have property down there."

"They had bought the lot down there for $500," Tolliver said. "And the last offer, they asked me—?"

"I think the last offer we had was $90,000–$95,000," said his son. "We built, but we're tearing it down. We had an old verbal covenant. See, we were beachfront. There was about 400 or 500 yards to the beach from our place."

"We needed it in writing," Tolliver said.

"The relatives sold that strip of land behind us, right?" Tolliver's son asked. "They cut a road between us and the beach, and so I think you and Harold Jenkins went down to St. Joe's and tried to fight it."

"Tried to fight it; we didn't have it in writing," Tolliver said sadly. "It was a handshake. That was a man's word, the law we were using."

"And so now they get to have half-million-dollar houses behind us," his son said.

As for moonshiners, "we had one on every corner," Tolliver said. "We had a sheriff named J. P. Lovett, a regular old pistol. He'd come around, he'd say, 'It's the Bible,' he said, 'I'll tell you what, you come by a house and you see somebody come out the back door and spit [throw up], that's a moonshiner.' They don't water it down any."

Tolliver knew about slave raids along the river before statehood. "Oh yeah. One house right down the end, there are slave quarters in there.

"My mother was born in 1908, and she was born in Petersburg, Alabama," he added, recalling steamboat frontier days that brought immigrants down river. "Rousters, they had to throw more wood, throw more wood on the boiler." He sang an old rouster's song: "I got a gal in Georgia, hey, hey honey.

I got a gal in Georgia, hey, hey honey. I'll see her 'fore the sun go down, hey, hey honey.

"Oh, the museum down here got some of the pictures of them rousters. Yeah. Dr. Gorrie made the first ice machine. He made it in Apalachicola. Preceded air-conditioning.

"[We] didn't know about air-conditioning," Tolliver added. To keep cool, "we would go flying with the wind, never knew when it would rise. And so we ran around here barefooted in regular shade, and then you run some more.

> You'd go downtown, swim right through.

"We walked far to the beach," Tolliver added. "We walked right straight out there in the woods. Out there Hog Run Beach. They called it Hog Run because there was a hog pen out there. You'd go out there and swim, swim all day long, summertime. You'd go down to the mill pond and swim all day long. You'd go downtown, swim right through. If you'd'a lived around here, you'd'a known that. If you didn't live around here, you didn't."

As a city and county commissioner, "[my] big issues and concerns were my people," Tolliver said. "I have been pretty good, by whites, [too]. But I wanted my people to be treated good, and they weren't being treated good. I tell you what, [politicians would] come over here to get one man. They buy a vote from one man. I didn't like that idea. You give one man all the money; he take you for a ride and turn around and be a jerk. I wanted to change the middle man had that one vote himself. One vote, one person. They changed that."

"You could get a lot of half pints of liquor down here," his son added. "They were trading their votes for liquor at election time."

"Oh, right here. A lot of cheap liquor," Tolliver said. "They'd bring down a half pint liquor maybe the night before election. You'd pass it around and get your vote like that. I tried to educate the people not to choose their man that way. I tell them [vote for] the man that votes like you want 'im to."

Robert Howell: Paper Boy, Mayor, General

The late General Robert L. Howell was twice elected mayor of Apalachicola between 1990 and 1998 and was credited with discouraging graft and dissolving city debt. Nearly simultaneously, he served at-large on the governing board of the Northwest Florida Water Management District for two four-year terms between 1991 and 1999. Earlier he was hospital superintendent at Port St. Joe, then clerk of circuit court for twenty-seven years. He retired as assistant adjutant general of the National Guard in 1983. In his 1989 video

Fig. 10.3. General Robert L. Howell died on July 26, 2005. Photo by permission of Milo Stewart.

interview with ANERR's Frances Ingram, he recalled his boyhood in Apalachicola during World War II.

"I'm Robert L. Howell. I was born [in Apalachicola] in '29 and finished high school here and went to Florida State, the first class of 1947, [with classmates] Steve Roux, Helen Porter, and Doris Johnson.

"'Course, when I grew up in Apalachicola, Sheip's Lumber Company was about the biggest employer here. They had a commissary up there, and the old Belvedille Bar was out there just about where Don Lanier built his house years ago.

"'Course, there wasn't a lot of cars in town. Everything was pretty tight until World War II, 'til 1942 when the air base opened up here; [then] they were parking on both sides of Main Street. The ambulance came in 1942, and they closed in '46. The air base was the main authority at that time.

"Sheip's Lumber Company left here in about '46 or '47 and moved to Chattahoochee. Sheip's was located right about where the commercial boat basin is right now. Mr. Calloway ran the commissary, and Freddie Richards worked for him.

"Sheip's Lumber Company paid off in jugaloo—half cash and half token—and you could spend the token at the commissary. You couldn't spend 'em any place else. 'Course, a lot of the town people traded up there because it was one of the best meat and grocery stores in the county.

"Uncle Floyd's daddy worked there, ten hours a day, and they made 80¢ a day, or 8¢ an hour. And I remember Uncle Bert tellin' us that. He worked for

We re-did that whole courtroom and made it into a Teen Town.

the Corps on a dredge. But the money went down, and they'd laid off the crew of the dredge, and then he went to work for Sheip's.

"The old depot was down there and the Old Riverside Café. John Ida owned the Riverside Café down there, and he made all of his lemon pie and his coconut pie, and I would be delivering papers there at 4:30–5:00 in the morning. I'd go by there and that smell would [be the] purtiest of anything in the world. Didn't have a dime to buy a piece, and he would say, 'Hey boy, come and tell'a me how good this'a pie is.' And he'd cut [a piece], and I'd say, 'That's good.' And he'd say 'That's'a the one I needed to know.' He ran the café right there by the depot.

"'Course the Fortunases owned the fish place right across the street. The old Acme 'Pack Me' Company was right where Cleve Randolph owned the Standard Oil dock down there next to the Rainbow Motel. Those were pretty big places then. But the Riverside and the old depot were probably the places to go in those days.

"We had a coach here named Paul B. Stephens, and he coached us all the way through all of our sports in high school. The old courthouse was right in the middle of where the hospital is right now, right in the middle of Eleventh Street and upstairs was the old courtroom. We went to the city commissioners. They turned the building over to the city, and we asked the city to let us fix the upstairs for the Teen Town. They agreed, and Coach Stephens, old man George Sizemore, and a lot of 'em donated the paint, and we built scaffolds in there, and we re-did that whole courtroom and made it into a Teen Town. And we had our own little stove where we cooked hot dogs and hamburgers, and we had our own jukebox.

"Julia Hampton—'course, she was Julia Bowers then—and Coach Stephens danced all the time. She was in about the tenth or eleventh when we did that, a year or two ahead of me. But we all worked real hard. It was a prize for us, and it was a privilege for us to have done what we did, and that was ours. We never opened it that Coach and his wife, Elizabeth, wadn't there. They were great people in our life as kids comin' along. That was probably the greatest thing we did.

If we could get Bob Sikes [Cut] open, we had a vision that this could once again become a seaport.

"The Christmas dance used to be held here in the armory every year, and all the people would come back, and you would see who was here. It was always Christmas night, and I guess that was a custom that was the only one carried forward.

"Didn't have a Seafood Festival then. That came later. I'm gonna say that the Seafood Festival came in '46 or '47, but it was called Harbor Day at that time, and Newt Creekmore was a big pusher of that. He was the city manager at the time. Newt never got the credit he deserved for what he did for Apalachicola. He was just a great person, and he probably started the forerunner to the Seafood Festival.

"It was called Harbor Day because, if we could get Bob Sikes [Cut] open, we had a vision that this could once again become a seaport. So this was going to be the harbor. But that was before anyone knew anything about ecology. We didn't worry about the intrusion of salt water into the sanctuary; we didn't worry about things like that. Didn't know anything about things like that. We tried to put emphasis on getting the politicians here to see what we needed to create a harbor for shipping and everything. That was the purpose of it.

"The first few Harbor Days, the fish fries and all were free. The city, I assume, paid for 'em, or donations came through. Newt handled all that, and the paying came later.

"One of the saddest things that you can think about in Apalach was you had giant people then that you don't see now. You had the Mannie Brash and Bob Medley and Gene Austin and Mr. Joe Spear and Mr. Buzzett—Bill Buzzett—and Rod Porter and Mr. L. G. Buck. You had these people that were in business, and they were sorta giants in the community. I know Joe Maloney, when he got the newspaper, he called 'em the Mutual Admiration Society, but we also admire them, and we haven't had anybody to take their place since they've been gone. But also the small-town business left. 'Cause you got to remember they received their greatness in business with no transportation. You couldn't get to Panama City and Tallahassee. You had to stay here and shop. Now everybody gets in a car and drives to Panama City or Tallahassee. It's harder to be in the business world today in a small community.

"My father was a disabled World War I veteran. He was hurt in the navy in World War I. He was a total invalid and received some meager pension—$17, $18, or $20 dollars a month. I don't remember what it was. How he ever got by, I don't know. But my grandfather was a sheriff, and my grandmother was a schoolteacher. They helped us a great deal, and my mother never worked outside the home until after Dad died in 1945. [Then] she worked at different seafood houses. But my grandfather did more to help our family, to keep us going, because Dad couldn't do anything.

"Probably the most important thing that unified people was baseball. I played on the old Apalachicola Town Team. All these great businesspeople would buy us uniforms and pay for us to play, and Mr. Bob Medley and L. G. Buck and Gene Austin, Manny Brash, all of 'em, put up the money. We had a Gulf Coast League, and we had quite a few good ball players. Probably there wadn't a pitcher in the country any better than ol' Connie Hendels was. He could hum one. And other people—L. O. Macrae was a great catcher. Mr. Willie Fred Randolph was a great ball player. I know in the twilight of his career, and the beginning of mine, I pitched to him and Frances Bloodworth and all of 'em. Everybody played. You played every Sunday and every Wednesday, and nobody did anything but go to the ball game. 'Course, that was before television.

"The hospital was first opened up, I'm gonna say in '47. But it was opened up out at the air base. It was an old Apalachicola Air Base Army Hospital, and V. G. Sangaree was the real person behind that and of course Willie Fred Randolph. Both of 'em were county commissioners. Mr. Willie Fred, I'm sure, was just as involved, but V. G., being kinfolks, I knew more about it from V. G. But they got that building, and Joe McDonald, [V. G. Sangaree's] son-in-law who married Madeline, was an X-ray technician over there, a medical technician at Camp Gordon Johnston before he went overseas. So V. G. got them to bring Joe back, and Joe started the first hospital out there.

"And then we built a new hospital about 1959. I was clerk of the circuit court when we built that, and we moved it from out at the air base in approximately 1959. And that was an ol' Hill-Burton Act, where the feds put up 75 percent, and we, in the local, put up 25 percent, and I signed those bonds for the bonded indebtedness, and it was something like $75,000 to $80,000. That was a lot of money then. It was a very successful move at the time.

We used to row over to St. George Island.

"When we were kids we used to row over to St. George Island. We didn't have any motors. The first time I can ever remember going to St. George Island in a motorboat, we had a senior party over there in 1946 or '47. A shrimp boat took us all over there for a senior picnic.

"Now, we rowed over there many, many times. We'd go swimmin', and we'd go dove hunting. That's what we really went over there for. We'd spend the night over there, take us some tents and camp out. All during World War II, that's what we did.

"The happiest days of my life were spent right there at the high school. [They] tore down a good school and built a piece of junk. Only one man around town had enough guts to get involved and try to save it, and that was Jack Cook. They dug sand outta the back and built that other little ol' school in it, and I got real disappointed 'cause I knew that when it rained, it filled up with water where they were diggin' the sand out. Then that school lasted about ten years before they tore it down. The old Chapman High School, it was a sound educational building.

"Going to school here was a great experience. I played baseball and basketball, football and track, and we just had a great deal of pride. In 1939, they built the new gym out there, and until that time we played basketball here in the armory. Then they built the auditorium on it. Then they tore down the baseball diamond to build that school and never had a decent baseball diamond since.

"I popped popcorn and took up tickets [at Dixie Theatre] during World War II. George Fotunas's daddy owned it. During the war he had two projectors up there, and then Miss Josephine, George's momma, sold tickets and Ruth's sister and Miss Anderson. You could smoke upstairs. During the war, we ran two shows a day, and it would be full the entire time, soldiers from Camp Gordon Johnston and also from out at the air base.

"The old Coombs house up here on the hill was probably one of the most beautiful houses in the community. I delivered papers there every morning. 'Course, the old Chapman house, at the time Lizzy Cooper lived in that house, and that was always a beautiful house. To me the most beautiful house was the old Ruge place right next to Herbert Marshall that a fella by the name of Willis owns now. That house had a lot of character to it. But when I was growin' up that was closed; they had it boarded up. Mrs. Rustmire moved back after World War II. But that was my dream to own, which I never did.

"[My wife,] Rosemary, came here from Vicksburg, Mississippi. Rosemary graduated from Belhaven Presbyterian College for Women in Jackson. Then she came here in 1954 and was teachin' school, and I was superintendent of the hospital down in Port St. Joe. She was livin' in the Zingarelli apartment. Boz Nichols and Tom West had been datin' a couple of girls, and Boz called me in St. Joe and said: 'Come on down. Tom and I are goin' to go out, and we want you to meet this girl.' So we all went out, and that's when I met Rosemary, and then later we got married and had our two children. Then in 1956 I ran for clerk of the circuit court and then stayed here for twenty-seven years as clerk. We moved to St. Augustine, and we're ready to come back home [The Howells moved back to Apalachicola on March 1, 1989.]

"[I remember my mother] givin' me the devil for stayin' out late at night. She thought you were supposed to be in at eleven o'clock, but we were a very close family. We had the Mahons here, which my grandfather was a Lovett and the Mahons' mother was a Lovett, and we had a big family.

"'Course, there were twelve Mahon children, and then my granddaddy had two children—one was my mother. And we stayed pretty close, all of us. Jack Mahon was my age, and there was somebody in the Mahon family that was everybody's age. They just came along like doorsteps. We just had so much love in the family, and all of 'em are about gone now. The only one of the Mahons left is Jack, who's my age, and Verna and Ferrell; but it's sad.

"We used to all come here, and when you sat at our table you sat in two rooms 'cause it just wouldn't hold everybody, and you'd eat in shifts, and you couldn't ever hear what was goin' on, everybody was talkin' at the same time. And everybody was married, and they brought their children, and our house was a meeting place. 'Course there's six bedrooms in that house, and everybody would come in, just everybody, come in and change clothes. We would go to Eileen's, or we would go around and meet everybody in town and say hi. But that was probably what I miss more than anything was the size of it, and they were great.

"The first house I can remember [living in] is Cecil Gibbs house right there. It's a little house right in front of the cemetery right behind the Coombs house. And then we moved up to the old place that Papa bought about 1934, which was at the corner of Avenue C and Tenth Street, and later Frances Lovett built his home right across the street. But there was an old two-story house there, and we moved in that little ol' Egbert house, right to the rear of Henry Porter, and that's where I spent my life.

"'Course, my grandfather's home was right down on the corner where my mother lives now on Avenue E and Tenth Street. I was born in the front bedroom of that house, my brother and I were. They tell me we later moved into the ol' Coombs house.

"Oh, I'm still sure [ending the war] was the happiest days of my life. The war was a terrible thing, yet it was an exciting part of our history. I remember we were playing football in front of my grandmother's house or Mr. Charlie Schoelles' house, which was Roland Schoelles's granddaddy, and I can remember Mark Rogers was playin' and Roland Schoelles and Jack Schoelles and my brother, myself, a boy named Herman Newnan, and a boy named Mike Machado. We were all out there playin', and we all called Mr. Charlie Schoelles 'Uncle' Charlie. And your [Frances Ingram's] uncle was out there, Rocky Donato. So we had all gone to church and then had dinner, lunch. And then we went across the street and were playin' football on Uncle Charlie's lawn, and he walked out and he said, 'Boys, the Japs just bombed Pearl Harbor.' Somebody said 'Uncle Charlie, where's Pearl Harbor?' I was twelve at the time, and he explained it to us. And I remember that like it was yesterday.

"[Rocky] was in the National Guard, but he was home that weekend; he was federalized in 25 November 1940, and they had come back home that weekend. It was a very vivid thing.

"This was a bustling town at the time; air base here and Camp Gordon Johnston, and the Coast Guard had a big station here. Everybody was workin'. I had three jobs. I worked at the theater, the A&P, and the air base. You could get all the jobs you wanted, no problem. It was just a great time—

and a terrible time, because all of the men were gone and the families were split up, and yet it was a time to remember.

"I started deliverin' papers when I was ten years old. We started at 4:30 in the mornin'. My brother and I delivered five hundred papers a day. We rode on our bicycles. If you didn't have somebody's paper at the house by six, they'd quit it. You got to remember that most people workin' in stores were women, and we would go in there and stock the shelves, and I'd work at night at the A&P. Mr. O. N. Taylor was the manager. It wadn't uncommon for any kid to have three or four jobs.

"What money I got, I made, or I didn't get any. What clothes I had, I made the money [to buy]. We had a bicycle, we bought it. We had a new pair of shoes, we bought it. We had trousers, we bought it. Whatever we had, we bought. We had to come up with the money, so we worked. So we worked, didn't hurt me."

Kathleen Hays: Teacher, Gibson Inn Proprietor

Kathleen Reams Hays, a Gibson Inn proprietor and Apalachicola teacher, was interviewed and videotaped in 1989, also by Frances Ingram. We present a portion of Mrs. Hays's oral history here.

"I came here to teach school in the 1930s, and I was Kathleen Reams, and I fell in love and married Pat Hays. We married, and I moved into the Gibson Hotel with him. He had been livin' there since he was fifteen years old. He had gone to Georgia Tech and had come back to live in Apalachicola after he graduated. He was responsible for running the hotel with his aunt, Sunshine Gibson. His mother, Annie Gibson, had remarried and was living in Tallahassee. We had our first daughter, Patsy, while we lived in the Gibson. When Patsy was four years old, the army took over the hotel for an officer's club for Camp Gordon Johnston, and we bought the house behind the hotel.

"We had some interesting days in the hotel. After the Gibsons bought the hotel, Edison Marshall spent a week in Apalachicola. He was a well-known writer for the *Saturday Evening Post*. He liked the hotel and the small-town atmosphere, so he came and spent a week at the hotel. We had quite a lot of interesting people stay at the Gibson Inn because when you came to Apalachicola, you usually had to stay more than one day because it was hard to get in and out of town.

"When my mother-in-law got married, she had formal invitations with a formal wedding gown and the invitations said six o'clock in the morning. We asked her why in the world she married at six o'clock in the morning, and she said: 'Well, the *Crescent City* left at a certain hour,' and they had to go

Fig. 10.4a.
Kathleen Reams
Hays, age twenty-
one, an Apalachi-
cola teacher and
Gibson Inn pro-
prietor. By per-
mission of
Kathleen Hays.

on the *Crescent City* to Carrabelle, and then they would catch a train in Carrabelle and to Tallahassee. They would then change trains in Tallahassee to go to North Carolina. The best way to leave Apalachicola was by boat across Apalachicola Bay to Carrabelle, and you had to plan around the *Crescent City* schedule. The only other way out was by car, and you had to go west to Port St. Joe, up to Wewahitchka and Chattahoochee, and the roads were very, very bad back in 1905. So they did marry at six o'clock in the morning at the First United Methodist Church.

"The church burned in 1900, and they built it back in 1901 at a cost of $3,500, which included all those stained glass windows. We have recently done a little bit of work on the church that has cost us $20,000, so it shows you the difference in the cost in 1901 and now.

"My father was in the turpentine business. I was born in Greenville, Florida, but I came here right out of college, and I taught the second grade

Fig. 10.4b. The Gibson Inn, photographed here in January 1918, was built in 1907 by James Fulton Buck and purchased in 1923 by sisters Annie Gibson Hays and Mary Ellen "Sunshine" Gibson. It was purchased again in 1983 by brothers Michael and Neil Koun and Michael Merlo and reopened on November 1, 1986. Photo courtesy of Florida State Archives.

three years before I was married and five years afterwards. I was here when the first Gorrie Bridge was built. We had some changes in the town.

"When I came here, they had more businesses than they have now. They had a lot of two-story stores downtown. People shopped locally back then because it would take you all day to go from here to Panama City because the roads were sandy. You'd have to get out and push half the way there. When I came here they did have paved roads, but my mother-in-law would tell me stories about the unpaved roads. You had to go from here to Port St. Joe and Wewahitchka and Blountstown to get to Tallahassee. It was more than a day's trip to Tallahassee because of the roads.

"We had some very, very good department stores in Apalachicola back then. Montgomery's was where the Dallas Furniture Company is now. Then after that it was Austin's, and they carried real smart clothes, as smart as you could get in Tallahassee, LilyAnne's and things like that. The businesses were more thriving then than they are now. Since I have lived in Apalachicola, we had two or three drugstores. The city paved the streets before I came here, and if the street was paved in front of your house, you had to pay for the pavement. The cost of the paving was included as part of your taxes. We had

Fig. 10.4c. Patsy Hays Philyaw with son Palmer at a Gibson Inn dual mirror vanity in the mid-1950s. Photo courtesy of Florida State Archives.

to pay the assessment on the hotel for the pavement. When we moved to the Buck house behind the Gibson in 1942, we had to pay for the assessment also.

"My husband moved to the hotel about 1920. The hotel had run down, and it didn't have a very good class of people that stayed there. He and his grandfather slept over there because there was a big street carnival in town. They used to have street carnivals that would stay for a week or two right in the middle of the streets. [It] had all kinds of merry-go-rounds and [games] where you knock down balls and shoot the rifle for different prizes.

"They had a dining room open in the hotel, and for $4 a night you could get a room and three meals. [Pat] said a lot of traveling salesmen would not eat anything until they got to the hotel that night, and then they would order steak, fried shrimp, fried oysters, and anything else that they could.

"They used to have dances in the hotel. The entire front of the hotel was lobby so they would have dances in the lobby. And we had quite colorful bellboys. The most colorful was Shug Jones, and he was quite a character. That was during Prohibition, and so Shug would go get the patrons some moonshine.

Street carnivals . . . would stay for a week or two right in the middle of the streets.

Fig. 10.4d. An antique bedroom suite at the Gibson Inn in the mid-1950s.
Photo courtesy of Florida State Archives.

"One night this man asked him to get him a pint of moonshine, and he got it, and the man said: 'Shug, this is the worst stuff that I ever drank in my life. You can have it.' So Shug drank the whole glass down, and he smacked his lips and said, 'Mister that was just right.' And he said, 'What do you mean just right?' Shug said, 'Well, if it'd been any better you wouldn't have given it to me; if it'd been any worse, I couldn't have drunk it.'"

"Well, my husband's uncle could've bought St. Vincent's Island for $10,000. And Alf Landon [the powerful Republican presidential candidate in 1936] and he went over to St. Vincent's several times. He was interested in buying it. He didn't, but he did stay a week at the hotel.

"Pat's grandparents came here from Columbus, Georgia, I guess the 1880s or 1890s by riverboat and decided they liked it. So they [got] on the riverboat and come down here. Pat told how, as a child, he loved riding the riverboats, and he thought the cookin' was just fantastic. He would go up and spend the weekend with Captain Magruder. He was Nell Murrow's father, and Pat would go on the riverboat with him sometimes and spend a week at a time.

"Ned Porter was a real good friend of [my husband's], and Bill Norton was another good friend and Veto Sangaree. He had a lot of real, real close friends. Ned pitched for the Giants, and they drafted him when he was a freshman in college. Every spring he would go to Lakeland [to] their spring training, and my husband would go down with him, and he got to meet Babe Ruth and all those big-name players back then. So he had a really good time with that.

"[Pat and his friends] would get up before day, before school, and go duck hunting down at the lagoon, and then come back and get here in time to go to [Chapman High] School. He said [the school] was cut in sections and sold. And some of the houses here in town now are part of the schoolhouse. But which houses? When I came here it had been torn down for a lot of years.

"The *Apalachicola Times*, in that one big building was the ice plant when I came here. They still packed shrimp and canned and everything. They had some big packing plants here down on the river.

"After the cotton, they had lumber mills that came in. They had Sheip's Lumber Mill, and then there were several others. I think there was a Fulton that came here and had a lumber mill.

"Cars had been in a long time when I got married. [Pat] had a real, real big Studebaker that had belonged to his uncle, Nick Hays. He died, and Pat drove the car. It was about half a block long.

"Captain [Barrow] of the *Tarpon* was a very special friend, and he ate supper every Thursday night at the Gibson's. When we married he gave us six sterling silver knives. He was a big man, and the *Tarpon* was the only [merchant] boat comin' in the Apalachicola when I came here.

"[It went down] during a storm. I'm not sure [where], but Zuliene Lovett's father was on that boat when it went down, and I think he drowned at that time.

"When I first came here, the only way you could get [to St. George Island] was by a boat. John Howell had a boat for charter, so Bill Norton and Pat took Grace, Bill's girlfriend, and me to St. George Island. We packed a lunch and spent the day. As far as I could see, we were the only people on the island.

"There was only one building over there, and that was the old hotel. When my husband was a little boy, about nine or ten, he spent a summer on the island with a Miss Herring Brook Smith. She was from Ireland, but she loved Apalachicola. She rented that hotel and was going to try to do something with it, but I don't think she ever did.

"Before St. Vincent's was bought by the government, they had lodging over there that had three rooms with private baths. They were three apart-

Fig. 10.4e.
Kathleen Hays at
age eighty-two.
By permission of
Kathleen Hays.

ments really. They had a living room and bedroom and a bath. And it was all on one big porch, and on the other side they had the kitchen and the dining room. We went over there with Elgin and Eunice Wefing. Elgin had charge of the island, and Pat would shoot doves. We used to have a lot of doves coming through here on the island but not anymore.

"[During World War II] was the first time in our life that the hotel made any real money. The government took it over during the war. They needed it for Camp Gordon Johnston because the wives would come, and they didn't have a place to stay.

"During the Depression they built Chapman Auditorium. It was my understanding that it was built with WPA [Works Progress Administration] help, and they stayed at a CCC [Civilian Conservation Corps] camp up on the Sumatra road. Many of them were well educated. They were college graduates, but they just couldn't get a job. One of them just played the piano beautifully. He had a degree in music, and he would come in the hotel on Saturday night and sit down at the piano and play for hours.

"A Mr. Doorman built the Ruge house. He was a stranger from out of town, and he did perfectly beautiful woodwork. It's in the Queen Anne style. I suspect that it was built about 1887, and Mrs. Neate's home, that was the other Ruge house. You had two Ruge brothers here in the seafood business. Van Russell lives in the second Ruge house now, and it was built in 1889.

"Years ago, I think the Catholic Church put on a carnival, and they had a king and a queen. When my husband was a little boy, about nine years old, he was the king, and Dorothy Wefing was the queen. The carnival was held in the armory and they had a grand march and festivities, which ended in a dance. [In the Grand Dance] they would walk all the way around the armory with your dates in a parade of peace.

"When I came here Dr. Munroe lived in the Raney house. We had [three] very good doctors, and they all seemed to make a living, and they all got along beautifully, and we were fortunate to have 'em. We did not have a hospital until after the war, and then the barracks was made into a hospital out at the air base, and that was before we had Weems Memorial here in town.

"My first daughter, Patsy, was born in Thomasville. The hospital in Tallahassee was just a little wooden shack. Thomasville had Archibald Memorial Hospital then, so Patsy was born there. Frances was born there eight years later because my doctor was still there. Quite a number of Apalachicola children were born in Thomasville.

"They used to have a lot of dances and teas, and people had big, big bridge parties. You would have ten tables of bridge and think nothing about it. They were just partying all the time. When I came here I didn't know how to play bridge, but everyone would ask me. Because I was a new schoolteacher everyone would ask me to the parties. Now I could play every day.

"They are still using the [pre–Civil War] cemetery. You can still be buried there, but they don't have any more plots to sell.

"We always had a lot of riverboats coming in and out of Apalachicola before they had the highways. Back in the cotton days they had a lot of river boats comin' in. I've always heard that [the wide streets were for rolling cotton bales].

"The St. Joe train, the Apalachicola Northern, would change [direction] at the Y, then back into town and be ready to go right out. We had a nice big, big depot. Of course, they let them take it away, and now that's a shame.

"In the summer, they would go to Port St. Joe on the train because the roads were so bad the cars couldn't go to the beaches very well. They would have one big, big picnic, and all the people from here would go to St. Joe on the train. There was a park down there and also a place [where] everyone could swim. Everyone would ride back on the train in the afternoon.

"When Pat was a little boy, his grandmother would give him a nickel, and he could buy two or three doughnuts. There was a bakery, probably where the Gulf filling station is now. He would go there every Saturday and get bakery goods for a nickel." Bakery scents drench Apalachicola's history, but cotton goods also persisted.

Clifton Lewis: "High Cotton" Proprietor, "Walking Island" Matriarch

The Apalachicola Bay has been a seasonal retreat for dozens of north Florida and south Georgia and Alabama families since the Civil War. In summer of 1873, a resort was founded between Alligator and Turkey points named St. Teresa on historic maps, said Clifton Lewis. This bluff drew Tallahassee families looking for more affordable vacations than the ones traditionally taken to Virginia and North Carolina.

Arvah Hopkins opened a large house on the beach to boarders. A 10-ton sloop, the *Kate B* (Lewis also recalls her mother mentioning the *Walka-tumpka*), connected passengers between St. Marks, St. Teresa, and Apalachicola. Overland, travelers took a ferry across the Ochlockonee River.

Medical doctor Flavius Augustus Byrd and his wife, Catherine Blake Byrd of Miccosukee, were among the early settlers of St. Teresa. Their son Tom built a cottage at nearby Lanark, and their daughter Lina Clifton and her husband, Dr. William Van Brunt, bought a St. Teresa cottage, possibly at the same site as the original Byrd cottage, which had been destroyed by hurricane. They called it Camp Itldo, and this was where daughter Clifton spent an idyllic childhood. After World War II, Clifton and her husband, George Lewis, heir of the state's oldest bank, Lewis State Bank, bought a cottage on nearby Dog Island.

Clifton Lewis's story was recorded in Tallahassee on January 29, 2002, at her leaf-shaped, hemicycle house designed by Frank Lloyd Wright. She wore pioneer-style bonnet, dress, and apron designed by her daughter, Byrd. During the 1970s, Ms. Lewis promoted local crafters and artists at her boutique, High Cotton, at the Gibson Inn.

At age eighty-two, she recalled sailing in *Clifton*, the boat her husband built, and their retreats to Dog Island, which is "walking" toward Carrabelle. As a widow, she had to sell the Dog Island home to re-roof her Wright house. Her children were enriched by collecting arrowheads and potsherds on St. Teresa, a historic Indian hunting ground, she said. Screened from U.S. Highway 98 by pines, it is changing as development creeps into the region, she added.

Fig. 10.5. Clifton Lewis at her hearth in her Frank Lloyd Wright home, January 29, 2002. Photo by Faith Eidse.

"There's seven generations of my mother's family who have enjoyed being part of the old St. Teresa community. And there's a book, *The Tides That Bind*. It's memories [by] the Byrd family. It [reprints] letters from what would be my great-grandfather, who went to St. Teresa before the Civil War.

"And he went by boat from the St. Marks River and found this beautiful bluff with trees goin' right down to the beach in a place [protected by] Alligator Point and Turkey Point, and a sand spit. And marvelous seafood. Before the dredging of Alligator Channel, the sand spit [Bay Mouth Bar] would come out at low tide [stretching] a half mile from St. Teresa with scallops and flounder and pin cushions.

"When I was very small I went with my father, William E. Van Brunt, to the courthouse in Apalachicola, and there, in a handwritten records book, [were] the purchases of the property he had bought when I was just four years old. A summer cottage that'd been built by the indigenous carpenters between 1913 and 1916 for a cousin of my mother's, Dr. George Gwynn.

"My mother had been brought up as a little girl in generations going to St. Teresa. She was born in 1887, '88. And so her first memories of the coast were at St. Teresa, and in the late 1800s, there was a terrible storm, and the Byrd cottage was demolished. St. Teresa was abandoned, and the family moved to Lanark.

"What I saw in that old record book was that a Scotsman had come to

Florida, and he had platted eight, 100-foot-wide lots by about 123 foot deep, and then there was a road parallel to the beach, and then there were back lots. [Ours were] on the front. And my brother Van and his family are homesteading there now in this marvelous summer house.

"And the indigenous carpenters knew how to build because they [knew] that the strongest roof for hurricanes is four-hipped. And this house had overhangs. It's built [with ancient] 2-by-4 pine. And there's no inside plaster or anything. It's called a two-by-four." It's 40-foot square with a 20-foot-square central room. "Architects are just fascinated with it because it has survived so many hurricanes that [blew away] other houses that are tightly built. And this is more like a great screened porch with an inner room. You just have to see it to believe it.

"The old families who lived in Florida who had come from Virginia had enough sense to do what the Indians used to do. In the summer they'd go to the mountains, they'd go to North Carolina. And in the winter they'd come back to St. Teresa. After the "late unpleasantness"—and I assume you know that's the Civil War—the families didn't have the means to go to the mountains and so [they] started going to a place called Belle Air, south of town. There were great oak trees, and under the oaks it was very cool. And there may have been a pond there or some water. But they went to escape malaria and to . . . get away for a little breather.

"But then this great-grandfather discovered old St. Teresa. And my husband's grandfather and my grandfather were very good friends and did experimenting with plants. They used to bank this celery to make it white. I can't imagine why, but I definitely remember the first green celery I saw. And celery was always a very special Christmas dish."

"But the sort of marvelous importance [of a river] to the fertility of the land and the whole ecosystem is such a miracle of functioning, if man doesn't interfere. It took us a long time to know that damming was a terrible thing. There are areas that should flood. It's that fertile soil that's made such a marvelous difference.

"We went by barge from Eastpoint to St. George Island. We must've gotten off and walked on St. George, and that was a fantastic experience to me because the sand at St. Teresa and on Alligator Point is fine and white as sugar. Well, St. George's sand is beigy, is coarse, and it's beautiful, but the reason it's like that is the tannic acid from the river. On a very rainy season on Dog Island if you're on the west end, the water will not be clear; it will show that tannic acid.

"Jeff [Lewis, George's brother] bought Dog Island with his friend Richard Weeks. And he said in the war he [and] Richard were flying the hump of

Himalayas, taking supplies to China. [They] said, 'We're gonna get us a place on the Gulf of Mexico,' [so] families can go and fish and swim.... The Island is now the Jeff Lewis Wildlife Preserve.

"Mr. G. E. Lewis [George and Jeff's father] is a banker from Florida's oldest bank. His grandfather [Benjamin Cheever Lewis] came from Massachusetts in the early 1830s. Tallahassee became [the capital] in 1824. So the early thirties were a shock, in my opinion, to this Yankee who came down as a seventeen year old from Lynn, Massachusetts. And one myth is that he, maybe, walked [down]. He was very young, and he worked in a drugstore in Tallahassee, and he started being a banker out of his pocket.

"And then he started B. C. Lewis and Son, which became Lewis State Bank. And his son George Lewis [was] sent to Key West for his health. Nobody said TB, but that's prob'ly what it was. So he was down there, and his wife, Betty Douglas, was pregnant, and so this bachelor brother, Edward, lived with her and helped take care. And so when she had the baby, they named the baby George Edward, and that's my husband's father.

"When we had our firstborn, George said, 'Oh, I've always wanted a little boy to name for my father.' So he's George Edward Lewis II and has a son, George Lewis III.

"We found Indian sherd [at St. Teresa] and arrowheads, and our oldest son, George Edward, was 'specially interested, so [Great Aunt] Mamie Lewis took [him] with his sherd to see Dr. G. Hale Smith, head of [the] anthropology department at FSU [which also houses her basket collection].

"Well, it turned out that some of it was Weeden Island pottery, and some was from North Carolina. And the arrowheads, see, were made out of the stone from North Carolina, and what he found out was that the Indians would come to St. Teresa in the winter, and they'd go back to the mountains.

"There's a man in Apalachicola, if he's still living, who says he lives in the oldest house in Apalachicola. It's a little house [in back of] the Raney House. That man, of Greek heritage, had grown up being fascinated with the old bottles, and the old Indian sherds and the shells. The Indians would take a conch and cut it a certain way and make a stick and it would be a hoe. The conchs were heavy and big. We find these shells cut this way even today.

"Our family would go to St. Teresa to my family's cottage for our summer vacation. And George would commute, and he designed and built a great sailboat. George had grown up sailing. And the first time George asked me for a date it was to go sailing with him.

"Well, this gorgeous sailboat, the *Clifton*, was about 19 [or 20 foot]—and it was a cat boat with a simple rig. He started building it in his family's carriage house after he was graduated from college in May, and then he didn't go to work in the bank until his birthday on November 4. He had finished the hull and the cabin when World War II came, and he pulled it out when VJ [Victory over Japan] Day came. That day they said, 'George you're not goin' get it out.' I think he had an eighteenth of an inch, but he got it out of there and pulled it to our yard in Los Robles. And he hopped on that boat and finished it. And then we launched it, and we would keep it at wonderful Spring Creek.

"In the fall we'd come in at night to Spring Creek, and there's a Willie Spears, [an] old fisherman [whose youngest son] Doodlebug was just [scootin' around] with his little tiny motor and his boat. But Willie Spears had found a mastodon skeleton in a spring. He called him a monster. And in the side [room of his house] for 25¢ [you could see it].

"[Spring Creek] is the closest freshwater to the Gulf. So in the winter we would keep the boat at Spring Creek, and we would go and sail out of Spring Creek, around Bald Point to St. Teresa for the summer. And George said in freshwater, worms get in a boat; in salt water, barnacles. So the salt water would kill the freshwater worms, and the freshwater would kill the barnacles.

"Van, our son, apprenticed [with] Mr. Lolly, [a boat builder in Carrabelle] of Greek heritage. Mr. Lolly built—without drawings, as his father had done—the boats that were used by the crabbing people and the shrimp people and the research people. Because he built wooden boats that were seaworthy and appropriate to the waters.

"Oh, and in the summer, we sailed the *Clifton* around Cape San Blas, out from Alligator Point, to St. Teresa and sometimes go to the Econfina [River]. There's a time in the fall when the redfish go into the rivers.

"Oh yes, High Cotton. The Gibson hotel was in tremendous disrepair. An attorney had bought it. . . . And we drove by the Gibson, and there were two young men [out]side, one with an old felt hat, and he was blond, and then a brunet with a beard. And it turned out to be Mel Livingston, and the brunet was Tom Cardinal.

"And so I said, 'George! Something's going on.' Well, I was just so glad to see this great old hotel was getting attention. It had four-footed tubs, and it had [metal] vanities with beveled mirrors and shelves [on both sides]. There was a tiny little beauty parlor around the back. So I asked the lawyer who owned it if I could have that center main entrance with those beautiful beveled glass doors. This space was just a shambles.

"So I readied that central place, and I asked Tom Cardinal and Mel Livingston—told them how I wanted to do it. Those men took the old paint off and got back to wood, beautiful beveled wainscoting. They [uncovered] the old brick vault floor from all the debris. The walls were painted white,

My shop . . . was a little museum of the beautiful work . . . done in the area.

and I had them make horizontal strips to hang pictures—'cause I wanted a gallery. I had the Little Gallery at the Lewis State Bank for years.

"I was determined to have nothing but natural materials. I wanted indigenous crafts, and I wanted them to be useful. It had to make sense to me, plus it had to be beautiful. So I sent word out to my friends in Apalachicola for the artists. I said, 'Where is there a weaver?' I [found] a young [weaver] from Hungary who was in Tallahassee, and I said, 'I want a raw silk, I want a cotton,.I want a denim stole.' I still have the elegant raw silks.

"I found out there was an old English sailor who was painting the mural on the side of Wefing Marine Hardware. He wove gorgeous mats out of old rope. I think they're called lover's knots. They're an oval shape; I sold the footmats he made—very fine. The rope was as round as a large thumb and saltwater- and sun-bleached. The mats had 'shubui,' as the Japanese say, meaning a beautiful patina.

"Byrd was a single parent, and she supported herself and her young son making her designs. And I had the 'George' suits and the beautiful dresses. Her dresses for 'small' people," Ms. Lewis said ironically, "were even more beautiful."

"I chose the watercolor paintings, and people began to bring me things. And I had to be [careful] 'cause I have a kind heart, but [I wanted] to be just the cutting edge of what's beautiful and neat.

"George Griffin, the potter down at Suncat [Ridge] going to Sopchoppy, started just pottin' on his own, and he had made these beautiful big bowls, pitchers, cups and saucers, and he had made a kiln that fired them so hot that they were ironstone. You could bake with them.

"One young man in Wakulla County did beautiful woodwork, and he made a high chair that you could flip the seat over and it became a library ladder. He made 'em out of the native woods, perfectly beautiful, with solid brass hinges. All of these young people knew what they were doing. They were very talented.

"What my shop turned out to be was a little museum of the beautiful work that was being done in the area. I lived in Tallahassee, and so what I had to do," she laughed, "was hire people to keep the shop. And the bank down there in Apalachicola called me and said, 'Ms. Lewis, your shop is overdrawn.' That young woman had put [deposits] where it was s'posed to be debits. She didn't do it maliciously. And what I realized then, here was this beautiful thing that was not really working.

"What the owner of Gibson said was, 'Clifton, you were just ahead of your times.' You know the tourists hadn't started coming to Apalachicola; the Yankees hadn't started buying the houses and having bed and breakfasts; and the

Fig. 10.6. Apalachicola merchant Homer Marks was born in Apalachicola on August 20, 1903, and lived to be over one hundred. He worked as a shipping clerk, delivering feed from his father's wholesale grocery, Marks Brokerage Company. It was 1914, and "everyone in Apalachicola had a chicken and milk cow in the backyard." He got two trips to Columbus as striker on the steamer *City of Eufaula*. "On the long straightaways," the pilot would "go sit down and leave me up there holding the wheel straight." He remembered the steamer *Tarpon*, which later sank, blowing as it came through West Pass, and having to rush from dinner to take delivery of dry goods and coarse sea salt, used to salt down mullet. Marks established the Evinrude Motor Co. dealership, which supplied the boat motor that Neel Yent used, and bought the Apalachicola Ice Company.

rest of the hotel was in shambles except for . . . the little beauty parlor, High Cotton, and, right next to me, was Shaun Donahoe's wife, and she started The Gibson Girl. Young girls had to come to Tallahassee and go to Panama City to buy real purty bathing suits and shorts and costume jewelry, so she started the boutique—fun and business.

"I do not regret my work with the Gibson because it was sheer delight. . . . I ended up with things that I had chosen and paid for, which is real smart if you're gonna start a little shop and can't be there.

"Oh, and then Kristin Anderson . . . she hit Apalachicola and she just said, 'This is where I wanta be . . .' And she's the one that helped rescue the *Governor Stone* [schooner] and get it going and all. And [Dan] Tonsmeire used to pilot the *Governor Stone*. And [his son] Christopher would be his first mate. And the *Governor Stone*, at the [Apalachicola] Seafood Festival, would come into port. It looked so beautiful. Historic Preservation [status] with the National Trust for Historic Vessels was awarded to the great *Governor Stone*.

"Tonsmeire's older brother was on the board of Nature Conservancy and gave Tonsmeire the job of running the Pelican Inn [on Dog Island]. There was no restaurant. Each apartment has a kitchen equipped. And you bring your own food. There are no stores on the Dog Island.

"So I guess as far as Apalachicola itself, the city wouldn't be there without that river. I was at the [Apalachicola] Seafood Festival [one] November, and an interesting-looking man came up. He had a beard and his bright blue eyes. [This Mr. Ralph] Clark turned out to [have] written a definitive [report] on barrier islands. And the Indians called Dog Island, the 'Walking Island.'

[Barrier islands are] also walking toward the mainland.

"They said it was walking towards the west. They had prob'ly watched the island. But what barrier islands do, when the waters come and they churn out underneath and then they build up on the other side. So they're also walking towards the mainland. But depending on currents and things, in this case, Dog Island, they're also walking toward the west. Well, I'm sure the [waters] must have made that tremendous channel between St. George and Dog Island on the west end where people have lost their lives fishing, the current is so swift.

"There's another book that's written about the history of Dog Island. And you know how it got its name? It's not shaped like a dog. One was that when the Indians were there they had dogs. The most likely is that as, off England, there's a Dog Island, and off, I think, Scotland, there's a Dog Island. And Jeff found a French map in the 1500s where the French called it Iles des Chiens.

"But anyway, this Iles des Chiens in the French map of the 1500s, which also had St. Teresa and St. Augustine. Raymond Williams, [retired] boat captain [and] Franklin County commissioner for a while, told me that there was a native Carrabellean who said, 'It don't make sense: St. Augustine, St. Teresa, St. Joseph, St. George, Dog Island?' He had a friend that lived in Mexico, and this friend collected old maps, and on the old Spanish map [Dog Island was] St. Catherine.

"The people of Apalachicola have always known how to really enjoy living in good times and hard times. And so many of the old families had experienced both, as so many people in the South did. . . .

"My High Cotton was an attempt to make a market for native crafts and art. What memories I have of gracious old Apalachicola and its inhabitants!"

Notes

Chapter 1

1. Stein, Kutner, and Adams 2000.
2. Leitman et al. 1986.
3. Hipes 2003.
4. Means 1991.
5. Milner 1998, 48.
6. Light, Darst, and Walsh 2002.
7. Brose and White 1999.
8. Gibson et al. 1980, 125.
9. Milner 1998, 36.
10. Sakim 2001.
11. Rogers and Willis 1997, 16.
12. McCarthy 2004, 31.
13. Wright 1986, 199.
14. Loomis 1816.
15. Rogers and Willis 1997, 16.
16. Milner 1998, 45.
17. Wright 1986, 240–58.
18. Spires 2002.
19. www.geocities.
20. Milner 1998, 46.
21. McCarthy 2004, 44.
22. Huang, Jones, and Saquibal 1998.
23. Menzel, Hulings, and Hathaway 1958, 1966.
24. Lipford 2004, 5.
25. Keyser 2002.
26. Niesse 2003.
27. Leitman et al. 1986.
28. Light et al. 1998.

Chapter 2.

1. Willoughby 1999, 5.
2. Gibson et al. 1980, 106.
3. Ibid., 113.
4. Ibid., 105.

5. Ibid., 105.
6. Wright 1986, 239.
7. *Time* 1978, 59.
8. *Appalachicola Times* 2004.

Chapter 3.

1. Gramling 1980, 224.
2. Ibid., 228.
3. Willoughby 1999, 105.
4. Ibid., 155.
5. Ibid. 167.
6. Ibid., 137.
7. Rogers and Willis 1997, 126.
8. Willoughby 1999, 170.
9. Ibid., 172.
10. Ager et al. 1986, 79.
11. American Rivers 2002, 1.
12. Struhs 2003.
13. Westphal 2000, 1.

Chapter 4.

1. Light and Darst 2003, 1.
2. White, Knetsch, and Jones 1999, 148.
3. Light and Darst 2003.
4. Wells 2003; Ritchie 2005.
5. Wright 1986, 190.
6. Word 2002, 18.
7. Ibid.
8. Nessler 2002.

Chapter 5.

1. Adlerstein 2002, 1.
2. Coleman et al. 2004, 1.
3. *See also* Loller 2003, 3.
4. U.S. Constitution, Amendment 14.
5. Hauserman 2003, 1.
6. Putnal 2002.
7. Tonsmeire et al. 1996, B-43.
8. *Florida Fish and Wildlife* 1997.
9. Neils 2003, 23.
10. Livingston 1983, 38.
11. Ibid.

12. Tonsmeire et al. 1996, G-5.

13. Unger 1998.

Chapter 6

1. Hurston 1935, 69.

2. Blount 1993, 2.

3. Ibid.

4. Ibid., 3.

5. Ibid., 54, for more on debt servitude.

6. Ibid., 50.

7. The U.S. Department of Labor created a Wage and Hour Division when the Fair Labor Standards Act was passed in 1938, which was followed by numerous clarifying amendments during the late 1940s.

8. Kindell and Wojcik 2000, 21.

9. Ibid., 26.

Chapter 7

1. Tonsmeire et al. 1996, 2.

2. Ziewitz and Wiaz 2004, 64.

3. Penson 1996, 11.

4. Roberts 2000, 2.

5. Cleckley 2004.

Chapter 8.

1. Fishman 2000, 162.

2. Ibid., 177.

3. Kimball in Nichols 2004, 1.

4. Ibid.

5. Johnson 2003, 2.

6. Fishman 2000, 158.

7. Leitman et al. 1986, 256.

8. Means 1991, 25.

9. Middlemas 2001, 1.

10. Blackwell 2001, 3.

Chapter 9.

1. USGS data shows a brief drop in 1932 river flow to nearly 5,000 cubic feet per second, the corps proposed minimum currently in litigation.

2. White, Knetsch, and Jones 1999, 147.

Chapter 10.

1. Aguda in Todd 2003, 38.

2. Davis 2004, 5.

Glossary

andropogon an important genus of grass (a subgenus is sorghum, from which come millet and sugarcane).

Archaics people from the North American period, 8000 to 1000 BC.

basin a landform that drains all water within its boundaries to one point.

bay up how catch dogs trap a hog.

billy log raft.

bur (or **burr**) a rough or prickly envelope of a fruit; a plant that bears burs; a hanger-on; a small rotary cutting tool.

cant a log sawed with one or more squared edges.

catch dogs dogs used to catch hogs, usually charging from three sides of a bayed-up hog.

croker sack an alteration of crocus sack; from 1895, chiefly Southern.

cull what's left of the original growth.

deadhead a felled, sunken log, usually cypress, that makes high-grade, flexible lumber.

depauperate impoverished; to fall below natural development, number, or size.

dioecious having male reproductive organs in one individual and female in another.

disjunct disconnected; formed into separate groups.

double-ender (1) a man who works both the engine room and the wheelhouse of a steamboat; (2) a slim, 16-foot boat used for cutting cypress out of swamps. It was braced at each end and in the middle with seats, and men lived aboard, stowing food under the seats and stretching out between seats at night. At night, alligators sometimes stole food off their boats. Loggers didn't have to turn the boat around in tight spots; they simply turned themselves around and paddled out.

duff partly decayed organic matter on the forest floor.

effluent something that flows out as (1) a branch of a main stream; (2) waste material discharged into the environment.

flambouies a homemade torch created by filling a glass jar with kerosene and adding a wick of pine needles; possibly from French *flambeau.*

freshet a flush of high water on a stream, from an archaic word for stream.

gator tail saw used for girdling.

Gibson girl the fashion ideal for American women in 1900, created by illustrator Charles Dana Gibson.

gig a pronged spear for catching fish.

girdle to cut a ring into a tree to make sap or gum run.

hill, the dry land, as seen from the open water.

jook forerunner of the juke joint; a place to eat, drink, dance, play card games, or, at C. C. Land still on Sundays, worship.

jugaloo tokens or scrip, made of wood, aluminum, or brass. Workers were paid a portion in cash and a portion in jugaloos, which could be spent only at the company store, where prices were controlled.

keystone species a species on which associated entities depend for support.

lightered Resinous pine used for kindling; a knot of wood used as a night light.

logging ditchy-do pulling so many trees on one cable that their weight carves a ditch.

Lord God bird the large, boldly colored ivory-billed woodpecker, which elicited the exclamation "Lord God" from people who saw it. Since that bird's decline, the moniker has been transferred to the pileated woodpecker, which also has a bold red crest, a large wingspan, and a distinctive call.

mechanical redistribution Engineer Alton Colvin's term for pushing dredged sand back into the river during high water.

negative estuarine system having no freshwater inflow.

nor'wester a strong northwest wind.

OPS (Other Personal Services) temporary employment without benefits.

pecky old or sunken cypress riddled with irregular-shaped holes.

peonage the use of laborers who are bound in servitude by debt.

pitcher pump pump with a lip or spout to direct water.

pitty-pat small motorboat.

porgy (also **pogy, pogies**) a blue-spotted crimson percoid food fish; also any of various teleost fishes, such as menhaden.

pull hulls scars in the earth made by pulling logs with a steam-driven winch.

rasher perhaps from Middle English, *rashen*, or cuts, meaning several slices of bacon or ham.

relict a persistent remnant of an otherwise extinct flora or fauna or organism.

river stage the height of the surface of the river above an arbitrary zero point.

roe the eggs of a fish, especially when still in the ovarian membrane.

roe season a period when fish are depositing eggs.

rogue it up to push up soil to make a road, perhaps derived from the verb *rogue*, meaning to weed out (1766).

scrip a token issued for temporary use.

selective snagging engineer Alton Colvin's term for removing only the snags in the navigation channel.

Senator Cypress this record 138-foot cypress was struck by a hurricane in 1926 and lost 30 feet. www.visitseminole.com/what/entertainment/unusual.asp.

singletree (also **whiffletree**, from *whippletree* [ca. 1828]) the pivoted swinging bar to which traces of a harness are fastened to draw a vehicle.

spat a young bivalve (such as an oyster).

stevedore a shiphand who loads and unloads cargo.

strong back a crosspiece to which logs are wired for rafting downstream.

Torreya taxiflora a small evergreen blighted by a fungal disease of the stems and endangered in its natural habitat, the steepheads of the Apalachicola River's eastern banks. However, healthy plants are growing in botanical gardens elsewhere. It is also known as Florida torreya or "stinking cedar" due to its resinous odor. (For more, see *National Audubon Society Field Guide to North American Trees, Eastern Region.*)

trotline (1) a short setline used near shore or along streams to catch fish; (2) one of the short lines with hooks that are attached to a trotline at intervals.

trotting to ride, drive, or proceed at a trot, as when floating logs are moved quickly with the current.

tussock upended tree roots that wild hogs sometimes back up to when set upon by catch dogs.

walking catfish *Clarias batrachus* arrived in America from Thailand as a pet-store novelty, reports Florida Fish and Wildlife Conservation. It also stocked commercial fish farms near Deerfield Beach and Tampa until it walked away. It has become one of the most widespread exotic fish in the state. Its voracious appetite categorizes it as biological pollution since it outcompetes native species, but drought keeps it from moving since it needs moisture in the air to keep skin moist.

watershed all water within its boundaries drains to one point.

wetlands transitional lands between uplands and open waters that are inundated long enough to support a predominance of plants adapted to these conditions.

windlass a horizontal barrel supported on vertical posts and turned by a crank so that the hoisting rope is wound around the barrel.

within-bank disposal Engineer Alton Colvin's term for disposing of dredged spoil inside the banks of the river, to avoid filling the floodplain with it.

woodsriders overseers on horseback who followed turpentine workers through the woods and into town.

Source: Webster's Eleventh New Collegiate Dictionary. Springfield, Mass.: Merriam-Webster Inc., 2003.

Bibliography

Adlerstein, David. 2002. *Apalachicola Times.* May 30. http://www.apalachtimes.com/leadstoryselect.php?id=63.

Ager, L. A., C. L. Mesing, R. S. Land, M. J. Hill, Mike Spellman, R. W. Rousseau, and Karen Stone. 1986. *Five-Year Completion Report: Fisheries Ecology and Dredging Impacts on the Apalachicola River System, July 1981 through June 1986.* State of Florida Game and Fresh Water Fish Commission.

American Rivers Media Advisory. 2002. "River in Florida on 2002 'Most Endangered' List." Washington, D.C. April 2. <http://www.americanrivers.org/site/DocServer/mer02final.pdf?docID=671>

Apalachicola Times. 2004. "Joseph McMillan, Sr." *Local Events.* July 16. <http://www.apalachtimes.com/localevents.html>

Barkuloo, J. M., L. Patrick, L. Smith, and W. J. Troxel. 1987. *Natural Resources Inventory: Apalachicola-Chattahoochee-Flint River Basin.* U.S. Fish and Wildlife Service.

Blackwell, Marilyn. 2001. "An Apology." *Franklin Chronicle.* February 9.

Blount, Robert S. 1993. *Spirits of Turpentine: A History of Florida Naval Stores, 1528–1950.* Florida Heritage Journal Monograph No. 3. Tallahassee: Florida Agricultural Museum.

Brose, S. David, and Nancy Marie White, eds. 1999. *The Northwest Florida Expeditions of Clarence Bloomfield Moore.* Tuscaloosa: University of Alabama Press.

Cleckley, William. 2004. Personal e-mail. November 5.

Clewell, Andre F. 1986. *Natural Setting and Vegetation of the Florida Panhandle.* Mobile, Ala.: U.S. Army Corp of Engineers.

Coleman, Felicia C., William F. Figueira, Jeffrey S. Ueland, and Larry B. Crowder. 2004. "The Impact of United States Recreational Fisheries on Marine Fish Populations." *Science,* August 26.

Davis, Ronald L. F. "Creating Jim Crow: In-Depth Essay." *The History of Jim Crow.* New York Life. August 4, 2004 http://www.jimcrowhistory.org/history/creating2.htm.

Donoghue, J. 1987. *Evaluation of Sediment Loading Processes in Apalachicola Bay Estuary.* NOAA Technical Report Series, OCRM/SPD.

Edmiston, Lee R., and Holly A. Tuck. 1987. *Resource Inventory of the Apalachicola River and Bay Drainage Basin.* Apalachicola: Office of Environmental Service, Florida Game and Fresh Water Fish Commission.

Fishman, Gail. 2000. *Journeys through Paradise: Pioneering Naturalists in the Southeast.* Gainesville: University Press of Florida.

Florida Fish and Wildlife Service. 1997. "Florida's Endangered Species, Threatened

Species, and Species of Special Concern." http://floridaconservation.org/pubs/ endanger.html.

Florida Game and Fresh Water Fish Commission. 1981–86. "Fisheries Ecology and Dredging Impacts on the Apalachicola River System."

Gibson, Jon L., Robert B. Gramling, Robert J. Floyd, and Steven J. Brazda. 1980. *Cultural Investigations in the Apalachicola and Chattahoochee River Valleys in Florida, Alabama, and Georgia: History, Archeology, and Underwater Remote Sensing*. Report No. 6. University of Southwestern Louisiana Center for Archaeological Studies.

Gorsline, D. S. 1963. "Oceanography of Apalachicola Bay." In *Essays in Marine Geology in Honor of K. O. Emory*, edited by T. Clements. Los Angeles: University of Southern California Press.

Gramling, Robert. 1980. "Criteria for Underwater Cultural Resource Significance Assessment." In *Cultural Assessment of the Chattahoochee and Apalachicola River Valleys in Georgia, Alabama, and Florida: History, Archeology, and Underwater Remote Sensing*, edited by Jon L. Gibson et al. Report No. 6. University of Southwestern Louisiana Center for Archaeological Studies.

Hall, Rubylea. 1947. *The Great Tide*. New York: Duell, Sloan, and Pearce.

Hauserman, Julie. 2003. "Land Sale Might Open Door to Development." *St. Petersburg Times Online*. July 28. http://www.sptimes.com/2003/07/28/State/Land_sale_might_open.shtml.

Hipes, Dan. 2003. Florida Natural Areas Inventory tracking list. Personal e-mail. December 12.

Huang, Wenrui, William K. Jones, and Jerrick Saquibal. 1998. *Three-Dimensional Modeling of Circulation and Salinity for the Low River Flow Season in Apalachicola Bay, FL*. Havana: Northwest Florida Water Management District.

Hurston, Zora Neale. 1935. *Mules and Men*. New York: HarperPerennial.

Johnson, Kathy S. 2003. "To Honor an Indefatigable Field Botanist and Chattahoochee's Most Famous Citizen . . . Angus Gholson, Jr. Nature Park of Chattahoochee." *Twin City News* 56, no. 12 (March 6).

Keyser, Robert. 2002. ACF Stakeholders Public Meeting, Columbus, Ga., December 5. http://www.sam.usace.army.mil/briefings/ACT-ACF/ACFMtg12-05-02Transcript.pdf.

Kimball, Winifred. 2004. "Life of Dr. A. W. Champman." Excerpted in "Apalachicola Diary by Jimmie J. Nichols." *Apalachicola Times*. September 23 and October 7.

Kindell, Carolyn, and Jamie Wojcik. 2000. *Historic Vegetation of Tate's Hell State Forest*. Tallahassee: Florida Natural Areas Inventory.

Kurz, Herman, and Robert K. Godfrey. 1962. *Trees of Northern Florida*. Gainesville: University of Florida Press.

Leitman, H. M. 1983. "Forest Map and Hydrologic Conditions, Apalachicola River Floodplain, Florida." *Bulletin of Marine Science* 32, no 4: 807–22.

Leitman, S., T. Allen, K. Brady, P. Dugan, A. Redman, M. Ednoff, and J. Ryan. 1986. *Apalachicola River Dredged Material Disposal Plan*. Office of Coastal Management, Florida Department of Environmental Regulation.

Light, Helen, and Melanie Darst. 2003. "Assistance to the Northwest Florida Water Management District in Evaluating Restoration Alternatives for the Apalachicola River and Floodplain."

Light, Helen, Melanie Darst, and Steve Walsh. 2002. "Apalachicola River Floodplain: Importance of River Flow to Biological Communities." Paper presented at ACF Florida Stakeholders Meeting, October 7.

Light, H. M., M. R. Darst, L. J. Lewis, and D. A. Howell. 1998. "Aquatic Habitats in Relation to River Flow in the Apalachicola River Floodplain, Florida." U.S. Geological Survey Professional Paper 1594.

Lipford, Jody W. 2004. "Averting Water Disputes: A Southeastern Case Study." PERC Policy Series, Issue No. PS-30, February. http://www.perc.org/pdf/ps30.pdf Apr. 25, 2005.

Livingston, Robert J. 1983. *Resource Atlas of the Apalachicola Estuary*. Florida Sea Grant College, Report Number 55.

Loller, Kevin. 2003. "Young Fish Victim of Net Law." *Franklin Chronicle*. May 16.

Loomis, J. 1816. Letter excerpted in "Destruction of the Negro Fort in East Florida," *Franklin Chronicle*. September 17, 2004.

McCarthy, Kevin M. 2004. "Our Florida Heritage: Florida's Legends of the Nineteenth Century." *Florida Monthly* 24, no. 8 (August): 31.

McClellan, Pete, and Marie McClellan. 1831. Land Abstract. Calhoun County, Fla.

Means, D. Bruce. 1991. "Florida's Steepheads: Unique Canyonlands." *Florida Wildlife*, May-June.

Menzel, R. W., N. C. Hulings, and R. R. Hathaway. 1958. *Causes of Depletion of Oysters in St. Vincent's Bar, Apalachicola Bay, Florida*. Proceedings of the National Shellfish Association 48:66–71.

———. 1966. *Oyster Abundance in Apalachicola Bay, Florida, in relation to Biotic Associations Influenced by Salinity and Other Factors*. Gulf Resource Report 2, no. 2:73–96.

Middlemas, Kendall. 2001. "Environmental Tests Set for St. Joe Mill." *Panama City News Herald*. October 3.

Milner, Richard S. 1998. *Northwest Florida Place Names of Indian Origin*. Parthenon: Yanosochee Books.

Neils, Parker. 2003. "Seascape Sanctuary: The Madison-Swanson Reserve." *Research in Review* (summer 2003). Tallahassee: Florida State University. http://www.research.fsu.edu/researchr/summer2003/grouperridge.html.

Nessler, Lisa. 2002. "City of Tarpon Springs." http://www.ci.tarpon-springs.fl.us/tourism/epiphany.htm.

Niesse, Mark. 2003. "Rural South Georgia Strains Water Supply." *Tallahassee Democrat*. January 26.

Penson, Georgann. 1996. "Caring for Our Forests." *Florida Water* 5, no. 2 (fall/winter): 11.

Public Meeting on Apalachicola River below Jim Woodruff Lock and Dam. 1973. Marianna, Fla., June 27.

Putnal, Bevin. 2002. ACF Stakeholders Public Meeting, Columbus, Ga., December 5. http://www.sam.usace.army.mil/briefings/ACT-ACF/ACFMtg12-05-02Transcript.pdf.

Ritchie, Bruce. 2005. "Dredging Study Fuels Opposition." *Tallahassee Democrat.* http://www.tallahassee.com/mid/tallahassee/news/local/11356514.htm.

Rivers, Larry E. 2000. *Slavery in Florida: Territorial Days to Emancipation.* Gainesville: University Press of Florida.

Roberts, Gordon. 2000. NWFWMD Governing Board Meeting Minutes, April 27.

Rogers, W. W., and L. Willis III. 1997. *At the Water's Edge: Pictorial and Narrative History of Apalachicola and Franklin County.* Virginia Beach: Donning Company.

Sakim, Charles Randall Daniels. 2001. http://www.tfn.net.us/Museum/index.html.

Spires, Byron. 2002. "McLane Family History Revisited." *Gadsden County Times,* online edition. http://www.news.mywebpal.com/news_tool_v.2cfm?show=archivedetails&pnpID=582&om=1&ArchiveID=898931.

Stein, B. A., Kutner, L. S., and Adams, J. S., eds. 2000. *Precious Heritage: The Status of Biodiversity in the United States.* New York: Oxford University Press.

Struhs, David. "Statement by Florida Department of Environmental Protection Secretary David B. Struhs Regarding the Conclusion of the ACF Compact." Florida Department of Environmental Protection. September 1, 2003. http://www.dep.state.fl.us/secretary/comm/2003/sept/0901.htm

Time. 1978. "Robin Hood of the Bench: Some Gothic Politics in Backwater Florida." September 18.

Todd, Kim. 2003. "Interview: 'Water is the Blue Soul of the Planet': A Spanish Economist on Things That Can't Be Bought or Sold." *Sierra Magazine,* September/October.

Tonsmeire, Dan, Duncan J. Cairns, Ellen Hemmert, and Patricia L. Ryan. 1996. *Apalachicola River and Bay Management Plan.* Havana, Fla.: Northwest Florida Water Management District.

Twain, Mark. 1883. *Life on the Mississippi.* Boston: J. R. Osgood and Co.

Unger, Brent. 1998. "Death in the Morning." *Panama City News Herald.* March 11:1E.

U.S. Constitution. Article 2, section 1.

U.S. Department of the Interior. 1966. *Proceedings: Conference in the Matter of Pollution of the Interstate Waters of the Chattahoochee River and Its Tributaries, from Atlanta, Georgia, to Fort Gaines, Georgia,* vol. 2.

U.S. Department of Forestry. http://www.fl-dof.com/state_forests/Tates_Hell.htm.

U.S. Department of Labor. 2002. "Wage and Hour Division History." http://www.dol.gov/esa/aboutesa/history/whowhahist.htm.

U.S. Environmental Protection Agency. 2000. http://.a.gov/pls/tmdl/waters_list.control?huc=03130001&wbname=CHATTAHOOCHEE.

Watts, Betty M. 1975. *The Watery Wilderness of Apalach, Florida.* Tallahassee: Apalach Books.

Wells, Deena. 2003. "Florida Reaffirms Commitment to Protect Apalachicola River: Officials Call for End to Dredging." DEP Press release, July 30.

Westphal, Joseph. 2000. Letter to Senator Bob Graham. August.

White, Nancy, Joe Knetsch, and B. Calvin Jones. 1999. "Archaeology, History, Fluvial Geomophology, and the Mystery Mounds of Northwest Florida." *Southeastern Archaeology* 18, 2 (winter): 142–56.

Willoughby, Lynn. 1999. *Flowing through Time: A History of the Lower Chattahoochee River.* Tuscaloosa: University of Alabama Press.

Word, Ron. 2002. "Tarpon Springs Is Rich with Greek Heritage and Sponges." *Florida Daily News.* December 6. ActivePaper Edition: 18.

Wright, J. Leitch, Jr. 1986. *Creeks and Seminoles: The Destruction and Regeneration of the Muscogulge People.* Lincoln: University of Nebraska Press.

www.geocities.com/heartland/Bluffs/3010/tractdoc.htm.

Zeiwitz, Kathryn, and June Wiaz. 2004. *Green Empire: The St. Joe Company and the Remaking of Florida's Panhandle.* Gainesville: University Press of Florida.

Index

126, 188, 250; development impact, 114–15; famous, 8, 209, 259; freshwater needs, 1, 8, 78, 112–18, 118–19, 131, 154–59; leases, 112, 116; Popham, 277; swamp-fed, 35–36

Panther, Florida, 48, 157, 160, 185; attacks, 162, 168

Pinhook: current gave out, 65, 113, 118; drought, 131–32, 138

Pirate, 6; treasure hunt, 140–41

Pitcher plant, xv

Polio, 66; vaccine, 72; syndrome, 73; tupelo cure, 235

Pollution, 159; causes, 130–31, 137; chemicals, 155; dam traps, 152; nutrients, 132; worse than nets, 124

Protection, preservation: 3, 9, 106, 110, 117, 120–21, 158–59, 160–67, 263

Railroad, 8, 49, 89; Apalachicola, 67, 147, 266–67, 280, 295; Chattahoochee, 66; cotton, 42; deregulated, 71; detective, 186; Harbeson City, 182, 191; narrow gauge, 104; not subsidized, 104; St. Joe, 263, 295; seafood, 119, 266–67; tram roads, 191, 206

Ramsey: Bo Landing, 58; Honest John, 16; Louis Joe, 58, 62; Ndola, 16; uncles killed, 18; Wisa, 15–16, 18

Red tide, 112, 130–31; oysters, 126

Rice: cultivated, 57; wild, 28

River: Junction, 6–7, 8; Styx, 35, 37, 64, 251

River uses, 8, 69–70; recreation, 78; reservoirs, 76

Roosevelt, Franklin D., 91; welfare, 179

St. George Island, 8, 298; rowed, boated to, 285, 293; development, 124, 130; hotel, 293

—Little St. George Island: military training, 143, 180–81, 193, 262; Marshalls, 143–44, 257–62; turpentine, 179, 183, 187; cattle, 186–87, 257–62

St. Joe Company, 30–31; failures, 222; steepheads, 223; train, 295; workers, 38–39, 126, 275–77

St. Teresa, 296–97

St. Vincent, 8, 190, 292; lodging at, 293–94; Sound, 113

Sand: blocks creeks, 100, 188; buries nutrients, 36; destroys willows, 92; fills rivers, 35–36, 85; kills tupelo, 36; Mountain, 37, 75–76, 78; pumped, 36, 86; spoil wash, 251; white at St. Teresa, 298. *See also* Sloughs

Sawmill: Blountstown, 210–11; Graceville, 210–11; Hosford, 210–11; cypress, 33, 181–82; electric, 87, 182; fence post, 243–44; Fulton, 293; Harris worked, 242; lucrative, 201; Sheip, 87, 91, 128, 269–70; skidder, 181; steam-driven, 195; Stem Red, 114; portable, 181–82, 202; Tildon, 196, 275

Schuler: Pat, 57–58; Bub, 61

Scott, R. W., Lt., 6–7

Scott, Tom, 65

Scott Ferry, 31

Scrip: peonage, 183–85; Sheip, 269–70; jugaloo, 282

Sea Dream, rescued sailors, 143; Captain Randolph, 267

Seafood: Buddy Ward and Sons, 113–14, 118–20, 138; business, 19–20, 119, 136–39, 149–53, 158; canning, packing, shipping, 117, 119, 148, 151, 267; festival, 263–64, 277, 283–84, 303; Hurricane Alberto, 125; Island View, 149–53; Leavins, 55; Lloyd Fish Market, 127; workers, 2, 153

Seagrass: Alligator Harbor, St. Joe Bay, 161

Segregation: Apalachicola, 280; separate beaches, 280; crosses burned, 279; fishing, 279; schools, 276, 278; theaters, 277; upheld, 273–75

Seminole: chairman, 17; Creek runaways, 6; escaped slaves, 6; Hitchitis, Miccosukee, 15; killed Blount's family, 14; Second War, 6; Wars, 6–7, 85

Sharecroppers, 237–48

Sheip, Jerome H., 87, 91; after cotton, 293; dangerous work, 147, 276; scrip, 269–70, 282; tore down, 128

Shrimp, 135–36; 100 boxes a day, 138; down "the Miles," 113–14; freshwater, 2, 118; Mosconis family, 105–10; red tide, 208; sea bob, 141; small nets, 133–34; TEDs, 123–24

Sikes, Bob, 249–50

Sikes Cut, 43, 76–77; drains freshwater, 152; drains pollutants, 131–32; Gulf access, 113, 115, 264; mistake, 179; salt intrusion, 115, 264

Slaves, 6; graves, 188; raids, 280

Sloughs: blocked, 21, 81–84; Gum Drift, Maddox, 36; no fish access, 38, 188; Roberts, 29

Snakes: abundant, 158; control rats, roaches, 158–59; cottonmouth moccasins, 171–72; bit soldiers, 180–81

Sneads, 6; port, 67; populous, 70

Snyder, Henry: pilot, 49

Spain, 6

Species, endangered: 107 plants listed, 157; conservation, 112; gopher tortoise, 218; mussels, 104; torreya, croomia, 217–19

Sponges, 42; TEDs help, 123–24; Greek immigrants, 106–10, 182, 264–66, 272

Springs: Blue, 103, 243; Defuniak, 181; Roberts Slough, 32; Spring Creek, 218, 221, 300; Tarpon, 106–7, 109–10, 272; under dam, west of river, 97–98; Wakulla, 186

Square Ground: Pine Arbor, 17; Creek, 20–21; ceremonies, 21. *See also* Boggs Pond

State Roads 20, 12, and 67: built, 60–61

Steamboats, 42–43, 47–55, 251; *Barbara Hunt*, 48; *Beulah Ray*, 48; Blountstown, 58–59; Bristol, 56; *Callahan Jr.*, 42, 53, 67, 249, 255–56; captains strike, 49; carried dancers, shoppers, mail, 42–43, 56, 90; *Cherokee Princess*, 54–55; *Chipola*, 42; citrus, 168; Colvin, Master of *Arrow, Albany, Guthrie, Montgomery*, 73; cordwood-fired, 51; *Crescent City*, 169–70, 288–89; *Eva*, 105; glitzy, 254; *Jesse May* ferry, 268; *John W. Callahan*, 45, 53, 170, 269; *Louise*, 46; *Midnight Mist*, 51–52; paddlewheel, 148; Pilot Dudley, 48–49; rousters, 48, 280–81; *W. C. Bradley*, 45, 47, 49–50

Steepheads, 3, 220–21; botanized, 217–19; refuge, 159

Sumatra: CCC camp, 294; Cebe Tate, 162

Sugarcane: grinding, 170–71; lunch, 184

Swamp: dying, 35–37; in Apalachicola, 281; logging, 88, 89–91, 148, 162–66, 181, 198, 207, 210, 211–13, 216; survival, 19–20, 29–31, 34–41, 167, 171–72, 174, 186, 188, 213–14, 237, 247–48

Sweetwater Creek: Creeks killed, 18; steepheads, 220–21, 223

Tall Timbers, 221

Tallahassee, 170; *Democrat*, 28; *Springtime*, 17

Tarpon: arrived Thursdays, 147; Capt. Barrow, 170, 293; from Mobile, 269; naval stores, 180; sank, 293

Tate's Hell State Forest: C. C. Land Still, 177–87; fishing, 183, 187; Harbeson City, 181, 191–92; hunt in, 120, 174; lost in, 183–84; restoration, 162–67; road-building, 188–93; snakes, 158–59; submerged, 191; timber, 181–82, 188–93

Taunton: Abigail, 30; Family Children's Homes, 29–30; truss plant, 30

Telogia, 60–61

Theatre, Dixie, 268; World War II, 286

Thirteen Mile, 114; Seafood Company, 115, 118–20

Development Association: Three Rivers, 43; Tri Rivers Waterway, 68

Torrey, John, 217

Torreya: State Park, 221, 236; taxifolia, 3, 217–20, 222, 224–25, 227–28

Tourism, 100, 124, 150–53, 161

Transportation, 2; Apalachicola, 147; bus line, 270; mule, 245; rail, road, 32, 42–43; river, 10, 20, 24, 42–43, 53; Tri Rivers Waterway, 68; truck, 43, 47, 49; wagon, 137, 144; walked, 246; Zeppelins, 270

Treaties: Adams-Onis, 7; Moultree Creek Treaty, 6

Trees: black gum, juniper, 191, 200, 248; citrus, 37; champion, 215; dwarf pond cypress, 188, 191; grafting, 182; ironwood, 36; longleaf pine, 182; mulberry, pig nut hickory, 243; pine, 188–93, 200, 206; saltwater slash, 180; "Senator" cypress, 207; tupelo as polio cure, 235; "Unreachable" cypress, 206–7; virgin, 345; yew, 218, 224

Tri-state negotiations, 138

Tug, 67; Sheip, 91, 114; hazards, 106; captain's son, 113–14; to Panama City, 114

Faith Eidse, public information specialist at the Northwest Florida Water Management District, was raised in Congo/Zaire, where her linguist father recorded oral histories along the Kwilu River basin. She is a former journalist and magazine editor, a 1996 Kingsbury award winner, coeditor of *Unrooted Childhoods: Memoirs of Growing Up Global,*and contributor to *Between Two Rivers: Stories from the Red Hills to the Gulf.* Her essays, short stories, and poetry have appeared in scholarly and literary journals around the world. She has also taught at Florida State and Barry universities.

Titles of related interest from University Press of Florida

Death in the Everglades
The Murder of Guy Bradley, America's First Martyr to Environmentalism
Stuart B. McIver

The Everglades
An Environmental History
David McCally

Florida's Megatrends
Critical Issues in Florida
David R. Colburn and Lance deHaven-Smith

Highway A1A
Florida at the Edge
Herbert L. Hiller

Journal of Light
The Visual Diary of a Florida Nature Photographer
John Moran

Key West
History of an Island of Dreams
Maureen Ogle

Land of Sunshine, State of Dreams
A Social History of Modern Florida
Gary R. Mormino

Outposts on the Gulf
Saint George Island and Apalachicola from Early Exploration to World War II
William Warren Rogers

River of the Golden Ibis
Gloria Jahoda

Some Kind of Paradise
A Chronicle of Man and the Land in Florida
Mark Derr

The Stranahans of Fort Lauderdale
A Pioneer Family of New River
Harry A. Kersey Jr.

Swamp Song
A Natural History of Florida's Swamps
Ron Larson

For more information on these and other books, visit our Web site at www.upf.com.